DARWIN, SEX, AND STATUS

JEROME H. BARKOW

DARWIN, SEX, AND STATUS

Biological Approaches to Mind and Culture

UNIVERSITY OF TORONTO PRESS
Toronto Buffalo London

© University of Toronto Press 1989
Toronto Buffalo London
Printed in Canada

ISBN 0-8020-5773-X

Printed on acid-free paper

Canadian Cataloguing in Publication Data

Barkow, Jerome H.
  Darwin, sex, and status

  Includes bibliographical references and index.
  ISBN 0-8020-5773-X

  1. Sociobiology. 2. Human biology – Social aspects.
  3. Human behavior. I. Title.

  GN365.9.B37 1989   304.5   C89-093684-6

For my father, Philip Barkow. I will forever wonder how much of all this he might have agreed with.

Contents

viii Contents

Part Four. Alternative Approaches and Maladaptation

xi Contents

Foci

Tables and Figures

Preface

ORIGINS

The kindling for this book was an anthropology course in 'Culture and Personality' taught by the late Gerald Henderson at Brooklyn College, back in 1962. He introduced me to the work of A.I. Hallowell and A.F.C. Wallace, and their ideas – especially Hallowell's thinking on the evolutionary origins of self and culture – have evermore influenced me. But the real genesis of this work was not quite so long ago. It began in the summer of 1965, at the University of Chicago. My eventual thesis supervisor, Bob LeVine, was collaborating with Donald T. Campbell (then at Northwestern University) in a major study of ethnocentrism. Campbell detailed me to study the evolution of ethnocentrism and its analogues in other species. To my everlasting regret, I never revised and published the monograph I wrote that summer; but in order to write it I read more than I ever had before, teaching myself the basics of animal ethology, evolutionary biology, and population genetics – and, equally important, becoming familiar with the thinking of Campbell (as will be evident in chapter 2). My reading qualified me for membership in a small group that formed around Daniel G. Freedman at Chicago's Committee on Human Development, a group that saw 'development' in terms of biological evolution. It was a heady time, and we shared the prescient conviction that Darwin was the key to understanding human behaviour.

A gestation period of more than two decades suggests rather low academic fitness. In truth, the path towards this book has included many zigs and zags. Fortunately, Dalhousie University is either a tolerant or a devious place. On the one hand, I was encouraged to design a course ('Human Nature and Anthropology') that reflected my own interests. On the other, there was no textbook suitable for the course, forcing me eventually to put my notes and lectures together and so write this book.

IS THIS BOOK ABOUT SOCIOBIOLOGY?

The answer to this question depends upon how one defines sociobiology, and there is no generally accepted definition. For some, the term connotes racism and a belief that complex human behaviours are simple, single-gene effects. If that is your definition of the term, then this book is not about sociobiology and please cross out all use of the word in your copy and replace it with 'the evolutionary theory of behaviour.' Please do the same if by 'sociobiology' you mean the practice of 'explaining' complex behaviours – and even culture traits – in terms of their effects on genetic fitness and without equally careful attention to the levels of processes between the genes and the behaviour. For others – including myself – sociobiology is a neutral and often useful retronyn (a renaming after the fact, as when the digital watch created the need for the term 'analog watch') for work in which many of us were engaged long before the publication of E.O. Wilson's monumental study, *Sociobiology: The New Synthesis* (1975a). There are some reputed to refuse to use the term because of a feeling that Wilson had no right to name a discipline. Others – including myself – often find the term useful but are sceptical that there has indeed been a discipline created. The evolutionary perspective, paradigm, framework, Darwinian approach – or whatever – continues to grow slowly in influence in the social- and behavioural-science disciplines, just as it did prior to 1975. Wilson has helped many of us catch up with developments in evolutionary theory and in ethology, and has added (along with popular interest and controversy) a new term to join the above list. I deeply regret that he has not (at least, not yet) succeeded in replacing all these various and vague labels.

WHAT KIND OF BOOK IS THIS?

Darwin, Sex, and Status is intended to be readily intelligible to the lay reader. At the same time, it attempts two academic tasks: to be an original contribution to scholarship, and to serve as a text or supplementary reading for courses in human sociobiology, human nature, culture and biological evolution, human ethology, and anthropological and sociological theory. *Darwin, Sex, and Status* was thrice vetted, prior to publication, in a year-long undergraduate course in 'Human Nature and Anthropology.' The students had exceedingly varied backgrounds and often enough it was a student majoring in a field not specifically discussed – such as nursing science or commerce – who would excel.

Darwin, Sex, and Status is not meant as a stand-alone sociobiology textbook (it pays insufficient attention to the animal behaviour literature for that purpose), but because of its focus on human behaviour at both individual and cultural levels it fits nicely with any number of other sociobiological works (I myself have used it in conjunction with material by Richard Dawkins and David Barash, among other authors). The style of writing is deliberately colloquial and is intended to enable students to discuss without self-consciousness such 'heavy' matters as the nature of the mind-body split or whether we may end war.

Darwin, Sex, and Status was as much woven as written. It is not so much a linear progression as a tapestry with recurring threads woven through it. To switch analogies, there are reiterated themes. One of these is the importance of sexual selection, and particularly of female mate preference, in hominid evolution. Another is the theme of the active, strategizing individual, sorting out and revising culturally/experientially provided information with each generation. A third is that our 'executive self' is part of our folk psychology but is mythical, and that awareness includes only a very limited and biased-by-evolution selection of information from the workings of the mind. (This last idea is the 'sleep-walking' theme, stated as a forceful conclusion only at the very end of the book.) There is the theme of complex sociocultural phenomena demanding complex, systems-theory-type explanations – simple causes, whether in terms of 'genes' or inclusive fitness optimization or ecology or whatever, are always wrong, or at best, very incomplete. There is the theme of complex psychology: simple ideas of global learning are barely mentioned except to be debunked, while domain-specific information-processing subsystems or modules are given considerable attention (even if, admittedly, they must usually be left as 'black boxes' with only slightly understood algorithms, an algorithm being a set of procedures and decision rules for problem-solving).

The plan of attack of *Darwin, Sex, and Status* is thus one of recurrence.

Important ideas are introduced in one chapter, reviewed and built upon in another, returned to later in different form elsewhere. This approach comes from the experience of teaching highly abstract material, material that needs time to 'sink in' to be absorbed. I have always found it much more effective to present complex ideas briefly but on several occasions, rather than to present them only once, even if in great depth. The book's organization lends itself to seminars, or to a discursive style of lecturing. Were I not the author, I would 'lecture' by explaining why I agreed or disagreed with the main points of each chapter.

Numerous footnotes suggest additional readings, and these are intended to help students assigned to write term papers. The *Human Ethology Newsletter* (published by the International Society for Human Ethology) is an excellent source of current bibliography for students, and pertinent articles frequently appear in (among other journals) *Ethology and Sociobiology*. The field of 'biopolitics' (political science and biology) might have been but regrettably was not included in *Darwin, Sex, and Status* and students concerned with this area may wish to consult Schubert's (1988) *Evolutionary Politics* both for its own sake and as a bibliographic source.

CITATIONS: DID THE GREEKS DISCOVER SOCIOBIOLOGY?

There are more than five hundred references in the references and several times that number of citations in the text and in footnotes. Were my memory better and my notes more thoroughly organized, there would no doubt be twice as many. Once one understands the basic principles of a field, much is readily apparent, and the individual to whom any particular idea first became obvious is often unclear. In practice, we tend to give credit to whomever we originally learned something from, provided we can somehow remember; to whomever we last read who said it; to those researchers who are also our personal friends; or to no one at all. In more than one case, in writing this book, I was struck by how one author seemed to parallel the ideas and material of another without referring, or referring only in passing, to the writer who seemed to me to have precedence. I suspect that, most of the time, what was going on was independent invention. I was myself occasionally chagrined to find ideas I have thought of as my own, and which I put in print many years ago, discussed without reference to my work. Often, the pattern of citations seems to tell more about social than about intellectual networks. I have come to understand that the Greeks must have invented sociobiology, for every 'new' idea has clear antecedents and in the end none of us is entirely original. This lack of originality is readily apparent when we look at the work of others, but difficult to see in the case of one's own work (a phenomenon explained in chapter 8, in the context of a discussion of why selection would have favoured our tending to exaggerate our own relative standing). At any rate, my regrets to any who feel they have been slighted – it has not been intentional.

In some places I disagree with those whose work I discuss. Often, the disagreement is the whole point of the discussion. But there has already been sufficient contention and contentiousness over Human Socio-biology, both within the field and from its critics, and I have tried to treat the work of others with respect. It is my hope that they will agree that I have done so.

ACKNOWLEDGMENTS

This book has been published with the help of a grant from the Social Science Federation of Canada, using funds provided by the Social Sciences and Humanities Research Council of Canada. Its first draft was written while I was the recipient of a Social Sciences and Humanities Council of Canada Leave Fellowship, for which I am deeply grateful. Since the research and thought in *Darwin, Sex, and Status*, whatever their merits, began in 1965, there are other agencies to thank as well, beginning with the u.s. National Science Foundation, which sponsored my early research among the Hausa, and several SSHRCC research grants that permitted me to do fieldwork in various parts of West Africa. A grant from the Harry Frank Guggenheim Foundation also permitted much thinking and research, while several small grants from Dalhousie University's Research Development Fund have been useful.

Many have helped me in my work. My children Philip and Sarah gladly modelled evolved behaviour for me. My spouse, Irma Juuti, put up with the new religion of the sacrosanct study and the mighty micro. Peter Richerson annotated the entire manuscript(!), while Dan Freedman, Michael Rose, Kathy Gibson, Sue Parker, Robert Boyd, Charles Lumsden, E.O. Wilson, Ron Wallace, John Tooby, and Leda Cosmides read and commented on parts of the manuscript: the remaining imperfections are in spite of their efforts (I have not always taken their advice). Colin Irwin was cheerfully available to work out an idea with, during the preparation of the first draft. Students in 1984–5 gave me their class notes so that some of my extemporaneous and ordinarily evanescent remarks could be incorporated into the work. Students in the summer of 1986 and during the 1986–7 and 1987–8 academic years used the draft manuscript as their textbook and, in the process, contributed to its final form.

DARWIN, SEX, AND STATUS

1

Introduction

This is a book about the dissolution of discontinuities between the social-behavioural and biological sciences. It explains the continuities among biological evolution, human psychology, conscious experience, and the societies and structures we build. It starts with genes and ends with cultures. Here is its framework.

VERTICALLY INTEGRATED EXPLANATION

Theory and data must fit together at multiple levels if they are to be acceptable – they must be what I have elsewhere termed *vertically integrated* (Barkow, 1980a). Suppose I wish to understand the human hand. I may review the genetics of finger length and even the number of digits. I will want to look at the hand in non-human primates, and will no doubt appreciate that the fingerprints evolved as part of our arboreal adaptation, as a means of ensuring a firm grip on slippery branches. I may trace the evolution of the hand as the thumb became increasingly opposable, rendering a climbing instrument into a tool-using one. I will want to examine the musculature and ennervation of the hand as well, its internal anatomy and physiology. I will look at the areas of the brain associated with the hand, and perhaps study how use of the hands develops in infancy and childhood. Finally, I may wish to review social-class differences in hand use, how different cultures categorize the hand, the extent to which in some societies tasks are assigned to one hand but forbidden to the other, and so forth.

Note that the various hand-related data and theory must all be mutually consistent – my genetics must not contradict my anatomy, my anatomy my understanding of growth and development, or my cultural anthropology my knowledge of neurophysiology. But no single type of account is privileged: no one kind of knowledge of the hand is deducible from any other kind, though all must fit together.[1] Different specialists will have different aspects of hand knowledge, though none will be truly expert in the hand itself: the anthropologist will know about hands in other cultures and the geneticist about hands among kin, but none will know all about the hand. A government agency that for some reason suddenly required an expert on the hand would discover no single individual but instead a variety of rival 'experts' from many different disciplines.

Perhaps I am interested not in the hand but in human dominance and prestige, or in sexuality, or in our species capacity for culture, or in self-awareness. Various chapters will deal with each of these topics, as well as with others. In each case, the emphasis will be on vertical integration, on putting together selection pressures, growth and development, psychological mechanisms, cultural differences, and analogies and homologies from other species. No one type of explanation will be shown as the key; all are needed. We will find gaps frequently enough, too, but the emphasis will be on compatibilities, on continuities. The topics may appear diverse but that diversity is precisely the point, for there are no natural breaks in the theories presented, theories that range from evolutionary biology to the generation of boundaries between ethnic groups.

The call for multiple-level, mutually compatible explanations of behaviour at different levels is not new. The ethologist Niko Tinbergen (1951, 1968), in a discussion more recently joined by Daly and Wilson (1978: 8–13) and by N. Blurton Jones (1982), suggests four levels, which I shall paraphrase (loosely following Blurton Jones) as follows: (a) the adaptationist or genetic-fitness account in terms of natural selection; (b) the account in terms of physiology or 'mechanism'; (c) an explanation of

---

1 Since my original (1980) work on 'vertically integrated explanations' I have moved the emphasis away from compatibility among *hierarchically* ('vertically') organized levels of explanation and placed it on the *compatibility*. True, chemical and physical explanations must be mutually compatible if both are to be correct, and true, too, their respective explanations are on different levels of organization. But psychological explanations in terms of mental processes must be compatible with neurophysiological explanations, yet it is not at all clear that they are necessarily at different levels.

how development or ontogeny occurs; and (d) a phylogenetic, comparative discussion of (homologous) behaviour systems in species sharing a common ancestor. Blurton Jones believes that the Tinbergian framework has done much to unify animal behaviour studies, so that workers at one level of explanation appreciate the meaningfulness of the research and theories of workers at the other levels. Blurton Jones laments that 'amazingly, diverse explanations of human behavior have become enshrined behind the walls of separate social or behavioral science departments' (p. 347), a situation that will be discussed and (one hopes) accounted for in the latter part of this chapter.[2]

WHY IS THIS BOOK NECESSARY?

The emphasis throughout this book will be on Tinbergen's first level of explanation, that of natural selection and biological evolution. Other levels will be incorporated to the extent possible, but evolution will here have a privileged position. This is because only if we begin with the biology will our framework be sufficiently broad to accommodate the social/behavioural sciences.

Science often consists of analysis, of seeking smaller and smaller units. For some of us, the understanding is in the detail and the finer the grain the better. But science also has to do with synthesis, with putting data into wider frameworks.

Imagine a Rorschach ink blot. Some of us will see a single, large image in it. Others will see numerous tiny, unrelated details. How we organize this bit of visual reality tells us something about how we approach problems, how we think about theory and data. The large-image types (like me) are happiest with synthetic, putting-together approaches, with broad and powerful frameworks. Others may find synthesis misleading and irrelevant, so engrossed are they in the details of their work. Both analysis and synthesis are necessary, of course.

This book is intended primarily for the large-image types, and for those for whom an effort at wider perspective seems timely. The perspective in question will be that of evolutionary biology. The recurring themes involve the evolution of the human capacity for culture and for self-awareness, our preoccupation with relative standing, and sexuality and sexual selection. For those who fear that such an

2 Blurton Jones (1982) optimistically believes that anthropology is an exception to the 'walls' problem.

approach will not lead to empirical research, please note that chapter 15's Focus 15.1 is a compilation of all the testable hypotheses found in the various chapters of this work. For those who do seek the details, the finer grain, footnotes frequently provide references.

ADUMBRATION

Chapters 2 and 3 will review evolutionary theory in a very basic way. Those already familiar with the fundamentals of evolutionary biology or with what many people nowadays term 'sociobiology' will find these chapters light reading. With chapters 4 and 5 comes a sketch of the mind, presented in terms of information-processing. Self-awareness will be presented as the most recent product of a process of natural selection that began with the rise of cognitive maps of geography. Along the way, we will have to rid ourselves of our folk-psychological ideas of 'will' and 'I.' One goal of this discussion will be to end the major gap between the social sciences and the biological sciences, a gap caused by the fact that one field uses people's subjective experience to explain behaviour – beliefs, attitudes, and so on – and the other uses biochemistry and neurophysiology. The relationship between the two kinds of explanations will (I hope) be made clear, though not without recourse to some philosophy. The other goal of this section will be to portray the mind as treating different kinds of information in quite different ways.

In chapters 6 and 7, we will see that the information of the systems we call 'cultures' can be divided into the same categories that the mind may use in processing information. We apparently filter and challenge different orders of cultural information in very different ways, as a result (as usual) of natural selection. Alternative ways of looking at evolution, individual psychology, and culture will be examined, but I will argue that the system developed here – one that divides culture into codes, goals, and plans – is likely to be the most productive for studying the actual behaviour of real people.

Chapter 8 takes us to a vertically integrated discussion of social dominance and human prestige. It will be argued that sexual selection was the key process in transforming primate dominance based on threat to human symbolic, culturally ordered systems of prestige. Along the way we will look at current neurophysiological research on dominance, at the relationship between cultural and genetic definitions of success, and at how the field of human ethology has treated the subject. Gaps –

such as a lack of research linking human self-esteem with primate dominance – will become apparent. Chapter 9 presents three case studies illustrating how interacting individuals, in their striving for prestige, generate sociocultural phenomena ranging from the spread of Islam to inter-ethnic conflict. The case studies will be drawn from my own fieldwork in West Africa.

In chapters 10 and 11 we will review in some detail alternative approaches to the evolution of human cultural capacity and the relationship between genes and culture. The work of Charles Lumsden and Edward Wilson will be discussed, followed by an analysis of the thinking of Robert Boyd and Peter Richerson. These two pairs of thinkers make use of mathematical models largely derived from the field of population genetics, and in order to do so have made some controversial assumptions about the nature of culture and of mind.

With chapter 12 we enter the realm of maladaptive behaviour. There are at least four processes that tend to move culture in fitness-reducing directions, while our individual decision-making, in similar fashion, frequently fails to be fitness-enhancing. Though an emphasis on genetic maladaptation may startle some evolutionists, it is a necessary corrective to an understandable tendency, among sociobiologists, to accentuate the adaptive. As we will see, the maladaptive consequences of our cultural capacity hardly outweigh its overall value, but instead constitute important selection pressures. Some of our psychological traits may reflect selection in favour of returning maladaptive culture traits to fitness-enhancing directions.

Chapter 13 brings us to scenarios about human evolution and the role played in it by sexual selection. Evolutionary scenarios (or narratives) are a rather speculative type of theory, but we will see that it is very likely that the differing fitness interests of males and females had much to do with our evolution. Human sexuality may as a result be as different from non-human primate sexuality as human culture is different from non-human primate protoculture. We will also see that the greater the importance we give to the role of the father in providing 'parental investment,' in our evolutionary scenarios, the less we expect to find major human sex differences in behaviour, particularly with regard to long-term rather than short-term pairing. Finally, we will review an important theory that suggests that, during a 'sensitive period' in childhood, we 'choose' one of two reproductive strategies.

Chapter 14 continues the analysis of human sexuality from an evolutionary perspective. Here, we will find that 'sperm competition' may account for the long penis and large testes of the human male. We will also analyse the differences between male and female sexual jealousy and review rape and incest from an evolutionary perspective. The chapter will end by presenting institutionalized homosexuality in Melanesia as an illustration of the limitations of purely genetic/ evolutionary approaches to culture (as opposed to vertically integrated approaches).

Chapter 15 will bring us to social engineering. This final and somewhat pessimistic chapter will explain how, in the light of the theories and data of this book, we can change culture. It will also suggest that there is little evidence that we wish to do so. (Note, however, that at no point will any effort be made to 'biologize' ethics or derive values or morality from biological evolution.)

EVOLUTION WILL NOT BE CHALLENGED

The evolutionary perspective, the adaptationist paradigm, is here assumed, and no attempt will be made to challenge it. Chapter 2 provides a more detailed discussion of this approach, but the stance will be that Darwin's theory of natural selection, with appropriate modifications and modernizations, underlies our understanding of the morphology and behaviour of all species, including our own. There have certainly been challenges to an exclusive emphasis on adaptation and genetic fitness, and, as we will shortly see, some have been justified. But the evolutionary perspective remains a powerful frame for the ordering of diverse data and theory.

Nevertheless, there is seldom justification for an automatic assumption of adaptiveness. Not everything is adaptive: chapter 2 alerts us to the problem of 'panselectionism' – the assumption that all aspects of all species are the result of natural selection and under the control of genes; chapter 4 explains why we should expect much human behaviour to actually reduce individual genetic fitness; while chapter 12 is devoted to explaining why cultures frequently include information genetically maladaptive for some or all of their participants.

As Gould and Lewontin (1979) have correctly, if rather luridly, pointed out, there can be real danger in the assumption of adaptive value. Given a good imagination, we can each be experts on evolution, advancing endless adaptationist explanations. But let us not overstate the risks. A practice of seeking vertically integrated explanation is likely to uncover cases in which the assumption of adaptive value is in error. In the meantime, adaptationism remains an immensely powerful organizational framework and generator of hypotheses. Here, for example, is an instance of how adaptationism furthers understanding in biological anthropology.

Adaptationist Explanations of Hair Loss
Suppose I notice that our fellow primates, the prosimians, monkeys, and apes, all have body hair or fur that we ourselves lack. Embarrassed over our nakedness, I decide to explain the evolutionary origins of human hair/fur loss. If my name is Desmond Morris, I might end up writing an entertaining popular book called *The Naked Ape*. Morris (1967: 38–44) provides a number of plausible evolutionary accounts for our missing hair. Here are four of the potential explanations he presents.

Why do we not have thick body fur or hair, as do other primates? Why, it must have been maladaptive. Dolphins are mammals without fur, too. Perhaps, like them (explanation 1), we once lived in the sea, where fur did us no good, and so we were selected against it. Or perhaps (explanation 2) our fur became a fire hazard, once we discovered fire, and selection favoured the less hirsute. Or maybe fur was a hazard to our health, not because of fire but because (explanation 3) we would soil ourselves, leading to discomfort and disease. Or was fur selected against because (explanation 4) it impeded the evaporation of perspiration, and the less hairy suffered less from heat exhaustion?

Is this, then, how we apply the adaptationist paradigm? Then what use is it? As Dennett (1983) argues, it is always possible to imagine a scenario in which whatever we think *is* must have evolved because it was optimal. We just have to keep on tinkering with the constraints we put in the scene, the design of the stage-set, until a hypothesis of optimal adaptiveness seems reasonable. Reverse the fur case, for a moment. Suppose we had after all retained our fur, what could be easier to explain? Even the tropics can have cool nights. Obviously, we must have needed the insulation back during the ice ages!

This is *not* how we follow an adaptationist paradigm. The goal is not to invent amusing scenarios for their own sake but to explain in a way that takes account of what we already know, and that organizes existing data and leads to new hypotheses. Morris reminds us, for example, that nothing in the fossil record supports the aquatic hypothesis (explanation 1). He might have added that some aquatic mammals, such as the seal, have retained their pelts. Morris suggests that the flame-proofing hypothesis implies that rather than being selected for the ability to quickly learn to avoid fire, and to teach this lesson to our young, our ancestors were for some reason selected to lose otherwise adaptive fur (explanation 2). This outcome seems unlikely. The fact that other primates have retained their fur renders the hygiene theory of fur loss equally implausible (explanation 3). The idea of hair loss as a product of selection for efficiency in ridding ourselves of excess heat (explanation 4), however, is consistent with the fossil record in that we did evolve in a tropical climate in which we very likely engaged in heavy, prolonged physical exertion as part of our foraging/hunting adaptation and as part of the carrying of foodstuffs and children back to a home base. This last explanation is also consistent with our profuse perspiration, another apparent adaptation to heat.

Of the four imaginative scenarios advanced to account for our bald skins, only one, therefore, the efficient evaporation account, is widely accepted among students of human evolution as worthy of continuing research. Hanna and Brown (1983: 262–4) review a number of studies dealing with hair loss, studies that address themselves to such questions as whether a rhesus macaque's fur, for example, is or is not a barrier to dissipation of heat compared to a human being's bald skin (fur is indeed such a barrier); and whether hairless skin actually absorbs more heat when exposed to sun than hair-covered skin (it does). On the basis of such empirical data, generated through the testing of adaptationist-inspired hypotheses, Hanna and Brown conclude (p. 263) that 'if heat tolerance and hair loss are related ... the selection must have occurred during bouts of strenuous activity when solar heat gain is less critical than immediate heat dissipation.' They suggest that such activity might have involved 'bursts of running in pursuit of game or strenuous digging of roots and tubers.' As their tentative phrasing indicates, research on the topic continues.

Adaptationism *works*, as Dennett (1983) points out. It organizes data and leads to further research. Suppose we uncover new information, findings inconsistent with the heat theory of hair loss but supporting the idea of our once having lived as do dolphins, what then? Why, then the biological anthropology textbooks would be revised. The adaptationist paradigm would still be working, still be ordering data and leading to more research, and that is all that is asked of paradigms and approaches. Those who wish Absolute Truth require religion, either divine or secular; but not science.

Even those strong critics of adaptationism, Gould and Lewontin (1979), as Rosenberg (1985a) and Dennett (1983) point out, are themselves adaptationists. Gould and Lewontin usefully remind us that modern evolutionary theory includes non-adaptive processes (for instance, gene drift, the loss of rare genes from a very small gene pool as the result of chance), but their final position is, reasonably enough, one of pluralism – we must not consider adaptationist explanations to the exclusion of all others. Evolutionary change often varies in rate, and developmental constraints may be more complex than most evolutionists imagine. But counsels of caution and complexity are hardly the equivalent of excluding adaptationist explanation (Dennett, 1983; Rosenberg, 1985a).[3]

Evolutionary theory, then, is a somewhat risky but immensely powerful scaffold.[4] It will serve for the chapters that follow, chapters that will illustrate the continuity between diverse fields. But why should this demonstration of continuity be necessary? Why do we need synthesis? Is not knowledge already seamless?

IF NO FIELD IS AN ISLAND
THEN WHAT ARE ALL THOSE FERRIES FOR?

Knowledge *is* seamless, continuous. It does not come in neat little bundles labelled 'disciplines.' The social and behavioural sciences flow from one to another and to the life sciences with no natural boundaries, no clear breaks, no real borders but the political. But ask any university undergraduate about the extent of overlap between, for example, the introductory psychology and the introductory anthropology (or sociology) courses and the answer will be that it is minimal. Similarly, evolutionary biologists who have dealt with human behaviour at times

---

3 Rosenberg's (1985a) analysis of the Gould and Lewontin criticisms is masterful, and makes one wonder why so much attention has been paid to them. For example, note his response to the familiar complaint that adaptationist accounts cannot be empirically disproved or 'falsified' (1985a: 166): 'If Gould and Lewontin's methodological criticisms are just the suggestion that adaptationalism is pseudo-science because unfalsifiable, then they cannot be taken seriously. For in their single-minded pursuit of the adaptationalist method, proponents of this approach are only doing what every rational scientist who embraces a theory must do: they are attempting to apply it, and are treating its problems as puzzles to be solved, not as anomalies that refute the approach.'

4 For those who would discard it, let them follow Alexander's (1974) advice, and seek a species whose members strive to enhance the genetic fitness of those with whom they share no genes, and who do so at no benefit to their own genetic fitness. Should such a species be found, then the adaptationist paradigm – biological evolution – must crash and I suppose we will all be fearfully re-examining creationism.

have complained that some of their colleagues felt this concern with our own species was somehow illegitimate for a *real* biologist, while many social and behavioural scientists know vanishingly little about human evolution.

Why should there be such gaps, and why should there be such bias against those who would bridge them? One answer is very general and has to do with the limitations of human intellect and the nature of bureaucratic organization. The second answer has to do with the specific history of the social-behavioural and biological sciences, a history of the abuse of 'evolutionary' explanation. Let us begin with the general problem of disciplinary boundaries and gaps.

The Reward System as a Gap Generator

Perhaps a Leonardo da Vinci could master all knowledge but the rest of us are more limited. Since we cannot master everything, we specialize. Once specialized, we find it most fruitful to collaborate with those with similar areas of interest. Historically, these specializations have grown into bounded disciplines. Disciplines and subdisciplines provide convenient limits to what non-universal experts must master and keep abreast of.

Universities, too, need neatly bounded disciplines. They are, after all, bureaucratic structures: how would one administer a large university without some kind of departments or divisions, some allocation of responsibility for subjects and topics? So we develop, as Donald T. Campbell (1969) and Murray Wax (1969) have explained (and I am indebted to them for all but the mistakes in the present analysis), the neat academic myth that knowledge comes in bundles, or boxes, or – to use a more elegant term – disciplines. In the social-behavioural and perhaps biological sciences, many disciplinary boundaries are arbitrary, accidents of history. Once embedded in the bureaucratic structure of a university, however, they tend to be permanent. Those socialized within the confines of such disciplines have a vested interest in treating neighbouring, overlapping fields as competitors, rather than allies. As a result, training in an academic discipline frequently involves indoctrination against neighbouring fields, as when sociologists confuse multiple levels of explanation with what they may term 'psychological reductionism,' or when biologists disparage colleagues' consideration of the behaviour of our own species. The attitude of colleagues is not a minor factor in determining the course of one's career. The sciences, after all, can reasonably be thought of as being organized around systems of scientists' reputations (Whittley, 1985).

If you want tenure and promotion, a non-voting intellectual collaborator or a publication in someone else's discipline is not in your career interest. Sharing with those in one's 'own' discipline is. The more one specializes in that in which others in one's discipline already specialize, the more reward-controlling allies one is likely to have. It is the members of one's own discipline who control one's employment, promotion, tenure, and (very often) access to research grants. Thus, the reward system of academia creates arbitrary disciplinary 'cores' that all practitioners are expected to – and had better – master. Specialize in one of these cores and you have a wider audience among those who will determine your rise or fall. Move to the periphery and you take risks. But it is on the periphery that the intellectual challenges are most likely to be found.

This condensation around often historically arbitrary 'cores' creates gaps in knowledge, gaps in which so-called 'interdisciplinary' studies are needed. Sometimes this push towards the interdisciplinary arises because challenging but previously unasked questions lie within the neglected-by-definition, between-discipline gaps. At other times an interdisciplinary or multidisciplinary team is generated by a real-world problem. Crime, overpopulation, the threat of war, poverty: no single academic discipline, in the social-behavioural-life sciences, is capable of dealing alone with problems such as these. Thus, dedicated researchers often permit their intellectual curiosity, or their concern with real-world problems, to push them into interdisciplinary (or multidisciplinary) studies. Sometimes new disciplines (or perhaps departments) result. There have been fads for interdisciplinary studies at various periods, during which university departments for 'social relations,' or 'area studies,' or 'human development,' have proliferated. During other periods careers can be damaged, since interdisciplinary work is often of lower prestige in academic fields than is 'core' research and theory.[5]

It is safest for interdisciplinary bravery to be shown by those who already have solid reputations in established disciplines. One thinks of Edward O. Wilson and his influential and highly interdisciplinary work, *Sociobiology: The New Synthesis* (1975a), for example. Donald T. Campbell (1969), himself one of the most interdisciplinary of senior American

5 I have my own doctorate from a multidisciplinary program (the University of Chicago's Committee on Human Development) but I was taught about the career dangers of being neither-fish-nor-fowl early in my training, and made sure that my professional identity as an anthropologist would be clear by doing rather traditional fieldwork and by publishing in anthropological journals. For young academics contemplating interdisciplinary careers I recommend this kind of strategy.

scholars, has long advocated a 'fishscale model' in which doctorates overlap other doctorates as do the scales of a fish, but without any arbitrary 'common core' around which all must lie. This is risky advice for young academics, but were it to be generally followed it would undoubtedly speed progress in the social-behavioural sciences, and probably in other fields as well.

Past Bad Biology as a Gap Generator
There is a special reason for the huge gaps between the social-behavioural sciences and evolutionary biology. It has to do with the racism of our intellectual grandparents. Chapter 8 will deal in part with the general tendency for human beings to take almost any attribute that in some way distinguishes them – or the groups to which they belong – from others, and to ascribe to it superiority. For our recent ancestors, a low melanin content of the skin was the sign of superiority.

The latter half of the nineteenth and first part of the twentieth centuries saw the development of a pseudo-biological justification for world domination by Western Europeans and their descendants, and for the domination of the poor by the wealthy. It was believed that 'white' skins were associated with an inherent superiority that at once was biological, psychological, moral, and cultural. The only real superiority, of course, was that based on military and economic power, but the social sciences had their genesis during this time of 'white' domination of many of the world's peoples. The theories of the early anthropologists were theories in part of 'racial' superiority and of magically pure or unpolluted founding 'races' (cf. Harris, 1968: 130–41). These theories served to justify both colonial conquest abroad and social inequality at home.

This book is not the place in which to review this racism to which we are the intellectual heirs; its history is readily available elsewhere. What is needed here is only a reminder that the apotheosis of that racism was Nazism and the Holocaust; and that much in the modern behavioural and social sciences stems from the bitter battle against the old theories, theories that justified so much racism, conquest, and murder. The bitterness has run especially deep among some biologists and anthropologists, I suspect, because immense horrors were elaborately justified and perpetrated by people who were members of these disciplines, as well as by physicians (Müller-Hill, 1988).

The biology was a bad biology, a pseudo-biology unsupported by any kind of scientific evidence. But the vocabulary *was* that of biology, evolution, and genetics. As a result, there has been and there remains –

for good reason – an extreme reluctance on the part of behavioural and social scientists to account for behavioural differences across populations in terms of actual or conjectural genetic differences. Research has moved in other directions, and those who have violated this near-taboo have found that their motives were instantly questioned, and that there are those who conclude quite automatically that these taboo-violators, if not necessarily closet Nazis, are at best dangerous fools.

That splash-and-thud you just heard was the old baby-out-with-the-bath-water problem. In retreating from the racist pseudo-biology and social Darwinism (more accurately, social Spencerism) of the past, the social-behavioural sciences locked themselves into an anti-biological environmentalism that is an intellectual descendant of eighteenth-century empiricism and the ideas of philosopher John Locke. Much of the present generation of social-behavioural scientists has been raised with the odd idea of the Lockean blank slate, the *tabula rasa* of eighteenth-century British Empiricism. Biological evolution in this perspective is fully respectable only when limited to the consideration of morphological traits, or to behavioural traits provided we are speaking of that long, vague period prior to the appearance of physically modern human beings, 100,000 to 200,000 years ago. After that point, goes the ideology, the only kind of evolution we need worry about is cultural, not biological. If biology is to be considered at all it should be limited to a few 'basic drives,' such as hunger and thirst, which are then 'moulded by culture' (for example, Malinowski, 1944: 75–90).

Anthropologists sometimes speak of their version of the *tabula rasa* as a belief in the 'psychic unity of man' (for instance, Harris, 1968: 15, and Wallace, 1961). The term means that all human populations are held to be psychobiologically identical except for the effects of culture and experience.[6] A member of our species is taken to be a *tabula rasa* upon which culture writes. This is not to deny that some genetic differences

---

6 As Harris (1968) explains, Morgan, the late-nineteenth-century anthropologist who originated the term 'psychic unity,' meant by it a postulated series of stages of development through which all human groups were believed to progress. The series began with 'savagery,' progressed to barbarism, and eventually ended with enlightened nineteenth-century European Man. This invariant sequence of development was believed to be at once biological, cultural, psychological, and moral. The conquered and colonized were therefore simultaneously inferior biologically, culturally, mentally, and, of course, morally. It was the 'burden' of the 'whiteman' (in Kipling's wonderfully unselfconscious presentation of military conquest as noble self-sacrifice) to rule and guide those darker-hued peoples who were still low on this evolutionary ladder, educating them to the extent their biological and moral inferiority permitted. Anthropologists today mean something quite different when we speak of 'psychic unity.'

may occur among individuals; but group differences in behaviour, culture, or society are never to be ascribed to differences in their respective gene pools, only to 'culture.' A sort of reified 'culture' takes plastic, malleable human beings and moulds them, shapes them as it will.

The behavioural-science equivalent of the 'blank slate' assumption has been the great emphasis on an undifferentiated idea of learning as a single process rather than as a loose term for a wide variety of environmental and experiential effects on behaviour, probably involving a host of specialized information-processors or psychological mechanisms, each of which evolved to solve a particular adaptive problem (Cosmides and Tooby, 1987; Symons, 1987; Tooby and Cosmides, 1989). As Cosmides and Tooby observe, 'The evolutionary function of the human brain is to process information in ways that lead to adaptive behavior' (1987: 282, italics omitted). Towards this end, the brain has evolved specific information-processing capabilities ('mental organs') to deal with particular kinds of data in the context of particular kinds of problems. There is little evidence for a global learning capacity, as opposed to specific capacities that have evolved in response to specific adaptive problems. To say that something has been 'learned' is therefore to say remarkably little (cf. Lockhard, 1971; Skinner, 1984). It is not enough to speak of a 'constraint' on learning: the implication, as Cosmides and Tooby (1987: 301) point out, is that the learning process would be very broad if only the constraint were removed, whereas there is no evidence of a global learning ability in the first place. Nor is it sufficient (though it is a good start) to admit, as most psychologists would nowadays, that learning is a product of a biological evolution process that shapes which aspects of the environment a given species will attend to, what it will learn readily and what with difficulty, and which stimuli it will find rewarding or 'reinforcing': what is needed is an understanding of the algorithms in terms of which particular kinds of information will be sought from the environment and then processed. Unfortunately, there is often a considerable lag in the diffusion of knowledge from one discipline to another, and many social scientists retain the simplistic view of learning and biological evolution now being discarded by many psychologists. Often enough, even today, social scientists believe that 'learned' contrasts with 'evolved' and that the two concepts represent alternative hypotheses (Cosmides and Tooby, 1987). (See chapter 5 for further discussion of how the mind may be organized.)

Whatever the problems of the concept of 'learning,' the total retreat from genetic determinism was probably needed: it was too easy to take assumed genetic differences as the primary rather than residual explanation for behavioural and social-cultural differences, and so leave off studying them. Whether the 'psychic unity' argument really is accurate is, of course, an empirical question, and will be discussed in chapter 11. But the 'blank slate' assumption has been quite harmful to our understanding of the nature of human nature. The assumption meant that 'culture' (often taken as *accounting for* patterned, socially transmitted behaviour rather than as being a way of distinguishing such behaviour from individual idiosyncrasy) could do almost anything: no theory of human psychology other than a simplistic version of learning theory was needed.

At times, anthropologists and other social scientists – particularly those influenced by Freud's *Civilization and Its Discounts* and by his *Totem and Taboo* (1961, 1950) – have even considered culture to be *opposed* to our biological nature, rather than an expression of it. Here, for example, is the noted anthropologist Marshall Sahlins, writing in 1960 in *Scientific American*: 'The emergence of human society required some suppression, rather than direct expression, of man's primate nature' (p. 77). Further on, he continues: 'Yet the remarkable aspect of culture's usurpation of the evolutionary task from biology was that in so doing it was forced to oppose man's primate nature on many fronts and to subdue it. It is an extraordinary fact that primate urges often become not the secure foundation of human social life, but a source of weakness in it' (p. 78).[7]

Now, perhaps, we are ready to understand how the oddity of a biology-free social science could develop; how in the social and behavioural sciences the only respectable biology could have come to be anatomical, physiological, or neurological, but never evolutionary; and how the social sciences could have largely ignored even this much biology. We have already discussed how academic disciplines have a built-in tendency to coalesce around historically arbitrary 'cores' and how the reward system may drown those who choose to work in the

---

7 There is a certain sense in which culture is indeed opposed to the satisfaction of human emotional needs, though I do not think this is what Sahlins has in mind. See Jules Henry's *Culture against Man* for this approach. For Henry (1963: 11), 'man *wrings* from culture what emotional satisfactions he obtains from it' (emphasis in the original). As we will see in chapter 12, there is no guarantee that our societies will make us either happy or healthy.

interesting oceans between these islands. Add to these processes the enduring effects of the bad biology of the past, when no explanation save that of birth seemed necessary, for many, to explain both population and individual differences in behaviour. If you can forgive the flood of metaphor, imagine evolutionary biology and population genetics as one island continent, and the social-behavioural sciences as another. Now is the time for ending false dichotomies and for emphasizing continuities. Now is the time to position the social-behavioral sciences in their proper place as seamless continuations of biology.

SUMMARY

1. This book is an attempt to integrate a broad swath of social-and behavioural science topics by placing them in the framework of biological evolution. Evolution is not a mere metaphor, in this context – I will be borrowing heavily from modern evolutionary theory.

2. Because the goal is a putting-together, a synthesizing, it will not be possible to detail many of the ideas and theories presented. However, all testable hypotheses have been collected and are presented together as chapter 15's Focus 15.1.

3. This book will deal with selected topics rather than attempt to integrate all the social-behavioural-evolutionary sciences. The topics will include the nature of awareness, emotions and irrationality, culture and gene-culture evolution, sexual behaviour, prestige and self-esteem, social change, and sociobiology and social engineering.

4. This book rests on the validity of modern evolutionary theory. At no point will any effort be made to challenge the adaptationist paradigm.

5. Even though knowledge is actually seamless, everywhere we find it divided into isolated islands called 'disciplines.' The general reason for these condensations has to do with the bureaucratic nature of the university – responsibility for subjects must be allocated, which requires boundaries – and of human limitations, since no one person can be expected to master everything. Once the boundaries among disciplines exist, however, the reward system of academia causes a turning inward within each field, as individuals turn towards those with whom they share the most intellectually and who also control their prospects for tenure, promotion, and prestige. As a result, gaps develop, though bridges across them are frequently built.

6. There is an additional reason for the gap between evolutionary biology and the social-behavioural sciences. It stems from the pseudo-biology of the past, a bad biology used to justify first colonial oppression and slavery and then the Holocaust. As a result, social-behavioural scientists turned strongly away from anything that smacked of 'evolution' or 'genetics.' They embraced the Lockean philosophical position that the mind was a blank slate written upon by experience. For social scientists, culture and society encompassed all the explanation they sought. Behavioural scientists made of 'learning' a simple process for which animal models were adequate, instead of appreciating it as a broad concept encompassing a variety of types of evolutionarily specialized information-processing.

Basic Theory

2

Darwin and Genes

BLIND VARIATION AND SELECTIVE RETENTION

Order arises from disorder through natural processes. No invisible hand must insert each atom into its crystal lattice. No mathematically modelling engineer need calculate the wind-resistance of a finch's feathers. Trial-and-error learning, crystallization, and biological evolution are examples of naturally occurring, order-generating processes. Underlying them all, according to Donald T. Campbell (1960, 1965), is the more fundamental process of *blind variation and selective retention*.

Begin with a source of variants. Call them ideas, or pieces of a puzzle, or even genes. Now we need a set of retention criteria such that some of these variants will be retained and/or propagated, and others rejected, in accordance with the criteria. Suppose we have a jigsaw puzzle. The retention criterion is that if a given piece fits a slot on the board it stays there. Shake the pieces on the board. Replace those that fall. Eventually each piece will have 'found' its proper place. Through blind-variation-and-selective-retention a puzzle has been solved yet no one has solved it.

Now, sit down at your new microcomputer and your new word-processing program and, by trial and error, find out how to delete a line. One and only one combination of keys will do this, so keep on striking combinations. These combinations are 'blind' variants, blind with respect to the retention criterion of deleting a line. Eventually you will hit upon the right combination. Retain it in your memory. You have now learned how to delete lines. You could, in principle, learn an entire word-processing program in this manner (though few have documentation quite so poor as to require you to do so). Many natural processes, like trial-and-error learning, argues Campbell, have as their heart blind-variation-and-selective-retention. It is, for example, the basis of biological evolution.

GENES AND EVOLUTION

Compare blind-variation-and-selective-retention to basic Darwin. For Darwin, individuals differ. These differences are the variants. Since offspring tend to resemble their parents, variants can be transmitted from one generation to the next. Some variants more than others increase the likelihood of an individual's surviving and reproducing, *in a given environment*. That is, some variants more than others meet the retention criteria of aiding individuals to achieve reproductive success. There are almost always surplus offspring, so that some but not all survive. Since offspring do tend to resemble their parents, with each generation those variants that meet the retention criteria of aiding reproductive success are retained and become more frequent in the population. In other words, inheritable individual differences that tend to increase reproductive success become ever more frequent. For the process to continue the environment must be fairly constant, so that the variations that increased the likelihood of reproductive success in one generation have the same effect in others. As the relative frequencies of variants alter, evolution takes place. Darwin's name for this differential survival and reproduction of varying organisms was 'natural selection.' The result of this process is biological evolution and the (relatively) gradual development of new animal species.[1]

Note that if the environment changes then so do the retention criteria and different variants will be favoured: the direction of evolution will alter. For example, if the terrain is usually snow-covered then selection

1 For a much fuller introduction to modern evolutionary theory, see any introductory biological anthropology textbook, for example, that of Bernard G. Campbell (1985). Note, too, that the extent to which speciation is or is not gradual has been controversial in evolutionary biology. Gould and Eldredge (1977) argue for evolution being not gradual at all but following a 'punctuated equilibrium.' More recently, however, the consensus seems to have shifted to the view that, properly understood, neo-Darwinian theory predicts that the rate of evolution will be highly variable, and that at times new species will arise with relative speed (Lewin, 1985).

may favour white-coloured prey species. Suppose the climate alters and there is rarely snow: now being white makes prey conspicuous, and selection will favour a different colour, one that provides better camouflage in the new environment.

The only variants of which Darwin was aware were the *phenotypic* differences among individuals, that is, differences in the observable or measurable physical and behavioural characteristics of their bodies and behaviours. Nowadays, of course, we understand that underlying these more apparent differences are differences in *genotypes*, that is, in the complement of genes organisms carry. A *gene* is a unit of the material of heredity. Think of these units as units of information. We have about 100,000 of them. Strictly speaking, a gene is a unit of information coded in the sequences of nucleotides (the bases thymine, guanine, adenine, and cytosine) composing a molecule of deoxyribonucleic acid or 'DNA.' Genes may have alternative forms called *alleles* that occupy the same position or locus on the DNA molecule and which code for very slightly different information.

The DNA molecule itself is a double spiral or helix, each strand of which coils around the other and is linked to it by its base pairs. Adenine pairs with thymine, cytosine with guanine. These links separate when cells divide, and each independent strand synthesizes its counterpart so that the original DNA molecule is duplicated. Thus, the genes are propagated.

One could argue, as does Dawkins (1976, 1982), that the organism is only a gene's way of making more genes. Our bodies exist only because the genes that help generate them thereby propagate themselves. But the distance between these coded nucleotide sequences and our actual bodies and behaviours is remarkably great, so great as to make the 'genes are our masters' idea entirely metaphorical.

A gene is a code not for a specific behaviour or part of the body but for a protein that serves as an enzyme controlling other biochemical processes that, in interaction with each other and with inputs from the environment, generate the organism's physical body and its functional properties or 'phenotype.' The environment of a gene includes both other genes and the external physical environment in which the organism finds itself.

The gene's ultimate effects on the phenotype depend on its interactions with its immensely complex environment. To ask what proportion of these effects is due to the gene itself and what proportion to the environment is to ask a dangerously misleading question, one that by implication reduces processes of extraordinary complexity to the simple blending of two ingredients. It is, of course, possible to ask how much of the *variability* (technically, the variance) of aspects of the phenotype is due to descent and how much to the environment. A statistical formula permits this calculation of the *heritability* of a trait, and it is easy to mistake heritability for a constituent element, an ingredient. But the fact that it is possible to partition variance does not magically transform genes and environments into ingredients. To say that a trait is highly heritable is simply to make the statistical observation that, if your close relatives mostly have the trait, you are likely to have it too. Heritability tells us nothing about the gene-environment interactions or the developmental processes involved.

A given gene may have multiple effects (*pleiotropy*) or, depending on its environment, no detectable effects at all. The complement of genes that the body carries about is its *genome*. In some instances, molecular biologists have actually determined the particular protein a specific gene codes for. In no case, however, have all the biochemical steps between a gene and a human behavioural ability been determined.[2] Given our general ignorance of the pathways between genes and our actual behaviour and morphology, and given the great controversy over the tightness of the links between genes and behaviour, for the purposes of this book it would probably be wisest not to speak of a *gene for* a trait but rather of a *gene influencing the probability of occurrence of* a behavioural or morphological character. The language of probability permits movement away from the outmoded idea that 'genetic' implies 'immutable' or inevitable. Admittedly, probability terminology fails to do justice to the immense complexities involved in gene-environment interaction: ideally, when we spoke of 'genes for' a trait we would be in a position to specify how the particular protein produced by this gene affects cells, tissues, and organs, in a given environment, in such a way as to influence the trait in question. Given the state of current knowledge, we are forced to speak of presumed 'genes for' increasing the likelihood of a particular developmental outcome. Since the vocabulary of probability theory can also be a bit awkward, at times, the term 'gene for,' wherever I do use it in this book, should be taken as shorthand for 'increasing the probability of occurrence of.' This last point requires expansion, for the failure of some to grasp it has led to much empty debate.

2 Research has tended to focus on the links between *dis*abilities and genes, as in such gene-linked disorders as hemophilia and phenylketonuria.

The 'Great Gene Myth'

Perhaps the blame for what Dawkins (1982) terms the 'great gene myth,' the fallacy of the 'super-deterministic gene,' lies with Gregor Mendel. Most of us probably first learned of genes in connection with his peapods and the single genes that alone seemed responsible for determining whether the pea would be wrinkled or smooth, yellow or green. The environment did not seem to be of great importance for the expression of these *single gene effects*. Some of my social-scientist colleagues still seem to have Mendel in mind when they hear the term 'gene,' and think that a sociobiologist writing of a gene 'for' aggression or for courtship behaviour means that these complex phenomena are single-gene effects in which it is safe to ignore environment, and that, say, human aggressiveness is of the same nature as colour in peas. Naturally, the social scientist protests. But no sociobiologist really means that complex behavioural traits are in any way comparable to the colour of peas, even when both are described as 'genetic.'

Complex characteristics are not single-gene effects; they are products of complexes of co-ordinated genes, sometimes known as 'polygenes.' And it is meaningless to speak of genes without discussing the environment. It is true that *all* behaviour is genetic, but not in a 'super-deterministic' sense, only in the sense that its probability of occurrence is indirectly affected by a host of genes, even when the pathways are extremely complex and the effect of any individual gene relatively slight. Playing the piano is in this sense genetic. After all, one's genetic background will certainly influence the probability that one will have sufficient manual dexterity to play, adequate auditory ability, and so forth. It is also true that, if you were born in the seventeenth century, the probability of your learning to play the piano was zero, regardless of your genes. We will return to the piano in a moment, after a discussion of sneezing.

The term 'gene' is sometimes linked to 'innate,' which has a strong connotation of immutability. An 'innate' behaviour is one that will manifest itself *not* regardless of the environment but within a wide range of environmental inputs. The distinction is crucial. All behaviours are the product of immensely complex gene-environment interactions. Suppose a given behaviour is vital to genetic fitness so that there is a strong selection pressure in favour of it: sneezing will do as an example.

Being able to sneeze is presumably a product of gene-environment interaction. Let us assume that people who cannot sneeze in response to nasal irritation due to dust get their respiratory passages blocked and in some situations may even die as a result. Let us hold environment constant, for a moment. People whose genes, in interaction with that fixed environment, generate the sneeze reflex are more likely to survive and reproduce than are others. People whose genes, in interaction with this fixed environment, do not permit them to sneeze are less likely to survive and reproduce than are others. Gradually, genetic variants (alleles) that in interaction with that environment result in sneezing will increase in frequency in the *gene pool* (the totality of genes of a given local population), and other alleles will decrease. We will all eventually be sneezers, even if only in that fixed environment.

Now, let us permit the environment to fluctuate slightly. We will add swarms of tiny gnats. Individuals whose genes, in interaction with the altered as well as with the original environment, *still* generate sneezing will be more likely to survive and reproduce than will others. Permit the environment to fluctuate even more. Alleles that in interacting with a wide range of environments increase the probability of sneezing will be favoured. If the selection pressure is strong enough and maintained long enough, selection will favour a constellation of genes that interact in varying ways with a varying environment to produce a relatively unvarying result: a sneeze. It saves a great many words to describe such behaviours as 'innate' but they are still totally dependent upon the environment for their appearance, even though a range of environments will do.[3]

By contrast, some traits require some very specific environmental inputs in order to manifest themselves. For example, learning to play the piano requires, at a minimum, a piano. But piano-playing is also genetic: there are certainly genes for piano-playing in the sense that they will increase the probability of your learning to play the piano, as was suggested earlier. But 'genetic' does not mean 'inevitable' or 'immutable' and does not contrast with 'learned.' Whatever your genes, you still need to have a piano, and unless you are very unusual, lessons and practice. Like sneezing, playing the piano is a product of gene-environment interaction. In a very real sense, sneezing and piano-playing are equally genetic. They differ in that the genes that make

---

3 In systems-theory terms, the gene-environment system that generates the ability to sneeze is an open system exhibiting *equifinality*. That is, the system may produce the same result with a variety of different inputs, following a variety of developmental paths. As von Bertalanffy (1968: 40) puts it, 'the same final state may be reached from different conditions and in different ways.'

piano-playing possible require some very specific and unusual inputs if they are to co-generate music, while genes for sneezing require only the usual human environment. Sneezing and piano-playing represent the end-points of a broad range of specificity of environmental input for behaviour to be manifested.

Panselectionism
Sociologist Howard L. Kaye (1986: 107) tells us that sociobiologists are often accused of 'panselectionism, in which virtually every characteristic of an organism – morphological and behavioral – is assumed, even in the absence of evidence, to be the product of natural selection and thus under the control of genes.'[4] If there are 'genes for' traits, does this mean that *all* traits are the product of specific genes that have been selected for? Recall the earlier mention of *pleiotropy*, the tendency for genes to have multiple effects. Perhaps a given trait is the product not of the particular effect of the gene being selected for, but of another, pleiotropic effect. The species bearing this trait will therefore have a characteristic that has not been selected for, and for which evolutionary (though not biochemical) explanations are invalid.

Sober (1984: 97–102) makes an often useful distinction between selection *of* genes and selection *for* their properties. For example, suppose gene 'A' has two effects, one of which is to make my chin more prominent and the other of which is to make hair grow on the back of my hands. That gene 'A' should have such evolutionarily unrelated effects is, we will further assume, a biochemical accident. Let us postulate that a prominent chin is a good buttress for the physical stresses of chewing and biting, and let us further assume that our diet is tough and coarse and requires a good deal of forceful mastication. People with prominent chins are (we are assuming) less likely to injure their jaws and therefore are slightly more likely to survive and reproduce than are others. Thus, genes for prominent chins will increase in the gene pool. There is selection *of* the genes underlying prominent chins.

But the gene for chins has that pleiotropic effect of causing hair to grow on the backs of hands. This second trait is *not* selected for but there is still selection *of* a gene causing it. Unfortunately, our evolutionist knows nothing about the molecular biology of chins and hairy-handedness. Though he or she may provide ingenious arguments for the adaptive value of hairy-handedness, these accounts cannot fail to be

---

4 Kaye cites, in this connection, those arch-critics of sociobiology Stephen J. Gould (1980: 280–3) and Richard Lewontin (1977: 293).

invalid. Of course, the sociobiologist will probably develop them anyway, for panselectionism is a sort of occupational hazard for the evolutionist: in this case, how would he or she know that, while there has been selection of the genes underlying hairy-handedness, there has been no selection for it?

Other non-natural-selection evolutionary phenomena, in addition to pleiotropy, may alter gene frequencies and therefore the distribution of traits. When a genetically isolated population grows very small, for example, genetic change can result because some alleles may simply be so low in frequency that they never happen to appear in a fertilizing sperm cell or fertilized ovum (genetic drift or the *Sewall Wright effect*).

Panselectionism leads to even more error when we invoke *emergence*. *Emergence* is a concept that in its simplest form simply means that the whole is greater than the sum of its parts. The term is closely related to the idea of the mutual non-deducibility of compatible explanations discussed in chapter 1. Higher levels of organization have *emergent* properties not predictable from lower levels – chemical compounds have characteristics not predictable from the properties of their component elements, for example. Used more loosely, the fact that the climbing organ known as the hand could later be used for tool manipulation is an example of emergence. Such an emergent property has not been selected for, originally, though selection may well subsequently work on it.[5] As we will see in chapter 4, it has been argued that human self-awareness itself is a product of emergence rather than of natural selection (though this argument will not be accepted). In much of the second half of this book, I will suggest that many aspects of human nature and culture have not been directly selected for at all, are frequently emergent in nature, and often enough may in fact be genetically maladaptive.

There seems to be no clear rule as to when we are to assume that a given trait is a product of natural selection and when we must not so assume. Thus, so long as we find the adaptationist paradigm as useful as it was asserted to be in chapter 1, we will run an unavoidable risk of panselectionism, that is, of generating false hypotheses. This hazard is of course reduced if we keep it in mind, but ultimately must be controlled by the usual process of challenge and counter-challenge of

---

5 See Buckley (1967: 110–11) for a discussion of the idea of 'emergence.' The specific example of emergence discussed here is an example of what some evolutionists term 'preadaptation,' a label that is sometimes frowned on because of its teleological connotations. Evolution is 'opportunistic' and new traits often develop from serendipitous 'side-effects' of old traits.

ideas and assertions by which science progresses, and by an insistence on vertically integrated explanation in order that accounts incompatible with other levels and kinds of explanation be identified and closely examined. Whatever the hazards of panselectionism, it would seem to be no more risky and far more fruitful a strategy than its opposite, an expectation that traits are *not* generally adaptive.

It is possible to misread some sociobiologists in such a manner that they appear to 'endow the commanding genes with consciousness and will and the evolutionary process with consciousness and purpose' (Kaye 1986: 109). As Dawkins (1982) protests, that is not what is meant. The fact that a given trait might well be adaptive for an organism (that is, increase the probability of its surviving and reproducing) does not somehow call that trait, and the genes underlying it, into existence. Recall the discussion at the beginning of this chapter of the blind-variation-and-selective-retention model underlying evolutionary theory: the genes are always blind variants and evolutionary theory, far from endowing genes with consciousness and will, shows how order and the appearance of purposefulness may be generated by natural processes. ('Blind' here, by the way, does not necessarily mean random, since some mutations occur much more frequently than do others: it means blind with respect to the retention criteria of differential survival and reproduction of the organism.) If there are no variants available that would produce a given trait then that trait will not evolve, no matter how useful it might be.

Natural Selection and the Resultant of Forces
Pleiotropy may at times defeat natural selection. Suppose gene 'Z' enhances resistance to influenza but lowers resistance to bacterial infection, in a given species in a given environment: will it increase in frequency in the gene pool? Actual gene frequencies represent a sort of *resultant of forces*, the result of evolutionary 'trade-offs': a given gene may be both selected for and selected against, and its eventual frequency in the gene pool will depend upon the relative strengths of the opposing selection pressures.

What applies to pleiotropic genes applies even more strongly to traits determined by constellations of genes. Suppose that larger size decreases the probability that wolves will attack members of my species, while aiding in heat conservation, important in our cold climate. Selection will therefore favour the increase in frequency in the gene pool of genes conducive to larger size. But suppose that there are periodic, catastrophic famines in our environment, during which only the smaller individuals can find enough food to survive: every few generations, selection will catastrophically decrease the frequency of the genes for large size in the gene pool – regardless of their ordinarily fitness-enhancing effects – and increase the frequency of genes for small size: once again, we have a resultant-of-forces situation, just as we did in the case of pleiotropy. All adaptations (as we will see in chapter 12) may simultaneously tend to increase and to decrease fitness, and may tend to do both in a variety of ways. It is usually impossible for biologists to be certain that they have identified all the selection pressures affecting the evolution of any given trait or the frequency of any given gene.

LEVELS OF EVOLUTION AND UNITS OF SELECTION

Natural selection is a blind-variation-and-selective-retention process, and I have identified the variants as genes or (more precisely) alleles: but are these the only variants, the only units of evolution? Could the unit of evolution not be the co-ordinated group of genes (the polygene or gene complex) that together give rise to a specific trait or structure? Alternatively, is not the entire organism subject to selection? Or could we not argue that selection operates among groups, that is, that the local population (*deme*) is the unit of selection? Perhaps selection operates in terms of entire species as units, and some are retained and some become extinct. This question of the level of organization at which natural selection operates, the question of what the unit is, is a highly controversial one, in evolutionary biology.[6] We cannot resolve it, but neither can we

6 For a full discussion of the unit-of-evolution debate, see Brandon and Burian (1984). For a philosopher's analysis of the problem, see the last three chapters of Sober (1984: 215–368). Sober finds great complexities and difficulties with the basic concepts that evolutionists have used in discussing selection. One of his key distinctions, for example, is that between selection *for* objects as opposed to selection *of* properties of objects. Thus, he can criticize Dawkins (1982) for assuming that a 'replicator' must also be the unit of selection, since while there is selection *for* genes (replicators), there is selection *of* its (presumably fitness-enhancing) properties (p. 251). Similar reasoning enables Sober to conclude that group selection does not necessarily mean that group properties are being selected for. I slight these (and many other) subtle arguments and distinctions, in the discussion that follows, on the grounds that they would distract from the task at hand, that of providing sufficient basic evolutionary theory to serve as a foundation for the theories of mind and culture to be presented in subsequent chapters. As an anthropologist, I can only hope that my treatment of major issues in evolutionary biology and biological philosophy does not elicit from members of those disciplines the same reaction of outrage that the treatment of the concept of culture by a number of biologists has elicited from many anthropologists.

ignore it, for the unit of selection of issue turns out to be closely linked with a major sociobiological topic, the evolution of *altruism*.

Altruism and Group Selection

Altruism means aiding another at one's own expense, and it has long been a phenomenon of considerable concern to evolutionists: at first glance, it should not exist. There has never been total agreement among evolutionists as to how to account for altruism, but for some years *group selection* explanations approached orthodoxy, particularly among naturalists (as opposed to population geneticists). In group selection, the variants upon which the selective-retention process operated are held to be local populations. Wynne-Edwards's (1962) massive and powerful study *Animal Dispersion in Relation to Social Behaviour* argued strongly that groups whose members behaved in an 'altruistic' manner were more likely to survive and reproduce than were other groups, so that the members of the species as a whole would come to act 'altruistically.' The latter term, in this context, tended to mean individuals apparently limiting their own reproduction in order to prevent the group as a whole from suffering from over-population. It was as if the individual, before acting, considered what would be 'good for the group' rather than what would be in its self-interest.

For example, many social species exhibit a status hierarchy in which high-ranking individuals have preferential access to some item of value, such as food or receptive females, and in which lower-ranking individuals usually yield access (and often physical place) to the higher-ranking without physical violence. For Wynne-Edwards, these hierarchies serve not just to control aggression within the group but to limit population: lower-ranking individuals often either make no attempt to mate or are prevented from doing so, potentially controlling over-population. As Wynne-Edwards (1971: 94) put it, 'the greatest benefits of sociality arise from its capacity to override the advantage of the individual members in the interests of the survival of the group as a whole.' This perspective is remarkably similar to the old structural-functionalism of sociocultural anthropology and, like that paradigm, is no longer widely accepted. Instead, the theory of selection at the level of the individual gene has ascended.

In 1966 came the publication of Williams's *Adaptation and Natural Selection: A Critique of Some Current Evolutionary Theory*, which argued persuasively against group selection.[7] The problem with group selection

7 The reader Williams subsequently (1971) edited gives both sides of the controversy but it is clear that his side prevailed.

is a matter of simple logic. Individual genes for 'altruism' are continually lowering their own representation in the gene pool, since their bearers are less likely to survive and reproduce than are others. These genes, after all, lead individuals to give up some of their own opportunity to reproduce, thereby benefiting the group as a whole by lowering the pressure on resources. As a result, groups with a high frequency of individuals with 'altruistic' genes are more likely to survive and reproduce *qua* groups than are other populations. The group may thrive but the genes for 'altruism' that are the cause of this thriving are constantly being lost because it is their bearers who are least likely to have offspring. 'Altruism' is therefore selected *against* at the individual level but is selected *for* at the group level. Mathematically, for most species, it turns out that the rate at which groups either propagate themselves or become extinct is unlikely to be sufficiently high to maintain appreciable frequencies of 'altruistic' genes in the species as a whole, given the rate at which 'altruism' genes are lost.

Migration presents an additional problem for group selection. As Peter Richerson (in a 1987 personal communication) points out, groups with a high proportion of individuals with 'altruistic' genes may be invaded by individuals from other groups with 'selfish' genes. Altruism by definition has costs, so that these non-altruistic, 'selfish-gene-bearing' invaders will out-reproduce the altruistic 'natives.' Soon enough, the non-altruistic genes will dominate.

If group-selection accounts of altruism turn out to be flawed, we need alternative explanations. For example, in the case of the social hierarchy, Williams (1966) explained that its members were aiding themselves by avoiding aggressive encounters that they were unlikely to win. A potentially violent encounter risks fitness-reducing injuries, or even death: unless one has a very good chance of winning, selection actually favours taking a subordinate position. But a more general explanation of 'altruism' is available.

Altruism and Selfish Gene Selection
The alternative theory, now widely (though not universally) accepted in evolutionary biology, involves a rethinking of individual-level selection that takes into account selection at the level of the gene. This approach is based on the work of Haldane (1955), Fisher (1930), and Wright (1969), but in its current form was developed largely by Maynard Smith (1964, 1971, 1976), Williams (1966), Hamilton (1964, 1970), and Trivers (1972). More recently it has been shaped by many others, including Dawkins

(1976, 1982) and West Eberhard (1975). Evolutionists who emphasize evolution at the level of the gene and de-emphasize group selection sometimes but by no means always refer to their work as 'sociobiology' (as was discussed in the preface and in chapter 1).

Sociobiology 'solves' the problem of altruism by redefining it to mean 'genetic selfishness' on the part of individuals. (In point of fact, the biologist's 'altruism' is not ordinary English 'altruism' at all. Obviously, any gene that 'altruistically' caused its bearer to sacrifice some of his or her fitness would necessarily be lowering its representation in the gene pool.) Any two individuals from the same population (or even from the same species) share most of their genes. Each of your offspring, however, shares with you an additional one-half of the genes you would not share (on a statistical basis) with a randomly chosen, non-related individual. For the sake of brevity, let us just say that your offspring shares one-half of your genes, that is, that your coefficient of relatedness or consanguinity (r) with your offspring is 0.5. Evolution, we know, has to do with changes in allele frequencies (an allele, as indicated above, being an alternative, or variant, form of a gene). An allele that increases the probability of your survival and reproduction increases the probability that it will increase in frequency in the gene pool because it has a 0.5 probability of being replicated in each of your offspring. In short, if an allele increases your chances of having offspring it increases its chances of increasing in frequency in the gene pool. Obviously, natural selection must favour reproductive success.

From this perspective, selection should favour individuals who act so as to maximize their genetic representation in the next generation, their *inclusive fitness* (Hamilton, 1964). The older 'synthetic' theory of evolution (synthesizing Mendelian genetics with Darwin) had individuals striving to leave as many surviving offspring as possible, that is, to maximize their *reproductive success*. Differential reproduction was the key to evolution, in Darwinian terms. It remains of great importance in sociobiology (particularly since measuring actual inclusive fitness is extremely difficult both practically and conceptually). But a sociobiologist would argue that natural selection favours reproductive success only because your offspring share a portion of your genes.

Cost-Benefit Analysis
Your offspring are not the only relatives with whom you share genes. As will be discussed more thoroughly in chapter 3 (under the heading of 'genes recognizing their replicates'), your full siblings each have, on the

average, 50% ($r = 0.5$) of your genes. By encouraging their survival and reproduction, you, in effect, increase the frequency of a portion of your genes in the gene pool. Selection, in short, has to do with individuals striving to enhance their *inclusive* fitness, that is, their genetic representation in the next generation as calculated by their own immediate offspring and the additional offspring their kin have had thanks to their ('altruistic') efforts (cf. West Eberhard, 1975).[8] Inclusive-fitness selection is also known as 'kin selection.'

This kind of approach results in the *cost-benefit* analysis typical of sociobiology. It is as if, before being altruistic, you had to weigh the potential cost to the 100% of the genes you carry vs. the potential benefits to whatever proportion of those genes your possible beneficiary carries. For example, suppose you are an expert swimmer. Your full sibling is drowning, even though the water is calm. Saving the sibling would entail little risk to you but would have a considerable probability of permitting your sibling to reproduce. Each additional niece or nephew would represent an addition of one-quarter of your genes (one-half of one-half) in the gene pool. At slight potential cost, therefore, you might well reap a large increment in inclusive fitness. Jump in!

This example is not meant as parody. The behavioural traits of all species are directly or indirectly the products of genetic evolution. The sociobiologist assumes that these traits – including the psychological dispositions of your species – reflect relative allele frequencies.[9] Alleles that cause you to act *as if* you were performing this kind of cost-benefit analysis will increase in relative frequency in the gene pool. In chapters 4 and 5 we will discuss some of the mechanisms that more proximately generate this approximation of cost-benefit analysis, but for the moment, what is important is this: *you* did not solve the jigsaw puzzle discussed at the beginning of this chapter; a blind-variation-and-selective-retention process did. You did not deduce how to use your word-processor program; that knowledge was generated by a blind-variation-and-

---

8 Of course, you need to recognize your kin. In our own species, we apparently take those with whom we have been socialized as kin. The problem of altruism and kin recognition will be returned to in chapter 3. For a thorough discussion of the mechanisms by which various species solve the kin-recognition problem, see Sherman and Holmes (1985).

9 This assumption entails the risk of panselectionism, discussed in chapter 1. The assumption is worth the risk for, as we shall see, it permits the generation of much theory and testable hypothesis.

selective-retention process. You did not just do a cost-benefit analysis about whether saving your sibling was worth the risk, either: the gene frequencies that underlie the systems and subsystems of your brain were generated by a blind-variation-and-selective-retention process which approximated a mathematical cost-benefit analysis. The mathematics of those gene frequencies, in this, as in all behaviour and morphology for all species, have been worked out, in evolutionary time, by the blind-variation-selective-retention processes Darwin called 'natural selection.' (The algorithms used by your brain in generating your behaviour are no doubt very different from the mathematics governing gene frequencies, but more about this in subsequent chapters.)

Thinking in terms of inclusive fitness – in terms of sociobiology – has become mainstream evolutionary biology and ethology. A glance at any issue of the major journal *Animal Behavior*, for example, will show a high proportion of articles applying sociobiological theory to various species and using empirical data to test the resulting hypotheses. Any controversies generated are productive, for they can be settled empirically so that theory and knowledge are continually expanded and corrected.

Multiple Levels of Selection
Even though selection at the level of the individual gene is the current orthodoxy, in evolutionary theory group selection is not and never will be out of the game. Evolution takes place at multiple levels: that is, we have a number of hierarchically ordered levels of variants. The unit of selection we emphasize will depend in part upon the particular question we are asking, in part upon our theoretical bias. There does not appear to be any final answer to the question 'what is the unit of selection?'

Recall, for example, the previous discussion of cost-benefit analysis. In that example, we explained aid to kin by focusing on the individual organism. Inclusive-fitness selection favoured your acting as if you were calculating your degree of relatedness to another prior to proffering aid, and then providing the aid only if the risk to your 100% was commensurate with the gain to the proportion of your genes shared by your relative. By implication, with this kind of explanation, the variant in the blind-variation-and-selective-retention process of evolution is the individual. This approach has much face validity to it.

By contrast, Richard Dawkins (1976, 1982) would focus on the level of the gene as the variant (or 'replicator,' in his terminology). For Dawkins, aiding kin is readily explained because any gene that increases the likelihood of its bearer aiding whatever individuals carry its replicates will increase in frequency in the gene pool. Hence, the gene is 'selfish' and the organism is a sort of 'gene machine,' a gene's way of making more genes. Whether a particular gene ultimately acts upon its own bearer or upon a bearer of its duplicate ('replicate') is not of great theoretical moment for Dawkins. The individual organism is not a replicator, he argues, but merely the 'vehicle' for the true replicators, the genes, which cause their vehicle to aid vehicles carrying duplicates of themselves. In similar fashion, even in group selection the gene remains the unit of evolution, the local breeding populations simply being 'vehicles' for the genes.

There is another way to deal with group selection. We will recall that the difficulty with the Wynne-Edwards type of group selection as an explanation of aid to others was that high rates of group extinctions and low rates of migration seemed to be needed. We will still need the low-migration-rate assumption here, but let us add to it an assumption that the group is fairly inbred. Now we get kin selection increasing the frequency of genes 'for' mutual aid and co-operation, and the result is a kind of group selection – 'family group selection' (Wade, 1978, 1979, 1980). Slatkin (1987: 789) argues that there is a continuum of selection, with kin selection on the one end and group selection on the other, the entire range being dependent 'on genetic variation within and between populations.'

This book is concerned primarily with theories and hypotheses about the evolved mechanisms underlying mind and culture. While evolution takes place at many levels, not all of these are equally relevant for a particular set of problems. For the task at hand, I will (provisionally) accept kin-selection theory, individual selection, and the vocabulary of inclusive fitness; I will reject explanations couched in terms of group selection, and will eschew speaking anthropomorphically in terms of 'selfish genes.' For my purposes, there is little difference between the statement 'genes that cause their carrier to aid the carrier of their replicates will increase in frequency in the gene pool' and its equivalent 'selection will favour the tendency for kin to aid one another': whichever kind of formulation seems likely to be most clear to the reader, at any given point, will be used.

HUMAN SOCIOBIOLOGY

A *human* sociobiology naturally generates controversy. I create interest only among biologists if I argue that alarm calls in ground-squirrels have been selected for not because they benefit the group but because the risk to the genes of the caller is less than the benefit to the proportion of its genes carried by those benefiting from the call. But I cause consternation everywhere if I claim that human beings have been selected to be nepotistic, or to favour members of their own group against outsiders, or to manipulate one another incessantly. Sociobiology seems to indicate that we act not so much selfishly as in *genetic* selfishness, and that our psychological traits are such that whenever it is in that genetic self-interest – that is, in the interest of our inclusive fitness – to be deceitful and manipulative, well then, that is how we are probably going to be. Sociobiology, in short, gives rise to a theory of human nature that, at least at first glance, seems depressingly cynical, a sort of original-sin version of humankind with no obvious hope of salvation short of our selectively breeding ourselves into a morally better beast (cf. Richerson and Boyd's [1989] domestication-of-genes-by-culture argument). I, at least, would have hoped that the controversies over a human sociobiology would have focused on that view of human nature. Such, however, has not been the case.

Controversies

Critics of a human sociobiology have argued that the field owes more to ideology than to biology.[10] Marshall Sahlins (1976), a noted anthropologist, looked at the cost-benefit aspect of sociobiology and apparently concluded that it must be an application of capitalist thinking pretending to be biology! Oddly, as we will see in chapter 11's discussion of Richard Alexander's work, some of Sahlins's own earlier theories in the realm of economic anthropology turn out to fit in quite exactly with sociobiological expectation.

The mainstream social and behavioural sciences remain largely environmental in their outlook, and anthropologists in particular argue

10 I will not provide an extended analysis of the controversy over sociobiology, since it is not germane to this book's emphases. However, for a recent example of this kind of debate, see the issue of the *Canadian Journal of Sociology and Anthropology* devoted to it (vol. 22, no. 2, 1985). For a sociological analysis of the debate and of the complex personal and intellectual relationship between its two chief protagonists, R.C. Lewontin and E.O. Wilson, see Segerstrale's (1986) insightful analysis. For a broader view of the controversy, see Kaye (1986: 100–35), who while criticizing Wilson for mistaking his personal values for the implications of 'science,' also argues that the stance that sociobiology is an apologia for capitalism is entirely wrong. Both Segerstrale's article and the number of the *CJSA* issue cited above provide a full bibliography for those seeking further material on the sociobiology controversy.

(as we saw in chapter 1) that we are *cultural* animals and that our cultures, not our heredity, determine our behaviour. Some have argued that the fact that we are a culture-bearing species means that the application of evolutionary biology to human behaviour and society – a *human* sociobiology – is invalid, however fruitful the approach may be to other species. That culture is a product of biological evolution is never denied by such critics, but the relevance of that fact is relegated to the dim past. Culture is viewed, from this perspective, not as an expression of our evolved human nature but as something somehow distinct from it and able to override it at almost any point, apparently with little cost. Chapter 10's discussion of the ideas of Marvin Harris will provide an example of this view.

For some social-behavioural scientists educated in the blank-slate days, the mere idea that we have an evolved human nature is in itself deeply offensive, since it seems to smack of the bad biology of earlier portions of this century. The suggestion that there may be some kind of biological basis to such phenomena as ethnocentrism, class conflict, kinship systems, incest avoidance, and sex roles[11] arouses considerable anger in certain social and behavioural scientists and biologists. There is a tendency to assume that 'genetic' implies 'immutable' (as it largely did in the racist literature of the 1930s); and that the hidden agenda of the sociobiologist is to justify existing inequalities by arguing that they are really 'biological' and the result of unequal 'genes' rather than unequal political power.

It is not too surprising, then, that there are those – including Lewontin, Rose, and Kamin (1984) – who fear that a human sociobiology is little more than a resurgence of the dark days of genetic determinism. Recall, however, that the label 'sociobiology' can be a slippery one. E.O. Wilson (1975a), who meant the term to refer to a new discipline, appears to include in it most of the biological, social, and behavioural sciences, from ethology to population genetics to a reworked sociology and anthropology. Lewontin, Rose, and Kamin, in their attack on sociobiology, seem to mean primarily human behaviour genetics, a field that seeks to account for differences between both

11 Some prefer to borrow the linguistic term 'gender,' in this context, in order to make the ideological point that the differences in question have no more to do with biology than do the genders of nouns in languages such as French or Russian. Use of the term 'gender' begs this empirical question, though, of course, so does use of the term 'sex.' I shall therefore use 'sex roles' and 'gender roles' interchangeably, in an effort to avoid bias.

individuals and groups on the basis of differences in allele frequencies. Robert Boyd and Peter Richerson, who have made a substantial contribution to human sociobiology's understanding of gene-culture interaction, prefer not to apply that field's label to themselves at all (as we will see in chapter 11). While I have no aversion to the term, for me there are two issues at the heart of any human sociobiology: the evolution of human social psychology, including self-awareness; and the evolution of culture and the capacity for culture. Thus, this book will emphasize not the relationship between specific genes and specific behavioural traits but what comes between the genes and the behaviour, that is, mind and culture in the light of evolutionary biology (dealt with particularly in chapters 4 to 7).

My stance throughout this study is that 'species chauvinism' – the idea that evolutionary biology applies to every species on the globe except for *Homo sapiens sapiens* – is the modern version of the belief that the Earth is the centre of the universe.[12] We are products of biological evolution and no more exempt from its processes than from Boyle's Law. The real question is not whether sociobiology is applicable to human beings but how to apply it: how to apply sociobiology to a cultural animal. Part of the answer, as I indicated above, involves specific and detailed theories of both culture and 'mind,' that is, of the psychological mechanisms evolved to sort and order the various kinds of information of which culture is composed.

Culturally patterned behaviour is not something separate from our genetic evolution: it is the expression of that evolution, the expression of our genes, as mediated through evolved psychological mechanisms. This expression is not simple to understand for at least two reasons: first, the evolved mechanisms may have 'emergent' properties not reducible to the mere enhancement of genetic fitness (as discussed in chapters 4 and 5); and second, because culture too evolves, and its relationship with genetic evolution is sufficiently complex to justify the use of the terms 'coevolution' and 'dual evolution' and to permit at least some cultural traits to be genetically maladaptive for all or some members of a given society (chapters 6 to 11).

Evolution's wisdom is always past wisdom, of course, and genetic

12 Some religions, unfortunately, appear to justify species chauvinism with the contention that human beings but not other animals have an indwelling supernatural
attribute, the 'soul.' Sociobiology is of course profoundly materialist in orientation
and does not consider the possibility of supernatural differences between *Homo
sapiens* and other species.

adaptation can only be adaptation to past environments. Modern industrial society is distant from the hunting-gathering landscape of our evolutionary history: it is not at all clear that the evolved behavioural dispositions that (presumably) permitted our forbears more-or-less to maximize their inclusive fitness have any such effect today; nor is it even completely clear whether these behavioural dispositions are indeed those of our hunting-gathering ancestors at all, or whether they have themselves evolved since we left off foraging to become cultivators and herders (we have been industrialized for too few generations for this latest environment to have much affected gene frequencies; but see chapters 10 and 11 for discussion of the '1000-year rule'). Nevertheless, it remains true that our evolved social psychology – our human nature – is a product of past selection. As such, this social psychology must represent traits that, however modified by our present environment, were selected for because they tended to enhance the genetic fitness of our ancestors.

As social animals, one of our major means of enhancing our fitness is influencing – manipulating – the behaviour of others. Chapters 3, 8, and 15 deal in part with such manipulation. Because the vocabulary used will be quite anthropomorphic, let us conclude this chapter with a brief discussion of vocabulary.

Vocabulary and Genetic Selfishness
As scientists frequently do, sociobiologists often appropriate ordinary English words and phrases for use as technical terms, redefining them in unfamiliar ways. While the denotation of a term may easily be altered, its value connotations resist change. Still, there is much to be said for avoiding neologism.

In the following chapters, I will be discussing differing fitness interests while making use of an ordinary language vocabulary that will include such terms as deceit, altruism, bluff, strategy, and selfishness. The human behaviours labelled by these terms are not necessarily analogous to their animal equivalents, but you will readily understand what is meant by them. Coined words could be substituted, but such inventions often only annoy and confuse. Perhaps neologisms do succeed in avoiding the carry-over of value connotations that may accompany everyday English words: but it may also be that we learn a neologism only by memorizing an ordinary language gloss (for example, substituting ordinary-language 'threat' or 'aggressive action' for technical 'agonistic' behaviour) and so succeed only in gaining the annoyance of a new jargon term while retaining the misleading aura of connotational meanings of an ordinary-language word.[13] The best way to avoid any connotational confusion is to use vocabulary in the context of a multiple-level, vertically integrated theory of human behaviour. The effort to construct such a theory begins in chapter 4.

First, though, we need to know a bit more about those underlying selection pressures. Chapter 3 will explore the implications of our differing fitness interests and the kinds of behaviours that theory predicts we have been selected for. We must discuss deceit, sex, sibling rivalry, and (once again) altruism. Only then will we be in a position to develop a theory of the self and self-awareness, and of the nature of the information system we call 'culture.' We will be building a sort of social psychology, one that links awareness, consciousness, attention, and choice.

SUMMARY

1. Order arises from disorder through natural processes. D.T. Campbell has provided a powerful model for some of these processes, a model involving blind variation and selective retention. Variants are 'blind' with respect to selection criteria and are retained if they meet these criteria. The model underlies not just biological evolution but a range of phenomena, including trial-and-error learning.

2. In biological variation, genes are the variants. A gene is a code for a protein. In interaction with other genes and the environment, it is an important component of the process that generates the observable/measurable body and behaviour, the phenotype. Since we rarely know the precise pathway through which a particular gene operates, and since complex behavioural and morphological traits require complexes of genes, the term 'gene for' should be taken, at least in this book, for 'gene increasing the probability of occurrence of' rather than 'causing.'

3. Some people read sociobiologists as being 'panselectionists' who believe in 'super-deterministic genes' that cause all traits to be adaptive. Sociobiologists have also been accused of writing as if genes had consciousness and will, and as if they controlled all traits. Genes, however, are simply blind variants in the blind-variation-and-selective-retention process of evolution. Moreover, there are several processes, including pleiotropy, genetic drift, and emergence, that can cause

13 For a contrary view regarding the use of ordinary-language vocabulary rather than neologism, see Midgley (1978: 127) or Kaye (1986: 106).

non-adaptive and even genetically maladaptive traits to occur. Chapters 4 and 12 will consider maladaptive individual and cultural traits.

4. Some risk of panselectionism is unavoidable if we are to be adaptationists, but the usual process of challenge and counter-challenge in science and an insistence on vertically integrated explanation make the risk acceptable.

5. 'Genetic' vs. 'learned' is a false opposition, since all behaviour requires the interaction of both genes and environment. 'Innate' behaviours are those that strong selection pressure has permitted to manifest with a wide range of environmental inputs, while 'learned' behaviour is behaviour that occurs only in the presence of highly specific environmental inputs. In this sense, the ability to sneeze is innate, the ability to play the piano learned, and both depend on genes and environment.

6. Evolution takes place at multiple levels, and there has been controversy over which level is most germane to which phenomena. Evolutionists believed, in the past, that selection at the group level accounted for such 'altruistic behaviour' as the giving of alarm calls. At present, it is widely though not universally accepted that such apparent altruism results from selection favouring 'genetic selfishness.' Much 'altruism' represents the fact that animal social groups are often essentially kin groups. Thus, an 'altruistic' individual is in effect aiding that portion of his or her genes shared by the kin who are being helped. Organisms are selected so as to behave in a manner that increases their genetic representation in the next generation, their *inclusive fitness*, which includes not only the replicates of one's genes carried by one's offspring but the replicates carried by other kin who have received one's aid as well. To the extent that our aid to others will increase the frequency in the gene-pool of the genes we ourselves carry, to that extent our genetic interests coincide and selection will favour our aiding them. Since each individual (other than those who have an identical twin) has a unique, genetic complement, our fitness interests are equally unique so that in striving to maximize them we act in genetic selfishness.

7. While evolution takes place at many levels, not all of these are equally relevant for a particular set of problems. For the task at hand, I will (provisionally) accept kin-selection theory, individual selection, and the vocabulary of inclusive fitness; I will reject explanations couched in terms of group selection, and will eschew speaking anthropomorphically in terms of 'selfish genes.'

8. As we saw in chapter 1, the heritage of the 'bad biology' of the past

is controversy over any examination of the processes intervening between gene frequencies, on the one hand, and human behaviour, especially culturally organized behaviour, on the other. Many social scientists read 'genetic' to mean 'immutable.' Some reduce sociobiology to an attempt to explain complex aspects of human behaviour in terms of the 'causal' effects of genes. Behaviour genetics is not necessarily central to a human sociobiology, however, and this book will not deal with any one-to-one gene-behaviour effects, real or theoretical. Its focus is on human social psychology, self-awareness, and culture.

9. Culturally patterned behaviour is not something separate from our genetic evolution: it is the expression of that evolution, the expression of our genes, as mediated through evolved psychological mechanisms. This expression is not simple to understand for at least two reasons: first, the evolved mechanisms may have 'emergent' properties not reducible to the mere enhancement of genetic fitness (as discussed in chapters 4 and 5); and second, because culture too evolves, and its relationship with genetic evolution is sufficiently complex to justify the use of the terms 'coevolution' and 'dual evolution,' and to permit at least some cultural traits to be genetically maladaptive for all or some members of a given society (chapters 6 to 11).

10. Sociobiologists often use ordinary-language terms (such as 'deceit' and 'altruism') as technical terms with technical meanings, but the connotational aura of the more usual use of these words lingers and, some would argue, misleads. I will nevertheless be using the usual sociobiological vocabulary here, since neologisms are likely to be confusing and clumsy and, implicitly, to be understood in terms of connotation-packed, ordinary-language glosses in any case.

3

Differing Interests: Deceit, Sex, Rivalry, Influence, and Altruism

This chapter summarizes the core ideas of human sociobiology. Its theme is that different organisms have different fitness interests, leading to selection for various kinds of conflict, compromise, and mutual manipulation. Readers already familiar with basic evolutionary theory need only skim this chapter. Those preferring a more full introduction, or seeking greater emphasis on (non-human) animal behaviour, may wish to consult Dawkins (1976), Barash (1982), Trivers (1985), or Wilson (1975a).

MORE ABOUT GENETIC SELFISHNESS

Sociobiology's fundamental tenet is inclusive fitness, the principle that individuals have been selected to maximize their genetic representation in future generations. Since each individual's complement of genes is unique, however, the fitness interests of each individual are also unique. The result, as we have seen, is a genetic selfishness. We have been selected for psychological mechanisms that cause us to tend to act towards others more-or-less *as if* we were doing an endless series of cost-benefit analyses, with the 'benefit' including the possible fate of the portion of *our* genes that *they* carry. (Note that 'benefit' here has in effect been redefined to mean 'relative increase in genetic representation in the next or succeeding generation[s].')

The implications of our differing fitness interests are lurid: as we will see, it seems that selection has favoured our acting towards each other in ways that, in ordinary language, can only be called deceitful, duplici-tous, and manipulative; and especially so when it comes to sex. But note the distinction between a theory of selection pressures and a theory of the resulting, evolved psychological mechanisms that underlie human behaviour. The term 'as if' in the preceding paragraph is all-important: *this chapter does not present a portrait of human psychological mechanisms, that is, of our human nature; it presents a discussion of some hypothesized selection pressures that (arguably) gave rise to that nature, to those mechanisms.* Whatever other properties they have, whatever algorithms they use, our evolved mechanisms should tend to generate behaviour likely to enhance the fitness of people living as our ancestors once did. Mistaking a theory of the selection pressures likely to have produced those mechanisms for a theory of the mechanisms themselves, that is, for a theory of human nature, is an error sociobiologists and readers of sociobiologists often make (Barkow, 1980a; Symons, 1987a, 1989; Tooby and Cosmides, 1989). Sociobiology is not and cannot be a theory of human nature – for that we need vertically integrated, multiple-level accounts. The mechanisms, as we will see in subsequent chapters, have emergent properties not predicted by evolutionary theory (though not incompatible with that theory, either). Human nature itself – the *product* of selection pressures – is dealt with for the first time only in the chapter following this one.

Even as a picture of mere selection pressures, the image drawn here is not a particularly happy one for those who would like to locate the roots of our unkindness to one another in some place other than ourselves. We must discuss altruism and deceit, nepotism and sex.

Kin Altruism as Genetic Selfishness

We saved a man from drowning in the previous chapter. The cost to us of saving him (that is, the risk to our own genetic complement) was relatively slight, the benefit to our genes – the probability of an increase in frequency in the gene pool of the proportion of our genes our non-swimming relative shares – was great.

The save-or-let-drown case was an example of what sociobiologists term 'kin selection' or 'nepotistic altruism' or 'kin altruism.' I will use the last term. By 'altruism' I mean acting so as to lower one's own probability of reproductive success while thereby increasing that of another organism. 'Kin altruism' simply means altruistic behaviour towards a relative, that is, one with whom one shares genes by virtue of common descent. One way of discussing this concept (as we saw in chapter 2) is to emphasize the genes themselves rather than the bodies bearing them (following Dawkins, 1982).

Suppose we have a gene that can affect the probability of altruistic behaviour in a body other than the one in which it is housed. Think of this as a gene that influences the survival and reproductive success not just of its own bearer but of certain others. Let us call this gene a 'gene for altruism' (though what I really mean is 'a gene that will promote the development of a psychological mechanism likely to increase the probability of altruistic behaviour'). We will continue to speak in terms of costs and benefits, but for the moment we will mean costs and benefits to that particular gene itself. 'Benefit,' for a gene, refers to 'probability of increasing in frequency in the gene pool'; while 'cost' means 'risk of decreasing in frequency in the gene pool.' A gene for altruism will increase in frequency in the gene pool if the benefits of the altruistic acts it favours outweigh their costs.

If a gene for altruism is to increase in frequency, it must influence the development of a psychological mechanism, such as a specialized processor in its bearer's brain, that will tend to cause the bearer to act as if he or she had performed some very complex calculations. These calculations include assessing (1) the value of any aid to its potential recipient (that is, the extent to which the aid proffered would increase the inclusive fitness of the recipient); (2) the probability of risk to the donor of the aid (the probability that supplying the aid would reduce its fitness); and (3) the probability that the recipient of the aid does indeed bear a copy of the gene for altruism. (There is a fourth component to the calculation, involving the *fitness-investment-potential* of the recipient, discussed below.)

The first and second parts of the calculation obviously require what some would loosely term 'intelligence.' They imply that the organism must have been selected for the functional equivalent of an immensely powerful computer-simulation model, permitting the prediction of the probability of future events.[1] That model requires internal representations of both the potential aid recipient and the donor itself.

Part 1 of the calculation means that if the aid will have little benefit for the fitness of the recipient then there will be little selection pressure on the donor to provide it. If the aid would have major effects on the recipient's fitness, of course, then selection pressure in favour of the

---

1 Of course, it could be that this 'functional equivalence' is accomplished with relatively simple algorithms not comparable in complexity to the calculations of elaborate computer-simulation models.

donor's providing such aid will be great. Part 2 of the calculation means that if the risk to the donor is very great then selection will favour provision of the aid only under unusual circumstances.

Part 3 of the calculation is perhaps the most problematic, since it in effect requires genes to 'recognize' their replicates carried in other bodies. For example, in the drowning case we saw that the risk was small and the benefit great chiefly when we *assumed* that there was a high probability of the aid recipient really having a replicate of the donor's gene for altruism. How can a gene 'know' that, though?

Genes Recognizing Their Replicates
What kinds of evolved mechanisms could cause an individual to act differentially towards those who happen to carry replicates of his/her own genes? How do organisms 'know' what proportion of their genes is shared by another? Without such knowledge, after all, it is impossible to calculate 'benefit' accurately, and genes for altruism should decrease in frequency in the gene pool as they lead their bearers to risks without benefits. Selection must in effect cause the organism to act as if it were calculating the proportion of genes others are likely to share with it. To understand how this behaviour might be possible we begin by dealing with how the geneticist calculates the proportion of shared genes between individuals, that is, calculates their *coefficient of consanguinity or relatedness* (usually symbolized by r).

Let us begin with our parents – kin altruism is only a species of parental behaviour, after all. You received 50% of your genes from each of your parents, so that your relatedness to each of them would be 50%, or $r = 0.5$. For each further step away from oneself, keep multiplying by 0.5. If your child has 50% of your genes, your grandchild must have 25% and your great-grandchild 12.5%. Cousins are worth 12.5%. Your sibling and you each received 50% of your genes from each of your parents, so you and your sibling must share 50% of each other's genes. The child of your sister or brother has 50% of his/her genes from his/her parent, which means you share 25% of your genes with niece or nephew. You have an $r = 0.5$ for you and your parent, $r = 0.25$ for you and your parent's sibling, $r = 0.125$ for your and your parent's sibling's child (your first cousin), and so on. Suppose you only share one parent with a sibling? Your half-sibling and you share an r of 0.25.[2]

2 Strictly speaking, all members of a species share most of their genes simply by virtue of being members of the same species. The coefficient of consanguinity actually measures that additional proportion of genes shared by two individuals by virtue of their being kin.

We do not really go about calculating coefficients of consanguinity; nor can we necessarily act as if we had computed them with total accuracy. Selection will, however, favour genes for altruism that underlie mechanisms permitting us to act (very roughly) as if we had indeed done such calculations. In some social insects there is a 'hive smell' and it is possible to distinguish kin from non-kin with a fair degree of accuracy. Human beings, however, appear to lack genetically determined kin-identification odors.[3]

An obvious human mechanism for identification of kin involves familiarity and habituation. We tend to treat those with whom we are reared, and those who rear us, as relatives (Barkow, 1978c). (Presumably, they were so in the environment in which we evolved.) We also treat as kin those whom our cultures teach us to categorize as kin. There is rarely an exact correspondence between the kinship terminology of any particular culture and coefficients of relatedness (Sahlins, 1976), but social kinship and genetic kinship almost always bear a reasonably strong relationship (Alexander, 1979).

Aid and Inclusive Fitness
At first glance, one might think that we should have been selected to be altruistic to others in accordance with the proportion of *our* genes that *they* carry. Let us assume that the recognition problem is solved, for the moment, so that the organism can magically calculate its degree of relatedness with any other organism with which it comes in contact. We will also assume that the organism is very accurate in assessing the risk it runs in providing aid and the degree of benefit the potential recipient would derive from that help. Degree of relatedness now would seem to be the determining factor. But our calculations grow a bit more interesting than that.

Two kin may be equally related to you in terms of coefficients of relatedness, but the survival of one may have no implications for your inclusive fitness, while the survival of another may have major implications.

Back to drowning. Suppose the non-swimmer is your aunt or uncle

3 Nevertheless, odours do play a role in mother-infant recognition, and family members can recognize one another's odours. Thus, olfaction may play a (presumably subliminal role) in human social interaction. See Porter (1987: 193–7) for references and for a discussion of olfaction and other possible aspects of human kin recognition. To repeat a note provided in the previous chapter, for an excellent discussion of the problem of kin recognition in animals, see Sherman and Holmes (1985).

and that you therefore share 25% of your respective genes. You, yourself, are twenty years old and have a high probability of bearing or siring three offspring during your lifetime. You therefore have 50% × 3 or 150% of your genes in the next generation at risk. Your non-swimming aunt or uncle is sixty-five and has already produced as many offspring as he or she ever will and these children are now completely independent. This particular relative's survival would therefore enhance your representation in the next-generation by 0%. By jumping in you are putting at risk your 150% next generation representation for a potential benefit of 0%. The equation seems to say, 'Bon voyage, non-swimming aunt or uncle!' Less facetiously, the equation suggests that selection would favour psychological mechanisms in human beings that should make us unlikely to attempt rescue in such circumstances.

To digress for a moment, let us keep in mind that there is no chance that these mechanisms are carrying out the kind of simple arithmetic used above for illustrative purposes. Presumably, there is a particular subsystem of the brain making use of a complex algorithm to generate this kind of nepotistic altruism behaviour. We can predict that this algorithm will produce behaviour somewhat similar to that predicted by the arithmetic above, simply because the closer the behaviour produced by an algorithm comes to the arithmetic model, the stronger the selection pressure in favour of it will be. Since we are not perfect biological machines, however, actual behaviour will only be a rough approximation of the arithmetic. Moreover, the algorithm and its underlying neurophysiological bases may have emergent properties not predicted by evolutionary theory. The task of identifying the actual algorithm is one for the field of cognitive psychology, while that of identifying its neurological substrate is a challenge for neurophysiology.

Back to the arithmetic of altruism, and to a more complex situation. In two generations, we will assume, you will have a high probability of having six grandchildren. If your non-swimming aunt or uncle survives, the aid of this post-reproductive-age relative will permit you to increase the number of your eventual grandchildren from seven to eight (an additional 25% of your genetic complement). Your third-generation inclusive-fitness representation would therefore move from 175% to 200%. Let us also assume that your aunt/uncle's survival would permit him/her to help his or her own children to the extent that this aunt/uncle would have two additional grandchildren. The additional two grandchildren would total 50% of the non-swimmer's genes, or 0.25 × 50% of your genes, yielding an additional 12.5% of your genes. The benefit to you from saving your aunt or uncle would now be an additional grandchild for you and two additional grandchildren for the aunt/uncle, for a total 37.5% increase in your third-generation genetic representation. Now the equation is less unequal. You are risking the seven grandchildren you would otherwise have – 175% of your genes in the third generation – but your aunt/uncle's survival would give you 202.5% of your current genetic representation, two generations hence, so your potential gain is now up to 37.5%. Depending on how good a swimmer you think you are and how dangerous you judge the situation, you just might go to the rescue.

Suppose your aunt or uncle is only forty years old instead of sixty-five and has a high probability of having one additional offspring who would represent another 12.5 per cent of your genes: now the equation would be a little more strongly in favour of your risking your own potential progeny. Or, suppose the potential victim is not your aunt or uncle but your sister. If you attempt to save her you will put at risk the 150% of your genes that your own likely three offspring would carry. But assume that the probability is that your sister, should she survive, will bear four children, each of whom would represent 25% of your genes, on the average. You are still risking 150% of your genes but now the benefit would be saving 100% of them. Our evolved mechanisms governing altruism should lead you to be more willing to try to save the victim than you were when it was only an elderly aunt or uncle at stake.

The point of all this is that whatever algorithms the brain uses in determining kin-altruism behaviour, they must somehow take into account the *fitness-investment potential* (FIP) of a relative to be aided.[4] I use this term to indicate *the net extent to which an organism's inclusive fitness would be increased by its altruism to another*. ('Altruism' was defined previously, on page 47 of this chapter.) FIP is similar to the idea of 'reproductive value,' defined by Wilson (1975a: 93) as 'the relative number of female offspring that remain to be born to each female of age x.' FIP is a much broader term, however, since it applies to both males and females and is not a measure of remaining reproductive success but a return-on-investment sort of calculation in which the 'return' is a

---

4 What are the psychological mechanisms that presumably lead us to tend to treat kin as if we had calculated their FIP? A useful way of phrasing this question is to ask what subsystem of the brain, using what algorithms, provides the information behind FIP-related behaviour. Once again, we have a challenge for the neurosciences and for cognitive psychology.

measure of probability of increase of inclusive fitness. (The drawback of this term is that it would entail considerable methodological difficulties if used as an empirical measure.)

Notice how, for some examples, I discussed FIP in terms of a relative's increasing your genetic representation in the next generation, and for other examples I spoke of 'grandchildren' and your genetic representation two generations hence. We see here a major problem not of theory but of empirical measurement: at which generation do we measure inclusive fitness? There is no theoretical reason for specifying genetic representation after one generation, two generations, or five generations. For empirical researchers, the choice must be made in terms of practicality, and for most mammalian species it usually is hard enough to wait around for a single generation.

The measurement problem is especially difficult for human sociobiology. Aside from our being very long-lived creatures, we typically live in multi-generational kin-groups. Members of the grandparental generation may regularly provide much care for grandchildren and, in the form of inheritable wealth, can often supply 'investment' for many future generations. It would thus appear to be unwise to consider human genetic fitness solely in terms of the number of direct offspring. At a minimum, we should count the number of grandchildren who attain some given age. Studies that include only 'reproductive success' or 'number of surviving offspring' (including that of Barkow, 1977a) are therefore suspect, even if longer-term, more comprehensive surveys are exceedingly difficult to undertake.[5]

No matter what the problems for researchers of measuring inclusive fitness in terms of third- or fourth-generation genetic representation, the allele frequencies underlying our social psychology have nevertheless been determined in part by the fitness effects of cross-generational interaction. In other words, your aunts, uncles, grandparents, and perhaps even your great-grandparents have been and remain important for natural selection. What they do may affect your genetic fitness.

5 Borgerhoff Mulder (1987) and Caro and Borgerhoff Mulder (1987) discuss direct and indirect measures of adaptation and fitness. However, measuring fitness (or seeking an index of it) is hardly the only human sociobiological research strategy. Sociobiologists familiar with cognitive science might seek to develop algorithms for simulation models that approximate actual human behaviour, for example. Such models could be tested against behavior in real or contrived situations, and would also be expected to be fairly consistent with sociobiological expectation.

RECIPROCAL ALTRUISM: MORE CALCULATING[6]

Human social psychology reflects allele frequencies determined in part by the relative success of genes in causing our ancestors, back in past environments, to act as if they were running a sort of computer program before aiding others. That 'program' must have involved algorithms that roughly approximated calculating their own relative cost versus the relative gain of the recipient, their degree of consanguinity with the aid recipient, and the Fitness-Investment Potential (FIP) of the recipient. Now it is time to add another parameter to the calculation, *the probability of reciprocity*. Here, we move to a topic central to a human sociobiology (and to the social sciences in general): reciprocal altruism.

Back to drowning, but this time the potential victim is no kin of mine or yours: should we help him or her anyway? Our earlier simulated calculations would suggest 'no,' for our degree of shared consanguinity is zero: no replicates of our genes would automatically increase in frequency with the aid recipient's reproduction.

Suppose there is a chance that one of these days I will fall in the river and the stranger might pull me out: now, my aiding him or her should be determined by a simulated calculation of the probability of the recipient eventually reciprocating the favour. The concept of reciprocal altruism is one of the contributions of the eminent sociobiologist Robert Trivers (1971, 1985: 361–94).

Perhaps it is not particularly realistic to suppose that I will happen to reverse roles with today's victim, but think in terms of kin: human beings everywhere live in kin-dominated societies (and our modern industrial nations are hardly free of the importance of kin groups). The aid recipient may not help me personally, but perhaps he or she will eventually return the aid to one of my relatives, that is, to someone who does share genes with me. My calculation must take this possibility of indirect reciprocity into account, too.

Then there is the matter of *reputation*. If I have the reputation of aiding others, there is a considerable chance that someone will eventually aid me; but if I help none, the odds of my receiving help when I (or my kin) require it are lowered. Where did that reputation

6 A recent special issue of the journal *Ethology and Sociobiology*, edited by Michael T. McGuire and Charles E. Taylor (1988), is devoted entirely to reciprocal altruism and is an excellent source for current work on this topic. For an effort to specify the algorithms used by a hypothetical specialized processor in generating altruistic behaviour, see Cosmides and Tooby (1989).

come from? Human beings are long-lived creatures with even longer memories. Given memory, we can keep track of those who reciprocate aid and those who do not. Selection will favour our aiding only those who tend to reciprocate. Since receiving aid by definition enhances genetic fitness, selection will therefore favour reciprocators. Hence, our languages have proverbs like 'one hand washes the other' or 'you scratch my back and I'll scratch yours.' Trivers (1971, 1985) even argues that the emotions of sympathy, friendship, moralistic aggression, and the sense of fairness were selected for as regulators of reciprocal altruism. Presumably, these emotions are in some way linked to the psychological mechanisms we have evolved to permit us to maintain relationships of reciprocal altruism.

When, though, is reciprocity *unlikely*? How can the stranger, passing through, be in a position to reciprocate? Theory here predicts that hospitality and aid should not ordinarily be proffered to the stranger. This prediction may be true of many small-scale, low-technology peoples, but clearly is not accurate for all societies. The world's religions (Islam in particular) often put great stress on hospitality to the stranger. The unanimity with which the world religions (but not necessarily small-scale, 'tribal' belief systems) enjoin their adherents to show hospitality to strangers suggests that it may be that our common inclination is to withhold aid to the stranger, to victimize the traveller. The familiar person, the resident, the one with relatives in the area, or especially the individual with a reputation for reciprocity is the one most likely to receive aid when needed (and indeed, even when not needed, in order to establish a future basis for reciprocity when today's overly willing donor anticipates being the one in need).

The problem with the evolution of reciprocal altruism is that of the 'initial kick': once it exists it is easy to see how selection would favour its maintenance, but how would it have arisen in the first place? Trivers (1985: 362) argues that reciprocal altruism can evolve quite apart from kin altruism, while Breden and Wade (1981) argue the contrary.[7] For Breden and Wade, reciprocal altruism is much more likely to arise in an inbred population, and it seems reasonable to presume that ancestral hominids had this kind of population structure. Interestingly, both nepotistic and reciprocal altruism may have arisen long before there

---

7 The non-kin-related evolution of reciprocal altruism is usually discussed in terms of Axelrod and Hamilton's (1981) mathematical analysis based on a logical game called the 'prisoner's dilemma.' Boyd (1988) argues in support of this approach, while others have criticized it (see Boyd [1988] and Axelrod and Dion [1988] for references).

were hominids, or even apes: monkeys commonly exhibit nepotistic altruism and a social reciprocity that appears to be based on reciprocal altruism (Cheney, Seyfarth, and Smuts, 1986: 234).

Back to population structure: recall our earlier calculations in which degree of consanguinity had to be taken into account in order to determine whether kin altruism was to be proffered. Suppose we are dealing with a somewhat low coefficient of relatedness and the cost-benefit equation is almost in balance. Now, let us add to the benefit side of the equation the possibility that the aid will be reciprocated by either the recipient or the recipient's kin and to the donor or the donor's kin. This possibility does not need to be high in order to tip an almost balanced equation in the direction of aid. We have our initial kick, and reciprocal altruism has been born. A selection pressure exists, however slight, in favour of reciprocal altruism.

Is some degree of inbreeding absolutely necessary for the 'initial kick' towards the evolution of reciprocal altruism? Trivers discusses evidence for reciprocal altruism among such species as baboons, chimpanzees, vampire bats, and white-throated sparrows, and does not conclude that shared consanguinity is the evolutionary basis for reciprocal altruism. For example, baboon males form coalitions for mutual support, but these males are unlikely to be related. Moreover, argues Trivers, reciprocal altruism can exist even between unrelated species, as when 'species of small fish specialized as cleaners of other fish ... remove ectoparasites from the skin, gills, and mouths of various species of host fish' (Trivers, 1985: 47). The host fish reciprocate the aid by not swallowing their 'cleaners.'[8] For Trivers (1985: 362), the preconditions that may lead to the evolution of reciprocal altruism include long life span and low rate of dispersal (so as to increase opportunity for reciprocity), high 'frequency of interaction,' and 'kin-directed altruism.' But the last item is important *not* because it implies shared consanguinity, as one might expect, but only because (for Trivers) it requires that individuals interact frequently.

For our own species, I would guess, reciprocal altruism would probably not have been, initially, independent of kin altruism. Rather, the slight possibility of reciprocity would have been just one more complication in the calculations. It is difficult to imagine how, given the existence of kin altruism in a species living in fairly inbred (high mean

8 This kind of relationship is usually categorized by biologists as *mutualism*, the type of symbiosis in which each species confers a benefit upon the other.

coefficient of relatedness) groups with good memories, reciprocal altruism could have failed to evolve. Once it had evolved, of course, interaction with stable groups of non-kin would have further strengthened selection for it, in much the way that Trivers describes. (Thus, when we do find aliens among the stars, assuming their evolution has been anything at all like our own, our xenologists will probably find that despite tentacles and scales the aliens and ourselves share some basic moral values regarding reciprocity.)

Finally, note how readily reciprocal altruism is included in the FIP calculation, the 'fitness-investment potential' assessment of another. In addition to taking into account risk to donor, benefit to recipient, and degree of consanguinity between donor and recipient, the FIP calculation must now include the probability of reciprocity of aid by recipient to donor or to donor's kin, as well as the effect of giving or withholding aid on the reputation of the donor. In small-scale societies, at least, alleles that tend to increase the accuracy of FIP calculations should tend to increase in frequency in the gene pool. Our human psychology should reflect the high frequency of such alleles.[9]

SEXUAL SELECTION

It was Charles Darwin (1871) who first introduced the notion of sexual selection, in his *The Descent of Man, and Selection in Relation to Sex*. Darwin thought of sexual selection as distinct from natural selection. Distinct it may be, but both natural and sexual selection ultimately have to do with changes in the relative frequency of genes in the gene pool.

There are two types of sexual selection. The first involves members of one sex competing with one another, with the winners getting a disproportionate share of sexual access to the other sex. This form of sexual selection was originally termed by Darwin (1871) 'male-male competition,' but nowadays is usually known by the less sexist phrase 'intrasexual selection.' Perhaps Darwin may be forgiven his bias, for most forms of intrasexual competition do involve males. When stags compete for access to females by threatening one another with their antlers, or when male goats butt their heads together, this is intrasexual

---

9 Cosmides and Tooby (1989) have recently described in some detail the algorithms of the 'mental organ' underlying reciprocal altruism and, indeed, social exchange in general. They analyse the complex psychological mechanisms that human beings have evolved in response to selection pressures for reciprocal altruism, deceit, and the detection of deceit in others.

competition. Intrasexual selection is often associated with sexual dimorphism (innate differences in morphology and/or behaviour between the males and females of a given species), particularly with respect to physical size and/or whatever structures are used in the competition. Thus, billy-goats have horns and stags have antlers, while male elephant seals and male savannah baboons are very large compared to the females of their respective species. In all four of these species, male-male competition in terms of threat and ritualized violence is a major determinant of who gets to sire the next generation. Since offspring resemble their parents, selection (sexual selection, in this case) favours the large or those well-equipped with horns or antlers.

The second form of sexual selection has to do with members of one sex choosing, according to various criteria, members of the other sex. This form of sexual selection is sometimes known as *mate choice*, though Darwin (1871) preferred to speak of 'charm,' while Huxley's (1938) term, *epigamic* selection, is also widely used. Whatever the label, this second form of sexual selection has to do with one sex evolving physical features and/or behaviour that influence mate choice by the other. Presumably, such features or behaviour are, at least initially, indicators of the genetic superiority – of the 'good genes' – of the displayer. A peacock's plumage and the ritualized courtship displays of many birds are presumably products of this 'charm' sexual selection. One could argue that, in our own species, culturally ordered decoration, dancing, contests of strength and skill, and athletic performances serve a similar function in that members of one sex display for members of the other, each displayer in effect emphasizing his or her 'good genes.'

Notice the possibility of a positive-feedback effect. Suppose that members of sex 'A' find certain traits in sex 'B' sexually attractive, presumably because these traits have been indicators of 'good genes.' Perhaps the traits involved glossy plumage or stored fat or whatever. Members of sex 'A' who succeed in getting especially attractive 'B' mates will have an added fitness advantage: not only will their immediate offspring benefit from these good genes, but those of the resulting offspring who are of sex 'B' are themselves likely to be found especially attractive by members of sex 'A,' because these 'B' offspring have the same trait that made their original 'B' parent attractive to the original 'A' parent in the first place. (Substitute 'male' and 'female or 'female' and 'male' for 'A' and 'B' to make the example more clear.) Whatever the traits in question were, with each generation they may intensify. In chapter 13 we will see that the evolution of the permanently enlarged breast of the human female may have involved the mate-choice form of sexual selection.

It clearly is in a male's fitness interest to win in intrasexual competition, just as it is in his fitness interest to be chosen in mate-choice selection. It is also in a female's interest to produce offspring sired by these winners. After all, in the case of intrasexual competition, the female by mating with the 'winner' is ensuring that her offspring will share the genes underlying their progenitor's success. Similarly, the female who chooses the most 'charming' male has thereby increased the probability that her male offspring will also be 'charming.' In both cases she is in effect acting to increase the number of grandchildren she leaves behind her.[10]

Why should sexual selection usually involve *males* competing for females? The answer has to do with the price of eggs. Less facetiously, it has to do with the relative cost of producing gametes. Ova are expensive, being much larger than the male gametes, the spermatozoa. Thus, for any species, a female in copulating is risking an expensive ovum, a male very inexpensive sperm cells. The amount of investment in potential or actual offspring any organism can produce is finite, and the female is putting at risk a larger proportion of her lifetime potential for reproduction than is the male. Selection therefore will favour females being more selective, perhaps looking for evidence that the male has the 'best' genes or is ready to invest in some way in her or in their potential offspring. Because the male risks little by copulating, selection will favour his being relatively undiscriminating. For many species, the cost of the egg is only the female's initial expense, and the costs of incubation and gestation, and possibly parental care, remain. Barash (1982: 310) explains that the female is less likely to desert offspring than is the male not because of her substantial prior investment, but because replacing the offspring would require a much heavier investment from her than it would from the male.

In the case of a human being, maternal investment will involve some

10 There has been difficulty in establishing empirically that such a thing as female choice actually exists. Majerus (1986), who reviews the topic, concludes that female mate choice has been demonstrated for at least a few species. There has also been some controversy as to whether the positive-feedback tendency of mate choice selection can result in traits that, aside from their attractiveness to the other sex, are deleterious to the organism. For further discussion of sexual selection, see Trivers 1972, 1985: 203–70; Wilson, 1975a: 318–24; Parker, 1987; Kodric-Brown and Brown, 1984; and Arnold, 1983.

nine months of gestation plus a (culturally variable) number of years of dependency. The male investment, however, may remain (facultatively) limited to his gamete. For species such as ours, we would therefore expect considerable female discrimination prior to permitting copulation.

Note that, in species such as the seahorse and the pipefish, in which it is the male rather than the female that provides the larger proportion of parental investment, and the male whose reproductive options following copulation are more limited than are those of the female, intrasexual selection involves female-female competition and it is the male who discriminates (Wilson, 1975a: 326; Trivers, 1985: 215–19). For our own species, the more parental investment the male is likely to provide the more discriminating he should be in mate choice and the more females should compete with one another to pair with him. (This topic will be returned to in chapter 13.) It is not maleness or femaleness per se that determines which sex engages in intrasexual competition or to what extent, it is the relative proportion of parental investment that each sex provides and the amount of reproductive potential each puts at risk with every copulation or fertilization. For most species, females provide a disproportionately large share of the investment.

Intrasexual competition can take place at a number of points during the life span and in a variety of ways. Parker (1987), basing her discussion on Alexander and Borgia (1979) and Borgia (1979), concludes that 'males [of all species with two sexes] compete through a variety of behaviors including territoriality, dominance, female guarding, nuptial feeding, and sperm production.' Thus, elephant seals compete for breeding territories, while (as we will see in chapter 8) many species of primates seek high position on a social-dominance hierarchy because such position is often associated with preferential sexual access to ovulating females. 'Female guarding' refers to the tendency of the male, in some species (possibly but not necessarily including our own, as we will see in chapter 14's discussion of wife seclusion), to attempt to keep other males away from a fertile female. 'Nuptial offerings' refers to food that the male provides the female and on which the female may feed during copulation. Thornhill (1979) explains that the offering may be prey, a bodily product (such as a glandular secretion), or the male itself (cannibalism). Sperm competition may take place when the female mates with more than one male, so that the spermatozoa of several males directly compete to reach and fertilize the ovum. Sperm competition in our own species has been offered as accounting for both female orgasm and male masturbation (discussed in chapter 14).

The implications for human beings of sexual selection (and its derivative, parental investment) theory have been analysed by Barkow (1981) and, in greater detail, by Symons (1979, 1980, 1989) and by Daly and Wilson (1978). I summarize below what might be termed the 'standard account': in subsequent chapters (6, 8, and 13) this account will be broadened (but not invalidated) in order to emphasize the importance of female choice and of distinguishing between long-term and short-term relationships. Though some controversy remains among those who dislike the implications of the portrait of sexuality and sex differences that the sociobiologists paint and though, as we will see, it is somewhat incomplete, the 'standard portrait' largely accords with the cross-cultural data (Symons, 1979).

The Standard Sociobiological Image of Human Sexuality
Since human beings are only mildly sexually dimorphic, we probably did not evolve in societies in which intrasexual selection was primarily about 'brawn' or the capacity for physical violence (though social rank, as we will see in chapter 8, is probably linked to reproductive success). However, given the very substantial differences between minimum male and minimum female parental investment in offspring, we would expect human males: (1) to seek far more sexual partners than do females; (2) to prefer partners who are young (and therefore more likely to be fertile and to live long enough to rear any offspring to the age of independence); (3) to prefer partners who are physically healthy (evidence of 'good' genes); and who (4) appear to provide a measure of 'paternity certainty.' This last phrase (sometimes put as paternity 'certitude' or 'confidence') refers to the probability that a male is actually investing in his own offspring rather than in that of another. For species in which male parental investment in offspring occurs (for example, by provisioning of the pregnant female and eventually of the young), selection will favour males with high paternity certainty. As a means of enhancing their paternity certainty, males should therefore prefer females who are 'virginal' or at least lack a reputation for having many sexual partners. The more the male is likely to invest in the female's offspring, the more selection will favour his being concerned with her behaviour.

Females, by contrast, should prefer 'good genes' males, that is, physically fit, well-co-ordinated individuals. They should also prefer those who control the resources required for paternal investment in offspring, that is, the wealthy, prestigious, and high in social rank.

Finally, they should prefer males who show some evidence, during courtship, of a commitment to a relationship. 'Courtship' refers to the period during which each sex is assessing the other. Cross-cultural standards of both male and female attractiveness, however variable, should have a 'good genes' basis.

DECEPTION

One of the most important things to realize about systems of animal communication is that they are not systems for the dissemination of the truth. An animal selected to signal to another animal may be selected to convey correct information, misinformation, or both. (Trivers 1985: 395)

Look at the green skin of a frog among the lily-pads – if you can spot it – and the truth of Trivers's statement is obvious. Look for your green and brown garter-snake in the grass, or the grasshopper, or the dun-coloured camel in the desert, or the white polar bear in the snow. Camouflage is a simple example of the 'misinformation' Trivers has in mind, the cryptic coloration that helps predator and prey hide from one another by communicating a deceitful 'nothing here' message.

The human- and animal-ethology literature is replete with examples of deceit (see, for example, Eibl-Eibesfeldt, 1975). Many animals 'puff up' in some way so as to give either a predator or a conspecific competitor the impression that they are larger than they are. Bullfrogs puff up with air. The male baboon's mantle of shoulder fur erects during agonistic (threat) encounters. Many species of birds fluff out their feathers in similar situations to achieve similar effects. In what Eibl-Eibesfeldt (1972: 17–18) suggests may be a cultural expression of an evolved behaviour tendency, human males in a number of cultures emphasize the shoulders with clothing and adornment (for instance, the wearing of epaulets).[11]

'Deceit' is freighted with negative connotations and with the idea of deliberate intention, but evolutionary theorists intend no moral judgment in using the term. All they mean by it is that 'misinformation is being communicated.' The neurophysiological processes that control the accuracy of the transmitted information evolved through the familiar blind-variation-and-selective-retention processes of genetic evolution.

11 Occasionally, in Western societies, women's clothing styles feature padded shoulders. One would hypothesize that men should find this style either unattractive or non-attractive, but should not prefer it.

Selection for 'deceit' is likely to produce a counter-selection in favour of the ability to detect deception. In response to cryptic coloration, predators may be selected to detect the slightest movement and then pounce. Prey may then be counter-selected to 'freeze' in response to the presence of a predator, and so on. This sort of dynamic situation in which different species generate selection pressures on one another results in the evolution of ecological systems. The process is one of many complex coevolutions in which a fair degree of relative stability will be reached, for a time, but never for all time. For our purposes, the most interesting selection pressures for deceit and deceit-detection occur within species.

To return to Trivers (1985: 395), that author goes on to discuss species in which 'males court females by offering them food.' He gives the scorpionfly as an example. The female who encounters a male carrying food in his mouth has been selected to communicate to him that she *is* female, which she does by lowering her wings. But a scorpionfly *male* who encounters another male carrying a nuptial gift of prey in his mouth will also often lower wings and otherwise behave as a female, apparently in order to gain that food. In 22 per cent of such encounters, the 'transvestite' male actually succeeds in gaining, and retaining, the food. In terms of the cost in time, energy, and risk of injury, selection favours this 'transvestism' (Trivers, 1985: 408).

In similar fashion, the mantis shrimp is highly vulnerable immediately after moulting, since it is temporarily soft-shelled. The frequency of its claw display increases at this time, and it may even lunge at intruders (Trivers, 1985: 409–10). It is behaving in a manner analogous to human 'bluffing,' a form of deceit. A reduced or even usual level of aggressive display would be more dangerous, to the just-moulted mantis shrimp, than is its deceitful 'bluff.'

The lexicon of every human language of which I am aware includes terms for lying, deception, and insincerity. It is very doubtful if there is any society in which parents do not have to train their children to truthfulness rather than to deceit. As we grow older we grow more skilful, avoiding the conveying of information rather than lying, substituting half-truths for untruths, subtly distorting by selective emphasis and careful choice of words.

In our earlier discussion of reciprocal altruism, we saw that selection favoured reciprocating, provided that there was a fair probability of aid being reciprocated to self or to kin in the future. We also saw that a reputation for being a reciprocator was in one's fitness interests. However, there are degrees of reciprocity, and Trivers distinguishes between gross and subtle cheating, the former being not returning the aid at all, the latter involving returning less than what was received but enough so that it remains in the interests of the cheated partner to maintain the relationship. For Trivers, reciprocal altruism is a sort of game in which it is in each player's interest to subtly cheat. This possibility is intriguing, since it is possible to hypothesize that our systems of trade and commerce, as well as many aspects of our political systems, are cultural elaborations of reciprocal altruism.

Fortunately, deceit generates a counter-selective pressure in favour of its detection. We are experts in noticing the non-verbal signs of stress associated with fear of our deceitfulness being detected. Trivers (1985: 415–16) speaks of the 'shifty eyes, sweaty palms, and croaky voices' that, in our own species, may signal the stress of deception to others. We learn to review the utterances of others for consistency and to put ourselves in the place of others so as to better understand where their interests and our own coincide and diverge.

Most of the time, truth rather than deceit is in our fitness interests. The reasons for this fact are twofold: first, there is reputation, and second, common interest. We discussed reputation in connection with reciprocal altruism, where the price for a reputation for deceit was likely to mean no longer receiving such altruism. This was a specialized case: think of the fate of the 'boy who cried wolf,' or of the hunter who repeatedly asks for help in carrying back to camp the meat of non-existent kills, or of the gatherer who frequently feigns illness in order to avoid work. In the small communities in which we evolved, and in today's distributed social networks as well, reputation was and is of immense importance.

Even if reputation were unimportant, however, *shared interest* would ensure that information would be more common than misinformation. In the case of kin, 'interest' here means genetic interest. Conveying to kin information likely to increase their genetic fitness is automatically likely to increase one's own inclusive fitness. Parents do not deceive their children about the dangers of fire and frost, for example. Teaching the skills of basket-making or flint-knapping accurately may mean more descendants for me. Even if the recipient of my true information is not a close relative, reciprocal altruism is still likely to result in my inclusive fitness being enhanced. Perhaps tomorrow I, or my child, will in turn receive true information.

Only in logic, however, are 'true' and 'false' opposites. Human communication is polyphonic, a many-voiced, multi-channelled medium of manipulativeness. Whatever the text of our words, our hands and feet and eyes, the posture of our bodies, the shifting tones of our voices, comment on our speech; and any child can effortlessly contradict his or her words with an expression, a smile, an artfully placed emphasis. The choice of words is itself communicative, and the selections of synonyms that our languages offer us represent not inefficient redundancy but a wide range of tools for specialized purposes.

If the 'orthodox' sociobiologists are correct, then what has been selected for, in human communication systems, is neither the conveyance of truth nor the transmission of falsity but the manipulation of the behaviour of others in our own fitness interests rather than in theirs. True, mother may warn the child of the dangers of frost and fire, but her fitness interests and his/hers overlap only by 50%, and the timing and phrasing of her warning may have as much to do with controlling his/her present behaviour in her interest as with the desire to keep him/her from harm.[12]

SEX AND DECEIT

Earlier in this chapter we discussed the differing fitness interests of males and females. Each copulation, in our species, puts at risk a large measure of a female's total reproductive potential but almost none of a male's. Thus, selection should favour males who are relatively undiscriminating in their choice of sexual partners. By contrast, selection favours females who are more discriminating. Females should prefer males who give evidence of having 'good' genes (by demonstrating a healthy and vigorous phenotype) and who also appear willing and able to invest in the female and her eventual offspring. Females who appear to be good 'paternity certainty' risks will also be favoured by selection (since males will be more likely to invest in their offspring). The cross-cultural data suggest strongly that, despite considerable variation in the patterning of sexual behaviour, this picture tends to be accurate (Symons, 1979). (However, as we will see in chapters 8 and 13, it is

---

12 See Markl (1985) for a sophisticated discussion of information exchange and manipulation in a variety of species. For a discussion of the cultural patterning of deceit in our own species (among the Cymba), see Anderson (1986). Note that the present discussion refers to selection pressures, not to human psychology. We need theories at that psychological level, theories of mechanism, before we can say how human beings are actually likely to behave. These theories, however, must be consistent with the theories of selection pressures here presented.

incomplete and may exaggerate some differences in male-female sexuality.)

Deceit enters the picture because selection favours appearance: for example, it favours males who can *appear* to be ready to invest in offspring, and who *appear* to be physically healthy (this being the only indicator of 'good genes' available to the female). When Goffman (1959) describes a paunchy man on a beach sucking in his abdomen as an attractive female passes by; when young men compete in athletic events or other forms of display; when men seem to fall readily in love with women: this is all deceit. Similarly, selection favours females who appear young and healthy; and discriminating in choosing partners even to the point of feigned virginity. It also favours females capable of appearing more likely than they actually are to permit copulation, so as to persuade males to continue to compete with one another and so to demonstrate their ability and readiness to invest parentally (that is, to continue to court), thereby enabling the female to make a more accurate assessment. As usual, therefore, each sex is under selection pressure to deceive, and each sex is simultaneously being selected to detect deceit in the other. Because courtship and sexual behaviours are so closely related to reproductive success, selection pressures in these areas are likely to be particularly powerful. (But note that the point of chapter 14's discussion of institutionalized homosexuality will be that even in the area of sexual behaviour, the psychological mechanisms underlying behaviour permit far more flexibility than evolutionary theory might lead one to expect.)

The most effective deceiver is apparently the one convinced of his or her own sincerity, so that we apparently have been selected for a strong tendency to *self-deceive* in matters of sex (and in many other matters as well).

Self-Deception

The selection pressures in favour of manipulating the behaviour of others, on the one hand, and of detecting and resisting such manipulating, on the other, exist in what an information theorist would term a 'reciprocal positive feedback' relation. This means that each maintains and strengthens the other. Perhaps only such a feedback loop could account for the evolution of the bizarre phenomenon of self-deception. In order to be a more effective deceiver, the organism deceives itself (Lockard, 1980; Sackheim, 1983)! The organisms in question may include our close relatives (the chimpanzee in particular) and certainly include ourselves.

Trivers (1971, 1985), who first discussed selection for self-deception, never explains what he means by the 'self.' The next chapter will include a theory of the evolution of self-awareness, but for the moment it is sufficient to suggest that 'self-deception' means that the organism's information-processing system is of sufficient complexity to permit it to encompass paradox, that is, to hold contradictory information. As we will see, there is empirical evidence to suggest that we human beings do indeed have that strange capacity. Presumably, one specialized processor of the brain holds an evaluation of the organism's capabilities and/or goals different from that held by another processor, one associated with the 'self.'

Although the organism evaluates itself as conveying accurate data, its communication (especially its non-verbal communication) transmits inaccurate, deceitful information. Our conscious experience, however, is that we are sincere. Keeping accurate information away from the self-representation permits it to evaluate itself as being truthful, reducing the stress and making the misinformation more likely to be accepted by others. In colloquial terms, no liar is more convincing than one who believes his or her own lies. Unfortunately, there is no clear demarcation between 'conscious' and 'unconscious' and 'in awareness' and 'out of awareness,' so that at times we may give conflicting messages. Self-deception may or may not prevent the lack of eye contact, shifty hands and feet, perspiring palms, and constricted voice that signal to others 'warning: deceit!'

Even worse, an information-processing system capable of maintaining contradictory data about both external reality and internal state and goals is inherently prone to malfunction. It may be that selection for self-deception is the ultimate cause of our species' tendency towards neurosis. The idea that 'self-deception' actually means that different subsystems of the mind hold contradictory information will be developed in chapters 4 and 5.

DECEPTION AND THE FITNESS INTERESTS OF OFFSPRING

We have already seen that, most of the time, selection favours the conveyance of accurate information. It would not be in an infant's fitness interest, for example, to falsify a distress call. It might, however, be in its interest to exaggerate the extent of its distress.

It is again Trivers (1972) who has explained parent-offspring conflict, weaning conflict, and sibling rivalry. Mother has a finite amount of 'parental investment' to offer her offspring. Investment in one child is therefore automatically at the expense of another child, regardless of whether that other child has or has not been born. Whom mother invests in and how much and when depends on her own inclusive-fitness interests. (More accurately, the probability that particular alleles will form part of her genome reflects their relative frequency in the gene pool, a frequency that, in turn, reflects the probability of their aiding the development of a psychological mechanism tending to lead a mother to partition her parental investment in a fitness-optimizing manner.) Mother's 'calculation' involves the costs and benefits of her investment in any one offspring as against the possible costs and benefits to that offspring's siblings, including the unborn siblings. Weaning provides a good example of the kinds of calculations that selection causes a mother to act as if she were making. (That is, selection will favour females who follow an algorithm for partitioning parental investment in offspring that approximates the calculations given below.)

The earlier an infant is weaned the sooner mother can bear more young and so enhance her fitness. Within limits, the longer mother delays weaning the greater the likelihood of the nursing infant surviving. Let us imagine, for a moment, that there is a gene that controls when mother decides to wean, a 'weaning gene.' Since full siblings have 50% of each other's genes, the frequency of a mother's weaning gene in the gene pool involves a balance between risking an offspring that has a 50% chance of carrying a replicate of that gene, against bearing a new infant who will also have a 50% chance of carrying that same gene.

That infant's situation is quite different. Let us imagine that the infant, like the mother, has a gene that controls when the infant decides to (self) wean. The frequency of the mother's 'weaning gene' will depend on an equation that weighs the 50% probability that it is being carried by the infant at the breast against the 50% probability that a new sibling will carry the gene. The infant's 'weaning gene' must weigh the 100% probability that the infant carries it against the 50% probability that the new sibling will also carry it. Therefore, the infant's weaning gene should 'decide' it is time to wean only long after the mother's weaning gene has come to the same conclusion. Of course, at a certain point, continuing to nurse would be against the infant's weaning gene's interest, since the infant would be gaining little from the additional milk while delaying or preventing the birth of a sibling who has a 50% chance of carrying a replicate of that gene.

If we think of individual rather than gene-level selection, then the equivalent argument is as follows: early weaning represents a risk to the mother of the 50% of her genes represented by the nursing infant. Her potential benefit is a hastening of the additional 50% of her genes that the new child will represent. The infant has its own 100% of its genes at risk by early weaning, while its potential benefit is identical with that of the mother. Since the infant in effect has more to lose, it should calculate that it is ready for weaning only after the mother has reached a similar conclusion. Hence, mothers typically must drive the infant from the breast. However, since additional siblings increase the genetic representation in the gene-pool of the nursing infant, both directly and indirectly (given the possibility of kin altruism, in the future), infants will eventually wean themselves, even if mother does not. (It is also true that, if the mother is nearing the climacteric and the nursing infant is likely to be her last, early weaning will not be in her fitness interests and she may nurse until the infant self-weans.)

Of course, these calculations have assumed that the nursing infant and the future sibling are full siblings and so share 50% of their genes. In fact, there is always a strong possibility that they will be half-siblings, sharing only 25% of their genes. Thus, the potential benefit to the nursing infant occasioned by the birth of a sibling will on the average be less than the 50% we have been assuming. (It will actually be 0.5 times the probability of both old and future siblings having the same father.) Nursing infants should nevertheless self-wean, eventually, but at a later point than would have been predicted if it could be guaranteed that the next sibling would share the father.[13] The infant at the breast should self-wean at the point at which continued nursing would provide only marginal increase in the probability of survival, a benefit by then outweighed by the benefit of a new sibling.

What is true of weaning is true of feeding in general. The infant is in competition with its siblings for investment from the parents – for food, care, protection. It is in its fitness interests to get more than its 'share' and alleles that cause it to manipulate the parents so as to get that extra will tend to increase in the gene pool. Its parents are related equally to each of the offspring and, from their perspective, it would make no

13 Selection would favour an infant permitting weaning at an earlier age if the next sibling will share the father than it would if the next sibling will have a different father. Thus, one might predict that a nursing infant exposed regularly to more than one adult male should be more resistant to weaning than one exposed only to a single adult male. Note that this is a testable hypothesis (though more readily testable with non-humans than with humans).

genetic sense for them to favour one 50% of their genes over another 50%, all things being equal.[14] Each offspring, however, is in effect 100% related to itself but only 50% (or 25%) related to its siblings. Naturally, therefore, selection favours it seeking parental investment at the expense of those siblings.[15] It is likely to do this by conveying misinformation as to the extent of its need. This apparent digression has, in short, returned us to the main topic of how differential fitness interests lead to deceit.

It is in the infant's and child's fitness interests to exaggerate weakness, hunger, alarm, and distress, at least up to a point. Thus, Claire Harkness (n.d.) finds that the child's development of language and other communicative abilities can be understood in terms of strategies to manipulate the behaviour of the parents. The strategies must be fairly subtle and responsive: excessive exaggeration of distress risks communicating to the parents that no further investment can salvage their offspring, and this might lead to abandonment. Still, it is only a slight exaggeration to suggest that, in general, selection favours 'cry-babies.' More formally, for young mammals, selection tends to favour an exaggerated communication of weakness and distress. This will be especially true in species in which parents are tending more than one offspring at a time, either because multiple births are the rule, or because, as in our own species, offspring remain dependent for extended periods of time. Parents, of course, are selected to detect deceit on the part of their offspring. Eventually, when the infant grows older and is no longer competing with siblings for parental investment, it will not be in its fitness interests to exaggerate its weakness. (Indeed, by adolescence the individual is more likely to be exaggerating strength than weakness, particularly when interacting with non-kin rivals.)

14 This discussion oversimplifies. For example, though each offspring has the same coefficient of relatedness to the parents, the parents do not necessarily maximize their own fitness by feeding each equally. The benefit conferred by a given amount of investment may be marginal for one offspring but make the difference between survival and death for another. Or, given shortage of food, a weak or simply very young offspring may be unlikely to survive even if given what is available, while additional food might permit a stronger offspring to survive. Thus, parents may favour some offspring over others, or even withhold any further investment from the weakest of a litter. See Wilson (1975a) or Trivers (1985) for further discussion.

15 Again, the discussion oversimplifies. Depending upon the ecology and social organization of a species, there may be substantial benefits (deriving from kin altruism) in having additional siblings. Thus, siblings may have been selected to be more 'altruistic' towards one another than the simple arithmetic provided here indicates.

INFANTICIDE IN LANGURS AS A TEST CASE

Let us leave human behaviour for a moment: after all, the differing-fitness-interests approach summarized in this chapter was developed by students of non-human animal behaviour. The strength of the approach continues to be most apparent, and its controversial aspects least distracting, when it is applied to species other than our own. This fact remains true even in discussion of the emotion-laden topic of infanticide.

Infanticide has been documented in a number of species, including the chimpanzee (Goodall, 1986), the prairie dog (Hoogland, 1985), the lion (Packer and Pusey, 1983), and the south Asian monkey known as the langur. It has been perhaps most intensively studied in the last-named of these species.

Sarah Blaffer Hrdy (1980) explains that the basic langur social unit consists of related females and their offspring. Each group will have a relatively transitory but dominant male attached to it. He is transitory because other males are continually attempting to displace him, and eventually one will succeed. Thus, the new male has a strictly limited period in which to maximize his reproductive success.

Langur females come into estrus – become sexually receptive and able to conceive – soon after their offspring are weaned. When a new male enters a group, he naturally finds that existing infants and fetuses are the product of his successor. It is obviously in this new male's fitness interest for the resident females to come into estrus as quickly as possible. He cannot hasten weaning, of course, but he can accomplish the equivalent: he can kill the suckling infants. By destroying existing infants – who were sired by his defeated rival – the new male increases the number of resident females who will conceive and bear him offspring. Moreover, the sooner they can be born, the more time his own offspring will have to grow into juveniles and thus be relatively resistant to the infanticidal efforts of the next new male.

Selection naturally favours nursing females attempting to protect their offspring, often by temporarily leaving the group. However, this strategy presumably exposes them to greater predator pressure. Oddly, they may be in a better position to protect their unborn than their nursing offspring. The new male will not destroy infants born to a female with whom he has previously copulated. However, he is not able to count the months required for gestation. Selection has therefore favoured pregnant females coming into a sort of 'pseudo-estrus' upon the arrival of a new male and copulating (infertilely, of course) with him. In this way, he becomes unlikely to destroy their young. Once again, we have an example of selection favouring deceit because of differing fitness interests.

Do human males practice infanticide in a manner similar to that of male langurs? Such a question is beyond the scope of the present discussion but is dealt with at length in Hausfater and Hrdy (1984). Certainly, Daly and Wilson (1981, 1982) find that stepparents, particularly stepfathers, are more likely than are genetic parents to practise child abuse.

Finally, a note about controversy: Sarah Blaffer Hrdy's research on langur infanticide was strongly attacked by the eminent American political scientist Glendon Schubert (1982), who had previously rejected the sociobiological paradigm upon which it was based. (But see his recent important book, *Evolutionary Politics* [1988], for his current position.) Such attacks on the youthful field of human sociobiology have not been rare. Blaffer Hrdy's work was vulnerable in that she had never personally observed infanticide but had in part inferred it from other aspects of behaviour and in part relied on the observations of others. Thus, some, like Schubert, felt that her conclusions were unreliable. Paul N. Newton (1986), however, with little fanfare but with a methodologically extremely careful research design, has since independently observed infanticide by male langurs while they were attempting to 'take over' a group. Blaffer Hrdy's work and conclusions have thus been corroborated. (Newton adds the interesting suggestion that non-resident, rival males may, by regularly killing the infants sired by the resident male, so lower the fitness benefits of occupying that position that selection may favour the incumbent quitting rather than fighting to the death to maintain a status deprived of fitness benefits.)

ARE THE FOUR DNA BASES REALLY THE THREE FATES?

Genetic Selfishness: Is Sociobiology Cynical?
The sociobiological image of *Homo sapiens* is that of a strongly proactive, strategizing species, highly complex in psychology, selected to weigh and measure incoming information in the pursuit of goals ultimately linked to genetic advantage. The portrait is one of dynamism, true: but is it not cynical as well?

The mechanisms of the mind are the product of selection for genetic selfishness, with the clear implication that *human beings should be manipulators in our social relationships.* After all, the fitness interests of all human beings (with the exception of identical twins) differ. Each of us represents a unique genotype, a unique constellation of genes. If evolution means that we have been selected to maximize our own genetic representation in the next generation, then apparently we should either aid or oppose one another depending on which tactic is most likely, in the long run, to enhance our inclusive fitness.

This motif of genetic selfishness recurs frequently in the work of human sociobiologists (for instance, Alexander, 1979, 1987; Barash, 1982). But it is not quite accurate: what is true is that *to the extent that current environment approximates that of our ancestors in terms of particular parameters*, to that extent the evolved processors of our brains, *whatever their other properties*, should lead us to tend to aid, ignore, injure, or influence others in ways that would have tended to enhance the inclusive fitness of our ancestors.

Notice that this wording opens three questions: (1) What are the relevant environmental parameters (informational inputs from the environment) to which our evolved processors react? (2) What algorithms do they use? (3) What other properties do these processors have? This book will in various places make some tentative efforts to answer these questions, but this volume's goal is not so much to provide answers as it is to establish a framework in which such questions can be asked, while the purpose of the present discussion is to counter the frequent confusion in sociobiology between a theory of human nature and a theory of natural selection.

This chapter has *not* argued that human beings are selfish, deceitful, and manipulative. It has argued that important selection pressures on our ancestors favoured the evolution of neurophysiological mechanisms embodying algorithms that provide a capacity for such behaviour in certain situations. The distinction between a theory of selection pressures and a theory of human psychology – of human nature – is crucial here. This chapter has dealt with *genetic* selfishness, not with *selfishness*. Genetic selfishness has to do with selection pressures, with allele frequencies. The term is just another way of saying that selection favours behavioural predispositions that maximize *my* inclusive fitness rather than that of another. Actual human behaviour is the product of a myriad of 'modules' or subsystems, each processing information in terms of algorithms solving problems of the kind that have faced our ancestors (chapter 5; Tooby and Cosmides, 1989). These evolved systems no doubt have properties that would not be predicted from study of the selection pressures alone. The important role of socially transmitted information, of culture, adds an additional order of complexity to our behaviour (chapters 6 through 8).

It will surprise no one that we are capable of selfishness, deceit, and other such behaviours. It should not be surprising that the capacity to act in such ways is a product of natural selection. Whether or how such behaviour can be moderated or even eliminated depends on the nature of the mechanisms that produce it – our psychology – and not on the selection pressures that produced the psychology. This distinction, between our evolved behavioural mechanisms – our social psychology, our human nature – and the selection pressures that have generated them, is crucial. All that we have said about the human-nature level of explanation (the psychological or individual level) is that we expect it to produce behaviour very roughly similar to the way we would act if we spent our time doing calculations of potential cost and benefit to our inclusive fitness for our every action. As we will see, the actual human nature produced by selection pressures is far more complex, perhaps, than the selection pressures themselves. Human psychology is a product of natural selection, but human behaviour hardly reduces to a calculus of selection pressures. Properly understood, there is nothing particularly cynical or pessimistic about a sociobiological view of human nature.

Many of us have probably read Erving Goffman's (1959) *The Presentation of Self in Everyday Life*. Here is an image of human behaviour and motivation entirely consistent with sociobiological expectation. Here is the individual enormously concerned with how others view him/her, utterly preoccupied with self and with staging dress and appurtenances so as always to appear in the best possible light (to fall into Goffman's dramaturgical metaphor). Far more than does any sociobiologist, Goffman accentuates the negative.

For those who do not read Goffman, we can take a look at classical economics's image of ourselves as endlessly greedy. Or we can glance at both ethnography and literature to see precisely what a sociobiological perspective would lead us to expect: people everywhere concerned with relative standing, with status and prestige (Barkow, 1975a); people preoccupied with sexuality and with the sexual and resource-related activities of those around them; people everywhere forming coalitions and categories and competing with other groups, coalitions, and categories for the control of the resources necessary for parental investment. Surely the literature on social conflict and inequality portrays a humanity whose *behaviour* is consistent with the tenets of evolutionary biology, even if social scientists habitually account for that behaviour in environmental rather than in evolutionary terms. Sociobiology's view of human nature is neither more nor less cynical than that of (other?) social-science views of our species, and fits in especially well with sociology's 'conflict theory.'

Free Will and Ethics

E.O. Wilson (1975a: 564) attracted much attention with his proclamation that ethics were to be 'biologized.' At one point (1978: 196) he even appears to believe it may be possible to use sociobiological insight to make our behaviour *more* ethical. He writes: 'The principal task of human biology is to identify and to measure the constraints that influence the decisions of ethical philosophers and everyone else, and to infer their significance through neurophysiological and phylogenetic reconstructions of the mind.' The 'constraints' are 'not so tight that [they] cannot be broken through an exercise of will.' Similarly, Lumsden and Wilson (1983: 179) argue that the evolved 'epigenetic rules' of the mind 'only bias development; they do not determine ethical precepts or the necessary decisions in a fixed manner. They still require that a choice be made, and in this sense they preserve *free will*' (emphasis added).

Wilson and Lumsden clearly wish to steer clear of the idea that biology somehow *determines* either ethical systems or conformity to such systems; but in their effort to avoid such an implication, they fall into another morass, that of 'free will.' Nor are they alone. Richard Alexander, a major figure in human sociobiology, also seems to believe in something akin to Lumsden and Wilson's 'will.' Alexander (1979: 93) writes that: 'Whatever the extent or nature of biologically based constraints on the modifiability of human behavior, therefore, such constraints seem most likely to be effectively bypassed or superseded by humans who individually and collectively are aware of them and understand them well.' These sociobiologists never tell us what 'will' is or whether it can be selected for, and they never face the problem of intentionality. It sounds very much like, as Lewontin, Rose, and Kamin (1984: 283) point out, a return to a very simple sort of mind/body split, à la Descartes.

For Wilson, Lumsden, and perhaps Alexander, the sociobiological truth, it seems, *may* make you free. Their various phrasings are, however, quite cautious. Alexander, in the passage quoted above, for example, is making no promises, though he does believe that if anyone can overcome our evolved cognitive and motivational biases it will be someone who is at least aware of them. Those of us who find it difficult to diet successfully or to stop smoking or to fall in love wisely may be even more cautious than is Alexander as to whether knowledge and 'will' are sufficient to alter behaviour.

Neither Lumsden and Wilson nor Alexander are in any position to resolve the paradox of how 'we' who are apparently prisoners of our evolved psychology are somehow to escape it. What do we mean by 'will' anyway? Chapters 4 and 6 will deal with that specific question in terms of our own folk psychology, the 'mind-body' split, our unexamined beliefs about 'will-power' and the self, and current theory from the neurosciences. That discussion will be the prelude to a theory of self-awareness and of how we have been selected for an 'intra-individual' information-processing system with built-in goals and behavioural strategies. Questions about 'will-power' will then be discussed in terms of evolved attentional mechanisms that control the input of information into various subsystems. Finally, we will analyse how the intra-individual information-processing system interacts with the categories of the information pool we label 'culture.'

In the next two chapters the work of building a theory of human nature will begin. That theory must be consistent with our understanding of the selection pressures that resulted in our species but it cannot be reduced to it. One of the unpredicted-by-theoretical-biology properties of human nature, self-awareness, represents a challenging problem for human sociobiology.

SUMMARY

1. Even though every human being who is not an identical twin is genetically unique, we each share genes with one another. Aside from the overlap caused by our belonging to the same species, we overlap with others to the extent that they are our kin. The size of this overlap is determined by the coefficient of relatedness (r) between us. For parents and offspring, and for full siblings, $r = 0.5$; for half-siblings and between ego and parent's siblings and ego and grandparents, $r = 0.25$; for first cousins, $r = 0.125$. From this perspective, altruistic behaviour is just a form of genetic selfishness involving an implicit cost-benefit analysis. The 'benefit' is the probability that our aid to another will increase our own genetic representation in the gene-pool; the 'cost' is the probability that our representation will be reduced, perhaps because of harm related to our 'altruistic' act. Parental behaviour is the most straightfor-

ward form of aid to kin (which is at times called 'kin selection' or 'nepotistic altruism').

2. The coefficient of relatedness is one factor in nepotistic altruism. Another is the FIP or *fitness-investment potential* of a relative to be aided. This term refers to the extent to which an organism's inclusive fitness would be increased by its altruism to another. It is affected by such factors as the age of the aid recipient.

3. Selection will also favour our aiding others, regardless of whether they are kin, to the extent that they are likely to return that aid to ourselves or to our relatives. Selection has favoured us acting as if we were using reputation and personal familiarity as indices of the probability of return of aid. Outsiders and those with a reputation for lack of reciprocity are least likely to be aided. FIP calculations also take into account this probability of return of aid.

4. It is very often in the fitness interests of organisms to influence and manipulate the behaviour of others, whether members of their own species or not. From an evolutionary viewpoint, therefore, communication is primarily about manipulation and deception. Cryptic (camouflage) coloration is a common example of deceit. Such deceit is likely to produce a counter-selective pressure in favour of deceit detection. Within our own species, our differing fitness interests imply that selection will often favour our deceiving one another, and therefore we should tend both to deceive and to be skilled at detecting deceit. In order to influence more successfully other's FIP assessment, and to escape detection by our non-verbal 'leakage' of cues, we deceive ourselves. Thus, we human beings are notoriously self-deceptive.

5. Weaning conflict is a result of the differing fitness interests of mother and child. In terms of cost/benefit, early weaning puts 100% of the infant's genes at risk but only 50% of the mother's. In terms of benefit, early weaning means an additional 25% to 50% of its genes in the gene pool for the nursing infant (depending on whether the sibling is a half or full sibling), but an assured 50% of her genes for the mother. Thus, mothers should ordinarily be prepared to wean earlier than their infants are prepared to self-wean. Similar reasoning underlies sibling rivalry. However, individuals are not actually doing such calculations: the gene frequencies underlying their behaviour have been produced by such mathematical processes, working themselves out in a blind-variation-and-selective-retention fashion over the generations.

6. The sexes have sharply differing fitness interests. Selection favours the relatively promiscuous male, since a copulation puts at risk virtually none of his capacity for reproduction. A female, however, risks much of

her reproductive potential with a copulation. Selection therefore favours females who withhold copulation until they have obtained some evidence that the male in question has a good genotype (usually demonstrated by good phenotype – health and strength) and is both able and willing to invest in any offspring. 'Willing' here means apparently emotionally bonded to the female; 'able' means controlling resources, including subsistence-relevant skills. Thus, males are attracted by females showing cues of sexual availability, youth, and health. Females are attracted by youth and health, but also by evidence of control of resources (being of high status, usually) and signs of emotional bonding. Both males and females, in our species, can be expert at producing the appearance, in place of the reality, of these cues. We are equally expert at detecting such deceit.

7. All of these apparent calculations are models from evolutionary theory: they are not meant as models of what actually occurs in the mind. Selection would have generated psychological traits (specialized processors or some kind of neurological systems or subsystems) that should tend, more or less, to result in acting roughly as if we had done such calculations. We do not know the algorithms these subsystems use. We would expect the subsystems to have properties not predicted by evolutionary theory. There is an immense difference between a theory of selection pressures and a theory of psychological mechanisms. Human psychology no doubt has emergent properties not predicted by evolutionary theory.

8. In the south Asian monkey, the langur, local troops consist of females and their offspring, with a resident male battling against other, outside males. A new male will increase his reproductive success by infanticide, since the death of an infant – who would have been sired by his predecessor – causes its mother to return to estrus much earlier than she would have had she nursed the infant until it was weaned. That langur males practise infanticide has been challenged but has now been confirmed by new research.

9. Some sociobiologists have argued that an understanding of the evolved nature of 'human nature' may in effect permit us to transcend it through an effort of will. Such reasoning is confused, since no theory of a 'will' independent of that evolved nature is provided, nor is it at all clear what is meant by the folk-psychology term 'will.' We require a theory of human social psychology, including one of self-awareness and volition, if we are to make sense of the 'will.' We must begin by confronting the mind-body problem of Descartes. The following chapters will do so.

PART TWO

Mind and Awareness

4

Self, Soul, Brain, Body, Mind

The review of basic sociobiology is finished now. This chapter and the one that follows it presents the *intra-individual system*, a sketch of the human mind as standing between genes and culture, mediating their interaction.[1]

This sketch of the mind cannot really begin until three issues are dealt with, the three issues that are the focus of this chapter: (1) our folk-psychology ideas of 'will' and responsibility; (2) the problem of Cartesian dualism or the 'mind-body split'; and (3) the disjunction between a social-science explanation in terms of beliefs, values, and intentions, and an explanation in terms of neurophysiological processes. What does evolve, anyway, awareness or biochemistry? The chapter begins by asking why we need a theory of mind in a work focused on gene-culture interaction, and then goes on to introduce our 'triune' brain and its evolution.

THE NEED FOR A SKETCH OF THE INTRA-INDIVIDUAL SYSTEM

Some sociobiologists are content to speak of genes and behaviour and to de-emphasize that which comes between, the human brain. This can be a perfectly legitimate research strategy, provided that we remember that something does come between, and that a theory of gene frequencies is

---

1 Some of the material in this chapter has been adapted from Barkow (1983). It has been extensively revised.

not a theory of psychology. But it can be dangerous to omit the mind and brain, for at least two reasons. One has to do with the risk of the 'genes for everything' fallacy, the other with adequacy of explanation.

The adequacy-of-explanation problem is straightforward: it is simply not possible to 'explain' complex, culturally ordered behaviour patterns as the simple 'effects' of genes, because there are complex intervening processes between the genes and the final behaviour. Theory and data at the level of social psychology and of sociology/anthropology/history are needed. Population genetics is not enough (recalling chapter 1's discussion of vertically integrated explanation).

The special-genes-for-everything simplification is one that sociobiologists have learned to avoid. Yet, in the absence of adequate theory linking genes and behaviour, this error remains a danger and a temptation. Genes code only for proteins. We all know that, but if we have no theory of human cognition, of information-processing, of self-awareness – no theory of an intra-individual system – then we may fall easily into the trap of speaking about 'genes for behaviour': and those who read us either uncritically or over-critically may assume we believe that there really are genes for all sorts of specific behaviours. We may even come to believe so ourselves.

A common but dangerous way of avoiding the 'special genes' problem is to invoke the 'proximate mechanism' simplification. Proximate explanations are usually given as contrasts to 'ultimate' or evolutionary explanations, but the contrast is very inexact. The meaning of 'ultimate explanation' is quite precise: it is an evolutionary explanation, that is, one in terms of selection pressures affecting gene frequencies. 'Proximate explanation' is a much vaguer term and may involve physiology, sociology, psychology, history, or ecology. It is a grab-bag of levels and kinds of explanation. Appealing to the black box of proximate explanation or mechanism in human sociobiology is often a useful deferral of more detailed analysis, but is unproductive when it represents an avoidance of issues (such as those of mind and culture).

FITTING INTO NEUROPHYSIOLOGY

Despite great advances in the neurosciences (ably summarized by Changeux, 1985 and by Gazzaniga, 1985), the precise parallels and isomorphisms between the brain's architecture and human information-processing remain unknown. The problem is that the brain rather looks as if it was designed by a committee. MacLean (1973, 1978) presents the brain as a sort of unholy trinity, but his description does tie anatomy and function at least loosely together. Let us look at his picture of the 'triune brain' before going on to discuss some of the processes taking place within it.

Strange Television: The Triune Brain

Natural selection can only work on what is already there; and at every point in its evolutionary history, a species must be adapted to its environment. Oddly enough, these two statements explain why the eminent neuroscientist Paul D. MacLean can speak of our having *three* brains (or at least, three mentalities). To our first, 'reptilian' brain was added an old mammalian ('paleomammalian') brain and then, with evolutionary time, came the third or new mammalian ('neomammalian') brain.

The result is similar to what a television set might look like if we began with a crystal radio set, added vacuum tubes when they were eventually invented, installed a cathode-ray tube when it became available, put in transistors when they were developed, then added colour and remote control, until we eventually had a 'modern' TV with a crystal set at its heart. It is very unlikely that such a television would operate as efficiently as one designed and built *de novo*. The only advantage of an 'add-on' model is that our radio-television would have been able to operate at every stage of our tinkering. Our brains resemble that strange television set. Evolution never begins anew.

Natural selection cannot start growing wings on your back – or a unitary brain in your head – that would be utterly useless for one hundred generations, even if they would be wonderfully adaptive for the one hundred and first generation. After all, for the first one hundred generations (or even for just the first generation), there would be no selection pressure to cause alleles supporting the new structure to increase in frequency in the gene pool. If the alleles underlying the potential wings or brain did not increase then the wings or brain would never evolve. Variants whose accumulation might eventually become wings or a new brain will have to be adaptive (that is, will have to increase inclusive fitness) in the first and in every succeeding generation if we are to fly or to think.

Selection works only on what a species is already doing, even if it is doing it only to a very limited extent. One of the major problems in understanding the actual evolutionary history of species is the problem of the 'initial kick,' of just what began a positive-feedback process leading to flight, or efficient running, or very large brains, or to whatever structure or ability interests us. The origin of flight in birds, for example, remains the subject of much debate and controversy among evolutionists (see Lewin, 1985: 530–1). Perhaps the ancestors of birds solved the initial-kick problem by first being selected for wings that only helped them to glide down from trees they had originally climbed. Or perhaps the 'pre-wings' were stabilizers adaptive in a species of rapidly running (cursorial) reptile. Whatever wings were before they were wings, evolutionary theory insists that they must have been adaptive. Once an even roughly winglike shape was in existence, however, then the blind-variation-and-selective-retention process of evolution would have accumulated information about aerodynamics, generation by generation redesigning the wing.

Once a species has already been doing something, then, so long as the environment remains constant and that trait therefore continues to be adaptive, selection will continue to favour its doing that something. Its performance will continue to improve until all available genetic variation for improvement has been tapped. This process is sometimes known as 'orthoselection,' selection in favour of whatever a species is already doing, so that 'existing traits become more strongly developed' (Hulse, 1971: 506).

The human brain is an example of orthoselection, and it, too, evolved by transformation and accretion. Thus, at every step, our ancestors have had functioning brains adapted to their environment. But this means that the modified brains of our reptilian and early mammalian ancestors have never been eliminated in favour of a new start: they remain with us. The resulting human brain is not so much a product of efficient, unitary engineering as it is of tinkering with the equipment without shutting it down. It is a strange television.

Three Mentalities

MacLean calls the remnants of our ancestral reptilian brain the 'R-complex.' In mammals, it is 'represented by a group of large ganglia including the olfacto-striatum, corpus striatum (caudate nucleus and putamen), globus pallidus, and satellite gray matter' (MacLean, 1978: 42). It is involved with behaviours that MacLean associates with self-preservation or 'the survival of the species' but which nowadays we would probably refer to as 'inclusive fitness.' MacLean lists twenty such behaviours, including establishing and defending territories, routinized daily activities, forming social hierarchies (more properly, finding one's position in a social hierarchy), and courtship and breeding (MacLean,

1978: 43–4). These behaviours, at least in reptiles, tend to be stereo-typed, ritualized, and rather inflexible. (Some people like to refer to them as 'instinctive.')

The old mammalian brain has a greater capacity for learning than does the R-complex. This area of the brain surrounds the brain-stem in a thick lobe or cortex and has 'large, cable-like connections to the hypothalamus.' It includes the *limbic system*, the now widely used term that MacLean coined (in earlier publications) for that cortex and for the 'structures of the brain stem with which it has primary connections' (1978: 46). The limbic system 'derives information in terms of emotional feelings that guide behavior with respect to the two basic life principles of self-preservation and the preservation of the species' (which I am identifying with 'inclusive fitness'). The limbic system controls the 'four F's' – feeding, fleeing, fighting, and ... sex (Pribram, 1971: 201). It constitutes a substantial portion of the brain of 'primitive' mammals, such as rodents, and is of only somewhat less importance in primates such as ourselves. Interestingly, MacLean challenges the frequently made assertion that it is impossible to separate cognition (thought) from emotion. His argument is based on anatomy, since he believes that anatomically different structures are associated with emotion and cognition, respectively. Even more interestingly, MacLean remarks that the 'ancient limbic system has the capacity to generate strong affective feelings of conviction that we attach to our beliefs, regardless of whether they are true or false!' (1978: 47).

The new mammalian brain is found among the more 'advanced' mammals, such as the primates (the order to which our own species belongs). It consists of the neocortex, the greatly expanded part of the brain that makes us human beings such big-headed animals; and the 'structures of the brain stem with which it is primarily connected' (MacLean 1978: 49). The new mammalian brain deals with language, mathematics, abstract thought, and the use of symbols in general. It is linked to the senses that give us knowledge of the external world, including vision and hearing.

MacLean's triune-brain concept provides sufficient anatomy for present purposes. All three levels at once tend to be involved in our everyday behaviour. That colloquial concept, the 'mind,' should be identified only with the central nervous system as a whole rather than with any one of its components. It does not 'reside' in any one or pair of the 'mentalities' but in all three.

What of our conscious experience? Does that reside in the entire brain, or should we locate it in the neomammalian region of the brain? Where is the *self*? It is time to discuss self-awareness and our culture's notions of the 'self.'

SELF-AWARENESS

Between ourselves and our genes is our *self*, our self-awareness. This self-awareness creates an embarrassment of riches – we have one explanation too many to account for our behaviour. Behaviour is 'caused' by complex physiological and neurophysiological processes. It is also 'caused' by our *deciding* to act, by that subjective experience of volition known to philosphers as 'intentionality.'

The philosopher Alexander Rosenberg (1985b: 265) points out that the social sciences often account for behaviour in terms of the 'intentions' – the beliefs, goals, desires – of the behaving individuals. By contrast, biology and to a considerable extent psychology explain behaviour in terms of physical and neurophysiological processes. Thus, Rosenberg argues, social-science explanations are incompatible with the theories of the neurosciences. Human sociobiology, though, would seem to be in an even worse state. As we saw in chapter 3's discussion of human 'will' and whether 'we' could somehow 'overcome' our evolutionary heritage, human sociobiology flits from one type of explanation to the other. If we are going to be coherent, we had better resolve the disjunction between neurophysiological and intentionality explanations of human behaviour. What is the relationship between neurophysiological processes and our intentions?

We experience ourselves as active agents, as *doing* as well as *being*. We have a clear sense of an 'I,' a self that drives a car, looks for a job, falls in love, makes decisions. It is this 'I' that creates problems for human sociobiology (and for psychology and philosophy in general). Is a human sociobiology to account for the evolution of neurophysiological structures and processes, or is it to study my conscious experience and my subjective sense of *me*, of myself-making-decisions? Evolution has to do with gene frequencies, agreed: but do we discuss gene frequencies and the evolution of our awareness of being aware; or should we talk about gene frequencies and the evolution of the structures and functioning of the brain? This problem is a great deal older than sociobiology itself, for it is the problem of the mind-body split.

Coming to Grips with Descartes
Did 'I' press that button, or did an extraordinarily complex set of

neurophysiological processes just occur that resulted in an orchestrated sequence of neurons being triggered, causing the appropriate muscles to be flexed and stretched such that an arm was lifted, a forefinger extended, and (with input from a distal sense known as 'vision' and corrective feedbacks from the musculature involved) a button was pushed? Is sociobiology to account for the evolution of the physical brain and body and the operations they perform; or for my phenomeno-logical experience, my awareness of thinking, feeling, evaluating, deciding? Do we write in the passive voice or the active voice? If the neurophysiology is the 'real' explanation, then my subjective experi-ence is irrelevant and, along with behaviourist John B. Watson, we must rule it out of science. Sociobiology can, with much relief, ignore it. By contrast, perhaps we should ignore biological mechanisms and, follow-ing G.H. Mead (1934) and A.I. Hallowell (1959, 1960, 1961, 1965), think about how the 'ego' or sense of self can be a product of natural selection 'designed' by evolution to be shaped by the social influences that no doubt caused me to *want* to push that particular button at this particular time.

This confusion over cause stems from our culture's long history of belief in the body as almost non-alive, as machine-like unless animated by an indwelling, immaterial essence parallel to the body, a spirit or 'soul' or (to use a closely related but in principle non-supernatural term) 'mind.' This mind or soul (quotation marks omitted hereafter) was, and by many still is, believed to exist after death and for some even prior to birth. The seventeenth-century French philosopher René Descartes came to intellectual terms with these ideas by positing that mind and body were indeed separate, but that they interacted at the pineal gland.

Versions of this Cartesian approach (which is known as 'psychophys-ical dualism') remain current. For example, Popper and Eccles (1977) have invoked a 'mind' (they do not speak of 'soul' but appear to mean much the same thing) that interacts with the brain via the pyramidal cells of the vertical columnar arrangements of the sensory cortex of the dominant hemisphere. They hypothesize (and apparently conclude as well) (p. 355) that 'the self-conscious mind is an independent entity that is actively engaged in reading out from the multitude of active centers in the modules of the liaison areas of the dominant cerebral hemisphere. The self-conscious mind selects from these centers in accord with its attention and its interests and integrates its selection to give the unity of conscious experience from moment to moment. It also acts back on the neural centers.' It is not surprising that Descartes's mind-body split should remain alive among some philosophers and neurophysiologists, for it is an integral part of our folk psychology and underlies many of our ideas of responsibility, morality, and medicine.

Folk Psychology, the Self, and Responsibility

Our culture's folk psychology (or 'ethnopsychology') involves an implicit pilot-and-plane Cartesian model.[2] We tend to think of our bodies as machines, like airplanes, and our 'real' selves as the controlling pilots, the executive selves who dictate the actions. Other cultures have *healers*, we have physicians who have largely been trained as technicians. The mind-body split is so well-established in medical thinking that even some 'holistic' physicians tend to think of the mind's *effects* on the body rather than of the two as a single unit.

Not only are mind and body distinct, in Western thought, but the mind is expected to be in 'control' of the body, to be the body's pilot. As good pilots should, we take responsibility for our craft's actions and fear 'loss of control' perhaps more than death itself; hence our horror of mental illness, since it seems to involve such loss (Leighton, 1982).

When we do 'suffer' even a momentary loss of 'control,' we are contrite. If we overeat we must be apologetic for our lack of 'will-power' (one of the most revealing terms in our folk-psychology vocabulary). If we change jobs, end marriages, join political parties, or act against another, we must strive to present a public image of our having done these things after reasoned and reasonable thought.

When we cannot provide a non-emotional, instrumental-seeming response to the question 'Why did you do that?' we lose face and may pretend that somehow something else took control. Perhaps we remark, 'Sorry, I wasn't myself.' But if not oneself, then who? We no longer say, as our ancestors did, that 'the Devil made me do it.' Nowadays, it is the fault of the body: our 'irrational' but 'overwhelming' emotions – fears, envies, rages, lusts – come not from the supernatural but from the 'body.' This mind-body-split folk psychology helps us maintain our self-image of 'really' being rational and controlled (an image especially

---

2 Other cultures, too, often have some kind of spirit/body split. Indeed, the early anthropologist E.B. Tylor considered 'animism' – the belief in an indwelling 'soul' – as typical of 'tribes very low in the scale of humanity' and, in modified form, of more 'advanced' societies as well (1873; reprinted 1972: 11). For Tylor, this idea of the soul is inescapable because the stillness of the dead inevitably suggests that something has gone out of the body; and because the vividness of dreams lends itself to the idea of a spirit world. It is not clear (to me, at least) that other cultures share with our own folk psychology the notion of this indwelling spirit being the essence of the person, a controller of a machine-like, if often rebellious, body.

important to the middle and professional classes), regardless of how we actually behave. We blame someone else for our behaviour, only that 'someone' is our physical self.

There are of course subcultural and social class differences in the degree to which we are expected to maintain a 'rational' image, and our own culture does provide us with some socially acceptable reasons for acting irrationally. Alcohol, for many people, provides a socially acceptable 'time-out' excuse for being partially out-of-control, though there is real doubt as to the extent to which its effects are necessarily 'disinhibiting' (MacAndrew and Edgerton, 1969). 'Love' is officially considered unpredictable and, for many of us, 'falling in love' is a permissible reason for the 'pilot' to have lost control of the craft, particularly of its sexual apparatus. The rage of sexual jealousy, in many places, is considered a mitigating factor even in some crimes of violence (*crimes passionnels*).

These excuses reveal that even our own culture accepts at least implicitly that the pilot's control of the aircraft is often uncertain and, at times, not there at all. The craft itself – the body – is viewed as threatening the mind's – the pilot's – control. Somehow, our *bodies* are aliens able to influence our *real* selves. It is the source, in our folk psychology, of those disturbing influences, the emotions, the deadly emotions that put us off course, tempting us to sin and error. Chapter 5 will discuss why natural selection has so strongly limited our 'rational' behaviour and made 'us' subject to strong emotions. For now, it is sufficient to note that our mind-body-split folk psychology provides us with an 'out' whenever we violate our culture's norms by failing to present ourselves publicly as 'reasonable,' rational beings whose actions are explicable in non-emotional (non-body) terms.

In providing us with rationalizations for 'slightly-out-of-control' behaviour, our culture has at least touched reality: for the 'pilot' is never in control. Self-awareness is real enough, to be sure. As we will see, the illusion is the sense of being the executive, of being in control.

Begging the Question of Dualism
Theorists like Popper and Eccles (1977) do, at least, explicitly recognize that awareness is a challenging problem. Other theorists, however, including some who share with me the perspective of biological evolution, at times seem merely to retain an unexamined version of our culture's mind-body-split folk psychology, and to ignore the dual-explanation difficulty. Though there are some exceptions, theorists

often avoid the problem by, for example, writing about the evolution of intelligence while ignoring self-awareness (for instance, Humphrey, 1976, and Stenhouse, 1973). Others have written of the 'mind' or of 'consciousness' or of 'self-awareness' as having evolved because it was somehow adaptive, somehow related to intelligence, somehow inevitable (for example, Blakemore, 1976: 37).[3] Even the brilliant sociobiologist Robert Trivers (1985) writes of selection for 'self-deception' (to be discussed later in this chapter) without addressing the question of where the 'self' being deceived came from.[4] But as Hampshire (1978) puts it, to ignore the problem posed by Descartes is to be incoherent. If evolution is essentially about gene frequencies, and if the genes code for proteins that generate the physiological structures and processes of which we are composed, what explanatory need is there for any theory of 'self' or 'awareness'?

The most common way of bridging the mind-body split is by asserting that it is not really there because mind and body are essentially the same phenomenon, an approach taken, for example, by Rose (1976), by Lewontin, Rose, and Kamin (1984), and by Changeux (1985). This view, known to philosophers as the 'identity' solution, involves the expectation that 'thoughts, pains, and desires ... will turn out to be identical with special states or events of the central nervous system' (P.M. Churchland, 1979: 109).

In its most convincing form, identity theory involves finding isomorphisms (similarities in structure) between our phenomenological experience and the neurological architecture and processes identified by neuroscientists. There is little doubt that these isomorphisms are there and that the central nervous system is indeed the organ of conscious-

---

3 Sagan (1977) provides a very readable account of the evolution of human intelligence. Izard (1977: 131–61) provides a very useful overview of the various theories of the nature of consciousness. Changeux (1985) and Pribram (1976) provide the details of what we know of neuroanatomical functioning. Ryle (1949) gives us a powerful attack on Cartesian thinking, while Koestler (1967) writes a powerful rebuttal. Klein (1984) provides a comprehensive survey of how the concept of consciousness has been treated in the discipline of psychology. Kihlstrom (1987) provides an excellent introduction to consciousness and unconsciousness in contemporary cognitive science.

4 Of course, this may be preferable to the approach of writers such as Granit (1977), who argues that consciousness is an 'emergent,' the highest level of a hierarchical organization, and that 'conscious man makes use of neurophysiological mechanisms without being "governed" by them' (p. 73). It is difficult to say what this means or how this could be: Granit is aware of a problem but does not really give us any solution. P.S. Churchland (1986: 323–7) distinguishes among several different usages of the term 'emergence' in the context of the mind/brain problem.

ness and of information-processing. Thus, from this perspective, mind and brain may be identical in the way that 'mean kinetic energy of constituent molecules' and 'temperature' are identical (P.M. Churchland, 1979: 109). 'Mind' (awareness, including self-awareness) is therefore no epiphenomenon but identical to certain neurophysiological processes, another way of speaking about them. So far so good.

Our familiar, folk idea of temperature turned out to correspond to the findings of modern physics with sufficient accuracy to require no change in the way we are accustomed to speaking about it. Can we expect as much for our folk ideas of 'mind' and 'awareness'? Can they be shown to have neurophysiological equivalents? Suppose our folk psychology is wrong (cf. P.M. Churchland, 1979: 114–15; P.S. Churchland, 1986: 321–2)?

Let us repeat the folk notion of temperature versus the physics definition of temperature analogy, but this time substitute 'heat.' You and I usually mean by 'heat' much the same thing as we mean by temperature. The physicist, though, uses the term 'heat' to indicate quantity of energy: the temperature of a gas may be higher than that of an equal volume of liquid but hold much less heat. From the point of view of scientific physics, our folk physics (what an anthropologist would term our 'ethno-physics') is confused and inaccurate with regard to the idea of 'heat.' There is no way we can find an identity between our folk idea of 'heat' and the 'heat' known to physics.

Our folk-psychology 'mind' and 'awareness' are probably more like folk 'heat' than they are like folk 'temperature.' No matter how we search for the location of a self-awareness with intentionality, we will not find it. This is because the idea of a directive, decision-making self, an 'I' that takes moral responsibility, is inaccurate with respect to the underlying neurophysiological processes and, moreover, may well be a concept specific to our particular culture rather than a cross-cultural universal. As Hallowell (1959) put it, the self is 'culturally constituted' (a topic we will return to in chapter 8, in connection with the boundaries of the self). I will indeed present an identity solution to the mind-body problem, but only after developing a conception of awareness, and of its biological evolution, very different from our folk-psychology notions.

FINDING THE SELF WITH A MAP

This approach to integrating the evolution of our neuroanatomy with the evolution of our self-awareness begins (in the best psychological tradition) with the rat. A rat had better know its territory if it is to survive. Rats are small rodents that must frequently hide from predators, and must also be able to 'predict' where food is likely to be available. But for a rat to 'know' its territory means that it needs some kind of cognitive map, some kind of internal representation of local geography so that it can compute the best places to zig, zag, and go-to-ground when a fox or eagle or your pet feline is after it. Natural selection has presumably favoured those rats who are a little better than are others in developing and using such maps of local territory. Note that there are at least three aspects to this mapping: selection for *attending* to appropriate aspects of the environment; selection for *recording* them internally; and selection for *accessing* the recorded information. The discussion below will focus primarily on the 'attending' part of the mapping process.

For millions of years, rat alleles that give a slightly higher probability of a bearer successfully 'mapping' territory and utilizing the resultant internal representations for survival and reproductive success have been increasing in frequency in the rat gene pool. Laboratory psychologists, of course, take advantage of this evolved ability of rats when they 'run' them in mazes. Rats do not necessarily need an external 'reward' to run a maze – selection has made this behaviour 'self-reinforcing,' meaning that they do not require any external, associated reward to explore their territory (Lockhard, 1971).

Rats are hardly the only species with this kind of territory-mapping ability, of course. Peters (1978) points out that wolves (for example) have highly detailed and intricate internal maps of their home ranges. Presumably, selection would have favoured such ability. Wolf mothers unable to return to the dens in which they had left their cubs would thereby have lowered the frequency in the gene pool of the genes they carried. Individuals who were unable to recall sources of water or favorable sites at which previous kills had been made would have had a lower probability of survival and reproduction than would have others. Wolves whose alleles increased their likelihood of doing these things would have been the ones who produced the next generation, and since offspring resemble their parents ...

Our ancestors were not wolves. But they were gatherers, scavengers, hunters, and wanderers on a complex, three-dimensional terrain (three-dimensional, given the importance of trees for security, as places from which predators might spring, and as sources of fruit and nuts). No doubt they were selected for, and we are heirs to, the ability to attend to external geography and so internalize accurate and detailed cognitive maps or internal representations of that external reality (Wallace, 1989). O'Keefe and Nadel (1978, 1979) argue that this cognitive-mapping ability is associated with part of MacLean's neomammalian brain, the hippocampus.

Did you ever have the frustration of holding a perfectly accurate map in your hand but not knowing where on it you were currently located? Cognitive maps, too, need place-markers. Such a marker would be a kind of internal representation of the organism itself. Think of this representation as a locus in a data-processing system, something like the cursor on your monitor's screen.

But the internal mapping of a social animal is hardly likely to be limited to the geographic. Selection must favour the inclusion in the map of that which is relevant for survival and reproductive success: other organisms – potential mates, rivals, and offspring, as well as predators and prey – are clearly relevant (cf. Humphrey, 1983). Now we have moved beyond the idea of a relatively static 'map' and into something more closely resembling a computer simulation model, a moving model in which the solving of complex mathematical equations of present state and past experience permits prediction of the future. In this case, predictions are being made of future geographic location. Where will prey be likely to hide, for example? But just as the model is not limited to geographic landmarks, data about other organisms are not limited to physical location either.

What information about living organisms should representations of them include? Objects and organisms are internally represented in the first place only if they have some probability of affecting the genetic representation of the individual in future generations: similarly, selection is likely to limit the incorporation of 'other organism data' to those that are relevant to the encoding individual's fitness.

In chapter 2, for example, we discussed how social-dominance hierarchies had been interpreted by group selectionists as a means of limiting in-group aggression, but that current interpretations have more to do with inclusive fitness. Agonistic encounters have costs even to the victor. An individual who engages in them only when he or she has a high probability of winning will be more likely to survive and reproduce than an individual who always defers or one who always attacks. Evaluating the relative probability of winning requires data on relative size and physical condition, as well as memory of past encounters with this opponent. The internal representation of a fellow troop member will include at least these items.

What of the marker in the map, though, the representation of oneself? Data on fellow group members are useful only for evaluating their behaviour relative to one's *own* physical state and abilities, one's own past performance. The internal representation of self must be at least as differentiated and complex as is that of other internally represented individuals.

What is the subjective experience of a social animal with fairly complex internal representations of external reality, including internal representations of other organisms and of itself? Now I shall make a plausible but utterly unverifiable assumption: I assume here that such an organism experiences *awareness* (cf. Hallowell, 1959; Griffin, 1976, 1978). Awareness is not illusory (though the idea that awareness of self means that the 'self' is a miniature, controlling 'person,' a homunculus, is). Awareness, I am assuming, is a *property* of the kind of information-processing system described here in terms of cognitive maps and 'internal representations.' It is not separate or apart from the information-processing system, the central nervous system: it is a property of it (a version of the 'identity' response to Descartes).[5]

If these assumptions are accurate (and one must take them on faith, since they are not verifiable), then it is likely that all awareness includes at least some measure of *self*-awareness. But, as with a newborn infant, for most species there is probably no sense of 'me' and no idea of directiveness, of assertion, of volition. True self-awareness, I suggest, arises only when the internal representation of the organism grows complex indeed. Monkeys do not recognize photographs of themselves, though (interestingly enough) they can recognize the images and vocalizations of others. The great apes, when shown a mirror image of themselves, quickly learn to respond to it quite as a human being would – a spot of paint in the reflected image results in the hand exploring the paint-bearing portion of the face (Gallup, 1975 and 1979). Perhaps the distance between awareness and self-awareness is more quantitative than qualitative, though this is not yet clear.

5 For a recent and very technical philosophical discussion of the mind/body problem in relation to current advances in the neurosciences, see Patricia S. Churchland (1986). I believe, though am not certain, that she would categorize the position I take here as 'functionalism.' From my perspective, philosophical discussions of the mind/ brain that do not directly address the question of what it was evolving *for* are of limited relevance. No doubt some philosophers will feel that I am relegating to the footnotes what, in terms of their discipline and for their purposes, are major issues. My own purpose, lest the reader forget, is to construct a framework in which the continuities among the biological, psychological, and social sciences may be demonstrated and emphasized.

Selection pressures for the immensely elaborate human self-awareness were probably related to selection in favour of language and
self-deception. Before dealing with these factors in the evolution of
self-awareness, though, it is necessary to dispose of two distracting
issues: that of the previously discussed question of intentionality; and
the problem of the homunculus self.

Amending Folk Psychology's Self
Is the self a homunculus, a sort of bossy little person safely ensconced
somewhere in the brain, who makes the real decisions? Many theorists
of self-awareness (including Freud, if we assimilate his 'ego' to the
concept of 'self') seem to cast the self in this role. In the framework we
have been building in this chapter, though, self-awareness is not a
miniature of the organism, not a model of it. It is (depending on one's
taste in metaphor) the tip of an iceberg or an incomplete cartoon of the
real, unitary organism. *Self-awareness extends only to aspects of the self that
in our evolutionary past have strongly and directly affected inclusive fitness.*
Physical size and strength, current condition of health, evaluation of
ability vis-à-vis others, need for sleep or hunger – all these are directly
pertinent. We can do something about pain on the body surface and so
can precisely localize it. We can do little about internal pain, and are
quite likely to localize the pain of a heart attack very inaccurately (for
example, in the arms or elsewhere). Bilirubin count has no instant
impact on our inclusive fitness and so we have no automatic awareness
of it, or of countless other 'autonomic' processes. But when bilirubin
count is particularly high (indicating hepatic illness), or when other
autonomic functions are disturbed, we subjectively experience a sense
of malaise and are likely to avoid physical challenges. General data on
physical condition are certainly of importance, but there presumably
was no selection pressure for consciousness to include information
pertaining to the precise problems of specific biochemical systems.

Psychological anthropologist A.I. Hallowell (1959, 1960) concluded
long ago that the type and amount of data that are part of self-
awareness, or that are included in the internal representation of self,
have to do with culture and personal experience as well as with
evolution. As with other aspects of human behaviour, there is much
malleability built into self-awareness. The extent to which the self is tied
to a group or set of groups, the extent to which it includes family and
lineage, the extent to which clothing and other appurtenances are part
of the self, or even the degree to which body image is differentiated, are

all quite variable. Cultural differences in self-evaluation will be discussed in chapter 8, under the heading of self-esteem. At this point, it is only necessary to underscore that psychological studies of the peoples of diverse societies have led to the conclusion that the self is 'culturally constituted.'[6]

There remains the problem of our subjective experience of decision-making, of control. This, I would maintain, is largely an illusion of our culture. Yes, *I* make decisions if by *I* is meant my entire brain and body, not just some portion of this single organism. *I* am not the tip-of-the-iceberg phenomenon of consciousness. First-person singular in the English language is something of an illusion: 'I made a decision' is more properly rendered as 'I became aware that my brain-body information-processing system had arrived at a decision.' Information is being processed and decisions are being made and to a limited extent these processes may be reflected in self-awareness as the internal representations of external and internal reality are brought up to date. For those instants, 'I' am 'aware' of the decision.[7]

6 It may be that we could develop a culture in which socialization resulted in a self encompassing a large portion of the processes not considered 'under conscious control.' Perhaps it could even be possible to counter some of the built-in biases affecting information available to the self. Might one construct a religion able to do this, or are there already such religions?

7 Johnson-Laird (1983) presents a theory of awareness somewhat similar to that presented here and elsewhere (Barkow, 1978a; 1983). Johnson-Laird agrees that consciousness is a model of aspects of the organism rather than a homunculus (which would lead to a problem of endless recursion). But his conceptions of *self*-awareness and intentionality are quite different from my own. He writes: 'An intention is a conscious decision to act so as to try to achieve a particular goal. An organism can have an intention only if it has an operating system that can elicit a model of a future state of affairs, and decide that it *itself* should act so as to try to bring about that state of affairs' (p. 473) (italics in original). Johnson-Laird adds that 'the operating system only needs access to a model of itself in order to have intentions' (p. 473). For Johnson-Laird, 'will-power' has to do with 'the extent to which the operating system can enforce its decisions' (p. 469). Perhaps because Johnson-Laird is not working in the framework of modern evolutionary theory, he has no way to predict what that model might include. Moreover, his view of behaviour is that it is enforced from the top down, by the self (the organism's model of itself). I, however, am arguing that our subjective experience of volition is a culture-bound illusion. For a thorough discussion of intentionality and the neurosciences, see Sayre (1986).

Note that I am striving to avoid reifying the self: it is part of a process rather than a product or thing. Self-awareness and awareness of self are synonymous. The extent of self-awareness and what may be included in the process are highly variable across situations, individuals, and cultures. For an excellent analysis of the development of self-awareness in the young child, see Kagan (1981).

The next chapter will deal more fully with attention and the contents of consciousness, and with modular, parallel distributed-processing conceptions of how the brain is organized. The point of this chapter is that, in our culture, we learn to express the products of our information-processing in terms of a vocabulary of 'I decided.' More fatalistic cultures – and some individuals in our own society – may have fewer illusions over their own degree of 'self-control.' For example, though Buddhist thought certainly has a notion of a sort of executive self (otherwise its training would not emphasize efforts to erase self and will), it is doubtful that it places nearly as much emphasis as does our own culture on maintaining a self-presentation of the self as always being in full control of behaviour. The Judaeo-Christian tradition emphasizes perhaps more than do other traditions individual responsibility for one's own acts.

The tip-of-the-iceberg model of self-awareness may seem a sort of 'cop-out' to some, an evasion of personal responsibility. The approach is, however, very much in accord with the way we actually behave. 'I' may claim that I want to lose weight, stop taking drugs, fall out of love, not experience jealousy, and so on – but, in fact, a largely linguistic executive 'I' has no way to do these things. Feed data into the information-processing system such that the outcome decision is to love someone else or to ignore food or whatever, however, and the behaviour alters.

This last point, about 'feeding data into the system,' will be returned to, in the next chapter, for it is of considerable importance. It is the key to integrating the 'intentionality' of the social sciences with the neuro-physiological-process explanations of behaviour of the biologically oriented fields. For example, social scientists studying the relationship between 'belief' and behaviour are actually (implicitly) analysing how the processing of certain data by the intra-individual system affects behaviour. From this perspective, verbally elicited statements about 'beliefs' are imperfect indices of some of the data and processes of the intra-individual system, rather than 'causes' of behaviour. One implication of this approach is that the social scientist is gravely handicapped without some kind of model of the intra-individual system. Another is that the study of how knowledge is 'inputted' to the intra-individual system is vital if we are to understand changes in behaviour. This last topic will also be discussed in the following chapter, under the heading 'pay attention.' As we will see, the knowledge gates are very much the products of natural selection and have much to do with genetic fitness.

EVOLVED COMPLEXITIES OF THE SELF: DECEPTION AND LANGUAGE

Neither self-awareness nor language is a prerequisite for manipulation of the behaviour of others. Both frogs and human infants deceive, for example, one with camouflage and the other with exaggerated distress cries. But adult human beings are probably unique in the extent to which our inclusive fitness depends upon our effectiveness in influencing the behaviour of those around us. How others perceive and evaluate us, our reputations, our images, the gossip around us, all these are the real determinants of whether we receive aid when we need it, of the quality and quantity of our sexual and parental partners, and of the future of our children. The mechanism that selection has favoured in the human child and adult is neither the cryptic coloration of the frog's skin nor the wail of the discomforted infant, but the elaborate yet malleable self. This is because an extremely effective way to deceive others is self-deception, the inclusion of contradictory data in an information-processing system.[8]

Verbal and Non-Verbal Insincerity
Though personality theorists have long hypothesized that human beings can somehow hold various kinds of 'out-of-awareness' information (often using the vocabulary of our having some kind of 'subconscious'), only recently has experimental research confirmed that we can indeed both know and not know. Sackheim and Gur (Sackheim, 1983; Sackheim and Gur, 1978; Gur and Sackheim, 1979) took advantage of the fact that, when a person hears a voice, perspiration increases slightly, thereby increasing the electrical conductivity of the skin – the galvanic skin response or 'GSR.' The jump in conductivity is considerably greater for one's own voice than for a stranger's. Subjects asked to identify taped voices as being their own or as belonging to another made verbal mistakes. However, their GSR responses almost always showed the jump in conductivity associated with their own voice, *regardless of*

---

8 For further discussion of self-deception from an evolutionary perspective, see Trivers (1985) and Bond, Kahler, and Paolicelli (1985). The latter offer the interesting argument that the abilities to deceive and to detect deception are both under ongoing selection pressure, but that the ability to deceive always slightly outpaces its rival. Lockard (1980) presents possible neurophysiological mechanisms involved in deception, and discusses how it is that the two hemispheres of the brain may simultaneously hold different information. Krebs, Dennis, Denton, and Higgins (1988) and McGuire and Troisi (n.d.) review (in rather condensed fashion) the entire range of discussion of self-deception and evolution, and either is a good starting point for current thought and bibliography on this topic.

whether they had verbally identified their own voice correctly. Similarly, even when they incorrectly verbally identified a stranger's voice as their own, their skin still showed the small increase in GSR associated with hearing another's voice. In short, some subsystem of their brain-body systems contained accurate information even when their conscious awareness was in error.

The work of Sackheim and Gur does not really prove that there is something called a 'subconscious' but it does demonstrate that the human information-processing system can hold contradictory information. It also supports the argument that awareness is a 'tip of the iceberg' phenomenon (a conclusion that plays hob with our ideas of 'individual responsibility' and our 'selves' as decision-makers). But its most important implication, for this chapter, is the possibility that the highly differentiated and complex internal representation of self characteristic of our species may have its roots in selection for the ability to deceive verbally.[9]

We frequently lie, and the most effective liars are those who are able to convince themselves that their lies are the truth, so that their non-verbal does not contradict their verbal communication. Our folk psychology has long recognized this advantage, in the form of the adage about the danger of lying being that one comes to 'believe' in one's own lies (whatever 'believe' can mean in this context). It is usually in our genetic interest to believe ourselves larger, stronger, more attractive, and competent than we are.[10] Note how surprised and dismayed most of us are when we first hear our own voices. That one's recorded voice seems unfamiliar may be due to our ordinarily hearing it through bone conduction; but that it never seems nearly so mellifluous on tape as it

9 Language itself, it can be argued, may have in part resulted from selection to manipulate the behaviour of others. The evolution of language is discussed in Focus 13.1.

10 What of people with low self-esteem, who believe that they are less interesting and attractive than others may find them? Self-esteem will be discussed in chapter 8, but for the moment, recall the notion of a dominance hierarchy. Having a low position results in a self-representation that, it will be argued, is homologous (same evolutionary root) with low self-esteem. A realistically low evaluation of one's own capabilities, in the setting of a primate dominance hierarchy, is usually in one's fitness interests, since it causes one to avoid agonistic encounters and competitions that one would otherwise lose. The bias to evaluate oneself higher than others evaluate one must be limited if it is to be adaptive. In modern human beings, low self-esteem may or may not be fitness-enhancing, but presumably it is derived from a time when a lower self-appraisal was indeed adaptive for many. There may be a sensitive period for the setting of self-esteem (as will be discussed subsequently), and this would explain why it appears to be difficult to alter it after adolescence.

does in our own ears suggests self-deception. Imagine a world without mirrors: Would not most of us believe ourselves fair, even as we once believed ourselves well-spoken?

Our subjective sense of self probably can become as complex and differentiated as it often does at least in part because of selection to manipulate the behaviour of others (cf. Vine, 1987). In evolutionary time, the greater the complexity of our system of social relations grew, the more complex became the types of deceit that would have been possible, and therefore the greater the selection pressures in favour of a complex, differentiated, system of internal representations, including representations of the self. One might even argue that the primary evolutionary function of the self, in modern human beings, is to be the organ of impression management (rather than, as our folk psychology would have it, a decision-maker).

Costs of Contradictory Data

The cost of this complex sense of self, with its access to contradictory data, has been considerable. It may well be that much of the size and complexity of the neocortex is a reflection of the demands on an information-processing system that must hold much contradictory data in place. It may be, too, that much unhappiness – neurosis in particular – is a cost of this system.

One way to think of neurotic behaviour is as self-defeating behaviour that is not corrected by experience. The necessary information cannot move to the self: barriers that some call 'repression' and 'denial' are in place. In the framework constructed in this chapter, these refer to data available to some of the brain's specialized processors but not accessible to its internal representation of self. 'Repression' means the blocking of data about the organism's evaluation of itself, its own goals in particular. 'Denial' refers to data about external reality.[11]

11 For a fuller discussion of these Freudian defence mechanisms, see Freud (1946). For an alternative evolutionary approach to the Freudian defence mechanisms, see Nesse and Lloyd (n.d.). Kathleen Gibson (in a 1986 personal communication) suggests that I may have this account of defence mechanisms backwards, in evolutionary terms. Rather than selection for repression, the original state may have been each 'module' or 'subsystem' of the brain having a monopoly on information relevant to its own domain. Subsequent selection for sharing of information among the different subsystems would therefore have resulted in only partial rather than complete integration of information. 'Repression' may represent the normal state, and transmission of information from one module to another through various filters may be the product of relatively recent selection.

The capacity for repression and denial would have been an important aspect of selection for the capacity to distort and withhold information from the self so as to more effectively manipulate others. But once the corrective positive feedbacks are eliminated from any information-processing system, error is bound to result. One 'specialized processor' or 'subsystem' (to foreshadow chapter 5's discussion) of the organism may have a goal unknown to another subsystem, for example, or the effects of the organism's behaviour may be filtered and distorted by one subsystem so that another subsystem is in effect utilizing inaccurate data. The resulting complexity is orders of magnitude greater than any artificial intelligence program ever attempted. Somehow, the intra-individual system must tend – or at least have tended, in the past – to achieve its evolutionary goal of genetic representation in future genera-tions. But the process is mind-boggling, and the boggles often go by the name of 'neuroses.' From this perspective, psychotherapy consists of conveying (not necessarily accurate) information to the intra-individual system in spite of barriers. (How such information may be conveyed will be the subject of the discussion of 'Feeding Data into the System,' in chapter 5.)

'We' are the masters of our vessels – or pilots of our aircraft, to return to an earlier metaphor – only if by 'we' is meant the entire brain-body organism rather than a mythical homunculus 'self' piloting a machine-like body. Contradictory information is likely to exist at different levels in the organism's information-processing systems, and the line between 'sincerity' and 'insincerity' is nebulous at best. And yet, certain of our key social institutions – our legal system in particular – are built on the notion of individual decision and responsibility, a notion that rests on the foundations of a wholly inaccurate folk psychology.

SUMMARY

1. Understanding the evolution of human psychology and self-awareness is central to a human sociobiology. We need a theory of mind (an 'intra-individual system') between genes and culture or else we can fall into linking the two far more closely than we should, perhaps even imagining that there are 'genes' for all sorts of specific behavioural traits. Sociobiological accounts of human behaviour without specification of the psychological processes intervening between genes and culture are inadequate.

2. The intra-individual system cannot be tied tightly to current

neurophysiological knowledge but is compatible with Paul D. MacLean's notion of a 'triune brain.' This view stems from the observation that at every point in its evolutionary history an organism must be adapted to its environment. Thus, old structures cannot simply be discarded and replaced but must either have new structures added to them or be transformed into new structures, or both. The brain's evolution involved the last course, and its anatomy reflects both accretion and transformation. The brain is not a unitary system. The 'original' or 'reptilian brain' (the 'R-complex') remains with us and is associated with the brain-stem. It is responsible for life-preservation functions and what I would term (modifying MacLean's original formulation) inclusive-fitness functions. The old mammalian brain also remains with us and is chiefly associated with the limbic system and the latter's connections with the hypothalamus. It is closely linked to the emotions. The new mammalian brain has to do with the neocortex and is linked to cognition.

3. The social sciences tend to explain behaviour in terms of beliefs, values, *intentions*. The more biological sciences explain behaviour (at least in principle) in terms of neurophysiological processes. Human sociobiology tends to move from one type of these apparently incompatible explanations to the other. The problem stems from failure to confront the mind-body problem: Are we seeking to explain the evolution of neurological structures or processes, or of our conscious experience? As we will see, coming to terms with the mind-body problem will prepare us, in later chapters, to understand the nature of human social psychology, including self-deception, self-esteem, and culturally ordered prestige-seeking.

4. The problem of the mind-body split means that we can explain behaviour either in terms of physiological and neurophysiological processes, or in terms of our conscious experience, our *deciding* to act. The mind-body split probably arises from our culture's tradition of viewing the body as inert unless occupied by an immortal 'soul'; though, since Descartes, the secular idea of 'mind' has been substituted for that of 'soul.' Some philosphers and neuroscientists still believe that mind and body are separate and interact at a given point in the brain, though most do not. Instead, the 'mind' is held to be *identical* to some or all aspects of neurophysiological functioning. The intra-individual system approach taken here will propose a modified 'identity' solution to the mind-body split.

5. The mind-body split is central to our culture's folk psychology, a

belief system in which the body tends to be thought of as a sort of craft under the control of a pilot, the mind. The 'pilot' is expected to be in control of the craft at all times and is responsible for its operation. To switch metaphors, we tend to think of our minds as our real selves and our bodies almost as machines, as aliens with undue influence on these 'real' selves. This influence is thought of as taking the form of strong emotions or feelings. Our culture (especially for our middle and upper classes) emphasizes 'freedom' from these 'alien' emotions, so that we strive to portray our conscious minds as in control at all times, uninfluenced by strong emotion but instead calm and rational. When we are visibly not in control we lose face. We may therefore at times attempt to distance ourselves from our own behaviour by blaming it on such external factors as having been drinking alcohol.

6. Organisms act in a real world. To do so they require some kind of cognitive map, some kind of internal representation of external reality. Natural selection determines the kind of information to be included in the map, limiting it to information that in the past has affected inclusive fitness. No map is useful if you do not know your present location so this internal model will have a representation of the organism itself. But geographic information is hardly the only kind relevant to fitness. Potential predators, prey, and members of the individual's own species are also likely to be represented. The aspects of these external organisms incorporated in the internal representations are those relevant to the fitness of the mapping organism. Primates (including human primates), like wolves, live in societies in which alliances, relative position in a social hierarchy, relative size and strength, and past history of threat encounters are all likely to be relevant to fitness. Thus, we would expect the internal maps of such species to be highly elaborated.

7. Our 'cognitive maps' are probably not so much like maps of geography as they are akin to computer-simulation models with which predictions of the probable behaviour of other organisms may be made. The representation of the mapping individual itself within its own internal model will be similarly elaborated. This representation of self will not be some kind of miniature image, however, for like other representations it will include only fitness-relevant data. *An organism with a model of external reality that includes a representation of itself will experience consciousness. When that internal representation of self becomes sufficiently complex, it will subjectively experience self-consciousness or awareness.* Since this awareness is considered to be an aspect of a biological information-processing system rather than separate or apart

from it, it constitutes an 'identity' type of solution to the mind-body problem.

8. The resulting internal representation of self – the 'self' – is in our species culturally constituted, that is, within wide boundaries set by natural selection its contents can be quite variable. The 'pilot and aircraft' model of our own culture, though, with the 'pilot' taking all responsibility, is inaccurate, as is our vocabulary of decision-making. It remains valid to say that '*I* make decisions' if by '*I*' is meant the entire organism rather than that tip-of-the-iceberg phenomenon, consciousness.

9. The inclusive fitness of a human being depends very heavily on his or her ability to influence and manipulate the behaviour of others. This influence very often involves deceit. Self-deception prevents our non-verbal communication from 'giving us away.' However, self-deception means that the human information-processing system must be able to incorporate contradictory information, at different levels. Personality theorists sometimes speak of such distortions of information as 'repression' and 'denial.' Maintaining inaccurate or contradictory information in our information-processing systems exacts a heavy price, however, and probably lies at the heart of our species-specific disease of 'neurosis,' that is, of self-defeating behaviour that our filters on incoming data prevent us from correcting. It is possible to argue that the primary evolutionary function of the self is to be the organ of impression management (rather than, as our folk psychology would have it, a decision-maker).

5

Goals, Attention, Awareness

The preceding chapter gave us the beginnings of the intra-individual system and how it operates. We know about cognitive mapping of physical and social reality, and how it is related to self-awareness. We have left Cartesian dualism behind, and we understand that our folk psychology makes our intuitive ideas of how we arrive at decisions untrustworthy.

The present chapter will complete the sketch of the human mind and leave us ready for the topic of culture. To the ideas of cognitive map and self-awareness from the preceding chapter we will now add the notions of (a) goals built into the system by natural selection; (b) plans to achieve those goals (or to maintain goal-states within a given range); and (c) codes or communicational/organizational information structures. We will take a brief look at the ontogenesis of the mind (more properly, the 'intra-individual system') before going on to the important topics of emotion and attention. Finally, we will digress to look at a recent conceptual model of how the human brain may function, a model of 'distributed information-processing.' After chapter 6's introduction to the topic of culture we will return to the intra-individual system and see how its categories of data-processing coincide with the kinds of information of which cultures are composed. The 'coincidence,' as we will see, is a result of gene-culture coevolution.

'This Trichotomy is Provisional' is the heading of a discussion near the end of chapter 7, in the context of a theory of culture; but the title applies equally well to this chapter's analysis of the intra-individual system. The argument presented here that the brain appears to process information in terms of goals, plans, and codes is meant to be provisional, metaphorical, and heuristic. The trichotomy provides a way of talking about human behaviour that ties it tightly to culture. This tentative and trichotomous approach will permit, in subsequent chapters, close links to be drawn between culture conceptualized as information and the mind conceptualized as an information-processor. The framework (as we will see) is also broadly compatible with some current theory in the neurosciences. I do not argue that the mind actually works in terms of goals, plans, and codes: rather, I believe that the brain's functions are conducted by specialized processors or subsystems (some would use the term 'modules') that use algorithms that generate behaviour *usefully conceptualized* in terms of subplans and subgoals associated with adaptive problems.

THE INTRA-INDIVIDUAL INFORMATION-PROCESSING SYSTEM

Psychological theories of motivation have rarely paid more than minimal attention to the evolutionary perspective (cf. Bolles, 1975). The approach of John Bowlby (1969), however, is an exception. In the presentation that follows, I will be relying on many of his ideas, as well as on those of one of his own key sources – Miller, Galanter, and Pribram (1960).[1]

---

1 The portion of this discussion that deals with goals and plans has been adapted in part from Barkow (1977b).

Bowlby uses a good-for-the-species, group-selectionist evolutionary model, rather than the inclusive-fitness approach he would no doubt have used had he worked more recently. This lack in no way invalidates his general approach. Nevertheless, it would be very useful for someone to revisit Bowlby's work on attachment and to redo it in terms of the plans of mother and child reflecting their differing fitness interests. Trivers (1985: 145–68) presents an excellent discussion of the conflicting-fitness-interests framework in terms of which this task could be accomplished readily.

For work on goal-directed behaviour more recent than that of Miller, Galanter, and Pribram, see the collection edited by Frese and Sabini (1985). Unfortunately, their collection appears inadvertently to establish that, while progress in this field is being made, consensus as to the nature of goal-directed behaviour exists neither in psychology nor in the neurosciences. The sketch that I provide in these chapters does not (as far as I am aware) violate anything that is known about the actual functioning of the central nervous system and, one hopes, will be consistent with future research in this area.

Components
We have already introduced two of the key components of the intra-individual system. There is the cognitive map of external physical and social reality discussed in the previous chapter. Let us call this map the *mazeway*, in accordance with common anthropological usage. The mazeway includes the second key intra-individual system component, the *self-representation*, the information-processing system's representation of the organism itself. This representation, as we have seen, incorporates much distorted data and is both inaccurate and incomplete: only certain aspects of the organism are modelled in it, aspects that have been of particular evolutionary significance.

Three additional components remain to be discussed in the present chapter: *goals and $sub^n goals$; plans and $sub^n plans$;* and *codes and $sub^n codes$.* These components at their lowest level have been 'wired in' by natural selection; they are environmentally stable (meaning that they can maintain their stability in the face of a fluctuating environment). As we increase the value of n and the 'subs' reach higher and higher levels, the components become more and more labile, more differentiated by culture and by individual experience.[2]

GOALS AND SUBGOALS, PLANS AND SUBPLANS

Here in abstract, conceptual form is the organization of the goal/plan system. Some examples of goals and plans will be given later in this chapter, but it is only in chapters 7 through 9 that the operation of the system will be fully shown in its true, cultural context. First, we must be rather relentlessly abstract.

The goal/plan components of the intra-individual system may usefully be thought of as a hierarchical array of goals and plans, subgoals and subplans, subsubgoals and subsubplans, and so forth, the actual number of levels of subgoals/subplans being indeterminate. The entire array is goal-directed, with inputs from external reality permitting evaluation of whether a particular goal has been attained. When the subgoal of one level of a subplan is reached, control automatically switches to a higher level subgoal, or to one in the service of a different goal entirely. Failure may mean an alternative subplan is followed.

2 For the sake of simplicity, I am deliberately omitting any discussion of skills, what some theorists (such as Anderson, 1983) would term 'procedural knowledge.'

Conceptually, the system operates as if it were continually evaluating the success and failure of subplans in terms of whether their respective subgoals have been reached (or maintained), switching among them accordingly.

The basic goals and plans are environmentally stable and have presumably been built in by genetic evolution. As the individual matures, however, subgoals in the service of the original goals proliferate, and each subgoal may have a number of possible subplans. As subgoals/plans become more derivative (that is, as n increases in the $sub^n goals$/plans), culture plays an increasingly large role. At one end of the continuum is little response to local environmental contingencies and therefore cross-cultural universality; at the other end, great response to local environmental contingencies and therefore cross-cultural diversity. Choice of a subgoal/subplan is constrained by learning and attentional biases (more accurately, is the result of specialized processors). Since the biases are products of genetic evolution, they tend to result in our choices enhancing our genetic fitness (though as we will see in chapter 12's discussion of obligatory homosexual relationships in some human societies, this result is hardly guaranteed).

Ontogenesis
How does goal/plan behaviour grow and develop in the infant and young child? Ontogenetically, it is the product of complex, reciprocal feedbacks between a maturing central nervous system and external social and physical reality. The process is comparable to embryogenesis. For John Bowlby, each infant is born with a number of behavioural systems or plans, each system having a goal (or 'set-goal,' in Bowlby's terms). The plan Bowlby is particularly concerned with is that of 'attachment' of the infant to the mother, and he analyses in some detail the behaviours involved in the hierarchically ordered subplans in the service of that goal. As is often the case, the 'goal' or 'end-state' is actually the maintenance of a state rather than the attainment of some object or the discharge of some kind of 'energy.'

As the child's internal representation of external reality grows increasingly complex, he or she becomes increasingly capable of attaining his or her subgoals (even while these subgoals themselves alter).[3] The initial behavioural systems are what Bowlby terms 'environ-

3 I am aware that I am here slighting the entire corpus of knowledge concerning cognitive development. That field could and should be integrated with the theories of

mentally stable,' a phrase he intends as a replacement for 'innate.' They are in a sense 'built-in.' With experience and the development of his/her particular map of reality, however, the child's subplans and subgoals become increasingly labile, increasingly culturally specified (though still subject to evolved biases).

Since Bowlby is confining himself to what Miller, Galanter, and Pribram (1960) would consider a single, hierarchically ordered plan with the goal of 'attachment' to the mother, he does not need to consider the numerous other plans and subplans characteristic even of a child; nor need he concern himself with the extent to which the goals and subgoals of these plans/subplans are environmentally labile rather than stable. It would be consistent with Bowlby's framework, however, to think of much, even most, human behaviour as consisting of subplans derived from a limited number of plans. Each plan has an environmentally stable ('innate' or 'built-in') goal, while the subplans have subgoals that are generally environmentally labile (culturally, or more properly, experientially, determined).

Examples of Goals
There is a peculiar difficulty with this view of behaviour as essentially derivative of biologically evolved plans and goals: one is tempted to prepare an inventory. The resulting list of 'goal-states' to be maintained would resemble an old-fashioned list of 'personality needs.' Of course, the goal/plan framework is meant as a heuristic device, to let us talk about individual and cultural behaviour now instead of awaiting the day when we will (I have faith) have a concrete rather than merely conceptual idea of how the brain actually processes information. Still, one cannot avoid entirely the question of what some of the evolved goals and subgoals might be (in addition to the parent-child attachment goal with which Bowlby is concerned).

An important example of an evolved goal is that of being a member of a social group, a goal closely related to the goals of social prestige and self-esteem (discussed in chapters 8 and 9). As we will see, these goals

---

self-awareness, self-deception, goals and plans, and evolution, which I am here attempting to link together. For the reader who would like to attempt the integration, Case (1985) provides a state-of-the-art approach to cognitive-development.
MacDonald (1988) revisits the cognitive developmental literature on moral development, in the light of sociobiology. As yet, however, neither psychology nor the neurosciences has developed a consensus as to the relationship between cognition (schemata, representations, images) and motivation (goals, intentions).

are rather clearly linked to inclusive fitness. But the most familiar goals are probably those having to do with maintaining physiological homeostasis (nutrition, warmth, sleep, and so on). Another familiar goal involves sexual relationships – not merely having sex, but attracting mates who, in terms of the differing fitness interests of the sexes discussed in chapter 2, are likely in effect to enhance one's genetic fitness. Other goals might involve protecting one's offspring; maintaining a reputation for fairness (linked to reciprocal altruism); aiding members of one's group, one's kin in particular; and the mazeway-building goals that are discussed below. Goals are presented here not as 'drives' but as ends that most human beings in most human environments develop as a result of natural selection having so shaped our ontogeny. As we will shortly see, it is possible that particular goals are associated with a particular neurological subsystem or system, one utilizing a particular algorithm or set of algorithms.

The basic goals are probably cross-culturally universal. In many cases the plans may be as well (at least, they are if one is willing, for example, to define 'eating' as the plan linked to the goal of 'not being hungry'). But once we begin to speak about how we go about achieving goals (or 'maintaining goal-states'), we are in the realm of subgoals and subplans and of culture. You may, as we will see (in chapter 8), seek prestige through large harvests or a successful hunt; or by your claimed knowledge of the supernatural; or by an ability to mediate disputes; or by your having numerous offspring; or through the excellence of your crafts; or whatever.

The Mazeway and Goal Behaviour

A major and very broad human goal is what Eugene G. d'Aquili (1972; Laughlin and d'Aquili, 1974: 114–17) has termed the 'cognitive imperative.' It is the goal to map and order the physical and social universe and our own place in it. In short, this is the goal that leads to the development of the mazeway. Plans and subplans associated with this goal include much exploratory and play behaviour, beginning with the object and body manipulation of Piaget's sensorimotor stage and moving on to an interest in cosmology and eschatology. Every culture, as Murdock (1967) has shown, explains the nature of the universe and what happens to one after death. Mazeway goals also include keeping abreast of the relative standing and sexual activities of members of one's own group (hence, gossip). Much of the information in the mazeway is derived from the cultural information pool. Chapter 6 will explore the contents of the mazeway in some detail, drawing on the work of A.F.C. Wallace (1970).

Sensitive Periods, Alternative Tactics, and Learning

Are subgoals and subplans learned? As was discussed in chapter 1, there is a stereotype among the biologically ignorant that 'genetic' or 'evolved' behaviour is rigid and fixed for the life span: since an individual's genes do not vary over time, varying behaviour must therefore be accounted for in terms of 'learning' and the environment. Actually, for most species, selection has favoured those whose genes generate information-processing mechanisms permitting their behaviour to vary adaptively, over time, in response to environmental change. It is true that 'learning' is one term for the very wide range of evolved mechanisms that permit this adaptive behavioural variation during the life span (Roper, 1983): but (as we saw in chapter 1) the grab-bag term 'learning' has the drawback of at times being mistaken for a unitary and already understood phenomenon.

Caro and Bateson (1986) use the less assumption-laden phrase 'alternative tactics' in discussing variation in behaviour in the course of the life of individual members of animal species. Such variability is quite as much a product of evolution as are more fixed aspects of behaviour. Presumably, evolved, specialized information-processing mechanisms underlie the ability to choose among alternatives. Caro and Bateson discuss (among other topics) alternative tactics that are age-related, that is, individuals behaving differently at different ages; alternative tactics that are dichotomous – either one or the other, as opposed to an infinitely divisible range of variation; and alternative tactics that are reversible versus those that are irreversible. Some alternative tactics may depend on sensitive periods (to depart from Caro and Bateson). A sensitive period is a limited time during which specific experience has enduring effects, effects different from those the identical experience would produce at a different developmental stage. In evolutionary terms, sensitive-period mechanisms permit a single set of genes to generate environment-responsive alternative adaptive strategies.

The ways in which we process subgoals/plans/codes no doubt alter in a consistent manner as we grow, develop, and age, and in some cases are likely to involve mechanisms producing 'alternative tactics,' including sensitive periods. For example, early childhood is a sensitive period for the acquisition of language subcodes (and probably for other subcodes as well). *Attention structure* (discussed below) certainly varies with age and may involve sensitive periods.

Selection of sexual strategies may also be a sensitive-period phenomenon. As we will see in chapter 13, human beings have two (conceptually) distinct sets of reproductive strategies available, one of them based on a high probability of long-term male-female pairing and of continuing male parental investment; and the other based on repeated, short-term male-female pairings with unreliable male investment. It may be that some of the effects of what the literature rather misleadingly terms 'father absence' have to do with a sensitive period during which the child's perception of the availability of resources determines how his or her reproductive strategy is 'set.'

Because the framework of subgoals/plans/codes is new, we know surprisingly little of their acquisition by the child, of their possible dependence on sensitive periods, or of their reversibility. But given the great emphasis in the child-development literature on the 'primacy of early learning,' it is safe to assume that both sensitive-period and irreversible (or at least, difficult to reverse) acquisition of subgoals/plans/codes are common for our species.

Goals and Evolution

Reading this chapter probably will not increase the number of children and grandchildren you leave behind you, and you are unlikely to be reading it to aid your relatives or otherwise enhance your inclusive fitness. How is it, then, that you are reading it? The answer is that it is an error to expect all of one's current activity to be enhancing genetic fitness. It is not just that you are not your ancestors, and that behavioural tendencies that increased fitness in the past may not do so today; the more important reason to expect much behavior to have little direct connection with genetic fitness is that *fitness is the 'goal' of the blind-variation-and-selective-retention system called biological evolution, not your personal intention.* Of course, since you are a product of biological evolution, your conscious and unconscious goals presumably are linked to the kinds of activities that would have tended to enhance the fitness of your ancestors. This linkage – which may be exceedingly indirect – should be there regardless of the effects of your (sub)goals/plans on your current fitness.[4]

---

4 I am emphatically *not* arguing that we have some kind of 'unconscious' motivation to enhance our inclusive fitness. Such notions smack of the homunculus, of the mysterious and manipulative little person who fills our otherwise empty heads much as the ether once filled empty space.

The link between your goals and your genetic fitness may be completely cut (as when you copulate while using a contraceptive) without in any way invalidating the fact that, ultimately, your goals are products of evolution. Your current fitness, after all, can have no effect upon your ancestors, for whom the tie between goals and fitness would have been quite real.

Goals, Plans, Algorithms, and Ontology
I would like to identify 'goal' with some kind of identifiable-in-the-lab, neurophysiological end-state ... but I cannot. Because the 'ontological status,' the nature of the physical reality of goals, is unclear, it is safest to define them not in terms of neurophysiology but as evolutionary functions, as 'ends that we can reasonably link to the enhancement of fitness.' Goals are associated with and are products of the algorithms of specialized processors or subsystems, while plans, which are also generated by these algorithms, are the behaviours leading to the attainment of particular goals. The algorithms also generate subgoals, which in turn have subplans.

A 'plan' therefore involves behaviour in the service of a goal, behaviour that is generated by the algorithms associated with that goal. Plans, like goals, may or may not also be conceptual artefacts, useful hypothetical constructs. It may prove useful for us to speak of 'eating' as a 'plan' in the service of the 'goal' of nutrition.

'Plan' and 'goal' are functional concepts rather than physical units. Their underlying neurophysiological processes are no doubt of considerable importance for the neurosciences but are not vital to the present discussion. So long as the behaviours that the plans and goals refer to are reliably generated, the demands of evolutionary theory are met, regardless of the details of that generation.

The concept of 'goal' bears some superficial similarity to the idea of 'personality need.' The psychological theory that probably went further than any other with the need concept is that of Henry A. Murray. Focus 5.1 discusses Murray's 'needs' in the light of the intra-individual-system approach. His list of needs, lacking an evolutionary perspective, is both longer and more arbitrary than any list of adaptive goals or functions is likely to be. To be fair, of course, his goal was that of clinical utility rather than the building of elegant theory, and his framework provided a common vocabulary that permitted therapists to communicate with one another about patients and their problems.

The discussion of goals and plans will be returned to in chapter 7, in the specific context of culture.

focus 5.1

GOALS AND MURRAY'S 'NEEDS'

It is instructive to compare the kinds of goals mentioned above with the personality 'needs' of theorist and clinical psychologist Henry A. Murray. Contemporary psychologists appear to have forsaken the kind of all-inclusive theories of personality and behaviour once fashionable, and no longer attempt lists of 'needs.' Murray, however, took this concept further than did any of his contemporaries – perhaps as far as it can go. Hall and Lindzey (1970: 176–7) provide an 'illustrative list of Murray's needs,' adapted from Murray (1938). Table 1 includes Murray's original twenty needs (subsequently elaborated in later publications). Note that by 'infavoidance' Murray meant the avoidance of humiliation and embarrassing situations. By 'counteraction' he meant making up for past failure or overcoming fears and weaknesses. The other needs seem relatively clear in their meaning.

It would be slighting Murray to reduce his complex and subtle theory to a mere list of needs. The needs themselves were somewhat hierarchically ordered, and were classified according to whether they were related to basic physiological requirements for food and warmth, and so on ('viscerogenic needs'), or else were 'psychogenic' in nature. Some needs were proactive, some reactive, and some fitted into other categories. Unfulfilled needs could grow in strength, becoming 'prepotent.' Environmental factors, including other people, supplied 'press' that could either help or hinder the attainment of a goal and the fulfilment of a need. Murray's theory included an influenced-by-Freud theory of personality development, emphasizing the primacy of early experience. Above all, Murray's theory was meant for practising clinicians, as a guide to understanding their patients and to communicating among themselves.

From the perspective of evolution, however, what was missing in Murray's otherwise exhaustive approach was a notion of biological adaptiveness, of genetic fitness. His lists and theories operate in an evolutionary vacuum and must therefore strike the observer as arbitrary (however useful they may have been for clinical purposes). Other researchers have gone on to attempt to measure the strength of some of these needs in individuals and populations, as we will see in chapter 9's discussion of the 'need for achievement.'

In the framework developed in these chapters, most of Murray's 'needs' would probably be classified as sub^{n}plans in the service of sub^{n}goals. That is, they would be instrumental. For example, being deferential would be a subplan or tactic, rather than a goal or need. (Of course, for a given individual it may be a frequently used tactic in the service of a number of different goals and subgoals.)

TABLE 1
Twenty of Murray's needs*

Abasement	Harmavoidance
Achievement	Infavoidance
Affiliation	Nurturance
Aggression	Order
Autonomy	Play
Counteraction	Rejection
Defendance	Sentience
Deference	Sex
Dominance	Succorance
Exhibition	Understanding

*Adapted from Hall and Lindzey, 1970:
176–7

CODES

By 'codes' I mean the organizational structure of encoded knowledge. The capacity both to encode and to decode is neurologically based, presumably in an evolved, information-processing psychological mechanism. The deepest, most environmentally stable level of code is probably represented by the 'hard-wired' processes of the 'modules' that Fodor (1983, 1985; discussed below) argues are responsible for perception. Perception no doubt requires environmental input for its proper development but the computational processes responsible for our being able to distinguish among objects, or to see stereoscopically, for example, do not appear to be culturally variable. Any human environment will provide the necessary inputs.

Another example of a 'deep' and environmentally stable code would be colour detection, an apparently built-in process. Interestingly, though the ways in which we categorize colours are culturally variable, cultures label colours in a predictable sequence (Berlin and Kay, 1969; Rosch, 1975).

The most familiar case of a 'deep' code with a probably neurological basis would be the linguist Noam Chomsky's (1972, 1980) conception of human language as having a 'deep structure' (an argument now widely accepted in principle, if not always in detail). The range of logically possible grammars, it turns out, is far wider than the grammars we actually find in real languages. The linguistic processor of the intra-individual system constrains grammar. But grammar in the ordinary language sense is variable across cultures. It is a subcode, one further out on the environmentally stable/labile continuum than is the 'deep structure' of language code.

Cognitive anthropologists find complex logical structures inherent in myths and other cultural orders of information. These will be discussed in chapter 7; at present, it is necessary only to say that it appears that these complex logical complexes have an underlying deep code or structure, with layers of culture-specific subcodes above them.

RECAPITULATION OF GOALS/PLANS/CODES

To recapitulate, the organism's intra-individual system has been organized, phylogenetically, by natural selection. Biological evolution has so arranged our species that the system is generated through the ontogenetic interactions discussed above. The individual's behaviour is in the service of environmentally stable goals, each of which has an associated and environmentally stable plan. Interaction with the physical and social environment generates and elaborates both the mazeway and the various labile subgoals with their associated labile subplans.

The result is something like a computer program that elaborates itself in the process of running. It adds some subplans, alters others, and runs many plans and subplans simultaneously. Some of our plans and subplans have to do with the processing of symbolic data and many have goals that involve maintaining our *selves* in various states with reference to normative systems of evaluation (to be discussed in chapter 8). This sketch no doubt overstates the extent to which our stream-of-behaviour actually is rational and orderly, but the model presented is, after all, deliberately designed to order behaviours produced by our various specialized processors/modules.

We have now introduced the major components of the intra-individual-system framework. Next we must deal with the nature of attention, with the strong emotions, and finally with a model of brain function involving 'distributed processing,' and with that model's relationship to the trichotomy.

PAY ATTENTION!

In our folk psychology, the homunculus self controls attention. When someone does not pay attention to what we wish them to attend to, it must be because they do not *want* to. Thus, we feel justified in being angry at them, in accusing them of moral failure. Old-fashioned schools in North America and elsewhere were based on this folk-psychology notion of attention, and children were punished for failing to *attend*.

'Attention' is simply a communications concept. It means something like 'channel open, ready to receive' (Barkow, 1976a). The organism's information-reception channels are an aspect of its intra-individual system. It is the latter, and not an illusory homunculus self, that determines which channels are open and to what they are attuned. We can no more decide what we will pay attention to than we can decide whom we will love.

If appropriate information is fed into the information-processing system as a whole, that data may then alter the direction of attention in a predictable manner. For example, if attending to school work or whatever becomes an aspect of a subplan related to the goal of, say, prestige or sexual attractiveness, then the individual will indeed attend to school work. But if a given task is related to none of the individual's plans or subplans then the communications channel will not remain attuned to that task. Punishment is likely to turn attention to the goal of avoiding the punishment rather than accomplishing the work. By contrast, when a task is part of a subplan, not only is threat or punishment unnecessary, but both the attention to and the accomplishment of the task are likely to be experienced as pleasurable and rewarding.

Attention, like the rest of our sensory or information-reception apparatus, has been organized by natural selection. For example, we do not apprehend the entire electromagnetic spectrum, being blind to both infra-red and ultraviolet radiation. The extremes of the spectrum had relatively little to do with our ancestors' fitness, compared to those wavelengths that permit us to map physical features of the environment with some clarity – wavelengths that natural selection therefore permits us to refer to as 'visible light.' In the same way, we attend most readily to stimuli that, phylogenetically, have affected our inclusive fitness. For example, we detect motion automatically, since movement would have been of profound importance for the fitness of our ancestors. We are less likely to perceive subtle differences in static shapes, unless doing so is part of a plan associated with a goal. Of course, we can learn to make such discriminations, possibly because selection may have favoured such a learning capacity in our forager ancestors.

The structure of the mazeway reflects the nature of our attention, which is primarily social. Even more than motion, we attend to other animals, particularly to members of our own species: our internal representations of others require continual bringing-up-to-date. These 'others' include potential mates, rivals, and (occasionally) allies. Their appearance, stature, achievements, and, above all, sexual activities are universally fascinating for us. We attend especially to those of their activities likely to affect our own inclusive fitness.

Gluckman (1963) has argued that gossip defines the community: knowing the gossip establishes one's group membership. The contents of that gossip are the activities and achievements of members of our own group ('troop,' for our protohominid ancestors), since these are likely to be relevant to our inclusive fitness. Our fellow group members, after all, are probably our relatives, our rivals, our children and our potential mates: we need accurate internalized representations of them and so 'gossip' about them is fascinating in a way that gossip about strangers can never be. Gossiping is a plan in the service of the goal of maintaining the mazeway.[5]

Of course, nowadays, the professional entertainers and politicians about whom we frequently gossip and read about so avidly are 'strangers': but somehow they do not *feel* like strangers to us. The modern media serve to convince many of us that the important people in 'our' group are individuals whom we have never in fact met and who, often enough, are soap-opera personalities with no objective existence at all. Yet, in our minds, they are more relatives and neighbours than are most of the people who actually surround us, such being the power of film, television, and the press. Their success in getting information into the intra-individual system, into the mind, will figure in chapter 15's discussion of how we engineer social change.

Hedonic and Agonistic Attention
There are probably many different types of attention but the distinction that Chance and Jolly (1970: 176–7) make between *hedonic* attention and *agonistic* attention deserves special emphasis. Agonistic attention is fear-constricted attention, attention narrowed to information having to do with danger and threat. Hedonic attention is broad and permits a wide flow of information. Chance and Jolly typify chimpanzee attention structure as primarily hedonic, that of the baboon as primarily agonistic.[6] Human attention obviously may be either. Attention may be a *sensitive period* phenomenon.

5 Gossip is notoriously inaccurate, of course. After all, it is communication, and (as we recall from chapter 3), communication is about manipulating the behaviour of others in our own fitness interests.
6 Nowadays, we would characterize both species as utilizing both modes of attention, depending upon the situation and environment.

Childhood experience may set the individual's attention structure in an enduringly agonistic, or else hedonic, mode. If this hypothesis is accurate, then, to the extent that most children in a particular culture have similar socialization experience, they (and the adults they become) will be marked by a distinctive attention mode. Thus, each culture would have a predominant attention mode. Unfortunately, developmental psychology has not, as far I know, addressed itself to the question of whether human beings do have cross-situational attention structures *per se* and, if so, whether these are the products of early experience during a sensitive period.

Attention structure may be closely related to *cognitive style*. The relationship between the two is discussed in Focus 11.2 (chapter 11), in connection with the work of Boyd and Richerson.

Feeding Data into the System

'Attention,' as we have seen, has to do with how the intra-individual system receives data. Rather than speaking about 'learning' and the morass of psychological theories involving this one-term-fits-many-processes approach, it may be preferable to think in terms of how the intra-individual system acquires data, or how we would go about feeding information into this evolutionarily organized, immensely complex information-processing system that is capable of holding contradictory information and whose input gates depend on paying attention. I write these words by inputting data into a microcomputer via a keyboard: I am typing. But how do I type, how do I input data, into the central nervous system? How, in short, do I get its attention?

From an information-processing perspective, 'therapy' and 'learning' are simply ways of inputting information into the intra-individual system. The new data may cause the system to change the subplans by which subgoals are to be reached, or at least to alter the evaluation of the relative success of existing subplans. At the same time, the new information may also be successful in altering some of the subgoals (or, at least, their relative weighting). It may even succeed in reducing conflict between subplans with mutually exclusive subgoals.

Therapy techniques are ways of getting our attention, that is, ways of getting information into the intra-individual system. In behaviour therapy, for example, the technician (therapist, animal trainer, whatever), rather than verbally dealing with a largely illusory executive 'I,' provides a series of rewards contingent upon increasingly specific behaviour. The effect is to feed information into the system: 'Do such-and-such and this is the result.' Alternatively, a series of punishments may be used. For some people, a carefully designed relationship with another individual (as in psychoanalysis) may open communication channels, permitting the input of information. Some of these therapy and counselling techniques may operate by taking advantage of our hedonic attention capacity. Typically, this sort of 'psychotherapy' relies on the establishment of a relationship of what might be termed 'hedonic dominance' between therapist and client. The therapist is at once (relatively) non-threatening but superior to the client in status. In many cases the individual may function better when the repressions and denials, and the misinformation they protect, are retained. (One example of this functional misinformation involves the maintenance of self-esteem, discussed in chapter 8.) Religious ritual, for some, appears able to feed very large quantities of culturally ordered information into the intra-individual system.

To summarize, even though teachers throughout the world believe that attention *should* be under conscious control, it is clear that it is not. If attending to a particular information source is an aspect of a subgoal/plan in the service of an evolved goal, then the attention will be there and information may enter the intra-individual system. If the potential information source is not related to a subgoal/plan or in a 'general interest to mazeway' category (as with gossip), then it will be ignored.

An alternative way of making this point is to say that if a phenomenon tended to be relevant to the genetic fitness of our ancestors then we are likely to attend to it. If the phenomenon fits into no such category then attention will be problematic. Thus, we have no need to 'discipline' children to pay attention to their potential rivals, allies, and mates – that is, to one another. The evolved decision rules governing attention apparently guarantee this. Getting children to attend to an adult teacher whom they do not perceive as having high status, however, is extremely difficult and is usually accomplished by transforming the teacher into a source of danger, often of physical danger. But the resulting attention is agonistic in nature. The children will be geared to placating the teacher rather than to acquiring a broad range of knowledge. Such teachers are likely to stress rote memory and highly specific responses to predictable questions rather than creativity, curiosity, problem-solving, or sensitivity to the feelings of others.[7]

7 Regrettably, this discussion relies on personal experience rather than on scientific study. A program of research on attention in natural settings, with particular attention to pupil attention to teacher in the class-room, is badly needed.

CONFLICTS WITH MR SPOCK: EMOTION AND RATIONALITY

The intra-individual-system framework accounts for what our folk psychology encourages us to treat as an ironic misfortune, our frequently acting 'emotionally' rather than 'rationally.' As we saw in chapter 4, folk psychology views emotions as external agents, overpowering us. Now we will see that folk psychology's approach is not entirely inaccurate.

Pleasure and Pain and Limbic-System Overrides
Plans, we have seen, have goals. Whatever the neurophysiological concomitant of goal achievement, we subjectively experience maintaining a goal-state as *pleasurable* and we seek that pleasure. Plan-failure tends, subjectively, to be associated with pain, discomfort, unhappiness. Natural selection has determined which stimuli are experienced as pleasurable and which as painful. In the course of seeking pleasure and avoiding pain, we in effect follow phylogenetically organized plans that tend to lead to the maximization of inclusive fitness. Thus, behaviourist psychologies, which emphasize how reward or pleasure can alter behaviour in rats and human beings, very often work despite their extreme simplicity.

But sometimes the path to inclusive fitness is through pain. At such times, behaviourist psychologies have little to say. Protecting my offspring, for example, may not be in the interests of avoiding pain and injury, but is usually in my inclusive-fitness interests. So may be my challenging another male who is attempting to mate with the female to whom I am bonded. Sharing when I am hungry, in order in effect to gain for my line a reasonable expectation of reciprocity, is another somewhat painful but in-own-inclusive-fitness example.

Now, let us think of the new mammalian brain as having evolved as a sort of portable computer, an information-processor capable of doing simulations with great speed and clarity. It is 'programmed' to calculate the path of least pain and greatest pleasure. But, as we have seen, the resulting calculations at times fail to enhance inclusive fitness. *At such times, selection will favour the 'overriding' of the new mammalian brain.* The override may operate through the differential weighting of subplans and goals (experienced as 'I want that more than life itself') or through the distortion of information ('I am tougher than he is!'). *We experience these overrides, subjectively, as emotions.* This does not mean that this is all there is to the emotions or that they serve no other functions, of course, but they do seem to be associated with what it is tempting to think of as limbic-system overrides of the neocortex, of the old mammalian brain overriding the new.

Why should such overrides exist? Well, the creators of Mr Spock wisely present his non-emotionality as a result of ideology rather than evolution. Aside from the fact that the pointed ears of the Science Officer of the Starship Enterprise would have been selected against in any climate that included a winter, Mr Spock's ancestors, had they resembled him, would have made complacent cuckolds. Sexual jealousy is 'illogical' because it causes pain while resulting in no material gain. But, as we saw in chapter 2, selection rather strongly favours male adultery (and only somewhat less strongly, female adultery, discussed in chapter 13). Male sexual jealousy, in such a context, is selected for as a means of increasing the odds that one's offspring are one's own. A male lacking in sexual jealousy would presumably invest in other males' offspring a fair proportion of the time, and would therefore have far fewer offspring than males who did their best to maintain exclusive sexual access to the females whose offspring they would be investing in. If Mr Spock's 'logical behaviour' precluded sexual jealousy, and his ancestors resembled him, they would have been selected against. Hence, Mr Spock could never have evolved.[8]

What about a 'Ms Spock'? Selection favours females who mate with males who subsequently invest in any resulting offspring (see discussion in chapters 3, 8, 13, and 14). Lack of female sexual jealousy would have meant that Ms Spock's ancestresses would have enjoyed less male investment in their offspring than did more jealous females, and therefore would have had relatively lower reproductive success. But this presumed ancestral lack of sexual jealousy is only one reason why we have neither Mr nor Ms Spocks among us.

Emotions[9]

Sexual jealousy is one example of an override of the new mammalian brain by the old. But all our strong emotions (and I discuss no other kind here) – rages, panics, lusts – represent such overrides. In a certain

---

8 Several of my 'trekkie' students have reminded me, since this writing, that Vulcan male sexuality is periodic in nature and that, during the sexual phase, Vulcans can indeed show great jealousy.

9 This treatment of the emotions is deliberately cursory. The topic enjoys a vast literature replete with controversies. For a sociological approach to emotion, see Kemper (1978) or Hochschild (1983); for a (sociocultural) anthropological perspective, see Lutz and White (1986); for psychological approaches, see Plutchik and Kellerman

sense, they are the levers by which our genes control our behaviour, the levers by which our evolutionary past controls our present (cf. Plutchik and Kellerman, 1980: 139). Strong emotions may well have other evolutionary functions, of course, but exerting genetic leverage over 'logic' and rationality is clearly one of them.

Another function of emotion seems to be the regulation of reciprocal altruism. As Trivers (1971) points out, gratitude ensures that we will repay aid, thereby making it more likely that we will receive it again in the future. Anger and resentment – holding a grudge – ensure that we will not offer aid again to those who have not reciprocated it. And both of these emotions ensure that we will maintain a reputation as a reciprocator but not as a 'mark.'

Emotions have other functions. Infatuation – falling in love – facilitates bonding in that the lovers find it relatively easy to cope with problems and faults that otherwise might preclude the pairing. The choice of partner is 'blind' only in the sense that the decision rules governing it are products of evolution's blind-variation-and-selective-retention process and appear to be mediated by out-of-awareness processors. Presumably, however, we tend to choose partners whose attributes would, back in our hunting-and-gathering evolutionary environment, have enhanced our inclusive fitness. As Symons (1979) argues, males prefer younger females (who would have a longer remaining fertile span) to older ones, healthy ones to the ill or crippled. Females prefer males able to invest in offspring – high in status or in control of material resources – and pay less attention to age than do males. But a healthy phenotype is the best available indicator of a healthy genotype and females also prefer the strong, the fit. That males engage in competitive physical display before females in so many of the world's societies is unlikely to be a coincidence. (Mate-choice sexual selection will be discussed again in chapters 8 and 13.)

DISTRIBUTED INFORMATION-PROCESSING

Bowlby's approach to the brain (as well as that of Miller, Galanter, and Pribram) emphasized hierarchical functioning. These thinkers gave us a model with levels of goals and subgoals, plans and subplans. At first

(1980), Izard (1977), Averill (1982), and Mandler (1984); for the view, from (European) ethology, see Lorenz and Leyhausen (1973); for a biological view combining both physiological and evolutionary perspectives, see Konner's (1982) thorough and readable *The Tangled Wing*.

glance, this view seems at variance with a powerful conceptual model of brain function and consciousness presented by Baars (1983). The two approaches are, however, compatible, as we will see at the conclusion of this chapter.

For Baars, the brain includes a number of *specialized processors* that perform particular functions and that can operate in parallel (in effect, simultaneously).[10] Hence, information-processing is described as being 'distributed.' Each specialized processor or subsystem is relatively independent of the others but some of them in effect 'try to act as a governmental executive toward the others' (Baars 1983: 45). The definition of a 'specialized processor' is not anatomical: to the extent a given process is 'autonomous,' to that extent it is under the control of a specialized processor.

One test of 'autonomy' is whether the process impinges upon awareness. For example, the child's acquisition of the grammar and phonology of a language is an automatic process, the domain of a 'linguistic processor.'[11] Similarly, riding a bicycle, once one has learned how to, becomes the domain of a specialized processor. It is autonomous and does not impinge on awareness. But during the training-wheels stage the specialized processor has not yet developed, so that riding is definitely not autonomous and every small wobble and pedal-pressure impinges on awareness. Note that some autonomous processes would appear to be 'innate' and have been explicitly selected for, as in the case of the 'linguistic processor' of the previous example; while others are more dependent upon specific experience, as in the case of bicycle-riding.

A key concept in this approach is that of 'global data base,' which is 'essentially a memory to which all processors in the system have potential access' (Baars, 1983: 46). Specialized processors make their own selection of data from this global base, and also add to it. A

10 Parallel, distributed information-processing has become a topic of considerable current interest in cognitive science. See Johnson-Laird (1983, 1988), Rumelhart et al. (1986), or McClelland et al. (1986) for a full treatment of this subject. See Ballard (1986) for a discussion of the neurological structures that may underlie parallel processing. See Kihlstrom (1987) for additional bibliography.

11 My five-year-old daughter (as of this writing) would not know what a grammatical rule is, yet her speech is very rule-bound. For example, she often conjugates irregular verbs regularly (for example, 'I hanged it up,' 'I catched it'). Her linguistic processor is clearly at work and has formed a rule about the phonemes ('d/t') that, in final position, usually put a verb into the past tense; but she has not yet sorted out the irregular verbs to which the usual rules do not apply.

linguistic processor, for example, will 'tune in' to the linguistic information and also will add to it, since such data is within its domain. The same information may be in the domain of a number of specialized processors simultaneously but, since the system operates in parallel rather than serially, this presents no problem. There is a distinction between 'local' and 'global' information. Local information is that processed within a single specialized processor. The data that a processor *adds* to the global data base is 'global information.'

Baars agrees with other theorists (for instance, Kihlstrom, 1987) that most information-processing is not part of awareness (consciousness). He cautions against equating awareness with the global data base. But *'conscious experience of some content involves … a coherent representation that provides global information to the system'* (Baars, 1983: 72, italics in original). In other words, when one of the specialized processors (subsystems) puts information into the global data base, we consciously experience the injected content. For example, we know that the tree is an oak but are not aware of the specialized processor(s) whose domain is categorization and labelling of flora. Recalling chapter 4's discussion of self-awareness, we might add to Baars's formulation that it is information likely to affect inclusive fitness that tends to enter the global data base. It was also suggested, in that chapter, that it is more accurate to say 'I became aware of having made a decision' than to say 'I made a decision.' In Baars's terms, the decision would have been made by a specialized processor. Information-processing by specialized processors is not only non-conscious but generally quite rapid, since a number of these subsystems can operate at once (in parallel).

Conscious processing is relatively slow for several reasons. First, it is slow because it can only take place in series, that is, can only deal with one thing at a time. This serial nature stems from the fact that conscious processing involves the global information base, and while there are many specialized processors, there is only one global information base. Conscious processing may also be slow because it must involve an indefinite number of these specialized processors. Hence, paying attention to a usually habitual sequence of actions – one ordinarily under the control of a specialized processor – will tend to make the sequence slow and clumsy.

Baars's treatment of *attention* is somewhat cursory. For Baars (1983: 75, emphasis in original), attention 'involves a set of systems able to *select and maintain* some particular conscious content, either voluntarily or involuntarily.' In similar fashion, goal-directed behaviour is dealt with by the statement that 'an *intention* may be considered a specialized kind of problem context, one that serves as a global goal to mobilize and organize a large, diverse set of action specialists to prepare and execute an action' (Baars, 1983: 74–5, italics in original).

To what extent are Baars's 'specialized processors,' these subsystems for specialized, non-conscious information-processing, to be identified with specific neural anatomy? Baars is vague on this point, probably because his emphasis is conceptual rather than anatomical. Even the manner in which Chomskian linguistic 'deep structures' are represented (some would say, computed) remains quite controversial (see the discussion by Stabler, 1983, for example). However, Jerry A. Fodor has recently argued in favour of the 'architectural' existence of specialized processors, which he refers to as 'modules.' A module is, at least in part, 'an informationally encapsulated computational system – an inference-making machine whose access to background information is constrained by general features of cognitive architecture' (Fodor, 1985: 3). It is interesting to note that Fodor considers the issue of parallel-versus-serial (sequential) processing of information as separate from that of modules, though some (for instance, Kinsbourne, 1985: 23) would argue that Fodor's approach gains greatly in power if parallel processing is incorporated into it (a position with which I would agree).

For Fodor, perceptual processes are 'modular' in nature, that is, they are specialized processors that cause perception to occur automatically and in a fashion relatively uninfluenced by the organism's other information-processing. One of the arguments he provides for the relative autonomy of modules is adaptationist in nature: 'Prejudiced and wishful seeing makes for dead animals' (Fodor, 1985: 2).[12] Language perception/processing would also be, for Fodor, a module. Perception is not to be considered cognition, however, even though it is indeed 'computational' in nature.

Fodor (1980) is one of those responsible for the gradual retreat, in psychology, of the myth of a generalized learning capacity. Selection, he and others (for example, Cosmides and Tooby, 1987, 1989) argue, favours specific information-processing abilities for specific purposes, moulded by specific selection pressures. As Fodor puts it, 'a truly *general*

---

12 This comment is ironic in view of chapter 4's argument that self-awareness is intimately linked with self-deception. Apparently, some modules are mostly accurate, for instance, those having to do with vision. By contrast, some modules are likely to be systematically biased, for example, those having to do with evaluating one's own relative standing.

intelligence (a cognitive capacity fit to discover just *any* truths there are) would be a biological anomaly and an evolutionary enigma' (p. 333, quoted in Symons, 1989). How could such an apparently inefficient mental organ have evolved, rather than a specialized processor for a specific function? Fodor's modules and the more enduring of Baars's specialized processors are presumably the mechanisms underlying these specific information-processing abilities.

Finally, note how readily a distributed-information-processing model disposes of the problems associated with Freudian topological models of 'consciousness' and 'unconsciousness,' and of contradictory information held in the mind. Presumably, different specialized processors may hold different and perhaps at times contradictory information. Rather than conscious and unconscious 'layers' of the mind, Baars's approach permits an image of awareness as the continuously altering product of continuously altering processes.

ASSEMBLING THE SKETCH OF THE INTRA-INDIVIDUAL SYSTEM

The various components of the intra-individual system have now been described. The structure resides in the triune brain and, like its anatomy, is neither unitary nor elegant. The functioning of the structure may usefully be thought of in terms of a loose hierarchy of subplans, and sub^{n}plans. Plans have goals, subplans have subgoals, and so on. The further we go down this hierarchy, the less environmentally stable and more environmentally labile sub^{n}plans and sub^{n}goals become. The goal of not being hungry is very stable. So is the plan associated with it, eating. The subplan of buying food and the subgoal of gaining money with which to buy food are quite labile. Even more labile is the subsubplan of working and the subsubgoal of finding and keeping a job. The more labile the subgoal and subplan, the larger the role played by culture and by social organization. A major goal of the intra-individual system involves the acquisition of what may be termed 'reference' or 'background' data, that is, data used to develop the mazeway, the cognitive maps of physical and social reality.

The stability/lability continuum is a simplification. Human beings have numerous ethological mechanisms that operate to push subplans in fitness-enhancing directions. The most dramatic of these is the limbic-system override, as when we panic or fall in love or experience other strong emotions. The tendency to self-deceive, discussed in chapter 5, is another mechanism that tends (or at least tended) to enhance genetic fitness. Much of our non-verbal communication, and reactions to that communication, represent similar ethological mechanisms – we cringe, we 'eyebrow flash' in greeting, we gaze-avert or stare, we show a 'win face' that intimidates an opponent, and so on (Eibl-Eibesfeldt, 1975; Zivin, 1985).

There are weak ethological mechanisms as well. Like the 'weak forces' of particle physics, they may be crucial and yet very difficult to detect empirically. These weak forces may involve subtle biases in attention. We seem to attend more readily to the high than to the low in status, for example, and find the activities of the former far more 'interesting' than those of the latter. We tend to define practice in skills crucial to the hunting-gathering ecology of our ancestors as 'play' because we find these activities rewarding. Social contact with others results in our learning the skills of communication-in-own-interest, skills that amount to manipulation of one's own appearance and of information conveyed to others, including deception. But perhaps most important, we find some of the subplans and subgoals derived from the cultural pool of information in which we live more appropriate than others. Our selections are biased. This is a topic that will be discussed at much greater length in chapters 10 and 11, in connection with the relationship between genes and culture, and with the work of Lumsden and Wilson (1981) and of Boyd and Richerson (1985).

The sketch of the intra-individual system passed over how we switch from one plan or goal to another – the question is important but I have no answer. To postulate some kind of 'centralized co-ordinator' or switching system is to risk putting the homunculus back into the intra-individual system. Presumably, the limbic system, interacting with the frontal lobes, is intimately involved in determining what gets accepted as a subgoal and which goals and subgoals get priority when. This is quite clear in certain situations, associated with strong emotions, when the limbic system seems to override whatever else is going on in the intra-individual system. But the hierarchical organization of plan-goal behaviour is very much overstated in this sketch (in order to create an approach useful for chapter 7's treatment of culture as a pool of information). We follow many plans and goals simultaneously and relative priorities may shift from instant to instant. Subplans and their subgoals may be tenuously – or even ludicrously – linked to their ultimate goals. Chapters 8 and 9, which deal with prestige and self-esteem, will provide examples.

So loosely organized is the hierarchy of goal-plan behaviour that it may simply be a product of multiple and reciprocal feedbacks among Fodorian modules or Baarsian specialized processors/subsystems. Thus, it is by no means necessary to assume that each of what we may conceptualize as a 'goal' or a 'plan' be associated with a single specialized system and a single algorithm. But until we begin to understand the brain in terms of its actual processors and algorithms, it will remain convenient to discuss behaviour in terms of evolved goals and subplans, and their derivatives. After all, it is hardly coincidence that the components of what I call the intra-individual system should interact in such a way as to tend to generate plan-like, apparently goal-oriented behaviour: the system as a whole is ultimately the product of biological evolution. Individuals whose intra-individual systems failed to provide behaviours that resembled successful plans in the service of fitness-linked goals tended not to become our ancestors.[13]

As Baars argues, awareness has to do with specialized processors putting information into the global information system. These specialized subsystems are busy ones, for a major task of the intra-individual system is to map fitness-relevant aspects of physical and social reality. 'Self-awareness' results from the fact that the intra-individual system develops a highly elaborate internal representation of fitness-salient aspects of the organism itself. The scope and much of the contents of that representation – its size and boundaries – are culturally determined.

I suspect that moment-to-moment conscious experience depends on what proportion of the subsystems of the intra-individual system are organized in the service of a single subplan, at any given time. Hence, the intensity of consciousness waxes and wanes. There is no dichotomy between 'conscious' and 'unconscious,' but merely a continuum (though Kihlstrom [1987: 1446] might disagree). Our most intense subjective experience probably occurs during 'limbic system overrides,' when many of the subsystems are put in the service of a single plan (for instance, flight), and many of the others appear to shut down.

'Attention' has to do with communications channels. We attend most

13 Hence the point made earlier, that the plan/goal approach is a conceptual rather than anatomical model of human behaviour. It permits us to discuss actual behaviour – particularly culturally ordered behaviour – in a way that the modular or specialized-processor model cannot. But it is the latter that is the more likely to be linked, eventually, to neurophysiological processes. The two approaches have been developed for different purposes, one for understanding the link between brain and behaviour, the other for understanding the link between the individual and culture. See the discussion in chapter 6 headed 'This Trichotomy Is Provisional.'

readily to that which is fitness-salient. Danger, for example, makes us more alert, particularly for cues associated with that danger.[14] The breadth and focus of the currently receptive communications channel implied by the term 'attend,' and the kind of 'filters' put in place, may usefully be thought of in terms of 'hedonic' versus 'agonistic' attention. Note that these terms are probably ends of a continuum rather than binary in nature. Note, too, that there are probably a good many other attention filters. If a plan needs some missing thing or person for success then we actively scan the environment for that which is missing. If the active plan has to do with food, for example, then we are hyper-alert for signs of something to eat. If the plan involves sex, then ... but there is no need to belabour the obvious. Attention is closely related to 'interest.' We tend to be interested in phenomena in some way linked to a plan in the service of an evolved goal, and find it hard to attend to anything that is not so linked.

The intra-individual system frequently incorporates inaccurate and even conflicting data. In later chapters, we will see that some of the inaccuracies have to do with our having been selected for the capacity for culture, a capacity that often involves our accepting socially transmitted information that is untested and often untestable. Other inaccuracies are probably the result of the equivalent of 'computation errors.' However, much of the distortion and tolerance of contradiction characteristic of the intra-individual system appears to be systematic in nature and linked to our fitness interests (or at least, these kinds of inaccuracies seem likely to have been in the fitness interests of our ancestors).[15] Such distortions often bear on the individual's relative standing vis-à-vis others and thus result in self-deception: self-deception

14 Of course (as Michael Rose, in a 1985 personal communication, reminds me), danger may also make us 'freeze up.' It is tempting to argue that instant motionlessness as a first response to possible danger was highly adaptive for our ancestors. Many prey animals exhibit this response today, after all. But for neither human beings nor other species is freezing an adaptive response to an automobile coming at one at high velocity.

15 This adaptationist analysis of the intra-individual system obviously risks running afoul of Dr Pangloss. It may well turn out that some of these traits in fact are not adaptive at all. Nevertheless, as I argued in earlier chapters, an adaptationist stance is highly powerful – it did, after all, generate this sketch of the human mind. No doubt the sketch, which in any event is intended to be quite tentative, contains errors. No doubt, too, these errors will eventually be revealed by the usual processes of scientific research, given the vested interest that rival researchers have in building upon one another's work and (I am afraid) proving one another wrong.

appears to be the most efficient way to deceive others, and it is very often in our fitness interests to so deceive. Where fitness-relevant information is concerned our evaluations are often very inaccurate, especially when it comes to the sexual and status activities of rivals and relatives. We attend to friends, relatives, and rivals and gossip about them: the subjects we gossip about are precisely the sex-and-status topics about which we are most likely to distort information. Now we have sketched the intra-individual system. Before we can return to it we must first look at culturally ordered behaviour, and at culture itself.

SUMMARY

1. This chapter introduces the three remaining components of the intra-individual system: *goals and sub^{n}goals*; *plans and sub^{n}plans*; and *codes and sub^{n}codes*. These components at their lowest levels are environmentally stable, but as we increase the value of n and the 'subs' grow further removed from their origins, they become more and more labile, more differentiated by culture and by individual experience. Note that these concepts are intended only as useful metaphors: the brain presumably operates in terms of specialized processors and systems that actually generate the behaviour conceptualized here as goals, plans, and codes.

2. This approach owes much to John Bowlby and to Miller, Galanter, and Pribram. It views the intra-individual system as consisting of a hierarchical array of plans, subplans, subsubplans, and so on. Each plan or subplan is associated with a goal or subgoal likely to involve the maintenance of a state rather than the attainment of a finite end. Goals tend to be built-in to the organism, but subgoals and subplans are culturally/experientially determined. The intra-individual system has the capacity to follow a number of plans simultaneously, continually shifting the priority of various goals and subgoals and modifying and shifting among plans and subplans. Goals are best thought of as evolutionary functions, though they presumably have not-yet-understood neurophysiological correlates.

3. The ways in which we process subgoals/plans/codes alter in a consistent manner as we grow, develop, and age. For example, early childhood is a sensitive period for the acquisition of language subcodes (and probably for other subcodes as well). There may also be a sensitive period for the 'setting' of one's predominant sexual strategy.

4. Maximizing inclusive fitness is the goal of the blind-variation-and-selective retention process called evolution, not anyone's personal goal. There is no 'drive' or 'instinct,' in human beings, to maximize fitness. But, since natural selection was the organizing process that gave rise to the intra-individual system, it is biased in favour of goals whose attainment tends to result in enhanced inclusive fitness (or at least once did, for our ancestors).

5. A list of goals superficially resembles the lists of personality 'needs' that psychologists once drew up, but those need lists, lacking an evolutionary perspective, appear at once to be both longer and more arbitrary than any list of adaptive goals or functions. Focus 5.1 discusses need-theorist Henry A. Murray's approach in some detail. Some likely intra-individual system goals include: maintaining physiological homeostasis (nutrition, warmth, sleep, and so on); attracting mates who, in terms of the differing fitness interests of the sexes discussed in chapter 3, are likely to maximize one's genetic fitness; protecting one's offspring; maintaining a reputation for fairness (linked to reciprocal altruism); aiding members of one's group, one's kin in particular; and mazeway-building goals such as keeping abreast of the relative standing and sexual activities of members of one's own group (hence, gossip) and maintaining an accurate internal representation of physical reality (curiosity, exploratory behaviour). Such goals are presented here not as 'drives' but as goals that most human beings in most human environments develop as a result of natural selection having so shaped our ontogeny. It is not claimed that they are necessarily neurologically discrete units.

6. 'Codes' are communicational/organizational structures of information. The most 'hard-wired' example of a code would involve our perceptual processes, such as those that permit us to perceive the outlines of objects or enjoy stereoscopic vision. Chomsky's 'deep structures' of language would be another example of a deep code, with individual languages and dialects as subcodes. Subcodes are highly variable, cross-culturally. Cognitive anthropologists argue that many cultural domains have underlying codes.

7. Attention is a communications concept. 'Paying attention to' means keeping a receptive information channel open to a particular phenomenon or class of stimuli. Control over attention is not a matter of the 'will,' as teachers have tended to believe, but is phylogenetically organized and therefore linked to stimuli relevant to inclusive fitness. Thus, students attend to other children much more readily than they do

to notebooks, for example, the former having had rather more to do with the inclusive fitness of their ancestors than the latter. 'Gossip' is a cross-cultural universal that involves seeking and exchanging information about the activities of others likely to affect our own inclusive fitness (for instance, information about sexual activities and about possible changes in relative social standing.)

8. Michael Chance divides attention into the 'hedonic' and 'agonistic.' Hedonic attention involves a relaxed and broad receptivity to information emanating from a particular source. Agonistic attention has to do with fear and is a constricted information channel primarily open to data about possible danger emanating from the individual to whom attention is being paid. Human beings are capable of both modes of attention, though it is possible that there are cultural differences in their relative prominence. It is possible that an individual's predominant mode of attention may be set during a sensitive period.

9. It is probably more useful to talk about 'feeding data into the intra-individual system' than it is to speak of 'learning,' as if the latter were a single process. Psychotherapy involves feeding data into the system. One form of it involves a hedonic relationship with a high-status individual (for instance, a psychoanalyst). Another involves another person's deliberate manipulation of rewards and punishments (as in behaviour therapy) so that data enters the system to the effect that 'if I do A then B will follow.'

10. Organisms have been selected to find pleasurable (rewarding) stimuli and activities phylogenetically likely to enhance their inclusive fitness. Conversely, organisms tend to find painful activities and stimuli likely to reduce their inclusive fitness. The neomammalian brain has been programmed to maximize pleasure and minimize pain and in this way tends to cause the organism to enhance its fitness. However, in some cases the path to inclusive fitness involves pain. Challenging another individual in order to improve one's relative standing, preventing another from copulating with one's mate, protecting offspring and other relatives – these and many other activities may enhance fitness but also are likely to cause pain. As a result, selection has favoured the limbic system's overriding the neocortex in such situations. We experience these limbic-system overrides as strong emotions. They cause us to behave in 'illogical' or 'irrational' ways (that is, to fail to maximize our own pleasure and minimize our own pain and risk). They also fuel the folk-psychology illusion of an executive self assailed by the body's emotions (discussed in chapter 4).

11. A conceptual model of brain functioning presented by Bernard J. Baars makes use of the concept of 'distributed information-processing' to account for a number of important phenomena, including limitations to conscious awareness. From this perspective, much of the brain's information-processing utilizes specialized subsystems that can run simultaneously (in parallel) and that make use of and add to a 'global data base.' Consciousness is related to additions to and changes in this information base. Baars's approach requires integration with theories of neurophysiological structures and processes. More important, it requires a much more developed theory of goal-seeking behaviour. With relatively minor changes, however, it is compatible with the Bowlby cum Miller, Galanter, and Pribram approach presented in this chapter.

12. The intra-individual system resides in the triune brain. It is useful to think of it as organized hierarchically, in terms of plans and various levels of sub^{n}plans, and goals and sub^{n}goals. As we descend these hierarchical levels, we move from more environmentally stable to less, from less culturally/experientially organized to more. Many ethological mechanisms, including much of our non-verbal communication, may also serve as automatic aspects of plan behaviour. The limbic system is intimately involved in assigning strengths to goals and subgoals. It also can override – that is, interrupt – the operation of other plans in what, in evolutionary terms, are emergency situations in which fitness is at severe risk. But the hierarchy of goal/plan behaviour may simply be a product of multiple and reciprocal feedbacks among specialized processors and subsystems, 'designed' by evolution to in effect emulate a loosely hierarchically organized system even though, in terms of neurological functioning, it may be no such thing. In other words, plans, goals, and even codes may simply be useful hypothetical constructs. Awareness may have to do with specialized processors putting information into the global information stream. Alternatively, one could argue that it involves the plurality of subsystems functioning in the service of a particular subplan/subgoal. Hence, the intensity of conscious experience waxes and wanes, depending upon how much of the intra-individual system as a whole is organized around a single goal/plan. Finally, the intra-individual system has much inaccurate information – in part because it is impossible for any organism to verify all socially transmitted data, in part owing to what might be considered 'computational errors,' and in part as a result of selection for efficient deception.

PART THREE

Culture, Prestige, and Self-Esteem

6

Culture:
An Introduction

The boy's arms, sweeping through the fine, dry dust, made a soft sound. He was swimming, but that was probably not what had awakened me. Probably it had been the earnest beseeching of his father, who was trying to persuade Sarkin Rafi, King of the River, to dismount from the boy. No musicians had played the spirit's praise-song, and the boy had not been dancing for him. But sometimes a spirit will just choose to come, and the mount has little say in the matter. Eventually, the spirit agreed to leave and the boy fell into a deep sleep. The next morning he still seemed a bit dazed, and he never did discuss the incident with me. It is well known that those ridden by the spirits recall nothing of what has passed. (From the author's unpublished field notes)

THE CONCEPT OF CULTURE

Culture is a system of socially transmitted data. Culture is an organized array of symbols. Culture is ... a concept easily made dry as the dust in which the Hausa-speaking boy of Kaduna State, Nigeria, had been swimming. Culture is the third information system discussed in this book. The first involved genetic evolution, the second the human mind; and now we must deal with the data, the symbols, the culture we transmit from generation to generation.

Definitions of Culture
Blurry though it be, the concept of culture is central to sociocultural anthropology. Definitions abound. Kroeber and Kluckhohn, back in

FOCUS 6.1

DEFINITIONS OF CULTURE FROM KROEBER AND KLUCKHOHN (1952)

Few (if any) genuinely new definitions of culture have appeared since Kroeber and Kluckhohn's exhaustive effort. The categories below are those used by them. (Please note that the page number following each definition refers to Kroeber and Kluckhohn [1952] and not to their source.)

I. *Descriptive*. Kroeber and Kluckhohn give us some twenty definitions in this category but the first, that of Tylor, has undoubtedly been the most influential: 'Culture, or civilization ... is that complex whole which includes knowledge, belief, art, law, morals, custom, and any other capabilities acquired by man as a member of society' (p. 81).

II. *Historical*. Some twenty-two definitions are included in this category. The influential anthropologist Ralph Linton explained that 'the social heredity is called *culture*. As a general term, *culture* means the social heredity of mankind, while as a specific term a *culture* means a particular strain of social heredity' (p. 90, italics in original). As Kroeber and Kluckhohn point out, Linton is here making the important distinction between culture in general and a culture.

III. *Normative*. Kroeber and Kluckhohn further divided the twenty-five defini- tions in this category between those that place 'emphasis on rule or way' and those that place 'emphasis on ideals or values plus behavior.' The former group provides this example, from Bogardus: 'Culture is the sum total of the ways of doing and thinking, past and present, of a social group. It is the sum of the traditions, or handed-down beliefs, and of the customs, or handed-down procedures' (p. 95).

IV. *Psychological*. Kroeber and Kluckhohn give us four subcategories here: (1) 'Emphasis on adjustment, on culture as a problem-solving device'; (2) 'Emphasis on learning'; (3) 'Emphasis on habit'; and (4) 'Purely psychological definitions.' Together, these total some thirty-eight definitions. Ford provides an example that, though placed by Kroeber and Kluckhohn in the first subcategory, seems to cut across all: 'Culture consists of traditional ways of solving problems ... Culture ... is composed of responses which have been accepted because they have met with success; in brief, culture consists of learned problem-solutions' (p. 107).

V. *Structural*. 'Emphasis on the patterning or organization of culture' (p. 118). Of the nine definitions in this category, the most interesting may be that of Willey: 'A culture is a system of interrelated and interdependent habit patterns of response' (p. 118).

VI. *Genetic*. Kroeber and Kluckhohn do not mean 'genetic' in the biological sense here, but in the sense of 'how has culture come to be?' (p. 128). This category includes forty definitions divided into the following four subcategories: (1) 'Emphasis on culture as a product or artifact'; (2) 'Emphasis on ideas'; (3) 'Emphasis on symbols'; and (4) 'Residual category.' This large grouping merits two examples. First, from Wissler, comes 'a culture is a definite association complex of ideas' (p. 130). Because the anthropological study of systems of symbols has come to be a major endeavour within anthropology since Kroeber and Kluckhohn's time, it is worth citing at least the first half of White's definition, as well: "culture" is the name of a distinct order, or class, of phenomena, namely, those things and events that are dependent upon the exercise of a mental ability, peculiar to the human species, that we have termed "symbolling"' (p. 137).

Geertz's Definition
Since Clifford Geertz is considered by many to be the anthropologist's anthropologist, and his work has been of immense influence in both the social sciences and the humanities, it is worth noting his (1973:5) comment on the meaning of the term, 'culture': 'Believing, with Max Weber, that man is an animal suspended in webs of significance he himself has spun, I take culture to be those webs, and the analysis of it to be therefore not an experimental science in search of law but an interpretive one in search of meaning.' In effect, Geertz is taking the concept of culture from the social sciences and donating it to the humanities.

1952, prepared a review of definitions of culture so thorough that one hopes it need never be done again. These authors found some 154 definitions, which they then grouped into six categories. Focus 6.1 gives one example from each, and then quotes an additional conception of culture, one favoured by the influential American anthropologist, Clifford Geertz.

At least three ideas seem common to most of the various definitions of culture. First is the idea that culture is socially transmitted; second, that it consists of some kinds of information (techniques, norms, ideas, symbols); and third that it is ordered or organized in some way, that is, that it forms some kind of system or at least is in some way structured. Some might wish to add, as a fourth frequently included component, the notion that culture is *adaptive*. Culture *is* usually adaptive, in a variety of ways, but the nature and extent of that adaptiveness is sufficiently controversial (as we will see in chapter 11 and especially in chapter 12) that I will omit that point, here, because I do not wish to incorporate into a definition what would otherwise be a testable hypothesis.

We are left with culture as a system of socially transmitted information, that is, as organized data passed from generation to generation. It is transmitted within a specified population (or populations), is the largest such system so transmitted, and is inclusive of smaller systems (usually referred to by the loose term 'subcultures'). This definition in no way implies that the system of transmitted information is unchanging: I will eventually be arguing that every generation edits and revises received culture.

Other Species and Culture
Do other species have culture? Biologist John T. Bonner (1980), who emphasizes continuity and similarity among species, sees culture as occurring throughout the animal kingdom. Field-working anthropologists, however, immersed as we are in the complexities and subtleties of our host cultures, often find the idea of animal culture preposterous. Distinguishing between culture and *protoculture* is one way to deal with this disjunction. For me, 'culture' implies a large body of information that is in some way coherent, organized, structured. When only a few data bits are being socially transmitted I favour the broader term (often used by A.I. Hallowell) 'protoculture.'

Curiously, Bonner's (1980: 10) own definition of culture, since it omits the idea of structure, would be an acceptable definition of protoculture: 'the transfer of information by behavioral means, most particularly by the process of teaching and learning.' Boyd and Richerson's (1985: 2) definition of culture also seems more appropriate to protoculture: 'the transmission from one generation to the next, by teaching and imitation, of knowledge, values, and other factors that influence behavior.' The important work of these authors on the evolution of cultural capacity will be discussed in chapter 11, but here it should be noted that their inclusion of 'teaching and imitation' reflects their focus on social learning. Neither they nor Bonner are primarily concerned with pattern or structure in culture.[1]

In contrast, only when the information transmitted forms some kind of coherent, organized whole will I use the term 'culture.' When we are only dealing with socially transmitted information per se, I will use 'protoculture.' For example, the cross-generational transmission of complementary social roles would certainly imply organized, socially

---

1 Boyd and Richerson (1985: 38) seem to confuse the notion of the structure of culture at the level of the individual with that at the level of the group.

transmitted information and so would be diagnostic of culture. A variety of strategies for achieving a given end and rules for choosing among them would, similarly, be evidence for the existence of culture. The eating of a particular food item, even if socially transmitted, would not. But from protoculture to culture is a continuum and precisely where one draws the line is a matter of judgment.

Culture and the Mazeway: Individual and Population Levels
Culture is a population-level phenomenon. Individuals *participate* in a culture: they do not themselves carry it, any more than an individual can carry a gene-pool. Individuals select from information in the culture's information pool, refashion, re-create, invent, and synthesize the resulting data into a structure of knowledge termed by A.F.C. Wallace (1970: 15) a *mazeway*. We met the mazeway in chapter 4, where it was presented as the 'background' data of the intra-individual system. It is that, but it also has a certain relationship with culture. Wallace (1970: 15) explains: 'Mazeway is to the individual what culture is to the group. Just as every group's history is unique, so every human individual's course of experience is unique. As a product of this experience, every human brain contains, at a given point in time, a unique mental image of a complex system of dynamically interrelated objects.' The mazeway is a sort of 'map of a gigantic maze' (Wallace: 1970: 15). As we have seen, it is the intra-individual system's – the mind's – cognitive map of the physical, social, and supernatural universe and includes the self. Wallace provides a three-page outline of the contents of the mazeway. He sees it as including values positive, negative, and symbolic; objects, including the self and body image; other human beings; plants; animals; supernatural beings; 'statements of how entire sociocultural, natural and supernatural systems work' (p. 18); and techniques, including not just how to do things but in what order they are to be done, and including the various priorities of one's values.

Note that the structure and coherence of this cognitive map is quite distinct – and probably much greater than is the coherence of the information of which a culture consists. Of course, much of the structure of culture is probably related to the way in which data tend to be organized in the mazeway – that is, cultural structure is in part a reflection of the functioning of the intra-individual system (a position taken by Pulliam and Dunford [1980] and Laughlin and d'Aquili [1974]); but there is no necessary isomorphism (close similarity of structure) between the two levels of analysis. Culture systems are generated by interaction among individuals over the course of generations and reflect, among other things, the various compromises we self-interested human beings make with one another. A culture is not a single mind 'writ large' (Barkow, 1984).

Culture is not a 'thing,' not a concrete, tangible object. It is not a cause of anything. To describe behaviour as 'cultural' tells us only that the action and its meaning are shared and not a matter of individual idiosyncrasy. If you lie on the ground and make swimming motions, in our own society, this behaviour is idiosyncratic and not cultural: perhaps you are mad. In Hausa areas in West Africa in which the *bori* associations are active, you have mounted a god or a god has mounted you – the language permits us to put it either way – and your behaviour and attributes are for a time those of the god. The behaviour is 'cultural,' which explains nothing whatsoever about it except that it is a shared and socially transmitted pattern and not a psychiatric symptom (or, at least, not exclusively a psychiatric symptom).

A *society* is not a culture: the term refers to people living co-operatively in a single social organization, that is, following a given set of rules about their relationships to one another. Many societies have but a single culture, and in such cases no harm is done by using the terms 'society' and 'culture' interchangeably. Of course, different societies may share what is largely the same culture.[2] When a number of populations, each with its own culture, share the same political unit, then we may speak of a pluralistic society. (A nation-state, for example, is often a pluralistic society in which *citizenship* is independent of ethnicity.) Most contemporary societies are pluralistic (Japan being one of the exceptions). Pluralism is not to be equated with political instability: culturally homogeneous groups fission often enough, while the stability of pluralistic societies depends on many factors, from

---

2 Thus, anglophone Canada and the United States share what is largely a common culture, but live in different societies. Canadian nationalists often confuse the distinction between living in a separate society and having a separate culture, apparently in the belief that the latter is needed to justify the former. Thus, they tend to present subtle differences in aspects of the largely shared political subculture of the two societies as evidence for the existence of two different 'cultures.' (Of course, it is not impossible that the leadership of groups that mobilize political support on the basis of 'cultural' differences may succeed in creating such differences in reality, given that leadership's influence over propaganda and education.) But if Canada and the United States can be said to have different 'cultures,' then what term are we to use to describe the differences in the respective ways of life of, say, Trobriand Islanders in Melanesia and Inuit of the Eastern Arctic?

perceived benefits to coercion to the extent to which the constituent peoples have developed (or enjoy through common origin) some shared culture traits. In many cases, the original constituent cultures may be transformed into *ethnic groups*, in a process to be discussed in chapter 9.

CULTURE THE CREATOR

The human nervous system is curiously incomplete without its creator, culture (Geertz, 1962): *creator*, because the environment to which natural selection has adapted us is a cultural environment. We were selected for the capacity for culture (Spuhler, 1959), and the societies generated by our cultures were the environment to which natural selection adapted us. The idea of *Homo sapiens* as some kind of a deferred ape,[3] or worse, of our human nature as somehow being in opposition to culture, is highly misleading (as was discussed in chapter 1). There is no such thing as a functioning human being who does not participate in a culture.

Culture includes our social organization and our adaptation to physical environment – how we make a living, how we group and categorize ourselves, how we organize leisure, sex, violence. As we evolved, as our cultures grew in complexity, so did our dependence upon them. 'Dependence' on culture means strong selection pressure to acquire culture from others (usually but not always the older generation) and to transmit it efficiently to others (usually but not always the younger generation), all the while editing, revising, and elaborating cultural data in ways likely to enhance genetic fitness. These selection pressures meant the development of specialized mechanisms or processors capable of doing these things. Thus, the genetic and neurological bases of cultural capacity increased step-by-step with the elaboration of our cultures. As culture grew more elaborate and our dependence on it increased, the resulting selection pressures also increased our capacity for culture. Greater capacity for culture permitted the further elaboration of culture and an ever-growing dependence upon it for adaptation, resulting in greater selection pressure in favour of cultural capacity, which in turn permitted an increase in cultural elaboration ... These clumsy words describe a spiralling process, more properly termed (by Dobzhansky, 1963: 311) a 'feedback reciprocal relation,' a process of

---

3 Of course, if it is your opinion that knuckle-walking lies in our future, then you might consider *Homo sapiens* a 'deferred' ape.

reciprocating positive feedbacks between the capacity for culture and the body of transmitted culture itself.

This feedback relationship between culture and the genetic capacity for culture slowed – some would say ceased – with the rise of the first (anatomically) modern human beings, by at least 100,000 years ago. Whatever genetic changes have taken place in human gene pools in the past one hundred millennia, few would argue that they are of a magnitude comparable to the changes that have occurred during that time in technology, population size, economic systems, information-recording, and the sheer scale of society. We have gone from being skilled chippers of stone to being skilled makers of microchips. At least in terms of technology and adaptation to environment, culture 'took off' 100,000 years ago, and its rate of change has never been greater than it is in these waning years of the twentieth century.

Origins of Culture
Back in chapter 1, we looked at the evolution of the human hand. The hand moved from being the forefoot of a quadrupedal animal to being the branch-grasping organ of a tree-dweller, and thence to being a means of using tools for a terrestrial, cultural animal. Thus, different selection pressures shaped the hand at different times. What is true of the hand must be even more true for the myriad mental organs underlying the capacity for culture. This capacity, too, no doubt evolved in response to different selection pressures at different points in time. What were some of the likely pressures and processes involved?

Once we had at least some capacity for culture, it is easy to imagine scenarios in which its adaptive value was so great that the culture-capacity/culture-dependency feedback described above could have taken off. We will shortly be considering such scenarios. But this feedback process assumes that culture is already adaptive, at least to some slight extent. Some Promethean process must have already brought us to that point, the point at which the feedback process between culture and cultural capacity could have self-ignited. There are several interesting conjectures about what led up to that self-ignition, about the origins of the initial kick (to switch metaphors).

Primates are arboreally adapted creatures, meaning that our order (monkeys, apes, and human beings) largely evolved in the trees. The common ancestor we share with our very close relative, the chimpanzee, may well have been forest-dwelling, possibly similar in behaviour and morphology to the modern pygmy chimpanzee (Susman, 1987).

Why we left our tree homes remains a topic of debate, among evolutionists,[4] but there is consensus that we are descended from those who evolved to take advantage of a mosaic environment, one with woodlands, forests, and savannahs (Campbell, 1985; Pfeiffer, 1985). Food-bearing trees tended to occur in 'patches,' requiring walking from one grove to another. Thus, selection favoured terrestrial locomotion (moving on the ground).

Why walk on two legs, rather than the four ordinarily used by almost all other primates? Two legs may simply have been more efficient than four, in terms of the amount of energy needed to move from food source to food source (Rodman and McHenry, 1980). Bipedalism may also have been related to the freeing of the hands to carry food to females as part of courtship, or to carry it to home bases and the offspring therein. Walking quadrupedally, after all, makes it far more difficult to bear burdens. (We will be returning to this topic in chapter 13, when it will turn out that our choice of evolutionary scenario influences our views on the origins of bipedality.)

But if we are talking about carrying food to a home base, we may have already leaped over the initial kick question. Various theorists discussing the ultimate origins of culture have emphasized tool use (Brace, 1979; Washburn, 1960), home bases (Isaac, 1978a, 1978b), monogamy and the division of labour by gender (Etkin, 1954, 1963, 1964; Lovejoy, 1981), and the interaction of all of these factors. Kurland and Beckerman (1985) have argued that cultural capacity began when our newly bipedal ancestors found themselves in an environment in which food sources probably tended to be 'clumped' and 'very patchy.' These ancestors of ours, they assert (p. 74), would have coped with this problem by 'exchanging information,' thus providing an initial kick. In chapter 11 we will see that Boyd and Richerson (1985) present mathematical models in which cultural transmission is seen to be favoured by an environment in which individual learning is likely to be costly but social learning (cultural transmission), given a sufficient degree of environmental predictability, is likely to be both accurate and efficient. Chapter 13 will discuss Sue T. Parker's (1987) scenario for the evolution of human

---

4 My favourite explanation for our having left the branches of Eden involves our ancestors having been the least capable of the common ancestors of ourselves and our close kin, the chimpanzee. These ancestral failures would have been forced to the ground by our more able relatives, to adapt or die. While chimpanzees presumably would favour this view, we human primates may prefer to interpret the ancestors of our line as having taken advantage of a new opportunity.

cultural capacity (my personal favourite among current scenarios). (Once acquired, the taste for possible evolutionary scenarios of how we came to be as we are is rarely lost. For those with the taste, the volume edited by Kinzey [1987] is a good place to start.)

The Island Model and the Autopredation Hypothesis
However one accounts for the initial kick leading to selection for cultural capacity, why should we have subsequently gone on to develop so great a capacity to invent and transmit culture? One of the processes that may have been involved is that of the 'autopredation hypothesis,' which can be combined with the 'Sewall Wright effect' of gene drift. Let us begin with autopredation, or the notion that intergroup conflict served as a spur to human evolution.

Predation often results in very strong selection pressures. The predators cull the slower prey, or the weaker ones, or the ones with poor vision or hearing. The prey species therefore is selected for speed, or for some type of strength or general disease resistance, or for better vision or hearing. In the case of our own species, it has been conjectured that we were our own predators and preyed on ourselves.[5] We did not necessarily eat one another (though we may have), but we certainly could have warred on, raided, and competed with one another. Groups genetically likely to produce individuals who had more 'cultural capacity' – who learned more quickly – might have been better able to make weapons and other implements, and could have been superior in terms of grasping strategy and tactics, the ability to plan and to foresee contingencies, and in-group co-operation in general.

5 This possibility was originally advanced by Carveth Read (1917) and subsequently elaborated by Keith (1949), but has perhaps been best presented by Bigelow (1969, 1973), who, however, takes a group-selectionist stance. More recently, Richard Alexander (1971, 1974, 1975, 1979) has made the notion central to his thinking, while Pierre van den Berghe (1981) has given it some emphasis. For a discussion joining autopredation with the work of Sewall Wright, see Hamilton (1975).

Michael Rose (1980) argues that up to the Australopithecine level, selection for increased intelligence was due to ecological adaptation, then was 'amplified' during roughly the *Homo erectus* level through an interaction between ecological adaptation and autopredation ('intraspecific competition'), but slowed from that point on because autopredation continued but not ecological adaptation (presumably because of the costs, such as a larger brain, associated with increased intelligence).

Boyd and Richardson (1985: 230–40) seek to account for within-group co-operation. Rather than seeing this phenomenon (along with ethnocentrism) as the product of autopredation, they propose an alternative approach based on conformity and cultural group selection. Their ideas will be discussed in detail in chapter 11.

The autopredation approach looks like group selection and is certainly compatible with it if we think in terms of groups warring with one another to the point of extinction. More likely, however, groups in effect would have culled one another by raiding, which is more typical of small-scale society warfare than is simply wiping out the enemy (Otterbein, 1985). Individuals who had less cultural capacity than did others – and especially those individuals who tended not to co-operate with their fellows in the face of external threat – would have been the least likely to survive. In favour of the culling, as opposed to the group-selection, interpretation of autopredation is the likelihood of gene flow among groups, resulting not just from migration but from the incorporation into the 'victorious' group of captured females. Gene flow among rival groups would have greatly slowed the rate of evolution of cultural capacity through extinction of rival groups, but is compatible with the culling model.

Boyd and Richerson (1985) are critical of the autopredation scenario on the grounds that its hypotheses are 'plausible' but 'unattractive' (p. 231). They point out that the scenario must remain somewhat speculative, since 'we cannot observe human behavior under late Pleistocene food-foraging conditions' (p. 231). In a (1986) personal communication, Boyd and Richerson mention (as was noted above) that human warfare tends to result in substantial gene flow. They point out, as well, that we apparently do not see autopredation-type situations in other species, even though there presumably are other species who would 'get the same advantages from collective action in defense of territory.'[6] The alternative scenario they propose for the evolution of in-group co-operation, 'cultural group selection,' is discussed in chapter 11.

Do we see anything similar to autopredation among contemporary small-scale peoples? The best available data on homicide among a small-scale, low-technology group come not from a foraging people but from horticulturalists, the Yanomamö Indians of Amazonas (who, however, also engage in a considerable amount of foraging). Their homicides generally involve raiding and revenge killings between

6 If autopredation was indeed a factor in the evolution of our capacity for culture and co-operation, why have not other species evolved in a similar fashion? As presented in this chapter, autopredation is a second stage of the process of selection for cultural capacity. It can accelerate the evolution of cultural capacity only when a considerable amount of such capacity is already in place. Perhaps autopredation does not produce cultural capacity among other species because they do not begin with sufficient cultural capacity.

groups of kin. Chagnon (1988) finds that 44% of men of age twenty-five or older have participated in homicide. These men have more wives and children, on average, than do others, and also tend to enjoy higher prestige. Homicide accounts for some 30% of the adult male mortality rate.

How typical are the Yanomamö of small-scale peoples? After all, Chagnon's subtitle for his major ethnography of the Yanomamö (1983) was 'the fierce people.' Good-quality data on homicide in prior-to-European-control 'tribal' societies are unfortunately very scarce, as Chagnon (1988: 986) warns us, but he finds that the few trustworthy studies available do provide results consistent with his Yanamamö data. Chagnon believes that the Yanomamö's homicide rates and practice of revenge killing may have been characteristic of pre-colonial, small-scale, low-technology societies. One thing is clear: if our Pleistocene ancestors had a homicide pattern in any way similar to that of the Yanomamö, then autopredation would have been a powerful selective force among them indeed.

Autopredation is probably best viewed as likely to have been one of the processes involved in selection for cultural capacity, but not necessarily the most important such process and certainly not the only one. The autopredation hypothesis can be considerably strengthened if we make certain mathematical assumptions about population distribution and relative genetic isolation/gene flow rates among local groups (Hamilton, 1975), during the Pleistocene. Sewall Wright (1943, 1969) originally proposed an 'island model' in which local populations are small enough to be affected by gene drift (the Sewall Wright effect), so that chance produces in them considerable variability. Because these local groups are small, gene drift will often take place. This means that low-frequency alleles will tend to be lost simply because of chance, whenever the particular spermatozoa or ova bearing these low-frequency genes fail by chance to produce zygotes (fertilized ova). In other cases, local populations will be founded by a very small number of individuals, who will, again by chance, have a non-representative sample of the genes of the entire species' gene-pool. Thanks to this *founder's effect* and to gene drift, then, there will be a great deal of diversity among local gene-pools. But the model also assumes sufficient gene flow for adaptive alleles and allelic combinations to become fixed in the larger population. 'Adaptive' would, in this context, mean increasing survival and reproductive success in the face of intermittent hostility from neighbouring groups. Such traits collectively involve cultural capacity and would presumably include intelligence, co-operativeness with members of one's own group, and easily learned hostility towards other groups and their members. The latter pair of traits are aspects of the ethnocentrism syndrome.

The existence of the ethnocentrism syndrome makes the autopredation hypothesis a more convincing (if still impossible-to-prove) partial explanation for cultural capacity. LeVine and Campbell (1972: 12) provide some twenty-three defining features of ethnocentrism. These include the tendency for in-group members to see themselves as superior and virtuous, and to perceive their 'own standards of value as universal, intrinsically true.' In-group members are co-operative towards one another and there are negative sanctions for theft and murder if the victim is a fellow in-group member. In-group members are also willing 'to fight and die' for the in-group. In contrast, the out-group tends to be hated, there are no sanctions for theft and murder if the victim is an out-group member, it is virtuous to kill out-group members in warfare, out-group members are often distrusted and feared and blamed for the in-group's troubles. LeVine and Campbell proceed to analyse various theoretical conceptions of ethnocentrism and do find some contradictions as well as commonalities among them, but the syndrome clearly recurs with sufficient frequency to merit the label 'species trait' (van den Berghe, 1981). If the autopredation process actually did play a role in the evolution of our species, then our tendency towards ethnocentrism must be part and parcel of our capacity for culture.[7]

The plausibility of this argument for the autopredation hypothesis rests on the 'mathematical assumptions' mentioned above, assumptions concerning the genetic structure of ancestral hominid populations. We cannot go back in time, of course, but we can make the rather bold assumption that the genetic structure of contemporary small-scale hunting-gathering/foraging peoples in some ways resembles the genetic structure of the populations of our own ancestors.

Colin Irwin (1985, 1987) has examined available data and theory pertaining to the genetic structure of small-scale peoples in an effort to determine whether there is any real evidence for ethnocentrism having evolved in the manner suggested above. Most interesting is his analysis of materials dealing with the Netsilingmiut Eskimo and their neighbours. He makes use of both his own newly collected data and records

---

7 For an excellent source of sociobiological discussion of ethnocentrism, see the volume edited by Reynolds, Falger, and Vine (1987).

(particularly those of Rasmussen) stemming from the first thirty years of this century. These data deal with genetic variation (as inferred from genealogical data) among the local tribes, including migration, inbreeding, and outbreeding rates. It proved possible to calculate the extent of genetic relatedness both within and between local populations after n generations. Irwin (1985: 92) concludes that the genetic structure of these groups 'could precipitate the evolution of ethnocentric behavior.' Note that Irwin's conclusion here is based on empirical data rather than on (as is more common, in such discussions) plausible conjecture. Note, too, however, that if one rejects the assumption that Netsilingmiut Eskimo populations resembled those of our ancestors, then his conclusions must also be rejected. But our ancestors were hardly a homogeneous group living in one place and at one time: surely, during at least some of our long evolution, early hominids lived a life resembling that of the Eskimo.

Sexual Selection

Here is a second, and complementary, explanation for the growth of cultural capacity. Like the autopredation hypothesis, it assumes that there has already been an initial kick. Once our ancestors had gained some minimum degree of cultural capacity, then females may have selected males for increasingly high levels of cultural capacity simply by preferring the more successful males. Sexual selection, in short, may have been a major factor in the evolution of the capacity for culture. This possibility rests on several assumptions.

The story begins not at the very beginning but, as I suggested above, when we already had at least some cultural capacity, some socially transmitted, organized data.[8] As we saw in chapter 2, however, selection favours females who prefer the males best able to invest in offspring, that is, who are best able to provide resources (or access to resources) needed for the rearing of children, resources known as 'parental investment.' Such males will therefore be genetically successful, since females choose them. Let us assume (assumption 1) that, among our protocultural ancestors, those males best able to learn and to

8 Sexual selection for cultural capacity may have involved female preference for males able and willing first to provide 'nuptial gifts' of food, and eventually to provide parental investment for offspring. The latter topic is discussed at length in chapter 8, in the context of the transformation of primate agonistic social dominance into hominid symbolic prestige and self-esteem. The former topic is discussed in chapter 13, in connection with Sue T. Parker's (1987) evolutionary scenario.

transmit protocultural information tended to be the most able to provide parental investment and also to be the highest in status. That is, high male status, high cultural capacity, and high attractiveness for females may have tended to go together at a very early stage, perhaps from the very point at which males first began to invest parentally in their offspring.[9]

These early hominids or protohominids would have been foragers – scavengers and/or hunters. Presumably, if assumption 1 is valid, the best male forager would have been best able to provide parental investment. He would therefore have been of high status, preferred by females and therefore successful genetically. Now, assumption 2 is that he was the best forager because he had slightly greater cultural capacity than did others. He learned most readily how to make weapons and other tools, or how to predict where game would be found, or simply learned readily from his elders where to find water or roots or ripe fruit. He was also best at manipulating the behaviour of others so that they would provide him with advice and aid, rather than agonism. All this means that cultural capacity would have resulted in his having greater genetic success than did other males, thanks largely to female preference (and, of course, to the direct benefits he himself derived from his greater cultural capacity). Females therefore were (are?) in effect breeding males for cultural capacity simply by choosing the highest in status, since the high in status are the best providers, and they are the best providers because of their greater capacity for culture. Females would have been selecting males for 'cultural capacity' – for the ability to use cultural information for one's own ends, and in the process to innovate and resynthesize and add to culture.

This female preference for the high-cultural-capacity males may have been a major factor in the evolution of cultural capacity, but it is not a sufficient explanation. As was previously noted, the process could only have begun once we were to at least some measure dependent on culture. But given that measure, sexual selection would then have tended to favour cultural capacity.

Does this mean that females were essentially limited to the role of choosers and it was up to the males to be cultured? Hardly. Cultural

9 Note that I have here made an assumption of one of the major questions for human sociobiology, the extent to which culturally defined systems of success are also systems of genetic success. This question will be discussed in more detail in chapter 8, but here I am simply assuming that it is so, that cultural-success/genetic-success definitions do tend to go together.

capacity would have permitted females as well as males to be better able to invest in offspring, and the females would probably have invested more reliably as well. But females, in this scenario, would have had an additional role, that of choosing high-cultural-capacity males. Presumably, a female's own high cultural capacity would have been an asset in making her choice. Note that sexual selection (mate choice) and natural selection might have been acting in identical directions.

Would not males have been selected for preferring high-cultural-capacity females? The answer must be 'yes.' Males presumably had been selected to be opportunistic in choosing copulation partners, since, as was discussed in earlier chapters, copulation costs the male so little. But in choosing females in whose offspring he will eventually invest, the male who prefers the high-ability, highly skilled, high-cultural-capacity female will, all things being equal, thereby enhance his fitness in that the offspring will presumably benefit from the female's superior genes as well as from her relatively greater ability to invest parentally. We are led to a commonsensical but empirically verifiable hypothesis: *if youth and physical condition are held constant, then males should prefer the more intelligent, skilled (including socially skilled), resourceful, confident females, when choosing partners for long-term relationships.* I suspect that this is so.[10])

Yellow for Genetic Evolution, Green for Culture Change
We now have three compatible pieces of explanation for the evolution of cultural capacity: the 'initial kick' theories provided by Kurland and Beckerman, Boyd and Richerson, and others; the autopredation hypothesis; and sexual selection. What we do not have is a time sequence, or an association of particular processes with particular periods and ancestral hominid species. Was sexual selection important at the level of our early ancestor *Australopithecus afarensis*, for example, or only for the later species *Homo erectus*? When would autopredation have played a role? Unfortunately, we have no consensus among students of human evolution about the answers to these questions. For the purposes of this chapter, however, we do not need the answers: it should by now be very clear that culture and the capacity for culture arose as an aspect of the biological evolution of our species, even if the precise details of the processes involved remain uncertain.

10 For more about the importance of female choice, and of females in general, in human evolution, see the collection edited by Frances Dahlberg (1981), *Woman the Gatherer*. For further discussion of human evolution and sexual selection (including female choice) see Parker (1987); or see chapter 13.

Before we leave the topic of the origins of culture, however, we might pause to wonder why genetic evolution today moves sedately while cultural innovation explodes. Probably the major reason is that the genetic structure of our populations has changed and the Sewall Wright effect, except in isolated instances, has ended. The effect depends upon the population being distributed in small, semi-isolated groups (demes). Certainly by the Neolithic, if not earlier, human populations had largely ceased to be sufficiently small and sufficiently isolated for gene drift to be a major factor in evolution. At the same time, the domestication of plants and animals may have led to an acceleration of culture change. An additional reason for the slowing of genetic evolution of cultural capacity has to do with the source of phenotypic variation. As selection for cultural capacity continued, genotypic variation underlying this trait would naturally decrease, so that most phenotypic variation would eventually be non-genetic in origin, resulting in a weakening of natural selection for cultural capacity.

Only recently – between twelve and fourteen thousand years ago, for the Near East – did some members of our over 100,000-year-old species forsake a foraging way of life and settle down to become Neolithic farmers and herders. It is not clear why we should have done so. It probably was not the result of some genius noting that seeds planted in the ground eventually produced food. Hunter-gatherers have encyclopedic knowledge of their surroundings – they have to, if they are to live, and the idea that our early ancestors lacked knowledge of the possibility of gardening is unlikely. Nor is it at all clear that growing one's own food requires less labour than foraging for it – the opposite may be true (Lee, 1979). Flannery (1968) argues that agriculture probably began in the Near East, on the margins of stands of naturally occurring grain whose productivity could readily be increased by planting, once population expansion had made an increase in the food supply necessary. Note that agriculture and the domestication of animals arose quite independently and only somewhat later, in the New World, possibly (though not definitely) under comparable conditions of population increase and the inability to obtain sufficient food by foraging.

In any event, once food-growing became widespread, it made for great change. Raising food means relatively permanent residence, food storage, organizing to defend the food and residence, and, shortly, a surplus used initially to support the defence. In time, this way of life means kings, centralized administration, craft, religious, political, and military specialists supported by the surplus produced by the farmers, and the rise of civilization and the state.[11] Civilization – defined in terms of a system of writing, commerce, a division of labour including governmental and military specialists, and towns or cities – is extremely young. Industrial civilization is in its infancy, barely a few centuries old. Have there been important changes in the genetic bases of behaviour since our ancestors gave up the hunting-gathering life? Chapter 11 will discuss this question in some detail, under the heading 'genetic assimilation of culture,' but it is worth mentioning here that this possibility is quite unlikely. After all, we know that human beings from small-scale, low-technology cultures have no difficulty in adapting to large-scale, high-technology societies, provided they are sufficiently young when they make the transition. If there are genetically based behavioural differences across human populations, then we have yet to develop instruments sufficiently robust to detect them without ambiguity. Arguing that data for such differences are indeed strong is not in itself evidence of racism, though it is true that some racists do indeed so argue.

SUMMARY

1. At least three ideas seem common to most of the various definitions of culture. The first is that culture is socially transmitted; the second, that it consists of some kinds of information (techniques, norms, ideas, symbols); and the third, that it is ordered or organized in some way, that is, that it forms some kind of system or at least is in some way structured. A fourth frequently included component, the notion that culture is *adaptive*, is omitted from this discussion in order to avoid incorporating into a definition what would otherwise be a testable hypothesis.

2. Omitting the notion of 'structure' from the definition of culture leads to the conclusion that many species are cultural. I use the term 'protoculture' to refer to socially transmitted but unstructured information, and reserve 'culture' for those cases in which the information transmitted is in some way structured.

3. The mazeway is the intra-individual system's set of cognitive maps of physical, social, and supernatural reality. It includes the self.

4. Culture is not a 'thing,' not a concrete, tangible object. It is not a

11 For an excellent introduction to archaeology and the rise of civilization, see either Pfeiffer's *The Emergence of Society* (1977) or Fagan's *People of the Earth* (1985). For what came before society, see Pfeiffer's *The Emergence of Mankind* (1985).

cause of anything. To describe behaviour as 'cultural' tells us only that the action and its meaning are shared and not an individual idiosyncrasy.

5. There is no necessary isomorphism between the structure of the mind and the structure of culture. Cultural systems are generated by interaction among individuals over the course of generations and reflect, among other things, the various compromises about the acceptable roles and statuses that social interaction usually generates.

6. The capacity for culture and transmitted culture itself evolved in a 'feedback reciprocal relation,' a process of reciprocating positive feedbacks. But this feedback relationship slowed – some would say ceased – with the rise of the first modern human beings, perhaps 100,000 years ago.

7. Our ancestors probably became bipedal to take advantage of a mosaic environment requiring travel among food sources.

8. One scenario for the evolution of cultural capacity involves assumptions about autopredation and population structure. Predator pressure often is an important selection pressure in evolution. In our own case, we may have served as our own predators, with small groups occasionally attacking each other. Since cultural capacity was the most effective means of both offence and defence (assuming that the term implies abilities to co-operate and to make and use weapons and other tools), then we would in effect have been selecting each other's groups for cultural capacity by culling those lacking in this trait. If the population was distributed in terms of groups sufficiently small to permit gene drift to take place, but with enough gene flow so that chance-produced adaptive gene combinations would not be lost, selection for cultural capacity would have been even faster.

9. The ethnocentrism syndrome is consistent with this autopredation-plus-genetic-population-structure argument.

10. Early females may have selected males for increasingly high levels of cultural capacity simply by preferring the more successful males. Sexual selection may therefore have been a major factor in the evolution of the capacity for culture. Males, though sexually more opportunistic than females, would have been selected to prefer high-culture-capacity qualities in partners with whom they were likely to have longer term relationships.

7

Culture and the Intra-Individual System

Now we have defined culture and have a little understanding of how our species may have evolved the ability to create and transmit it. It is time to return to a question raised in chapter 5: What is the relationship between the information-processing of the intra-individual system and the socially transmitted and somewhat structured pool of information called 'culture'?

REVIEW

To review some of the points made in chapter 5: The intra-individual system may tentatively but usefully be thought of as a mazeway or cognitive map, plus various specialized systems and subsystems. These systems process information of various kinds, and culture *is* a structure of various kinds of information. The intra-individual system, it was argued, treats information in terms of codes/sub^{n}codes, goals/sub^{n}goals, and plans/sub^{n}plans. The superscript 'n' refers to the number of 'subs,' that is, to the number of steps between the original plan or goal or code and the subgoal/plan/code being executed. One of the intra-individual system's major goals involves incorporating information into the cognitive map or mazeway, the subsystem that (among other things) includes both physical and social background or reference data.

The basic codes, goals, and plans are likely to be quite stable, across cultures. Presumably, they develop in every normal human being in every culture, so long as the individual *is* raised in a cultural setting.

These basic goals and plans and codes account for much of the psychic unity of humankind. The 'subs' – the sub^ngoals and sub^nplans and sub^ncodes – vary enormously from culture to culture, and, indeed, from individual to individual. But various ethological mechanisms (such as those involved in much non-verbal communication), as well as learning and attentional biases and 'limbic system overrides,' cause commonalities across cultures even at the 'sub' level and tend to 'push' culture change in fitness-enhancing pathways.

CULTURE AS INFORMATION

The present chapter focuses on how the intra-individual system categorizes and processes cultural, socially transmitted *information*. The sources and forms of cultural information 'out there' are diverse and may include, for example, written records; tales and myths with moral lessons or with complex, deep, logical structures; implements whose design conduces to some techniques rather than others; and no doubt numerous other forms. But however cultural information exists 'out there,' my focus here is on how it is *received*.

I argue that it will be useful to think of cultural information as being received as sub^ncodes, sub^nplans, and sub^ngoals, and/or as mazeway data. The selection pressures that shaped the intra-individual system have caused it to treat culturally provided sub^ncodes, sub^ngoals, and sub^nplans quite differently from one another. Much of the vagueness and over-generalities of past accounts of the relationship between genes and culture, as we will see in chapter 10, may have been caused by trying to develop models that work for all three of these very different kinds of culturally provided information. For example, as will be discussed shortly, selection favours the ability to replicate subcodes with quite high fidelity and subgoals with somewhat lower accuracy; while subplans we often modify or even invent for ourselves.

Of course, all this is very provisional and there is no need to strive too ruthlessly for what would only be a spurious elegance. If the modular, parallel-distributed-processing model of the mind presented in chapter 5 does turn out to be accurate (as I expect and hope but cannot know it will), and if we eventually understand the algorithms of each of the brain's specialized processors or modules, then the theory of culture presented here will seem coarse and primitive indeed! Rather than dividing culture into three types of information, we may need to break it into as many different information categories as we have specialized processors, with each type of information potentially transmitted and received in a unique way. For the present, however, let us take a small and tentative step: How can we divide cultural information into the same categories that the intra-individual system was conceptualized as using?

Curiously, the debate in human sociobiology has centred not on whether there are categories of cultural information or what these categories may be, but on whether the information is particulate in nature. Is cultural information received by the brain as some kind of particles analogous to genes (discussed in chapter 10)? For those concerned with finding analogies between the processes of genetic evolution and those of culture change, this question may appear to be important. But if our goal is to understand the impact of cultural information on genetic fitness, then it would seem to be more productive to ask how the intra-individual system categorizes incoming information.

The code/plan/goal category set bears no particular relationship to ethnographic categories: religion, kinship and social organization, values and norms, social control, subsistence economy, technology, and the like. Ethnographic categories are chosen for the convenience of ethnographers, not for their possible correspondence with the functioning of the human brain.

GOALS AND PLANS

As we saw in chapter 5, the basic goals and plans can usefully be thought of as environmentally stable, perhaps even 'hard wired'; but with each new level of 'sub' goals/plans comes greater flexibility. Subgoals and subplans are the realm of culture. The prestige goal (discussed in the next chapter), for example, generates subgoals and subplans with major implications for our understanding of self-esteem, economic systems, identity, and group membership. Subgoals and subplans associated with how we get food or drink or warmth – the physiological maintenance goals – are equally basic to our understanding of cultural diversity and organization. Do we hunt, forage, beg, till the earth, steal? Do we keep warm by building a house, wearing clothes, making a fire, turning up the thermostat? Do we drink water, tea, kvass, or Beaujolais nouveau? It depends upon our culturally provided subgoals/plans.

With each step away from the original goal/plan, the amount of lability and the role of culture – and of individual experience in general –

increase. Suppose our goal involves eating and the sub^{1}plan is farming. Sub^{2}plan may involve acquiring land or animals or seed, sub^{3}plan may involve incurring an obligation to a kinsman in order to obtain these things, and so on. An immense variety of complex sub^{n}goals and sub^{n}plans may be pursued before we eat.

The various sub^{n}goals/plans provided by our cultures almost always serve a variety of intra-individual-system goals simultaneously. A job, for example, may have as much to do with self-esteem as with hunger. Hunting may have much to do with hunger, true – but also with goals associated with reputation, ability to aid relatives (kin or nepotistic altruism goals), sexual goals, and so on. Subplans in general tend to mesh together, to serve multiple goals, and to be co-ordinated with other subplans in the service of other goals. It is likely that subplans capable of serving multiple goals are the most likely to be adopted by individuals.[1] It is this co-ordination and multi-tasking of subplans that helps to prevent our stream of behaviour from being chaotic.

These preliminary examples are simplistic, of course. Only in chapters 8 and 9 will we see, in some detail, how goals and plans actually operate in the context of culture and social change. At that point, we will need some life-history data about actual individuals to make these abstractions more real.

More about Sub^{n}goals/plans
We need to make two additional points about sub^{n}plans, each one of which probably deserves but will not get a chapter of its own. First, every culture has distinctive sub^{n}goals/plans/codes that recur across individuals and settings. Anthropologists have had immense difficulty in discussing these, sometimes resorting to such terms as 'basic personality structure,' 'national character,' 'values,' and 'themes.' There has been a strong tendency to think of these recurring subgoals/ plans/codes as products of child training (which in a sense they are, since the intra-individual system has an ontogeny as well as a phylogeny); and to try to account for them in terms of Freudian and

---

1 Though Boyd and Richerson (1985) present many mathematical models for the spread of culture traits within a pool of such traits, they do not present one in which the relative frequency of a subplan capable of serving more than one subgoal is compared to that of a subplan limited to one subgoal. A reasonable hypothesis is that we have an evolved bias towards the former. Thus, we would be more likely to accept an occupation that offered both wealth and prestige than we would be to accept one that offered either alone.

neo-Freudian theories.[2] Why, for example, do we see much more physical violence in some societies than in others? Perhaps, in 'violent' societies, the subplan of physical aggression recurs frequently, in different contexts (cf. Daly and Wilson, 1988, 1989).[3]

Second, individuals favour a personal selection of the sub^{n}plans of their own cultures, a selection presumably reflecting their unique phenotypes. They utilize this limited set of subplans in the service of most or all of their goals and many of their subgoals. This recurrence of the same sub^{n}plans or tactics across many situations provides much of the integration of behaviour we often term 'personality.' Presumably, 'personality' would also include the rules for setting the priorities among goals and subgoals – the 'switching mechanism' that is part of the intra-individual system but about which I can provide no theory (as was mentioned in chapter 5).

CODES AND SUBCODES

The study of subcodes, in all their complexities, is the realm of linguistics and of 'symbolic' or 'interpretive' anthropology. The deepest level of code, the modules of perception discussed in chapter 5, are probably so environmentally stable that they have relatively little to do with culture. The best-understood subcodes are those of language. We have considerable knowledge, at least at the descriptive level, of how the child goes about decoding the grammar and phonology of the language he or she hears, while simultaneously learning to use these to encode meaning (Snow and Ferguson, 1977). We know much less about the presumably stable, 'deep structure' underpinnings of other cultural subcodes.

Cognitive Anthropology
'Cognitive anthropological analyses typically claim to present the calculus used by informants, *rather than some operationally equivalent*

---

2 The subfield dealing with these issues is known as 'psychological anthropology' or 'culture and personality.' For an excellent introduction to this subdiscipline, see Bock (1980).

3 I neglect aggression and violence, in this book, because I believe these behaviours are simply a category of human manipulative strategies and not fruitful theoretical concepts at all. Those interested in the topic, however, might see Daly and Wilson (cited in the text) and Eibl-Eibesfeldt (1975, 1982). For an environmental-determinist view of aggressivity, see the two volumes edited by Ashley Montagu (1973, 1978).

calculus' (Rubenstein, Laughlin, and McManus, 1984: 7, emphasis in original). Cognitive anthropologists seek the *'organizing principles underlying behavior'* (Tyler, 1969: 3, emphasis in original). Their goal is not surface description of specific spheres (such as how often crops are rotated or who attends a birth), but the underlying conceptual organization of behaviour. For example, some cognitive anthropologists (particularly those who use the term 'ethnoscience') analyse the concepts underlying local taxonomies. Let us take botany – or 'ethnobotany,' if we are seeking the local culture's equivalent of that field – as an example. Here, the investigator tries to discover the implicit rules underlying the local classification of plants. Are the categorizations being made on the basis of use, leaf shape, root shape, colour, taste, scent, or what? The next question is that of the logical relationship among these component principles. Ultimately, the observer hopes to be able to predict correctly the classification of any randomly chosen plant.

Claude Lévi-Strauss and his various schools of followers (usually known as 'structuralists') also seek the conceptual principles underlying various cultural domains.[4] They, however, conceive of such areas as mythology, pottery design – and kinship – as made up of irreducible elements that are in paired opposition to one another. These elements are seen as combining and recombining with one another in accord with a set of rules, so that the same logical structures recur not just in myth after myth but in domain after domain, within a given culture. This logical elegance is believed to reflect the nature of human cognition, though some (such as, Geertz, 1973: 359) suspect that it may be more in the minds of the analysts than in the minds of those who participate in the cultures analysed.

No doubt there are varying degrees of arbitrariness not just in structural analysis but in cognitive anthropology as a whole. But the field is probably moving in the right direction. Its confusion may well stem (as Lumsden and Wilson [1983] suggest) from the lack of an adequate psychological theory of human cognition with which to interpret findings. In other words, there is confusion about the nature of the subcodes because the more stable, underlying coding process is not yet understood. What does seem clear from the various contending schools of cognitive anthropology, however, is that much of culture may usefully be conceptualized as consisting of codes and subcodes.

4 For an introduction to the work of Lévi-Strauss, see Leach (1970) or Lévi-Strauss (1966). For an introduction to ethnoscience, see Goodenough (1970).

Symbolic Interpretations of Culture
At the labile extreme of cultural subcodes are those intricate layers of shared meanings that ethnographers delight to immerse themselves in, the meanings that permit us to understand one another when we participate in the same culture, and that lead to clash and shock when we do not. I classify these structures as subcodes because they are, in the last analysis, communicative in nature. They are Geertz's (1973: 9) 'webs of signification,' the 'thick structure' of human social life. They are different from subplans and subgoals because, as Geertz puts it (1973: 18), in his discussion of a multi-cultural misunderstanding in Morocco among Jews, Berbers, and the French military, 'as in any discourse, code does not determine conduct.' These codes of meaning make for so complex a bird's nest, that, explains Geertz, his business of 'interpretive anthropology' is more akin to an art form, or perhaps to literary analysis, than it is to 'science.' In the last analysis it is always an unfinished task: one more layer of meaning, one more interpretation, may yet remain.

Though Geertz himself might well disagree, woven through his tapestries of meaning are the sociobiological threads of plans and goals that can in principle be linked to genetic fitness. In the last analysis, even the most elaborate of subcodes represents a communicational structure being used by real people to do real things, things that can be thought of in terms of subplans and subgoals. As evidence, let us look at cock-fighting.

Cock-Fighting in Bali
A Geertzian portrait well known to students of anthropology is his depiction of the Balinese cock-fight. The cock is an obviously masculine symbol for the Balinese, explains Geertz (1973). Indeed, his predecessors in the study of the Balinese, Margaret Mead and Gregory Bateson, went so far as to describe the cock as a sort of detached penis. It is not surprising that the relationship between a man and his cock is intimate, and he will spend much of his time caring for it, preening it, preparing it. The cock stands for the man, and when it fights it is his pride (if its own blood) that is at stake. The owners fix sharp, pointed steel 'swords' to the spurs of their cocks, and betting is heavy. So, too, are the formal, detailed rules that govern the brief encounters in which one cock will maim or kill another, often in the presence of large, wagering crowds.

Geertz presents an apparent paradox: the fight and its bets (which at times are quite large) involve 'esteem, honor, dignity, respect ... and status' (p. 433). However, aside from 'a few cases of ruined addict gamblers,' 'no one's status is actually altered by the outcome of a cockfight; it is only, and that momentarily, affirmed or insulted' (ibid., emphasis added). What is happening, according to Geertz, is the reaffirmation of status. Prestige is central in Balinese society, he explains, and the cock-fight has to do with 'the necessity to affirm it, defend it, celebrate it, justify it, and just plain bask in it (but not, given the strongly ascriptive character of Balinese stratification, to seek it)' (p. 436). There are rules to be followed in betting at cock-fights. You do not bet against a cock belonging to a member of your kin group and you will usually support such a cock, just as you will usually bet in favour of a cock owned by a member of a kin group allied to your own. Similarly, if the match is between a cock from your own village against one from another village, you will of course support your own village's cock. When you have ties to the owners of both cocks you are likely 'to wander off for a cup of coffee or something' (p. 439).

Geertz tells us that most Balinese villagers can explain cock-fighting in much the way that Geertz himself has explained it – as a 'playing with fire only not getting burned' (p. 440), a way 'to activate village and kin group rivalries and hostilities, but in "play" form, coming dangerously close to the expression of open and direct interpersonal and intergroup aggression,' while studiously avoiding it. But, for Geertz, the cock-fight is also the equivalent of an art form, an emotional experience, a means by which 'the Balinese forms and discovers his temperament and his society's temper at the same time' (p. 451). It is a commentary on life and on his own society, much as a play by Molière or Shakespeare is for ours.

I probably do not do justice to Geertz's interpretation of the Balinese cock-fight, much less his 'interpretive' anthropology or to symbolic anthropology as a whole. But even this brief account teaches us two important lessons about cultural subcodes. The first is that they can be, at their most culturally labile and variable end, wondrously complex and subtle, interwoven with many meanings. The second is that, to repeat a previous quotation from Geertz, 'code is not conduct': we are here dealing with an analysis of code that is complex and multilayered, but code just the same.

The Balinese cock-fight is not merely a matter of complex subcodes of symbolic meaning, any more than language is nothing but grammar. If we stop to ask *why* the Balinese engage in cock-fights, why they find them emotionally engrossing, we find that we have asked a question requiring the concepts of goals and subgoals. Note that I am not asking why the Balinese engage in cock-fights rather than in contests of rhetoric as, say, Liberia's Kpelle might: that is a different question, one requiring history and ecology to answer. I am not asking why we human beings should have so much in the way of complex code in the first place. That issue has to do with both genetic and cultural evolution. What I ask here is what we human beings *do* with our complex codes and subcodes. The short answer is that we use them in the service of plans and subplans, goals and subgoals.

The cock-fight is, after all, about prestige, the seeking of which is one of the basic human goals. Geertz claims that nothing changes as a result of cock-fights but, with due respect to one who is, after all, a deservedly major figure in American intellectual life, I do not believe him. What, after all, would happen to one's prestige if one refused to cock-fight, or if one's cocks always lost? Would there be no implications for one's children and their social standing, or perhaps for one's attractiveness to women? Might not the outcome of cock-fights even affect one's inclusive fitness? These are empirical questions for which we have no data save the fact that Geertz does not ask them.

The Balinese cock-fight may also be interpreted as an example of culturally ordered male status display and competition. The goal of prestige or relative standing is one closely tied to genetic fitness, for many species, as we will see in chapter 8. In society after society, we find male-male status display and competition, for reasons that ultimately have to do with the much lower potential fitness cost of copulation for males than for females (as was discussed in chapter 2 and will be discussed again in chapter 13). The Balinese cock-fight uses unique subcodes; but if the Balinese had no cocks, would they not eventually construct other arenas in which males would compete, other idioms or subcodes, perhaps ones more violent than mere fighting among cocks?

The Overlap between Subcodes and Subgoals/plans
The distinction is this: subcodes tell us how to communicate and what the other is intending to convey. Subgoals/plans have to do with what we choose to do and why we choose to do it. For example, grammar is quite distinct from our reasons for saying what we are saying. It is a tool for the conveyance of meaning.

But the choice of subcode may itself be part of a subplan. After all, style of speech may emphasize solidarity, enmity, neutrality, sexuality, regality. This conclusion is a commonplace observation in the field of sociolinguistics (see note 5), but what of non-linguistic subcodes? If we think, for example, of dress and adornment as involving subcodes, then any particular subcode chosen may well be an aspect of a subplan. The possibility of the instrumental use of subcodes has, as we will see in the next section, important implications for the relative rates of change for subgoals/plans and subcodes.

SELECTION AND THE INFORMATION COMPONENTS OF CULTURE

The intra-individual system is a product of biological evolution. Selection has favoured our processing socially transmitted information – culture – in a variety of ways. These ways (this book argues) can usefully be construed as corresponding to the division of cultural information into subgoals, subplans, and subcodes. The tripartite division may be the product of genetic evolution, *for the selection pressures on the mechanisms underlying each information category appear to be distinct.*

Selection and Subcodes

There is an obvious fitness advantage in being able to acquire and utilize subcodes quickly and efficiently, and a disadvantage to using them poorly. But there is ordinarily little advantage in challenging, questioning, or revising subcodes for which n is low. A novel way to communicate would not work, after all, unless others simultaneously adopted the new subcode. Therefore, *there must have been and probably continues to be strong selection pressure in favour of acquiring low-n subcodes in an unproblematic and faithful manner, to permit individuals to communicate effectively.* I would expect the mechanisms underlying subcodes to ensure that they replicate with high fidelity, and their rate of change across generations should ordinarily be quite low. Compared to subgoals and subplans, subcodes should be the least often challenged aspect of culture and the most stable, provided the n in sub^ncodes is low. Codes themselves should be comparable to Chomskian 'deep structure.'

However, when n is sufficiently high, sub^ncodes may be quite labile, as is, for example, the slang of adolescents. High-n subcodes may alter even to the point of replacement, as a result of three processes: (1) transmission or replication error; (2) when new social groups are created; and (3) when use of one subcode rather than another becomes part of a prestige strategy.

(1) *Transmission error* can occur in any information-transmission system. Copying fidelity of subcodes is usually high but it is not perfect. People get something wrong and in transmitting it to their children, the error becomes a subcode variant. It is tempting to assume that

infidelities in subcode transmission are analogous to gene drift and the founder's effect (as Ball [1984] and Boyd and Richerson [1985] assume for culture transmission in general). If this analogy is accurate, then subcode change as a result of chance should be most common in small, isolated groups. It is possible that some grammatical and phonological changes are of this nature.

But the direction of replication error is in some cases predictable, at least when we are dealing with linguistic subcodes. Jacob Grimm (one of the two Grimm brothers of folk-tale fame) studied sound-system changes in pre-Germanic and Germanic dialects and languages and developed Grimm's Law: voiced sounds become voiceless (*b* becomes *p*, *d* becomes *t*); voiceless stops becomes fricatives (*p* becomes an *f*); and fricatives become voiced stops (*f* becomes *b*). Thus, Latin *pater* becomes English *father*, Latin *duo* becomes English *two*, and so on. Even the rate of change of vocabulary in languages may be fairly constant, or so Morris Swadesh has argued (Southworth and Daswani, 1974; Sturtevant, 1964). Swadesh (as well as other linguists) has estimated that 19 per cent of the basic vocabulary of a language is replaced every thousand years, so that two languages from the same root will, after one millennium, have 66 per cent of their vocabulary in common.

(2) When *new social groups* come into existence, new subcodes may be created. The subcodes may have to do with dress and deportment, or with art or myth or music, but, for clarity, let us again focus on linguistic subcodes. Adolescents, occupational groups, and others may evolve their own 'technical terms,' 'jargon,' and 'in-group slang.' This tendency obviously serves to set off groups from one another but its underlying mechanism is unclear and, therefore, whether it is a product of natural selection or simply an epiphenomenon is equally unclear. It may be related to the ethnocentrism syndrome (discussed in chapter 6).

We do know that, in some cases, there is a correlation between dialect differentiation and genetic differentiation (Irwin, 1985; White and Parsons, 1973; Crawford and Encisco, 1982). But whether the correlation is merely the result of geographic distance (Kirk, 1982) or of (genetic) selection for the 'green beard altruism effect' is not well understood.

The 'green beard altruism effect' is a term used by Richard Dawkins (1976: 96) and has to do with nepotistic altruism (discussed in chapter 3). This type of altruism requires that the potential donor have some means of estimating the extent to which a potential aid recipient is related to him/her. Having kin wear a green beard would solve the problem, suggests Dawkins. In lieu of a green beard, however, selection will favour some other type of recognition marker or badge. Familiarity is an obvious marker in our own species and, as I have suggested elsewhere (Barkow, 1978c: 13), 'we tend to be helpful toward those whom we are socialized with, those with whom we grow up or at least have become familiar.' Irwin (1985) suggests that dialect may serve a similar, broader, green-beard function.

Irwin (1985: 96) argues that 'tribal badges, such as dialect, by influencing mate choice, are one of the proximate mechanisms of tribal genetic differentiation' among the Netsilingmiut Eskimo populations among which he has found genetic and linguistic similarity to be correlated. This interesting possibility does not, however, solve the problem of whether we were selected to develop dialect differences under some circumstances *because* they serve as green beards for mate selection and nepotistic altruism; or whether they develop epiphenomenally, perhaps as a result of shared experiences or of isolation, and once they are established we use them as markers because they are a type of familiarity, just as similar gestures or garments would be. In the former case, dialect differentiation would have been selected for and presumably its proximate causes are psychological/neurological in nature; in the latter case, dialect formation results from chance processes, such as transmission error.

The argument that dialect formation has been selected for as a group marker and is not just a 'side-effect' is the more interesting. One could speculate that individuals forming a new social group or category have been selected to mark themselves off by altering high-n subcodes in several domains. For example, adolescents forming age-graded social cliques may distinguish themselves from other such cliques and from adults by developing distinctive slang, greetings, accent, taste in music, dress, and so on. Group formation tends to involve polarities to emphasize differences and thus the new boundary. Because the major group from which adolescents often wish to distinguish themselves is that of their parents' generation, it us understandable that adults often find the 'subculture' of teenagers strange and even offensive. Such 'teen-age subcultures' like more enduring ethnic differences, are a form of ethnocentrism.

(3) Probably the most common reason for rapid subcode change is *when the use of one rather than another subcode is a subplan in the service of a goal*, the goal in question usually being that of prestige. This process presupposes the presence of alternative subcodes that differ in associated prestige and/or are linked to particular social identities. Small-scale,

homogeneous societies may present few such subcode choices to their people, but this is hardly the case in culture contact situations, or during time of rapid social change in general. Whenever subcode alternatives exist, there is a strong tendency for one to be of higher status than another. Adopting the higher-status alternative is a common subplan in a prestige strategy, and results in borrowing from the higher- to the lower-status subcode. In some cases, subcode replacement takes place. This process is most clear when the subcodes in question are languages. Children of immigrants, for example, may reject the tongue of their parents if they perceive it as low-in-status.[5]

The fact that children acquire subcodes automatically when very young but with decreasing ability as they grow older is consistent with an evolutionary scenario in which assimilation into a new culture was a relatively rare event. Thus, selection favoured not the ability to assimilate into a new culture (with new subcodes) in adulthood, but, rather, early and accurate childhood subcode acquisition, followed by a diminished ability to acquire new subcodes. Ethnographers and immigrants, who must attempt to learn new subcodes (I do *not* say 'new cultures' because they are unlikely to be interested in the subgoals of their new societies and only occasionally are aware that their subgoals may be different from those with which they are familiar), are engaging in an evolutionarily unusual enterprise. Not surprisingly, they tend to find the task challenging, and frequently quite stressful and difficult. Sometimes, they fail. I doubt if any field-worker ever really 'goes native,' for example, though some do succeed in becoming bad imitations of indigenous people.[6]

Selection and Subgoals/plans
The selection pressures on the acquisition of subgoals and subplans are very different from those involving subcodes. For subcodes,

---

5 For more information on language and status, and on language and culture in general, see Hymes (1964, 1974) or Giglioni (1972).
6 Warning: throughout this discussion of codes and subcodes I have been making the implicit assumption that linguistic codes and subcodes (dialects) are comparable to the kind of subcode found, for example, in the Balinese cock-fight. This assumption appears reasonable to me, but there is the possibility of it being incorrect. Since we know very little about non-linguistic codes and subcodes, however, there seems little choice except to make the provisional assumption that they are similar.

selection involves competition for using the same subcodes better than do others. With subgoals/plans, selection involves competition in choosing the most effective (for oneself) alternative. Moreover, while novel subcodes are likely to be useless, newly invented subgoals/ subplans may be quite effective. Finally, as other aspects of the culture and environment alter, previously effective subplans and subgoals may be rendered ineffective. Thus, selection should not favour assimilating received subplans and subgoals unproblematically, but, rather, filtering, challenging, and editing them, and at times inventing one's own approaches.

Subgoals/plans are therefore not nearly as stable as are subcodes. The shaman who speaks Okinawan need have no doubt as to what linguistic subcodes (languages) her children will speak (Okinawan and perhaps Japanese as well), but has no such assurance that her daughter will also be a shaman – or farmer, or civil servant, or whatever. Individuals have unique genotypes and experiences, and selection favours their striving to find the subplans and subgoals that best serve their goals. This means that experimentation, trying different skills, and challenging the expectations of those around one should, within limits, be selected for. But sub*goals* should be more resistant to change than sub*plans*, since different means may serve the same end.

Selection and the Mazeway
The mazeway is reference data, among other things, and constantly revamping it would be immensely costly in terms of energy and time. It makes more sense for the mazeway's basic cosmology, the ideas of the physical and social universes, to be nearly (though not quite) as early-learned and as resistant to change as are the subcodes. Once beyond childhood, the individual's mazeway would still require updating but information would be added to a framework already built. Hence, the common observation that, though we can still learn as we grow older, what we learn adds to rather than replaces our existing conceptual frameworks.

The mazeway can, however, be rebuilt. Wallace (1970), who is responsible for the concept of mazeway, is also responsible for naming the *revitalization movement*. In these movements, social change drastically alters reality so that existing mazeways grow inaccurate. For the affected individuals, the universe ceases to make sense. Subgoals/plans fail and the mazeway's reference data are too inaccurate to make correction possible. Rates of deviant behaviour – alcoholism, crime, suicide – rise. When a sufficient proportion of the society has been affected, conditions are ripe for a 'revitalization' movement.

Typically, a central, often charismatic individual – the 'prophet' – experiences a spontaneous mazeway resynthesis, one that reassembles old and new cultural ideas into a new map in which the universe is again coherent and the prophet's own position in it is one of high importance. Since the prophet's problems are shared, his/her solutions may be too, and others therefore find the new synthesis satisfying. Early adherents become 'disciples.' They and eventually many others undergo a sort of religious conversion, except that this religion (or ideology) is new. Melanesian cargo cults, the Ghost Dance of the Plains Indians in the nineteenth century, and possibly the origins of Christianity are examples of revitalization movements.

Most revitalization movements fail, since the prophet's new mazeway tends to be quite unrealistic. Successful revitalization movements are those in which the prophet or, more likely, his disciples adjust their new vision to accommodate practical reality. The new religion or ideology usually accords fairly high status to the movement's adherents and to their society. Thus, in Melanesian cargo cults, it turns out that the attractive European/American goods are really made by the ancestors. In the Ghost Dance, the bison were to return and the whiteman be driven out. In Christianity, even members of the under-class (beggars, prostitutes, lepers) are taught that they are loved by an omnipotent, supernatural being.

It is tempting to argue that revitalization movements are evolved phenomena, a sort of 'emergency plan' built into the intra-individual system by selection. But there does not appear to be any way to determine whether mazeway resynthesis and revitalization movements are evolutionary phenomena or epiphenomena. As was pointed out in chapter 1, we cannot take adaptationism for granted. Would mass mazeway breakdown have been sufficiently common, in our evolutionary history, for selection for a built-in resynthesizing function to have occurred? After all, most of the revitalizations studied by anthropologists seem to have been direct or indirect effects of European cultural hegemony (if not conquest). Mazeway resynthesis may simply be a convulsive form of the general 'cognitive imperative' plan in which we are constantly striving to order our mazeways and accumulate data in them (cf. d'Aquili, 1972). Revitalization movements would therefore represent an emergent phenomenon, occurring when a substantial proportion of a local population experience severe change, so that their mazeways cannot track.

ECOLOGICAL CONSTRAINTS

Back in chapter 5 we saw that the subplans of the intra-individual system were constantly being evaluated as a result of feedback from the external environment. Those that work – in terms of achieving goals or maintaining goal-states – are retained and thereby enter or re-enter the information pool of culture. Those that are ineffective are likely to be discarded. Thus, culture is constantly in motion, particularly with regard to its store of subplans and subgoals. But why should some subplans/goals 'work' and others be 'ineffective'?

To a considerable extent, the external environment and the society's relationship with it seem to determine what works and what does not. At first glance, this seems quite obvious. A subplan for prestige that involves being a successful hunter in an area from which the game have long been gone will fail; but perhaps finding paid employment will now work. There is no need to discover through trial-and-error that a new subplan is needed, for the cognitive maps of the intra-individual system amount to powerful simulation models, often permitting accurate prediction of the relative efficacy of subplans/goals. Even if our prediction is wrong, others will see our failure and probably not repeat the error. In a given ecological setting, as individuals constantly revise and edit their subplans/goals, the cultural pool of information will grow increasingly adaptive, at least in the short term. (Long-term maladaptive consequences are quite possible, however, as we will see in chapter 12.)

If we hold ecological adaptation constant, for a moment, we discover that similar conditions have given rise to similar sets of subplans/goals even in widely separated societies. Indeed, for many features of culture (and social organization), simply knowing the subsistence economy (how people are making a living in a given environment) permits surprisingly accurate prediction.

For example, in this cultural analogue of convergent evolution, if we know that people 'A' live as hunter-gatherers we also know that they live in small, mobile, nomadic bands; that they stress egalitarianism as a value; and that they have indulgent child-rearing practices (Lee and DeVore, 1968). It appears that among hunter/gatherer peoples everywhere, subplans resulting in these culturally ordered behaviours have been more successful in achieving subgoals than have alternative subplans. Obviously, non-nomadic hunter-gatherers would quickly exhaust food supplies in their area and learn to move, to farm, or to starve. Non-sharing individuals would find that they could not share the food of others (given selection for reciprocal altruism, discussed in Chapter 3), and would have a very uneven food supply until they either changed their subplan or starved. Presumably, non-indulgent parents would find that their children grew up to be poor hunters and poor gatherers, since this way of life probably requires 'hedonic attention' (see chapter 5) if one is to learn enough about flora, fauna, and food acquisition techniques to be successful. So merely knowing that people 'A' get their food by foraging and hunting tells us a good deal about them. Ecological adaptation is thus a strong *constraint* on the cultures that human beings generate, because all cultural information must pass through the filter of the intra-individual system, and environment is a powerful constraint on the intra-individual system's revising, challenging, editing, and adding to the pool of cultural plans and subplans.

Ecological adaptation, by constraining selection among subplans/goals, is constraining cultural evolution. Similar constraints, and therefore somewhat similar cultures, appear in society after society that share not history but ecological adaptation. So strong is this effect that many theorists (for example, Steward, 1955; Vayda and Rappaport, 1968) see the ecological/technological factors as *determining* rather than as *constraining* culture. This viewpoint tends to hold particularly in cross-cultural survey or 'holocultural' studies (Barkow, 1967). A *constraint* emphasizes the impossible. It specifies what will not be. A *determinant* predicts what will be. Though there is little real difference between a strong constraint and a weak determinant, the term 'constraint' serves to remind us that we are not discussing mechanistic causes. Ecology constrains but does not determine culture. There is a certain tendency in anthropology and other social/behavioural sciences to equate 'determinant' with 'cause' and then to think in terms of old-fashioned mechanistic causes rather than in terms of complex systems that evolve under constraints and generate rather than 'cause' current structure.

THIS TRICHOTOMY IS PROVISIONAL

The distinction among cultural plans/subplans, goals/subgoals, and codes/subcodes, plus background mazeway data, is provisional. It serves its purpose of linking culture conceptualized as a pool of information with the information-processing characteristics of the intra-individual system (and thence to genetic evolution): but much finer distinctions may be needed in the future. We have already seen that the field of cognitive science is moving away from ideas of general learning abilities and towards domain-specific mental organs or modules. Not three or four but perhaps scores of domains of cultural information may eventually be posited, each with its specialized and evolved mechanism or processor. As Tooby and Cosmides (1989) put it:

In addition to whatever domain-general mechanisms may exist, the psyche is almost certainly comprised of a multitude of domain-specific, special-purpose adaptive mechanisms, organized into a coevolved, highly intricate architecture ... To the extent that the demands of different adaptive tasks are different in nature, and more efficiently solved using different means, psychological mechanisms will tend, over evolutionary time, to multiply in number and differentiate in procedure.

The analysis of these varied mechanisms is just beginning. Tooby and Cosmides offer visual perception and language acquisition as examples of the kind of mental organs they have in mind, and have analysed in some detail the algorithms involved in reciprocal altruism and social exchange (Cosmides and Tooby, 1989). One likely evolved psychological mechanism, to be discussed in chapter 13, involves the child's early experience 'setting' his or her future reproductive strategy. Another, to be analysed in chapter 14, is the Westermarck hypothesis of the mechanism underlying the incest taboo. As Tooby and Cosmides point out, the actual number of specific, evolved psychological mechanisms is no doubt immense. For example, it may be that the acquisition of *social norms* involves some specialized information-processing.

TESTING HYPOTHESES

If this chapter's arguments are valid, then some cultural domains should change more rapidly than others. In particular, domains clearly linked to subgoal/plans - domains such as prestige and status, economics, sexual behaviour, even marital and kinship patterns - should tend to be quite malleable. Code-derived cultural domains, however - spoken language, rituals of etiquette, pottery design, myth - should be much less labile, except when utilizing one subcode rather than another becomes a tactic in a prestige strategy (for instance, speaking a

FOCUS 7.1

TWO TYPES OF SOCIAL NORM?

Norms are part of the contents both of culture and of the mazeway. A norm is a 'should' or 'ought,' a prescriptive statement of how people expect others to behave in a particular situation. Norms refer to how one is 'supposed to' behave in a particular society, and cover most of life: what to eat and when, what to wear and where, whom to marry and how to court, what is to be condemned and what is to be praised, how to worship, and so forth.

In our own society, the norms about which we feel most strongly are frequently made into laws and their violation is 'punished' (negatively sanctioned) by the state. Other norm violations are punished more informally, perhaps by loss of social standing or reputation. People who violate norms are labelled by others as deviants, for instance, as criminals, witches, psychotics; or (if they are of sufficiently high status) as eccentrics. If I am a banker and wearing a tie to work is normative, then my failure to do so will only cost me some of my social standing and, at worst, my position. But if I violate the norm of protecting the bank's money by embezzling some, then I will be classified as a criminal and the state will provide the negative sanctions.

No sanctions are needed to keep me from eating insects or excrement. If I am an observant Jew or Moslem or Sikh, then not only are no sanctions needed to keep me from eating pork, but, should I consume some by accident, I quite likely will experience acute nausea (at the least). Some norms, in short, seem to be obligatory – their violation results in revulsion, even if the violation is unknown to others. Other norms are facultative – we follow them or fail to follow them more-or-less opportunistically, depending upon our assessment of the consequences; and we use them as aids in manipulating the behaviour of others in our own interest. Truth-telling, for example, is a facultative norm: we are expected to tell the truth even when doing so is not in our self-interest. Facultative norms are the type discussed in chapter 3, in connection with 'deception.' We may manipulate or violate them, at times, when our self-interest so dictates, but we nevertheless uphold them for others. Obligate norms are not manipulable.

From a sociobiological perspective, it could be argued that obligate norms are obligatory and not (manipulatively) facultative because their violation generally involves actual physical risk to life. Thus, those whose religion forbids eating certain foods react to these foods as if they had swallowed poison. Obligate norms are identifiable readily because the thought of their violation carries with it a physical revulsion. In contrast, the violation of facultative norms (by others) brings a sense of moral indignation. The two kinds of norms would presumably have evolved independently of one another and therefore are likely to be associated with different special processors. Their (respective) acquisition is presumably determined by different algorithms.

Obligate norms may be related to the mazeway's cognitive framework. Douglas (1966), for example, interprets the Hebrew dietary laws in Leviticus in terms of what fits into a classificatory system. Thus, the ancient Hebrews kept cattle and sheep, and for them a meat animal must therefore have cloven hooves and be a ruminant (chew its cud). Antelopes have both these attributes and therefore may be eaten. The pig has cloven hooves but is not a ruminant and therefore may not be consumed. Fish have fins and swim in the water and may be eaten. Shellfish live in the water but lack fins: they may not be eaten. One could argue that the feeling of revulsion that results from violating these injunctions is related to fitness not just in terms of poison avoidance but in terms of maintaining the integrity of the mazeway. That which violates the mazeway's classificatory system is an unpleasant challenge, to be avoided lest it render the entire system inoperative and so lower genetic fitness. Facultative norms, by contrast, may be learned as rules of behaviour but not become part of the cognitive grid through which the universe is ordered and perceived.*

The distinction between obligate and facultative norms has not yet been studied empirically and no doubt will prove controversial. It may be that, over time, some norms may pass from obligate to facultative status. But the point of this discussion of norms has been to illustrate that much work remains to be done on the trichotomy/mazeway conceptualization of intra-individual processing of cultural information. That framework no doubt will need to be enlarged as our understanding of specific psychological mechanisms increases. Eventually, the latter may replace the former. Until that time, however, the subgoals/plans/codes+mazeway approach remains a major conceptual advance over thinking of cultural information as having a single nature and being processed cognitively in a single manner.

*For a very different interpretation of religious dietary laws, see Harris (1985: 67–87), who sees food rules as reflecting ecological adaptation. Harris's views will be discussed in chapter 10.

---

higher-status language). While this hypothesis is in principle empirically verifiable, those who would attempt the verification should be aware of an apples-and-oranges comparison problem. How do we compare rates of change in dialect usage, say, or in cognitive classificatory systems, with rates of change in prestige strategies or subsistence techniques? Obviously, some equivalencies will first have to be established.

The second empirically verifiable hypothesis stemming from this discussion seems commonsensical: subplans capable of serving more than one goal should be preferred to subplans limited to serving only one goal. Presumably, genetic evolution has built this bias into us. A subplan that yields both income and prestige, for example, should be preferred over a subplan yielding either, alone. (See note 1 for further discussion.)

SUMMARY

1. This chapter focuses on the relationship between the goals, plans, and codes of the intra-individual system and the information content of culture. Cultural information occurs in many forms but my focus here is on how it is *received* by the intra-individual system. The argument made here is that this reception involves categorization of cultural information as subgoals, subplans, subcodes, and mazeway reference data.

2. The stable goals and plans and deep codes are the realm of human ethology and of the neurosciences. Subgoals/plans are the stuff of culture, and subcodes are the realm of linguistics and of 'symbolic' or 'interpretive' anthropology. With each additional 'sub' we move further along the stability/lability continuum, and the greater the lability the greater the role played by culture.

3. The various sub^ngoals/plans provided by our cultures usually serve a variety of intra-individual-system goals simultaneously. Subplans capable of serving multiple goals are the most likely to be adopted by individuals. This co-ordination and multi-tasking of subplans brings some order to our stream of behaviour.

4. Every culture has distinctive and recurring subgoals/plans that account for some of the integration of culture, a topic at times discussed under such rubrics as 'values,' 'themes,' and 'national character.' Similarly, each individual's limited selection from culturally available subgoals/plans lends a consistency to behaviour sometimes considered as part of 'personality.'

5. Cognitive anthropologists study the simple, underlying logical structures of cultural subcodes. Symbolic anthropologists are more concerned with the surface levels of subcodes, which are generally immensely complex and intricate. Subcodes are communicative structures and, like subplans, are used in the service of subgoals. Geertz's analysis of the Balinese cock-fight seems to deliberately de-emphasize the fact that, as Geertz himself suggests, for the (human) participants, the goal of prestige is what the cock-fight is all about.

6. The choice of one subcode rather than another is often a part of a subplan. This is particularly clear when the subcodes are dialects and one is of higher status than another.

7. The respective fidelities of replication of culturally transmitted subcodes, subgoals, and subplans differ in their implications for genetic fitness. Selection favours a relatively unproblematic replication of subcodes but a tendency to challenge subgoals and not only to challenge but to revise and reinvent subplans.

8. When subcodes do change it is as a result of one of three processes: (1) transmission or replication error; (2) the creation of new social groups; and (3) when use of one subcode rather than another becomes part of a prestige strategy.

9. The fact that children acquire subcodes automatically when very young but with decreasing ability as they grow older is consistent with an evolutionary scenario in which assimilation into a new culture was a relatively rare event.

10. Revitalization movements – mass conversions of the population of socially disintegrated societies into new ideologies or religions – are probably emergent phenomena stemming from widespread mazeway resynthesis. Mazeway resynthesis itself results when the mazeway is rendered highly inaccurate owing to rapid social change. It is probably related to the 'cognitive imperative' goal of having an accurate map of physical and social reality.

11. Ecological adaptation is a powerful constraint on the cultures that human beings generate because all cultural information must pass through the filter of the intra-individual system; and environment, by affecting the likelihood that subplans will succeed, partly determines how the intra-individual system revises, challenges, edits, and adds to the pool of cultural plans and subplans. So strong is this effect that many theorists see the ecological/technological factors as *determining* rather than as *constraining* culture.

12. Norms are part of the mazeway. Obligate norms are those whose violation automatically entails loss of genetic fitness. They are personally identifiable because the thought of violating them brings physical revulsion. Norms against eating insects or excrement are obligate norms. Facultative norms are of the kind discussed in chapter 3 in connection with deceit. We tend to violate and manipulate them whenever it is in our fitness interest to do so, while upholding them for others. Their violation brings a sense of moral indignation rather than physical revulsion. The distinction between obligate and facultative

norms is a new one and is presented here to illustrate how provisional the system of plans/subplans, goals/subgoals, codes/subcodes, plus mazeway, is.

13. Two testable hypotheses can be drawn from this chapter. (a) Fairly rapid change should occur in domains clearly linked to subgoals/ plans, such as prestige and status, economics, sexual behaviour, and even marital and kinship patterns. Code-derived cultural domains, however – spoken language, rituals of etiquette, pottery design, myth – should be more stable, the exception being when utilizing one subcode rather than another becomes a tactic in a prestige strategy. (b) We should have a built-in bias in favour of subplans capable of serving more than one goal rather than those limited to serving a single goal.

8

Relative Standing, Prestige, and Self-Esteem

Status, image, social class, politics, wealth, power, competition, rivalry, envy, greed, ostentation, impression-management, boastfulness, display, pride, arrogance, hubris, pretension, importance, worth, respect, honour, self-esteem, reputation: our vocabulary gives us away. Human language is cluttered with terms that have relative standing at their core. We hunger for prestige, and much of our behaviour is dominated by this goal and its varied subgoals and subplans.

The ubiquity of prestige-related behaviour makes that goal an appropriate test both for demonstrating the utility of the intra-individual-system approach presented in previous chapters and for illustrating the kind of 'vertically integrated explanation' discussed in chapter 1.

OUTLINE OF THIS CHAPTER

Human self-esteem and prestige seem to be largely symbolic in nature. In order to link that symbolic prestige with the evolutionary framework developed in earlier chapters, this chapter begins with a discussion of the selection pressures leading to dominance hierarchies. It then moves on to suggest that human prestige striving apparently evolved from (is homologous with) the general primate tendency towards social hierarchy. It touches at the physiological aspects of dominance with a

1 The general framework of this chapter is based on my 1975 article 'Prestige and Culture,' and on my chapter 'Prestige and Self-Esteem: A Biosocial Interpretation' (1980c).

presentation of research findings relating whole-blood serotonin level in vervet monkeys to relative status. Along the way, it reviews the argument and evidence for the proposition (predicted by evolutionary theory) that high rank should be associated with high reproductive success among primates (there is some lack of clarity in the data supporting this assertion, as we will see).

Human prestige is not quite the same as primate social hierarchy, for it is symbolic in nature. At some point in our evolution, hominid-line males began to provide parental investment to offspring. As a result, I will be revisiting the argument (first introduced in chapter 6) that selection is likely to have favoured females who preferred mates high not just in agonistic dominance but also in the subsistence-related skills and abilities necessary to produce investment. For such high-invest-ment-producing males, too, high-ability females would have been a scarce resource when they were seeking long-term (rather than short-term) mates. Thus, if this argument is accurate, sexual selection would have favoured both males and females competing intra-sexually not just in terms of primate-type, agonistic dominance but in terms of ability to produce resources and the displays indicating such ability. Sexual selection would therefore have resulted in selection for skills. Sexual selection, I will be suggesting, is largely responsible for transforming a primate tendency closely tied to capacity for physical violence into human culturally ordered, symbolic prestige systems. This transforma-tion may be recapitulated by children, who move from agonism to more symbolic social ranking.

Prestige can be symbolic because, in terms of the intra-individual system, it involves an ongoing comparison of the self-representation with the representations of others. The goal-state of prestige is maintained when the self-representation is ranked higher than the representations of others in one's social group or category. But *which* group or category? Each potential group/category has associated with it a set of criteria for the allocation of prestige. A universal subplan causes us to tend to emphasize the group/category – the social identity – in terms of whose prestige-allocation criteria we happen to do best. Because the criteria of prestige are symbolic and the evaluation internal, and ordinarily remote from the agonistic status-determining interac-tions of non-human primates, we can speak of the transformation of primate social dominance into human self-esteem. We use various cognitive distortions – what some term 'defence mechanisms' – to maintain self-esteem, that is, to maintain an evaluation of self as superior to at least some others.

The symbolic nature of human prestige ranking has meant that this single goal can have in its service a multiplicity of culturally ordered subgoals. The subplans associated with these subgoals involve activities that, among other things, generate our economic and political behaviours. This, then, summarizes the key ideas of this chapter. The next chapter will apply the framework to three ethnographic case studies.

DOMINANCE AND AGGRESSION

The cost-benefit mathematics of biological evolution are at the root of social hierarchy. Whatever resource I need is also needed by members of my own species, that is, by my *conspecifics*. We compete for food, for mates, and for nesting sites: but only rarely will it be in my fitness interests to attempt to destroy a conspecific. This is because competition that involves risk of physical injury or death may lower the frequency of my genes in the gene-pool in two ways. The first of these is obvious: it may remove me and the set of my genes that I carry, since my rival might win a violent competition. But the conspecifics with whom I compete are quite likely to be not just fellow members of my species but my kin as well. Damage to my competitor therefore removes whatever proportion of my genes this individual and I share, thus reducing my inclusive fitness (as was discussed in chapter 3). These potential costs devalue whatever genetic benefits successful competition might bring.

Under these circumstances, selection will favour our determining as efficiently as possible, with as little injury or risk of injury as possible, which of us would be most likely to win a physically violent encounter. The probable loser should then withdraw. Selection will also favour our using deceit – perhaps by raising our mantle of fur in order to look larger, or whatever – in order to win. The possibility of deceit, however, also means selection in favour of our being able to evaluate accurately in spite of such deceit. The result of these various selection pressures is that the expression of much intra-specific aggression among animal species has been *ritualized*, that is, the aggressive encounters involve stylized and conspicuous displays and threats but relatively little actual physical injury or death (Eibl-Eibesfeldt, 1975; Lorenz, 1965; Bastock, Morris, and Moynihan, 1953).

Suppose, however, that my conspecific rival and I often find ourselves together in a competitive situation. This will be the case if, for example, our ecology is one of 'clumped' resources, so that we may frequently feed together; or perhaps predator pressure has favoured our assembling in large groups for defence. In such circumstances of prolonged sociality, selection will not favour our continually repeating our initial encounter; rather, it will favour individual recognition of conspecifics plus a good memory. Thus, once our relative standing has been established, further agonistic (threat/aggressive) encounters will be necessary only if one of us tries to alter our relationship (Eibl-Eibesfeldt, 1975).

But this is not just *our* relationship – every dyad in our social group has a similar one. The results can approximate a linear hierarchy, as sometimes happens with domestic chickens. Indeed, the phenomenon was first studied in a barnyard by Schjelderup-Ebbe (1935), who noted that at the top of the hierarchy was a chicken who pecked all but was pecked in turn by none, followed by a hen who pecked all but the most dominant (or 'alpha') bird, who was the only one who could peck her; and so on, until at the bottom was poor omega hen, pecked by all but able to peck none. As every farmer knows, put a new hen in the yard and she will automatically be treated as the new omega and perhaps pecked to death unless she can quickly win some encounters and establish a position in the hierarchy. Of course, sometimes a hen has an 'off day' and loses an encounter to a hen who is subordinate to one that today's loser is dominant to, resulting in an imperfectly linear hierarchy; but the principle remains.

Primate dominance hierarchies are far more complex than are those of hens.[2] Old World monkeys and apes tend to be organized in 'female bonded' groups whose existence Wrangham (1980, 1983) explains in part as a product of the distribution of food supply, in part as due to the advantage of having the support of kin in one's competition with others for food. Males, argues Wrangham, are organized around females, females around the food supply. In many species (such as, rhesus macaques), a troop's composite matrilines are themselves ranked, and to a considerable extent social rank is hereditary (not through genetics but through the pattern of early interaction established between young members of powerful matrilines with members of less powerful groups [Hinde, 1983]). Dominant individuals often intervene in agonistic encounters between two lower-ranking individuals, while alliances and coalitions are frequently found, probably in part involving kin selection and reciprocal altruism (see Cheney, 1983: 278, for references). Goodall (1986), in her long-term study of the Gombe chimpanzees, finds that the alpha males are not the largest or the most aggressive but instead excel

2 Seyfarth (1981) provides a useful discussion of the complexities of the concept of dominance in primate studies.

in other areas, such as social manipulation. Finally, as we have seen in discussing Chance's (1967) concept of *attention structure*, for some species (such as the chimpanzee), agonistic encounters may often be so muted that the structure of relative standing may at times usefully be thought of as a matter of who *attends* to whom.[3]

Non-human primate dominance thus does not reduce to any simple agonistic 'pecking order.' But it retains agonism at its core: not agonism alone, but still agonism, and in this, I will argue, it differs from human prestige. Selection transformed agonistic primate dominance into human symbolic prestige. Before we can analyse how this may have happened, however, we must first branch to a brief discussion of the neurophysiological correlates of dominance.

NEUROPHYSIOLOGY

Rather than attempting to review the entire literature on dominance and biochemistry, I will limit the discussion to a single species about which, in a complex and still rather murky field, we have some unambiguous findings. As we will see, it is now clear that whole-blood serotonin level reflects social position in male vervet monkeys.

A number of studies (for example, Rose, Gordon, and Bernstein, 1972 and 1975) have sought to find an association between dominance and some physiological factor, usually testosterone level, but with often ambiguous results. Raleigh et al. (1984) concentrated on whole-blood serotonin level in vervet monkeys. Serotonin is a chemical associated with the platelets of the blood and is possibly involved in some forms of mental illness. Vervets are a species of Old World monkey and are widely distributed throughout sub-Saharan Africa. The dominant male, among vervets, copulates more often than do lower-ranking males and has preferential access to food suplies and sleeping places (McGuire and Raleigh, 1985: 458–9).

Raleigh et al. began by studying the relationship between serotonin level and spontaneous changes in dominance in captive male vervets. (Or perhaps 'semi-captive,' given the research setting). They went on to manipulate relative status by: (1) temporarily removing dominant males so that previously subordinate males could for a time occupy the alpha position; (2) placing the removed former dominants together in small

---

3 Hinde (1983: 179) suggests the possibility that 'the characteristics of individuals that attract attention are just those that are indicative of aggressive potentiality.' This observation merits treatment as a testable hypothesis.

groups so that they could form new hierarchies; and (3) isolating dominant males so that they could see their former groups through a one-way mirror but not be seen by them. In all cases, the whole-blood concentration of serotonin was high in dominant animals, fell sharply when they ceased to be dominant or were isolated behind the one-way mirrors, and rose when they became dominant either once again or for the first time. These results were the same for both spontaneous and experimenter-induced dominance changes. McGuire and Raleigh (1985: 459–60) postulate that the following 'behavioral mechanisms' underlie their findings:

a) A dominant male threatens a subordinate male; b) this agonistic behavior is associated with a specific cognitive-physiological state; c) if the subordinate male submits, a cognitive-physiological event occurs (e.g., hormone release) which contributes to maintaining elevated whole blood serotonin levels; and d) if the subordinate male does not submit, the cognitive-physiological event does not occur and whole blood serotonin levels begin to drop ...

McGuire and Raleigh (1985, 1987) emphasize the relationship between *cognition* and physiological response, thereby linking together (in good, vertically integrated fashion) hormones and psychological processes.

In a related study, McGuire, Raleigh, and Brammer (1984) studied dominance and basal cortisol level in vervets. Cortisol level is usually interpreted as a measure of stress. The authors found no consistent relationship between basal cortisol level and social rank: what they did find was that the level would rise in males in the process of gaining dominance. This was also true of formerly dominant males during the period when they were regaining their rank, that rank having been lost because the experimenters had removed them from their respective groups. One implication of these findings, the authors suggest, is that gaining dominance involves stress and is therefore 'costly' in physiological terms, a fact which may have evolutionary implications.

These researchers are not claiming that we now understand the physiology of dominance, or even the role serotonin or cortisol play in it. But, assuming that human beings are not totally dissimilar from vervet monkeys, we do now know that there *is* a complex physiology involved, as chapter 4's rejection of the 'mind-body split' would lead us to expect.

The vervet data are fascinating but limited because they *are* vervet data, and only on male vervets at that. Yet, the implications are impressive. For example, perhaps we may eventually end the problems of measuring dominance (discussed below) in non-human primates by using a biochemical assay. Perhaps, for human beings, we will find that the advantages of high social class are not merely material but also neurophysiological, and that the differences between officers and enlisted men, rulers and ruled, the successful and the failed, are biological (though not necessarily genetic). One can envisage research on drugs designed to raise self-esteem. Perhaps lack of 'ambition' will turn out to have a biochemical basis. All this is premature conjecture: at present, as far as our own species is concerned, we are justified only in saying that it is likely that status in human beings has neurophysiological concomitants.

THE TRANSITION FROM PRIMATE DOMINANCE
TO HUMAN SELF-ESTEEM

We retain much of the non-verbal communication of dominance of our non-human primate kin. For example, staring is a threat gesture we share with other primates, gaze aversion a shared form of ritualized appeasement. Make direct eye contact with a monkey or ape in a zoo: your cousin may gaze-avert but is equally likely to threaten you in response.[4] From Charles Darwin (1872) onward, human beings familiar with chimpanzees have found that much non-verbal communication – playfulness, fear, threat, laughter – is sufficiently similar to be readily communicated across species lines. But in spite of non-verbal commonalities and continuities, there is a profound difference between human self-esteem and prestige, on the one hand, and primate social dominance, on the other.

Agonism is at the root of dominance interactions among non-human primates: threat, the possibility of violence, or the memory of past threat and violence. This may be true of human children as well, but it is *not* true for most adult human relationships in most cultures.[5] When we do engage in agonistic encounters these tend to be culturally ritualized, as

4 I once performed this experiment at the London Zoo, with a barbary macaque. The animal stared back at me for an instant and then sprang directly at me. The glass between us stopped it but not before I flinched, a typical primate fear response.

5 Of course, agonism often lurks in the background, as witness the frequency with which spouse and child abuse and intimidation occur in our own society. Some cultures place a much greater stress on physical threat than does our own, the Yanomamö being a well-known example (Chagnon, 1974). Please note, as well, that one should not reduce the complexities and varieties of non-human primate social hierarchy to nothing but agonism. This statement is particularly true of our close relative the chimpanzee, a species that may also have some symbolic forms of dominance.

in our own society's organized athletics. The encounters involve display rather than efforts to kill and maim and are bounded by rules. Every society provides for retaliation against those who resort to (non-ritualized) violence, and in large-scale societies part of the definition of the state is its monopoly of such retaliation. Only in time of social disintegration, when polities cease to function and mazeways become inoperative, do adult human beings tend to retreat to status based primarily on the ability to offer physical violence to another. Human relative standing, ordinarily, is symbolic in nature.

It seems likely to me that *this transformation of primate dominance based ultimately on agonism to human prestige based on symbols has been primarily the result of sexual selection.*[6] Human males and females would have selected each other not just for agonistic dominance but for excellence – the ability to excel – in many spheres, spheres ultimately related to the capacity to provide parental investment. The process begins with the link between dominance and reproductive success.

Dominance, Reproductive Success, and the Provision of Resources
Discussions of sexual selection usually stress male-male competition and *female* choice of male. I will begin in this traditional manner for the sake of clarity, before moving on to the roles that *male* choice of *females* and female-female competition are likely to have played in the evolution of the human prestige goal.

As we saw in chapter 3, sexual selection may involve physical competition among males for females, with the more dominant individuals displacing lower-ranking males. But this *intrasexual* selection probably has not been as important, in human evolution, as was *epigamic* (mate choice) sexual selection, selection involving choice of mate on the basis of differences in attractiveness (the terms are those of Huxley, 1938). It is epigamic selection – selectivity in mate choice – that must have been involved in the transformation of primate dominance into human symbolic prestige.

There are three qualities that selection would have favoured proto-hominid females preferring in males. First, so long as there was any element of the 'brawn' sexual selection of male-male competition involved at all, females would have preferred physically superior males simply because their offspring, all things being equal, would have been likely to have greater reproductive success than the less 'brawny' males.

6 Chapter 13 will present Sue T. Parker's (1987) sexual-selection scenario for human evolution, and we will see how this process of transformation may have begun.

Second, of greater importance for human evolution, females would have preferred males willing to invest in offspring. This topic has been touched on in chapter 3 and will be discussed at some length in chapter 13. But for understanding the evolution of human prestige it is the third component of protohominid female mate choice that is the most important, preference for male *ability* to invest in offspring.

Given a growing readiness in protohominid males to pair with females and invest in their joint offspring, selection would have favoured those females able to choose as partners the males best able to so invest. *But what qualities determine a male's capacity for parental investment?* The answer depends on the nature of his society's economy. For our early ancestors, the relevant abilities presumably involved skill in scavenging, hunting, gathering, collecting and bringing back such resources, tool-making, and perhaps the ability to select a safe home base or 'camp.' What makes for such skills in a species moving from a protoculture to a culture? The answer is in large measure the host of cognitive abilities that permit social transmission of information. We have already discussed this topic in chapter 6 (under the heading 'Sexual Selection'), where it was assumed that 'among our protocultural ancestors, those males best able to learn and to transmit protocultural information tended to be the most able to provide parental investment and also the highest in status. That is, high male status, high cultural capacity, and high attractiveness for females tended to go together at a very early stage, perhaps from the very point at which males first began to invest parentally in their offspring.'

Why would high status and high ability/cultural capacity have 'tended to go together'? Selection would have favoured females who preferred not just males with high agonistic rank but males with high investment ability. It would also have favoured males who, finding themselves unsuccessful in competing in agonistic dominance, instead emphasized the procurement of resources. An alternative path to reproductive success was now opened for males, one involving not agonistic competition but competition for resources and in the tool skills associated with resource competition (cf. Alexander and Noonan, 1979: 453n). The more important male parental investment became, the more selection would have favoured females who preferred the most skilled and capable males and therefore the more males would have competed with one another *in terms of skills and abilities*. Primate agonistic dominance would have gradually broadened into the modern multiple-criteria sets of human prestige.

It is in the inclusive-fitness interests of males that their female kin pair with prestigious, resource-controlling males. Let us assume that a given male has at least some influence on his female relatives' choice of mate. If this is the case then it will be in his (inclusive) fitness interests to find prestigious the same resource-producing/controlling qualities in other males that females find attractive. It will also be in his fitness interests to entertain such males as possible allies or reciprocity partners, since they would be more valuable than are those who control no resources; and it would be in his interests to learn from such males (cf. Boyd and Richerson, 1985: 243). Thus, if sexual selection means that females should find a given trait preferable, so too should their male kin. Both men and women should find it easy to like, admire, and defer to those who demonstrate greater ability to control resources.

This scenario does appear to be what we find, even when the deference and liking are definitely not in our fitness interests and have no social legitimacy. Thus, hostages often speak well of their kidnappers, victims of airline hijackings well of their captors. Horribly, concentration-camp inmates were reported to ape their guards in manner and dress, and Solzhenitsyn makes the same observation for the inmates of the Siberian gulag (see Barkow [1976a] for discussion). We quite automatically tend to admire and imitate those who have power over us, a phenomenon Anna Freud (1946) termed 'turning against the self.'

SOCIAL IDENTITY AND SKILL CATEGORY

Multiple prestige criteria gave rise (at least in part) to the possibility of choice of social identity. A man might now compete with other men not just in terms of being the best hunter but, say, in terms of being the best butcher, or maker of tools, or best tracker, or best maker of snares. Colin Irwin, who has lived with Inuit in northern Canada for many years, describes (in a 1986 personal communication) just such a multiplicity of paths to prestige as characterizing these contemporary hunter-gatherers.

For our ancestors, the cognitive map of the local group was thus split into categories according to type of expertise, with the individual paying special attention to those with expertise comparable to his own (and to her own as well, as we will see shortly), and with whom he was therefore competing. Skill categories would have become cognitively comparable to ethnic categories, with the difference that while an individual is usually a member of only one ethnic group, he or she can be classified (in varying relative positions) in a number of skill groups. In order for one male to establish a relationship with another male, it became necessary to convey to that male – and to any observing females – what criteria for prestige-allocation one was attempting to meet, that is, what one was competing in, what social identity was now relevant. *The participants had in effect to negotiate an agreement as to the name of the game, and there were now a variety of games available, with agonism reduced to the game of last resort.* Communicating to others one's preferred game – the category and therefore set of status-allocation criteria one wished to be evaluated in terms of – may have been the origins of *social identity* and the preoccupation with conveying that identity which Goffman (1959) has described so well.

Within a single social-identity/skill area, men would have competed in terms of a shared set of evaluation criteria. But the available identities would themselves have been ranked, since some skills are more vital to subsistence than are others. Given the advantages of self-deception, however, each individual would tend to rank his own skill area as being of higher standing than other skill areas. We know from the work of human ethologists (Omark, Strayer, and Freedman, 1980) that children tend to rank themselves higher than they are ranked by other children;[7] I expect that adults would tend to rank their own social-identity/skill areas as higher in relative standing than others would rank them. (Note that this 'expectation' is a testable hypothesis.)

Selection for cultural capacity involved a transformation of male-male competition, which would have moved from agonistic rivalry to competition in the ability to invest in offspring, that is, the ability to produce resources. This means that, increasingly, competition involved socially learned, culturally transmitted skills and symbols of those skills. Evaluation would have grown ever more remote from agonism and become largely a product of complex cognitive processing, a transformation facilitating self-deception and related cognitive distortions.

MALES SELECTING FEMALES

Thus far the emphasis has been on male-male competition and on females selecting males. But females also compete among themselves

7 Their data are from several different cultures, and hence convincing. Human ethological data from single cultures can never be more than suggestive. The human sociobiological literature is replete with generalizations about human behaviour based only on the researchers' own culture.

and males, too, choose among females.[8] Female-female competition would have been quite similar to male-male competition, and male preferences for females would have been in many ways similar to female preferences for males.

At first glance, this statement appears to contradict the emphasis in the human-sociobiology literature on males being relatively unselective in sexual matters but on females being discriminating. Females, after all, are the scarce resource for males, for with each copulation a female risks a sizeable portion of her total reproductive potential but a male risks a vanishingly small portion of his. Thus, as the argument (presented in chapter 3) goes, females should be quite selective in mate choice, males relatively promiscuous. And so human males and females are, for *short-term* relationships.

But this analysis pays little attention to paternal investment in offspring. *The more important we assume male parental investment to have been for male reproductive success, in the course of hominid evolution, the more selective males should be in choosing long-term partners* (cf. Burley, 1977). Note the distinction here between short-term relationships involving copulation, but little male investment, and long-term relationships involving substantial male investment. Human males, as Symons (1979) and others have argued, have been selected to seek out short-term, relatively unselective relationships much more strongly than have females. But if paternal investment strongly increased the probability of the survival of offspring, then, since any given male is limited in the amount of parental investment he can provide, a male should reserve that investment for females who can supply not just confidence of paternity (discussed in chapter 3), but who are also themselves able to invest substantially in offspring; otherwise the male is likely to 'waste' his limited ability to invest on a female who contributes relatively little to their joint offspring. For males seeking a long-term relationship, high-investment-providing females are a scarce resource.

Which females are best able to invest parentally? Why, the females with the most skill and competence in subsistence activities. Which female should a male's kin prefer he pair with? Why, a female with a reputation for skill in subsistence activities. Females competing for mates, then, should compete with one another in terms of such abilities. As with males, the more we were selected for cultural capacity, the more these subsistence abilities became cultural in nature. Prestige criteria among males and females would therefore have been quite similar in

---

8 There is considerable evidence for fertility differentials and competition among non-human primate females. See Hrdy (1981) for references and discussion.

that both would in part be based on the culturally defined ability to provide resources for parental investment. Similar does not mean identical, since male prestige still includes more elements of agonistic dominance than does its female equivalent, and female prestige more elements of youth and ability to provide paternity certainty. But both sexes should value skill and control of resources when seeking a long-term relationship.

SELF-ESTEEM

Assessment of relative standing is always an internal process in any species, since it involves a comparison of the intra-individual system's internal representation of the organism itself with its representations of others. In many species, the criteria for the evaluation of relative standing largely have to do with agonism and the probability of success in agonistic encounters. When multiple criteria for the evaluation of relative standing are involved, however, the process grows more complex. For example, each member of a dyad may rank himself or herself higher than the other because each is using a different set of evaluation criteria. Self-evaluation is no longer tied to agonism and social dominance is no longer an appropriate term: now we must speak of maintaining *self-esteem*, of continually evaluating the self as being higher than at least some others, in terms of some set of evaluation criteria. Perhaps the prestige goal should be termed the self-esteem goal; but as we will see, seeking prestige remains the major subgoal in the pursuit of self-esteem.

Strategies for Self-Esteem[9]
Both human self-esteem and primate social rank involve the evaluation of relative standing. For primate social rank, the evaluation depends upon agonistic interaction with physically present others. But with human self-esteem, as we will see, those others not only need not be physically present, they need not have physical existence! This is because the evaluation that results in self-esteem is symbolic in nature, involving the application of criteria for the allocation of prestige. We need no longer compare ourselves directly with other flint knappers, for example, but rather assess ourselves (and be assessed by others) in terms of abstract criteria having to do with how well we knap flint.

9 For a thorough treatment of the concept of self-esteem and its measurement, see Wells and Marwell (1976).

Strategies for self-esteem involve just two fundamental parameters, each with two possible values. Self-esteem may be sought by the individual as an individual, or else as a member of a prestigious group or category. In either case, those who provide the standards of evaluation and potential approbation may be actually or potentially physically present, or else they may be permanently absent.

It will be useful here to distinguish between a membership group – a self-defined group of people who are in communication with one another (usually by physically meeting); and a reference group, the group in terms of which the individual evaluates his or her own relative standing. The reference group provides criteria for the evaluation of self and others. Often, of course, membership and reference group are the same, but they need not be. Criteria for the evaluation of relative standing in all cases are largely symbolic and only occasionally tied to agonism, as we have seen; and with the exception of those pan-primate aspects of non-verbal communication mentioned above, there is much culturally determined variation in the expression of both high and low standing.

In the simplest case, the individual's self-esteem strategy involves receiving the respect and deference of those physically around him or her, using the same criteria for prestige allocation that they do. In short, membership and reference groups are here the same and consist of those physically or communicationally present. This strategy is of course that of non-human as well as human primates, but in the latter case the prestige criteria need not involve agonism. Some individuals are highly dependent on this fundamental means of maintaining self-esteem and we are likely to label such people 'conformist': their sense of worth depends heavily on those with whom they daily interact.

Others of us maintain our self-esteem primarily through reference groups that are not physically present and that, indeed, may have no objective existence at all. For example, early socialization may have caused us to include in our mazeway a powerful reference group called 'ancestors,' among whom we hope eventually to be numbered and whom we perceive as constantly evaluating our behaviour in terms of 'their' criteria. Alternatively, the group may be termed 'spirits,' 'angels,' or 'gods.' Individuals who depend heavily on such physically absent reference groups may often be considered 'independent' or 'autonomous' or 'non-conformist' by others. They may maintain self-esteem in terms of prestige-allocation criteria quite different from that of their membership groups, at times even in the face of the strong disapprobation of these groups. In effect, physically absent reference groups

TABLE 2
Sources of self-esteem

	Present	Absent
Individual *strategy*	Membership groups (including kin)	Internalized others Gods and spirits Reference groups Ancestors
Collective *strategy*	Other groups (including kin)	Other groups

represent a means by which parents and other socializing agents may 'install' an enduring form of social control in the young.

For many people (and peoples), self-esteem is not sought primarily on an individual basis but as part of a group. We saw in chapter 4 that the scope of the self-representation is 'culturally constituted' and quite variable. In some cultures, early socialization results in the boundaries between self and group being vague and to some extent even coterminous. Self-esteem is maintained by membership in the group, and the goal of enhancing relative standing takes the form of striving to enhance the relative standing of the group vis-à-vis other groups. The group in question is most often a kin group; for China and Japan, argues Hsu (1971), it is the extended family. At least in the case of Japan, the self-definition may be transferred to include a larger unit, such as a nation-state or an industrial corporation. In North America and western Europe, socialization seems to produce people who seek self-esteem and prestige primarily through individual rather than group-oriented strategies. In group-oriented strategies, members of rival groups (nations, families, corporations) usually can be, at least at times, physically present. When such presence is generally lacking, rival groups are likely to be grossly misperceived. Table 2 provides a simple summary of this discussion.

No individual follows only one self-esteem strategy. Most of us belong to a number of groups, some with physical existence and some without, and the relevance of these various groups alters with our current situation and life-state. One moment I may be seeking self-esteem by communicating to all that I am a member of a prestigious group, that of the officer corps of our nation's army. Another moment I may be playing tennis with a subgoal of demonstrating to my opponent and to any onlookers that I am physically fit and coordinated, high in athletic ability; a missed serve and I may be proudly evaluating myself as a member of the respected social category, the 'good losers.' If I am a Japanese industrialist whose sense of self includes the Mitsubishi corporation, while striving to further its interests I am thereby simultaneously winning the respect and approbation of my fellow employees, so that I am at once necessarily pursuing both group-oriented and individual-oriented prestige strategies.

PRESTIGE AND ECONOMICS

It is this lability and multiplexity of prestige strategies that makes our economies work. People do engage in economic activity in order to garner the resources needed for subsistence and comfort; but beyond a rather bare subsistence level, our work involves subgoals/plans derived from the prestige/self-esteem goal. The relative importance of the goals of prestige and subsistence varies with the individual and the economic system. For the San hunters of Botswana, for example, Lee (1979) argues that the !Kung San hunt and gather enough rather than as much as possible. Given a norm of generalized reciprocity, so that sharing is widespread, it is not hunger per se that drives people to forage; to a considerable extent it is social pressure, that is, a desire for the respect and approbation of the members of one's group: prestige, in short.

Economic systems, when they work, harness our motivation for prestige. They can do so because we were selected to give respect to those who excel in control of power, resources, and – most germane in this case – subsistence skills. In hunting-gathering societies, men gain prestige through hunting (though not exclusively so, as we have seen); in agricultural societies, through farming. I have watched young Hausa men compete in hoeing contests and in the quality of their crops, their ambition channelled into subsistence because this channelling yields respect and prestige (and, not to oversimplify, funds needed for bride-wealth). In our own society, unemployment is often described as psychologically devastating because so many of us maintain our self-esteem (our internal assessment of our relative standing vis-à-vis reference and membership groups) and social identity in terms of our work. But it is doubtful that we are unique in withholding respect from those who can neither produce investment nor control the resources needed for investment. As the old southern Appalachian folk-song has it, 'a healthy young man who won't grow corn is the laziest man that's ever been born': we withhold esteem from the non-productive or they withhold it from themselves. I would suggest that in few societies are men or women who combine lack of productivity with lack of control of existing resources respected. (This is a testable hypothesis. Note that the warrior or soldier is an exception, here, because a soldier's prestige is related to agonism rather than to production. Elites, however, are not an exception, since while they do not necessarily produce resources they do control them.)

Surplus production equals prestige. This is a basic equation in sociobiological economics. It is also a fundamental tenet of the field of economic anthropology, particularly when systems of redistribution are discussed. Redistribution involves flows of wealth to a central figure (in New Guinea, the 'Big Man'), who in turn ostentatiously redistributes it in exchange for prestige. This system should incite the envy of economists concerned with the international balance of payments, for it automatically balances itself. One cannot exhaust the 'foreign exchange' of deference to the redistributor of goods.

The Pacific Northwest Coast and its potlatches provide one of the clearest examples of the equivalence of goods and prestige. Goods were amassed in order to be redistributed or destroyed in extravagant ceremonies termed 'potlatches.' The greater the amount of goods disposed of the more the chief and his followers holding them gained in prestige, at the expense of rival groups. Piddocke (1969) argues that potlatching functioned, in pre-contact times, to promote the production of surpluses that met the needs of occasional localized famines. While it is possible that potlatching did have this effect (or side-effect), Piddocke himself agrees that the conscious motive of a potlatching chief was always that of gaining prestige.

In our own industrial societies, charities provide the wealthy with the equivalent of a non-destructive potlatch. What do our wealthy do with their surplus wealth? They exchange it for prestige. They do so through charitable acts, such as endowments to hospitals and universities. Once again, redistribution of surplus goods equals prestige. Why, though, do the wealthy persist in accumulating such wealth in the first place, wealth often far beyond not merely their own needs but the needs of their children's children's children? The answer to this question requires a discussion of social identity.

IDENTITY AND CRITERIA FOR THE ALLOCATION OF PRESTIGE

We have already seen that, evolutionarily, social identity has much to do with the set of prestige-allocation criteria applicable to one. This topic merits further discussion: after all, who are you? In answering this question, you are telling me the name of the social unit whose criteria for the allocation of relative standing you use in evaluating yourself.

The amasser of incredible wealth does not compare himself or herself to a leper or to a university professor but to those who also have immense wealth and power. What does a billionaire need a second billion for? Why, to be of higher rank than a fellow billionaire who only has a single billion. Prestige and self-esteem are tightly tied to one's reference (comparison) group, a group that may or may not be the same as one's membership group (that is, the group to which one actually belongs).

The tendency to evaluate oneself not in terms of 'objective criteria' but in terms of the standards of a reference group was termed by David Aberle (1966: 322–9) *relative deprivation*. As he defined it, the term refers to 'a negative discrepancy between legitimate expectation and actuality, or between legitimate expectation and anticipated actuality, or both' (p. 323). The billionaire may indeed feel deprived because there are members of his or her group with more than one billion, and his 'legitimate expectation' was to at least equal them. But the peasant may not feel deprived compared to the lord so long as the peasant continues to think of the aristocrat as a member of another species, as a different kind of animal with whom comparisons may not be made. When such *encapsulation* of social groups takes place, *envy* is prevented (Aberle, ibid.; Barkow, 1975a). Encapsulation prevents comparison and there can be no envy without comparison, without a sense of essential similarity.[10]

Closely linked to envy-preventing encapsulation is *social distance*. The term refers to the effort of members of a group or category to avoid intimacy with those to whom they believe themselves superior. Typically, language implying equality is avoided, distinctions of accent, dress, deportment, and demeanour are cultivated, and the claimed 'higher' group strives to avoid being seen by members of the public in states that would emphasize their shared humanity, particularly states involving the display of strong emotion. Social distance serves to promote encapsulation and thus to persuade the less powerful to find comparison with the privileged unthinkable.

The English-language term 'honour' has to do with claimed member-

---

10 For a superb discussion of the cross-cultural ubiquity of envy, see Foster (1972). See, too, the discussion of envy and social engineering in chapter 15.

ship in a presumed-to-be-respected group or category. One has honour not in a vacuum but in the context of a claimed group membership or category inclusion: one may have honour as a chef, or honour as a man, or honour as a dentist, or whatever, provided one believes chefs or males or dentists to be respected social groups and one's social identity to be based on inclusion in the category. When the category is an occupational group we sometimes use the term 'professional pride' to connote honour but that phrase, too, conveys the idea that one is somehow *worthy* of membership in a prestigious group. When an obstetrician is criticized for performing unnecessary Caesarian sections, for example, his or her strong reaction is that of insulted honour, for his/her worthiness to be a member of a powerful and highly prestigious social group, that of the medical specialist, has been put in question.[11]

In small-scale societies, the choice of reference groups and associated prestige criteria is limited. For example, a woman may find her primary social identity involved with child-bearing and child-rearing, because in these often high infant- and child-mortality societies, these occupations are not only prestigious but nearly the only ones open to her. Among rural Hausa in northern Nigeria, for example, until the advent of modern opportunities a barren woman had only two potential ways to seek prestige, one through small-scale trading, the other through joining the spirit-possession (*bori*) association and becoming a type of healer/supernatural practitioner (Barkow, 1971, 1972).

The vast scale and complexity of modern industrial societies permit myriad potential physical and symbolic/categorical groupings and attendant prestige criteria. When coupled with our cognitive-distortion tendencies, members of these societies have a wide range of potential social identities or self-definitions, and therefore of ways of evaluating the self so as to judge it as higher than at least some others. This very wealth of choice presents problems, however.

Erik Erikson (1959) and others have noted that one of the 'tasks' of adolescence is the development of a stable sense of identity, of just who one is. In small-scale, stable cultures, identity is clear and, often enough, formal and public ceremonies (rites of passage) advertise to all what one's group affiliation is and which set of criteria for the evaluation of relative standing now applies. In contemporary Western society, however, a young person usually has to *make* choices of identity, choices of the set of prestige-allocation criteria to apply to him/herself. These

11 This discussion is based on Barkow (1975a: 556).

identity choices include those of social group or 'clique,' occupation, and (often) political and religious affiliation. The result can be an identity 'crisis,' a crisis caused by having to select, on the basis of uncertain knowledge, among a multitude of possibilities.

Our folk wisdom speaks of the young person 'discovering' who he or she really is, much as the sculptor may 'discover' the figure nascent in the stone. In terms of the present theoretical framework, however, the adolescent is actually seeking to determine which social and categorical, physically present and physically absent groups will accept him or her, and whether he or she wishes to be accepted by them. Presumably, there is a weighing of how high the group or category itself is vis-à-vis others, versus how high one is likely to rise within the group or category, a size-of-puddle vs. size-of-frog calculation.[12]

We split our society into an endless number of social circles and categories, each of which has its own criteria for the allocation of prestige. Birdsall (1968) has argued that our Pleistocene ancestors probably tended to live in same-dialect tribes of about five hundred, composed of local bands of about twenty-five. Though there is considerable variation, those hunter-gatherer groups of which we have direct knowledge have indeed tended to be organized in units of these sizes. We seem to continue to live in such small units, but today they are symbolically delineated. In a large city, group members share particular loci (restaurants, bars, 'turf') where they may congregate; they may share symbols of identity – clothing, hairstyles – and criteria for the evaluation of relative standing, such as speaking French, owning or not owning designer jeans, watching or not watching television. Even beyond adolescence, we may spend much time experimenting with membership in one group or another; or, finding ourselves failing to achieve high standing in terms of one category's criteria, redefine ourselves as members of another category (a transition sometimes labelled a 'life crisis').

If there are so many potential groups in terms of whose prestige-evaluation criteria one may evaluate oneself, why is self-esteem so common a problem in our society? Perhaps early experience in some way 'sets' the self-esteem level to which one aspires, and some of us have it set very low. Perhaps the very multiplicity of criteria means that

12 Presumably, an evolved specialized processor is operating, using an algorithm for weighing the relative status of a group vis-à-vis other groups, versus relative standing the individual is likely to obtain within each group. The result should be a trade-off between the size of the frog and the size of the puddle.

those without a very clear and definite social identity are unable to evaluate themselves in any consistent manner. But a detailed theory of self-esteem and socialization is beyond the scope of this work.

DOMINANCE, DEVELOPMENT, AND HUMAN ETHOLOGY

We have discussed how primate agonistic social dominance may have evolved into human culturally ordered and symbolically evaluated self-esteem/prestige. But how, developmentally, in each child, does this transformation occur? The hypothesis I will present is of the ontogeny-recapitulating-phylogeny variety. Dominance behaviour in the child begins agonistically, but over time grows increasingly symbolic in nature, gradually becoming a matter of culturally provided prestige subplans and subgoals and of self-esteem. The agonistic element never entirely disappears, however, and in some cultures (such as, the Yanomamö) may continue to be of major importance.

We have no developmental studies of the transformation of dominance in children and adults to prestige hierarchies in adults. Indeed, with the exception of Weisfeld, Omark, and Cronin (1980), we have almost no longitudinal, developmental studies of dominance at all. The field of human ethology, however, does provide us with some excellent 'snapshot' studies of dominance relations among boys and girls of various ages. D.G. Freedman of the University of Chicago, and his students, have long conducted research in this area, and the best sources of data and theory remain Freedman's 1979 work, *Human Sociobiology: A Holistic Approach* (which includes as appendices a number of separate studies), and the collection edited by Omark, Strayer, and Freedman (1980), *Dominance Relations: An Ethological View of Human Conflict and Social Interaction.* Where specific references are not provided in the discussion below, one or more chapters in the latter work is the source.[13]

Dominance relations among human children and adolescents are strikingly similar to those that ethologists find among non-human primates. This is especially true of facial expressions, gaze aversion and eye-contact, and posture – erect posture equals dominance. The 'win' or 'plus' face of one child in a dispute or rivalry with another is an excellent predictor of which will eventually win (Zivin, 1985). Relative position seems to be stable over time. The hierarchies of boys and girls are

13 For a more recent bibliography and a review of findings since the publication of Omark, Strayer, and Freedman, see Strayer and Trudel (1984).

distinct, with girls tending to be aware of the hierarchy of the boys but the boys much less knowledgeable about the hierarchy of the girls. Members of a group pay far greater attention to the activities of high-rather than low-ranking members. Dominance as measured by who can push whom or insult whom is correlated to varying degrees with physical aggressiveness, athletic ability, and desirability as a date, but the most aggressive is *not* the highest-ranking individual. When a new group of adolescent males is formed, the boys at the high and low ends are almost immediately apparent to all, including outside observers. Relative standing does not appear to be correlated with intelligence quotient.

An individual's past experience apparently strongly influences the relative rank he or she will seek in a new group. Some children and adolescents automatically expect to be alpha, some omega. It is not clear whether this is a sensitive-period phenomenon – whether level of expected rank is 'set' by a given age – or whether it is merely the effect of a repeatedly self-fulfilling prophecy that a break in the repetition could end. (This is, of course, a question of very great importance for those concerned with the clinical treatment of mental-health problems related to low self-esteem.)

While human ethologists study dominance rank in children, self-esteem is usually studied by personality and social psychologists. The result is (given chapter 1's discussion of disciplinary boundaries) that we have little empirical data on the relationship between dominance rank and self-esteem. Dominance is usually treated as a group phenomenon, self-esteem as a personality variable, and we can only speculate as to how the one affects the other. Presumably, any such effects are interactive. A related question would be what the relationship is between each and serotonin level (or some other biochemical indicator of relative standing).

We have neither theory nor data as to how and when the child/adolescent moves from group-oriented, dominance-type prestige strategies to those more symbolic in nature. Note that not just the omega but the alpha individual, too, eventually moves in this manner. One hypothesis, consistent with the earlier discussion of sexual selection and the transformation of primate social dominance into human multiple prestige-allocation criteria, is that individuals who tend to rank low in dominance (as a human ethologist would measure it) would compensate by seeking to be competitive in an ability sphere. This prediction does at least fit the stereotype of the socially maladroit child becoming

FOCUS 8.1

MORAL SUPERIORITY

Healthy human beings always find some way to maintain self-esteem, failure to do so usually being considered a type of pathology. As a last resort, one can always claim *moral superiority* over others.

The English-language term 'moral superiority' refers to an evaluation of oneself as intrinsically superior to others not on the basis of skill or beauty or family or wealth but on one of two grounds: (1) one's supposed stricter adherence to local social norms and/or (2) paradoxicallly, one's low relative standing in terms of any other criteria for evaluation. In both cases, a claim to esteem on the basis of moral superiority is often a last chance, to be used when one has little or no other recourse. Moral superiority is the residual strategy for self-esteem.

When a poor person disparages the rich because they have obviously gained their wealth dishonestly; when the low in power disparage politicians for their dishonesty; when the religious glory in their virtue and pity the sinners; when the slender patronize the overweight – in each of these cases, moral superiority is being claimed on the basis of adhering more strictly than do others to local norms of behaviour. At least until he or she is caught publicly violating a norm, almost any individual, lacking other sources of respect, can make this kind of claim for moral superiority, and so maintain self-esteem (or simply derogate a rival).

For the oppressed, the powerless, the defeated, the ultimate claim for standing is based on moral superiority: we are of greater moral worth than are our oppressors. Implicit in this stance is the claim that, had we powerless people the power, we would adhere to norms of conduct far more closely than do those who do, in fact, actually have control. The British philosopher/mathematician Bertrand Russell has referred to this claim as 'the myth of the superior virtue of the oppressed.' That the oppressed generally feel morally superior to their oppressors is quite likely a universal: what appears to be a distinctive Western trait is that onlookers tend to accept the claim. As a result, we onlookers are frequently disappointed to find that, when previously oppressed groups become empowered, they do not necessarily act more virtuously (that is, more in accord with local norms) than did their former oppressors. The Pilgrims who landed at Plymouth Rock may have been fleeing from religious intolerance, but the society they created was probably more intolerant than the one from which they were escaping (the difference being that, in their own settlement, the intolerance was directed at others rather than at themselves). The new African rulers of former European colonies did not necessarily show more respect for the norms of freedom, in terms of which they claimed nationhood and independence, than did the previous colonial masters. Students, when they themselves have become teachers, and workers once they have joined management, whatever past claims of moral superiority they may have made, do not necessarily observe local norms any more strictly than did those whom they have replaced.

---

the 'expert' computer 'hacker' or artist or writer. Perhaps low dominance rank in youth is related to later success in accruing or controlling resources – to wealth, in short. (This suggestion is reminiscent of Adlerian 'overcompensation' for an 'inferiority complex.')

DOMINANCE, PRESTIGE, AND REPRODUCTIVE SUCCESS

There is good theoretical reason to expect both male and female social rank to be correlated with genetic fitness in human and non-human primates. After all, since primates do strive for rank, one expects (in the familiar tautology of much evolutionary thinking) that selection must have favoured such behaviour. This 'expectation' is, of course, a testable hypothesis. To begin with non-human male primates, Cheney (1983: 235) and Gray (1985: 248) each cite several studies showing a clear relationship between male rank and either reproductive or at least mating success. However, Gray also cites studies with more mixed results, as do Fedigan (1983) and Berenstain and Wade (1983).

Studies correlating social rank and reproductive success for *females* are even less consistent. Gray (1985: 257) reviews a number of such studies and concludes that there is no evidence to support the prediction that 'female rank is positively correlated with mating success (e.g., number of copulations).' He appears to be emphasizing the negative, here, but the data are indeed unclear.

Much of the problem may be methodological (Bernstein, 1981). For example, there are numerous ways of defining 'dominance' operationally, ranging from attention to preferential access to a resource. Different studies often use different operationalizations of relative rank and these are not necessarily equivalent.

Perhaps the most serious methodological weakness of studies seeking to correlate rank and fitness is the difficulty in measuring the latter. It is rarely possible to do the multi-generational studies needed for accurate measurement of genetic fitness, so researchers are forced to fall back on imperfect indices, such as fecundity (number of offspring born to a female, without taking into account survival rate), or frequency of copulation. But neither copulation nor fecundity is identical to reproductive success.

For example, primate dominance may be correlated with age, with all males following a somewhat comparable career of low rank to high and back to low (Burd, 1986: 169). In that case, short-term studies of dominance and reproductive success would be very inaccurate because they would grossly inflate the importance of rank. Only a measure of fitness involving the entire life-span would be meaningful. Alternatively, suppose that rank increases access to a scarce resource such as food or water, thereby enhancing longevity. Short-term studies correlating rank and copulatory success, or even rank and fecundity, would miss this long-term relationship in which the increased genetic fitness would be the result of a longer life-span and, again, require a fitness-over-the-life-span measure to detect. In short, studies correlating rank with fitness may be seriously flawed. (This is not meant as a criticism of the researchers, though one can see why geneticists prefer short-lived creatures such as fruit-flies, for whom life-span measures of fitness may be readily made, to the much longer-lived primates.)

For present purposes I will assume that future research will establish that rank tends to correlate with long-term genetic fitness for both males and females (at least, in those species for which there is evidence that maximum rank is indeed sought by troop members).

Oddly enough, of all primate species the evidence for a correlation between rank and reproductive success is best for our own (Betzig, 1986), in spite of our multiplicity of criteria for the allocation of prestige. But is 'prestige' the same as 'rank'? Before discussing relative standing and reproductive success in *Homo sapiens* it would be wise to review some vocabulary.

Reproductive Success in Human Beings and the Vocabulary of Rank
Self-esteem, prestige, status, and power: these terms all have to do with relative standing in some kind of social group or collectivity. With which of them do we wish to correlate reproductive success?

Prestige is respect and approbation accorded to one by others. *Self-esteem* is an internal assessment that one's reference group (whether objectively 'real' or no) is according one prestige. *Status* sometimes means relative standing but may also refer to a formal position in a social organization, for instance, the status of priest or professor. Some statuses in the latter sense carry more prestige than do others (that is, are 'higher'), and this prestige tends to be allocated automatically to whomever occupies the status, so long as the individual carries out the behaviours (the social role) associated with it. A status may or may not have various kinds of *power* associated with it, that is, ability to influence others to act in ways in which they otherwise would not.

'Power' is the most complex of these concepts. It may operate through rewards, coercion, or a mixture of both. It may have much to do with formal status or nothing at all, relying instead on personal authority, that is, prestige; or on the personal ability to inspire fear. Some forms of 'power' are better thought of in terms of reciprocal and nepotistic altruism, even though they do involve influencing behaviour. Prestige, power, and status often but not invariably go together. An individual may have high prestige but low status and little power. Prestige, power, and status all tend to vary situationally – that is, an individual may be high in one of these in one situation but not in another, as when the prestige of the scholar becomes low when the group goes bowling and he/she shows little skill. Occasionally, a status and its associated level of prestige is overweening, relevant in virtually all social situations, as in the case of physician or priest in our own society, or that of 'untouchable' in Hindu culture.

The sexual-selection account of the transformation of primate social dominance into human symbolic prestige implies that genetic success and culturally defined success should be closely correlated, as we have seen. But by 'culturally defined success' do we mean self-esteem, prestige, power, or status? These are only somewhat correlated, after all, and each may vary independently of the others, depending on situation. Moreover, it was argued earlier in this chapter that, in any given society, the criteria for the allocation of prestige are multiple in nature, so that even attempting to consider prestige alone is quite difficult. As was the case in early studies of primate social 'dominance,' researchers appear to have used whatever operationalization of 'culturally defined success' they found convenient. This being the case, it is striking that the various approaches have nevertheless yielded converging results.

Power, Prestige, and Reproductive Success
We begin with Betzig's (1986) study of power and reproductive success. Betzig surveyed 102 of the world's societies, chosen from the 186-society Standard Sample of Murdock and White (1969). The Standard Sample is a representative sample of the world's cultures and has been used by

many researchers, so that for each society a variety of different ratings or codings are already available. It is ideal for testing hypotheses applicable to the human species as a whole rather than to any single population, and in which not individuals but cultures are the units of analysis. Betzig's 102 societies were those that earlier research had established as having been politically autonomous units at the time they were studied.

Betzig points out that 'Darwinian theory predicts that to the extent that conflicts of interest among individuals are not overridden by common interest, or by an overpowering force,' they will result in the reproductive advantage of one of the parties to the conflict (p. 9). She goes on to hypothesize that '*hierarchical power should predict a biased outcome in conflict resolution, which should in turn predict size of the winner's harem*, for men, a measure of success in reproduction' (ibid., emphasis in original). In other words, men in higher formal positions should tend to win conflicts and have more wives than do other men, and the more they are able to win conflicts the more they should have more wives.

Betzig reviews the societies of her sample and finds her expectations met. Men in high positions in social hierarchies win conflicts of interest, often through physical violence; and they overwhelmingly have more wives/concubines and offspring than do other men. Her (1986) cross-cultural survey establishes that in pre-industrial, autonomous societies, there was a strong association between physical power over the lives of others and number of wives and children: 'Not only are men [who are] regularly able to win conflicts of interest more polygynous, but the degree of their polygyny is predictable from the degree of bias with which the conflicts are resolved. Despotism, defined as an exercised right to murder arbitrarily and with impunity, virtually invariably coincides with the greatest degree of polygyny, and presumably, with a correspondingly high degree of differential reproduction' (p. 88). Betzig thus shows that, at least for non-industrial societies, cultural success as defined in terms of power (coercive power in particular) yields reproductive success.

Industrial societies differ, here, and will be discussed in chapter 12, under the heading 'Zero Population Growth.' But it is worth noting that Mealey (1985) has clearly established that the Mormon settlers of the Territory of Utah, during the years 1821–30, clearly fitted the pattern Betzig finds for non-industrial societies. Since the Mormons permitted polygyny during this period, the variance in male fertility is high. Male fertility correlates significantly with church rank, and this relationship 'was clearly due primarily to the fact that men of high rank had more wives than men of lower rank' (p. 251). Church rank at time of death even turned out to be a better predictor of male fertility than age at death.

Hill (1984), unlike Betzig, is concerned with reproductive success and *prestige* rather than power. In his discussion of some ten societies, he focuses on prestige in terms of skills and reputation. When he does mention hierarchical position, he emphasizes not coercive power but the prestige of the status. Both he and Betzig discuss the !Kung San and use the work of Richard Lee as their primary source, but where Hill stresses the prestige associated with hunting ability, Betzig stresses the relatively high homicide rate of this reputedly 'peaceful' people and the likelihood that the homicides have to do with disputes over women.

Hill concludes that, for eight of the ten societies which he reviews, prestige is indeed associated with reproductive success. The exceptions are the Tlingit (a Northwest Coast potlatching people) and the modern British peerage. The Tlingit data on reproductive success are very poor, however, while the discussion of the case of British peerage will be deferred to chapter 12's discussion of fertility in industrial societies. On the whole, then, despite very different approaches to cultural success – prestige as opposed to power – Hill and Betzig are in agreement. Both power and prestige correlate with reproductive success, for non-industrial societies.

Wealth and Reproductive Success

Irons (1979), in a pioneering study, analysed the relationship between wealth and reproductive success among the Yomut Turkman of Iran. Yomut culture encourages the pursuit of wealth, usually in the form of cattle. Irons found that the wealthy clearly had more surviving offspring than did the poor, in accord with prediction. He suggests that this link was due to such factors as the wealthy enjoying improved nutrition, polygyny, earlier remarriage if widowed, and less physically dangerous work.

But in any society in which polygyny is permitted and depends upon the ability to amass bride-wealth, it would be startling if wealth and reproductive success were *not* correlated. Reanalysing West African data collected many years previously, for example, I found that both for Moslem Hausa and for the non-Moslem, Hausa-speaking Maguzawa of northern Nigeria, wealth and reproductive success are correlated (Barkow, 1977a). As among Yomut Turkman, however, in both of these Hausa societies wealth is clearly valued and any man who can accumulate the necessary bride-wealth will probably be polygynous. Because in these cases wealth is obviously directly instrumental in enhancing male reproductive success, it is probably the least interesting way of testing the predicted correlation between culturally defined and genetically defined success.

Self-Esteem and Reproductive Success
What of cultural success defined in terms of high self-esteem, however? Unfortunately, while there are cross-cultural data available both for prestige and power/status, and for reproductive success, there are none for self-esteem. Here, however, is at least a testable hypothesis: for any given social group, in any given society, self-esteem should correlate with reproductive success.

Overview on Reproductive and Cultural Success
In every case for which the data are at all adequate (with the important, deferred exception of industrial society), cultural success – whether defined in terms of power, prestige, or wealth – is correlated with reproductive success, at least for males. The correlation is especially impressive because cultural success has been defined in three different ways, and because the multiple prestige systems of the various societies have been collapsed into a single ranking. This strong correlation between genetic and cultural success is precisely what the sexual-selection argument for the transformation of primate social dominance into human prestige would predict.[14]

The mechanisms underlying the link between culturally and genetically defined success, I have suggested in this and preceding chapters, appear to involve a powerful, built-in intra-individual-system goal of gaining the respect and deference of those around us, plus a built-in plan of using agonism to achieve that goal, along with culturally patterned subplans that include symbolic status. We clearly share both the root plan and goal with most non-human primates and it is apparent in human children. In children, however, the agonism plan soon gives rise to subplans in the service of subgoals related to ability and resource-control/acquisition competition (in line with the transformation-of-dominance-by-sexual-selection hypothesis). For both sexes, we put increasing emphasis on competing in terms of resource acquisition and

---

14 Of course, a Panglossian sociobiologist would make the same prediction, but would lack a theory of the 'proximate' mechanisms that lead to this convergence between culturally defined and genetically defined success.

control. For both sexes, too, the agonistic-dominance goal/plan remains in place but, depending on one's culture, is likely to be a 'plan of last resort.'

Could a cultural system of success *fail* to be associated with greater reproductive success? As we will see in chapter 12's discussion of maladaptive cultural traits in modern industrial society, the answer is yes, in some very special cases (for instance, when the society in question practises contraception and permits fertile females autonomy in deciding whether to make use of it). Ordinarily, however, the fact that human beings find both agonistic dominance and the ability to produce and/or control resources prestigious and attractive makes such failure unlikely.

UNANSWERED QUESTIONS

Many unanswered questions remain. For example, when is prestige more important, when power? We especially need data on gender differences in prestige evaluation, both across cultures and within cultures, both across the genders and within each gender. Is agonism always a 'last resort' in male relative-standing competition? In what ways is female intra-sexual competition in terms of sexual attractiveness comparable to male intra-sexual competition in terms of agonism? How important for relative standing is *male* intra-sexual competition in terms of sexual attractiveness? How important is *female* intra-sexual competition in terms of agonism? Lack of data has caused the discussion to slight these two important questions.

The relationship between dominance position in childhood and adolescence and later self-esteem and prestige strategy is a topic looking for a research literature (though Weisfeld and Billings [1988] do discuss, at least, the apparent continuity between childhood and adult relative standing). Perhaps the former young alphas later use their self-esteem to develop good social skills, utilizing the high self-esteem presumably generated by their past rank to convey to others non-verbally that they are indeed alpha. Are these the individuals who become our politicians, the 'big men' of both large and small-scale societies? Is this what 'charisma,' defined in one instance as the non-verbal communication of being alpha (Barkow, 1976a; cf. Larsen, 1976), is all about? Do those of us who ranked lower, in our early peer groups, tend to become those who excel in spheres not involving much public contact and display?

What of parents and the role of early experience in determining self-esteem and social rank? We know from studies of non-human primates, baboons and macaques in particular, that the rank of one's matriline is the major determinant of one's own rank, and that the determination involves frequent support from matrilateral kin from infancy on, in agonistic encounters. Perhaps, given the work of Raleigh et al. (1984) on serotonin and status, discussed earlier in this chapter, such aid influences not only the immediate social interaction but also the neurophysiological basis of 'self-confidence' and 'self-esteem,' of 'alpha-ness.' Does the knowledge of one's family standing have equivalent effects in human children? What is the relationship between family standing, child-rearing practices, relative position in the peer group during childhood and adolescence, and ultimate social rank?

Social scientists frequently study social stratification, the classes and castes typical of medium- and large-scale human societies. The frame-work presented here and the unanswered questions posed above are highly pertinent to any understanding of how social class is transmitted and how impediments to social mobility may operate. It may be that programs that try to foster mobility for the children of the 'disadvan-taged' (usually, the welfare-receiving underclass of urban areas) may be very much on the right track when they emphasize 'pride,' especially if it turns out that self-esteem and expected rank are indeed sensitive-period phenomena, or if they actually are in part dependent on serotonin or a related aspect of neurophysiology. 'Pride' might well turn out to be a precondition for successful skill acquisition.

In this chapter, then, we have looked at prestige and culture from a number of mutually compatible, vertically integrated perspectives, including those of (1) biological evolution and non-human primate homologues; (2) neurophysiology; (3) psychological mechanisms; (4) child development, particularly as dealt with in the field of human ethology; (5) symbolic anthropology; and (6) economics and political science. In the chapter that follows, ethnographic case histories will permit us to add the perspectives of (7) ethnicity and ethnic relations; (8) culture change; and (9) the actual behaviour of two ordinary people.

SUMMARY

1. Primate dominance hierarchies are far more complex than are the pecking orders of hens, often involving membership in a matriline or alliances with others. Nevertheless, they retain agonism at their core. This ordering must also have applied in the social hierarchies of our own ancestors.

2. The neurophysiology of relative rank in human beings is only

beginning to be studied. We do know, though, that change in position in the social hierarchy in vervet monkeys is correlated with a change in serotonin level. No doubt there are neurophysiological concomitants to relative standing in our own species as well.

3. Human relative standing has agonism at its core only among young children and, among adults, during times of great stress. Ordinarily, human social rank is symbolic in nature. This transformation of primate dominance based ultimately on agonism to human prestige based on symbols has primarily been the result of sexual selection.

4. The transformation would have begun with females selecting males able to invest in offspring. Non-dominant males, instead of competing agonistically, would have been selected to compete in terms of ability to invest, that is, in terms of skills in resource procurement (foraging, hunting, tool-making).

5. Males, too, would have preferred to reserve their limited parental investment for the offspring of females who also showed skill in resource procurement.

6. A single status hierarchy based on agonism would have been supplanted by multiple status hierarchies, each based on a particular skill. Thus, relative rank would have tended to vary situationally.

7. Individuals would have tended to compete primarily with those whose skill specialties were similar to their own. Individuals also began to divide their social world up into skill/prestige categories, and to develop social identities related to the categories in which they were competitive. Evaluation of others would have moved from being primarily agonistic in nature to involving complex cognitive processing of information relating to skill categories and relative standing within them.

8. Given the advantages of self-deception in manipulating the behaviour of others, individuals would have tended not just to rank themselves higher than others within their skill/prestige category, but also to rank their skill/prestige category as higher than the skill/prestige categories of others. This is what we do today. Since these assessments are covert and symbolic, and since in egalitarian societies we learn an etiquette of masking our assessment of the relative standing of others, we each can feel superior to the others with whom we interact, while they may feel superior to us.

9. Self-esteem involves assessing ourselves as holding high rank in a social group. Given the nature of the mazeway and of our ability to distort incoming information, we can assess ourselves as being of high

rank in groups not physically present and even in groups that have never had any objective existence (for instance, the ancestors look down on me approvingly). We usually perceive individuals dependent on non-present reference groups for their self-esteem as being independent and self-reliant.

10. We also can seek high rank by working on behalf of our group, rather than following an individualistic strategy. Usually, that group is a kin group, but it need not be (for example, in Japan it often is the corporation employing one). The ability to follow a group-oriented strategy is culturally determined and depends upon the inclusiveness of our self (of our self-representation in the intra-individual system).

11. Economic systems are linked to prestige systems. Surplus production can usually be 'traded' for prestige, causing us to produce above a subsistence level. In non-industrial societies, individuals tend to compete in terms of the skills needed for economic production (for instance, farmers competing in terms of crops and agricultural skills).

12. Even in our own society, individuals convert surplus production to prestige by charitable donations (that is, by redistributing goods).

13. Modern society includes a multiplicity of potential reference and membership groups in terms of which we may assess our relative standing. The billionaire is comparing his or her wealth to that of other billionaires, not to that of members of the middle class, and may strive mightily to amass yet more wealth because the competition is with other billionaires.

14. In hierarchical societies, envy and rivalry may be controlled by encapsulation, in which people from different social groups see one another as being almost of a different species. Thus, the peasant may perceive the aristocrat as another kind of animal and thus refrain from a comparison that would lower his or her self-esteem.

15. The term 'honour' has to do with worthiness to be a member of a prestigious group. One may have honour as a chef or as a physician, for example.

16. The 'adolescent identity crisis' in modern society may have to do with the search of the adolescent, who has to weigh the size of frog he or she might eventually be, in a given puddle, against the size of the puddle: how high-ranking a group one can obtain membership in and how high one is likely to rise within that group.

17. Self-esteem may be a sensitive-period phenomenon. It is possible that individuals with low self-esteem have had it 'set' low because of childhood or adolescent experiences.

18. Young children seem to move from an agonism-based social hierarchy to adult-style, symbolic status distinctions.

19. Sociobiology would predict a high correlation between rank and reproductive success. The data for non-human primates are ambiguous, probably owing to the difficulties of measuring fitness in long-lived species (especially when these are studied for only brief periods of time). For non-industrial human societies, cross-cultural studies show that prestige, political power, and wealth are correlated with sexual access to many females and therefore, presumably, with reproductive success.

20. This chapter has attempted to provide for social rank and prestige the kind of 'vertically integrated explanation' called for in chapter 1.

9

Prestige Processes in the Context of Culture

How do we apply evolutionary theory to culture? Some sociobiologists, as we will see in the next chapter, make the application tight, interpreting entire cultural institutions as almost a set of amplified strategies to enhance inclusive fitness. My own answer requires a series of multi-level, mutually compatible (vertically integrated) explanations that move from genes to neurophysiology to individual motivation to social interaction to sociology. In this effort, the goal is to demonstrate not the reduction of complex sociocultural phenomena to evolutionary biology but rather their compatibility with our evolved, fitness-enhancing, human psychology, itself the product of biological evolution: *the social sciences are not to be replaced by biology but to be made compatible with it.*

We have now developed, in however incomplete a form, a theory of how natural selection has led to a particular kind of human mind, one that sorts, selects, and edits the information of which cultures are composed. In the previous chapter, I focused on one aspect of the mind, goal-oriented behaviour, and on one particular goal, prestige-striving and self-esteem. It was argued that our socioeconomic systems in particular are in part generated by the interaction of prestige-seeking individuals.

The present chapter continues the focus on the prestige goal, but this time it narrows to the generation of major sociocultural change by individuals following their plans and subplans for prestige and self-esteem. We will analyse three case studies. The first of these deals with how and why the Hausa and the Ibo of Nigeria have responded so differently to the economic opportunities attendant upon British colonial conquest – differences that account to a considerable measure for the Nigerian Civil War (the 'Biafran' secession). The second concerns the spread of Islam in the Maradi region of Niger, as illustrated by the history of two men. The resurgence of fundamentalist Islam is of course a major historical phenomenon of our time. The third case history examines ethnicity and how an 'incipient ethnic split' developed between Moslem and non-Moslem Hausa in Nigeria's Kaduna state. In all three cases, we will see how social change can be generated by individuals seeking the basic sociobiological goal of prestige.[1]

DREAMS, DEEDS, AND WAR: HAUSA AND IBO IN NIGERIA

In the mid-sixties, Robert A. LeVine (then of the University of Chicago and now of Harvard University) conducted a study of the 'need to achieve' among the three major Nigerian ethnic groups: the Hausa, Ibo, and Yoruba. The notion of an 'achievement' motive derives from the work of psychologist Henry A. Murray (discussed in chapter 5), and was expanded into a virtual industry by David McClelland.[2] 'N-ach' (as it is often termed) has been correlated with variables from gross national product to school grades. McClelland and his collaborators have even attempted to promote economic development by training people to score higher on tests of 'n-ach.'

These 'tests' of n-ach usually involve some kind of fantasy material – typically, sentence completion tests or else stories told in response to a standardized series of pictures – that is then analysed for the number of mentions of achievement-related themes. LeVine altered this procedure by asking (male) children to write essays based on their dreams.[3] The results seemed to confirm the validity of the n-ach concept. The Hausa children scored low, the Ibo high, and the Yoruba between the two of them. The scoring system itself was adapted from McClelland's work by

---

1 The discussion of Hausa and Ibo differences in prestige-striving is adapted from Barkow (1975a). The discussion of two Moslems from Maradi is from Barkow (1975b). The discussion of the 'incipient ethnic split' is based on Barkow (1976b). For general ethnographic background on the Hausa, see Barkow (1978b).

2 See, for example, McClelland (1951, 1955, 1958, 1961), McClelland et al. (1953), and McClelland and Winter (1969).

3 This discussion of 'n-ach' deals exclusively with males, reflecting LeVine's focus. For those concerned with Hausa women and their paths towards prestige, see Barkow (1971, 1972).

Eugene Strangman, and LeVine (1966: 100–1) provides it as an appendix. The 'dreams' were rated for presence/absence of 'achievement imagery' on the basis of whether there was, for example, competition for a standard of excellence, unique accomplishment, or long-term involvement.

LeVine's (1966) results, *Dreams and Deeds*, appeared when the chain of events that would lead to the Nigerian Civil War had already begun, events that started with massacres of Ibo by residents of Nigeria's predominantly Moslem and Hausa-speaking northern regions. The Ibo fled back to their ancestral southeastern region, where they subsequently attempted to secede from Nigeria. As we will see, these initial massacres were the ultimate product of the very different responses made by Hausa and Ibo to the new economic opportunities brought about by British military conquest (termed 'pacification' by its apologists) and the subsequent era of 'modernization.' To simplify the tale I will omit discussion here of the Yoruba (and with no slight intended to this important people).

Cultural Prestige and Islam

The Moslem Hausa North had been notoriously slow to take advantage of the new opportunities attendant upon British rule, particularly the educational ones. Islam has long had immense cultural prestige in this region, and learning and education are closely associated with that religion even for the non-Moslem. The Hausa term for a Western, secular school, *makarantar boko*, connotes fraudulence, since true education is believed to be Koranic in nature. When the British urged the northern emirs to send their children to be educated in the early colonial schools, the children who were sent were often, in fact, the children of the emirs' slaves! Even by the time LeVine conducted his study, some years after Nigerian independence, the participation rate in (non-Koranic) education was much lower for the North than for the other regions of Nigeria. As we will see, however, Islam and attitudes towards education are not the entire explanation for the disparity.

Hausa civilization has over one thousand years of written (in Arabic) history and legend. So ubiquitous and successful have Hausa traders been, over the centuries, that their language has become a widespread trade language, a *lingua franca* spoken over large areas of West Africa and across the Sahara into Egypt. Hausa society was long organized in walled city-states, one of which, Kano, had a population of more than one million people even prior to British conquest. Perhaps not surprisingly (given our earlier discussion of ethnocentrism), the Hausa have a traditional contempt for small-scale, non-Moslem peoples. Among the peoples for whom they held this contempt were the Ibo.

British conquest found the Ibo participants in a small-scale, non-literate, low-technology society organized in terms of kinship and title societies and with a traditional African religion. But the Ibo were not slowed by a perception of European civilization as culturally inferior to their own: they seized with alacrity the opportunities the British brought. Ibo quickly adopted European clothing and competed energetically, first for access to schooling, then for civil-service positions and in commerce. The Hausa retained their traditional contempt for the Ibo but, in fact, the latter were soon providing them with government services, selling them their licences and postage stamps, and peddling goods by bicycle, deep in the most rural northern areas. Eventually, Hausa rioted and attacked Ibos in northern cities, and most Ibos fled to their eastern Nigerian homeland, there to secede under the name of a new state, Biafra. Did the Hausa-Ibo conflict really stem from ethnic differences in the 'need to achieve'?

Status Mobility in the Nineteenth Century
LeVine attempted to account for Hausa-Ibo differences in response to new economic opportunities not just in terms of n-ach but also as a result of their respective nineteenth-century 'status mobility structures.' To simplify somewhat, Hausa society was organized in terms of patron-client relationships. An ambitious Hausa man would seek to demonstrate his loyalty, obedience, and respectfulness to a patron who might accept him as a client. The client might seek to be set up as a small trader under a long-distance merchant; or he might seek to be the retainer of an important aristocrat. In either case, respect, obedience, and loyalty were the qualities required for success.

An ambitious Ibo man, by contrast, would seek membership in a title society. Such membership was highly prestigious but also quite expensive, since gaining it meant feasting existing members. Men would seek wealth in any way they could, individually, and if successful would convert their resources to prestige through the title societies.

Note that the prestige subgoals/subplans for Hausa and Ibo, in the nineteenth century, were very different. For the Hausa man, the subgoal involved clientship, a dependency relation; the subplan involved conspicuous displays of loyalty and obedience. For the Ibo man, the subgoal involved wealth, the subplan almost any kind of individual activity. But the McClelland scoring system is strongly biased in favour of Ibo-type, individualistic, entrepreneurial activity. Ratings involving 'competition with a standard of excellence, unique accomplishment, or long-term involvement' apply to Ibo but not to Hausa prestige strategies. Not only does the McClelland system fail to recognize the Hausa strategies for prestige as such, it actually rates them as evidence of a strong need for 'obedience and social compliance'! Thus, LeVine could conclude that the Ibo are high in the need to achieve while the Hausa are low in that need but high in the need for social compliance!

As others (such as, DeVos, 1968) have pointed out, McClelland's n-ach is better thought of as a need for *entrepreneurial* activity. It is a somewhat culture-bound concept, reflecting not the human universal prestige goal but mid-century, middle-class-American subplans/goals for prestige. LeVine, to his credit, recognized the limitations of the n-ach concept – it was he, after all, who felt it necessary to review nineteenth-century Hausa and Ibo 'status mobility structures.'

It turns out that traditional Ibo prestige subgoals/plans happened to result in high n-ach scores. More important, they lent themselves to the opportunities of a modernizing, capitalist economy. Hausa prestige subgoals/plans, as it happened, were maladapted to the new opportunities. In effect, the Ibo had to change tactics but not strategy, the Hausa had to change both tactics and strategy.

Inter-ethnic strife is common in much of the world today (perhaps it always has been). Commentators often ascribe such conflict to competition between groups for power, prestige, wealth, and territory, and this is a reasonable type of explanation, thoroughly consistent with an evolutionary view of human nature and society. In the present example, Hausa and Ibo were, after all, economic competitors. Perhaps, however, we need to ask why ethnic differences in economic success exist in the first place: how often can they be accounted for, at least at times and in part, in terms of differing culturally provided strategies for prestige? We need to learn how the existing prestige and self-esteem strategies of various peoples permit or impede their economic adaptation to modernizing structures of opportunity. The plans/goals/codes approach may prove useful.

TWO MOSLEM MEN FROM MARADI[4]

North of Nigeria lies a vast, sparsely settled young nation, the Niger Republic. Much of this country is Hausa-speaking, including the city of

---

4 This discussion is adapted from Barkow (1975b). For further discussion of Maradi, see the references contained therein.

Maradi. Maradi in many ways resembles its cousins to the south. It, too, was once a walled citadel, though it was founded only some years prior to 1830. The early part of the nineteenth century had seen a tremendous Islamic jihad in much of what is now Niger and Nigeria, a conflict associated with the Shehu Usman dan Fodio. Maradi was founded by royal refugees from the jihad-conquered Kingdom of Katsina, together with the autochthonous Hausa-speaking peoples of the Maradi region. Note, however, that the Katsinawa refugees considered themselves to be Moslems (whatever the opinion of the Shehu may have been), though apparently the original local population more-or-less adhered to traditional African religions at that time. During the period of European competition to control Africa, it was the French who gained control over the Maradi region. Most of Maradi was flooded in 1945, and the following year the French colonial authorities rebuilt the city in French fashion, in the shape of spokes radiating out from a central hub.

Maradi comes as a shock to one accustomed to the Hausa cities of Nigeria. It is not just a matter of the good quality French bread available everywhere, or the French-language loan-words of the local Hausa. In the early seventies, during my own visits, the conversation of junior civil servants seemed more like what one would expect of idealized French schoolchildren than of members of the élite of an African nation. Conversation was of French place-names, of towns, industries, geography. It was through such knowledge, I learned, that success in civil-service examinations lay. Though my own Hausa was more serviceable than my French, at that time, I discovered to my chagrin that, in the corridors of the government offices, one did not speak Hausa. Only later did I learn how the French (quite unlike the British, further south) had sought to suppress the Hausa language, even to the point of punishing schoolchildren for making use of the language of their own civilization, rather than that of their conquerors.

There was an additional surprise awaiting me. As I interviewed my way through social networks, I was startled to find no hint of resistance to Islam, despite the area's history. Instead, I found individual after individual who claimed to come from a deeply pious and scholarly Moslem family. In some cases I found myself sceptical, particularly after travelling to some of the rural villages from which several of my informants had originally come, discovering these to be non-Islamic, traditional-African-religion communities. Yet, in the town, the impress of Islam was overwhelmingly apparent, and I found that most people who claimed to spend hours each day in Islamic study actually did so.

The Two Men

In an effort to understand what was taking place, I sought to collect life histories, two of which we will discuss. One of my informants I will term 'Daya,' the other 'Shida' (the Hausa terms for 'one' and 'six,' respectively). Both men are descendants of the original founders of Maradi and have distant relatives who are members of the traditional aristocracy. Both were raised on the outskirts of the city and as boys would work daily in the fields.

Daya studied with a *mallam* or Koranic scholar from his earliest boyhood. At the age of sixteen he completed his reading of all sixty sections of the Koran (meaning that he had memorized and read them one-at-a-time rather than having to recite the entire Koran all at once). This accomplishment signals a graduation ceremony or *sauka*, literally a 'dismounting,' and is a proud achievement. Daya has never ceased to study the Koran, and was doing so for several hours each day during the period of the interviews. Shida, however, probably because he is of an older generation than is Daya, never received any Koranic education at all.

Daya continued to farm and study into adulthood. He also became the servant of the village schoolmaster, fetching wood and doing laundry for the man. He took advantage of a government-run adult-education program to become somewhat literate in his own language. At one point, Daya became a worker at the French uranium mine at Arlit. During his second year, however, he left off work and instead took his accumulated savings to the capital city of Niamey, where he bought goods to sell back at camp. He did this several times and, though during the period of interviewing the work at Arlit was at a low ebb and he no longer returned there, he nevertheless continued to support himself as a small-scale (petty) trader.

In 1974, Daya had two wives, three children, and a peddler's licence. By far his most profitable route involved purchasing goods at the Nigerian city of Kano, but he complained rather bitterly about problems with customs officials (colonial and now élite African authority having transformed the traditional Kano-Maradi trade route into one involving either smuggling or bribery or 'customs' – Daya does not distinguish between the latter two). But though Daya's financial position was precarious and he was quite hostile towards the official authorities, he was a very proud man. His opinion of the French-educated bureaucratic élite – who, in fact, very much run his country on their own behalf – was scathing. His respect is reserved for the Koranic scholars, and he was spending several hours each day studying with them, and shared much of his income with them.

Shida, as a young man, also left home, becoming apprenticed to a kinsman as a tailor, for a time, then working as a peanut buyer for another kinsman. The latter eventually put him in charge of a small cloth shop, but after approximately ten years Shida quarrelled with his patron. At the time of interviewing (1974), Shida had been supported for several years by his mother and by his wife, who earned small sums through the sale of cooked food. He lived in an inherited compound and received the charity of his kinsmen, despite his history of quarrelsomeness. A close friend of Shida's blamed his problems on his *zuciyar sarauta*, his 'nobleman's heart' that made him scorn the realistic avenues of petty trading or tailoring open to him. Shida himself would speak of grandiose plans to engage in large-scale commerce (Hausa vocabulary makes a clear distinction between large-scale and petty trading), but here he was entirely unrealistic. Unlike Daya, who conveyed an impression of energy and self-confidence, Shida seemed physically weak, stooped, and uncertain, his manner often cringing in the traditional behaviour of a low-ranking client in the presence of his actual or hoped-to-be patron.

Perhaps owing to their knowledge of their aristocratic origins, both Daya and Shida seem to have begun as rather ambitious men. Neither was content to remain a peasant farmer. Neither had the advantage of francophone education. Both followed traditional prestige strategies involving the pursuit of wealth. But Shida limited himself to the standard Hausa patron-client relationship and turned out to be unable to accept the role of client. He survives as the impoverished recipient of charity and with little respect from those around him. Daya, in contrast, was more innovative and enterprising. His knowledge of his religion gave him a great advantage, for he appears to have based his self-esteem on a conception of himself as a good Moslem.

At least at the time the study was conducted, Niger was a country run a by French-educated, bureaucratic élite. For this group, prestige accrues to those with high bureaucratic positions, and the key to such position was French-style education and the civil service exam. But for Daya – and for many others interviewed – only Islamic learning was worthy of prestige. Other kinds of learning, when discussed at all, were disparaged as just a means of getting money. Daya and the many like him were privately scornful of the francophone élite who, however, largely monopolized political power. Daya learned to protect his self-esteem by spending hours studying the Koran. He could evaluate himself as of higher standing than the ruling bureaucrats by using prestige criteria having to do with Islam. Shida, never having learned much more than the basics of that religion, was in no position to do the same. He was, then, a double-loser, both in terms of Islamic prestige criteria and in terms of French education and status.

Maradi society, at least during the time of this research, seemed in danger of splitting into two. One segment lived in the world of France and civil-service exams, the world of the bureaucratic élite. The other segment lived in the world of Islam and followed prestige-allocation criteria involving Islamic learning. Each group tended to consider the criteria of the other – and therefore the demands made by the other for respect – as illegitimate. Those with access to neither kind of education, like Shida, had nowhere to go. Not surprisingly, the Islamically inclined were rewriting their own history, emphasizing the antiquity of Islamic influence in the region and in their own family background, thereby confusing the visiting anthropologist, who was aware that Maradi was traditionally (but is no longer) relatively resistant to Islam.

Please note that I am not attempting to reduce all the social processes generating the current resurgence of Islamic fundamentalism to this simple case of rival sets of prestige-allocation criteria. Even for Maradi alone, more was going on. For example, the wealthy but non-francophone traders, the *alhazai*, were tending to marry their daughters to the sons of the bureaucratic élite. A new class structure seemed to be developing. Unfortunately, an unsympathetic funding agency cut off research support before this project could move into the survey research stage, when the hypotheses arising from the intensive analyses of a small number of people and their life histories would have been tested. Even so, Maradi is only one small corner of the Moslem world. Care must be taken to avoid reducing the rise of the Ayatollah Khomeini of Iran, for example, to nothing but these rival legitimacies.

Yet, it would be surprising if Maradi turned out to be the only region in which rival sets of prestige allocation played a substantial role in the resurgence of Islam. In societies in which those with Western education and skills are rapidly monopolizing power and prestige, it is predictable that those unable to compete in such terms will seek alternative ways to maintain their self-esteem. In Moslem nations, renewed allegiance to Islam will be for many an alluring alternative, one leading to pride and prestige. If a sufficient number of people choose this course, political repercussions are to be expected. Thus, the goals/plans/codes framework sheds some light on social/political/religious change in Maradi.

AN INCIPIENT ETHNIC SPLIT[5]

A strange problem awaited me, during my first fieldwork in the late sixties, in Nigeria's Kaduna State. I was living in a small, Moslem Hausa village of six hundred. Several miles' march into the bush was an even smaller, more scattered community of non-Moslem Hausa or Maguzawa. The Maguzawa insisted that they, too, were Hausa, even if not Moslem. The Moslem villagers, who had trouble understanding why I should be interested in Maguzawa, described the latter as *not* Hausa, and frequently said that they were like the 'Gwari' (literally, the Gbari, but usually meaning any very low-status, non-Hausa-speaking group). Careful ethnographic comparison revealed minimal difference between the two groups and supported what the literature gave me to believe, that is, that the Maguzawa were essentially a remnant population of intermingled resistant-to-Islam Hausa. The evidence of facial markings was unmistakable: these Maguzawa were nothing more than two groups of Kano and of Katsina-origin Hausa. The problem was, why should the villagers insist that their neighbours – their cousins – were anything else?

Historical reconstruction suggested that a long-term, conqueror-assimilation process had been at work and was generating something very much like an ethnic boundary. Like other peoples of the world, the Hausa had long been divided between metropole and hinterland. The metropoles were the walled cities, the bastions of Islamic learning and influence, the seats of power of the ruling aristocrats, the centres of craft, industry, and commerce. The hinterlands were by definition the more rural, less learned, less prestigious, and less Islamic areas. People tend to imitate and adopt that which is perceived as prestigious, and for most of us this means that symbols of status flow from metropole to hinterland, from urban to rural areas. In Hausaland, the eighteenth and nineteenth centuries had been periods of frequent warfare, so that rural villagers frequently would flock to the safety of the walled capitals. But British conquest, around the beginning of the twentieth century, had

---

5 This discussion is adapted from Barkow (1976b).

meant the recolonization of the 'bush' because the rural areas, with their plentiful land, were now relatively peaceful.

The flow of prestige symbols from centre to periphery did not cease, of course. Traits – almost always associated with Islam – continued to move. These traits included having some Koranic education, using a Moslem rather than traditional supernatural practitioner, wearing a turban, wearing a gown or robe of cloth rather than the traditional Hausa leather garment, constructing and then praying in mosques, giving alms, insisting that one's meat be ritually slaughtered and abstaining from pork and dog, not drinking the traditional millet or guinea corn beer, having no more than four wives, and keeping one's wife or wives in some degree of seclusion. By the first half of this century, most of these symbols had flowed to most rural Hausa villages. But many of them had not yet reached the most rural of all the Hausa, the Maguzawa in their dispersed, isolated compounds.

A symbol can give prestige only for a brief time, until its ubiquity dilutes its value. But a borrowed trait is not necessarily discarded; rather, it may now yield not so much prestige as social identity. Long after wearing a gown of cloth instead of a garment of leather had ceased to be anything other than standard Hausa dress, it was a sign that one was identifying oneself with Islam and was ready to be judged in terms of its prestige criteria. As Goffman (1967: 50) puts it: 'When a group of individuals become involved in the maintenance of rules, they tend to become committed to a particular group identity. In the case of their obligations, they become to themselves and others the sort of persons who follow these particular rules.'

Both rural and urban Hausa have come to be, in their own eyes, people who by definition are Moslem, who pray, who give alms, who do not drink millet beer. If this is who they are, then what are they to make of those most rural, most isolated speakers of Hausa who do not pray, who do not give alms, who do drink beer? These people must be different – they cannot be Hausa, these Maguzawa they must be like other non-Moslem peoples, they must be Gwari. As Barth (1969) theorizes about the generation of ethnic boundaries, we expect that 'new forms of behavior will tend to be dichotomized: one would expect that persons would be ... swift to classify forms of activity with one or another cluster of ethnic differences.'

All this left the Maguzawa a bit bemused, as I found in my working among them during 1968–9: they *knew* they were Hausa, and even what kind of Hausa they were (that is, either of Kano or of Katsina). But they also knew that they were not welcome in the village of the Moslems, where they were permitted to stay only in the courtesans' compound (and in that of the visiting anthropologist), and where they were treated as pariahs and shunned. Some had even come to accept a myth of origin in which they traced their beginnings to the first Bamaguje (the singular of the term Maguzawa). Bamaguje's full name was Bama-gujen-salla or Bama-runner-from-prayer, they say, and he was a follower of the Prophet who refused to pray and instead ran away, all the way to Kano, from whence come the Maguzawa. This false etymological myth suggests that, just as the Maguzawa represent a sort of 'negative reference group' for the Moslem Hausa villagers, some of the Maguzawa had accepted their identity as non-Moslems, defining themselves negatively.

By 1980, the government of Nigeria had taken two steps that in effect reversed the formation of the incipient ethnic boundary between Moslem and non-Moslem Hausa. First, they banned facial scarification. Maguzawa facial markings were extremely elaborate and visible from a distance; without them it is impossible to distinguish between Maguzawa and other Hausa. Second, the Nigerian government introduced universal primary education. Now the Maguzawa were no longer permitted to be deeply isolated – they must remain much closer to the Moslem villages, and therefore much more deeply involved with them. But even during a brief revisit in 1977, it was apparent that the Maguzawa were readily assimilating, most of them turning to Islam and a few others to Christianity. All individuals interviewed agreed that in the future there would be no more Maguzawa. The prediction was probably too harsh. Maguzawa as a discrete cultural and religious group may cease to exist, but they are likely to remain as one more ethnic group among the multi-ethnic Hausa, who already tend to have 'ethnic origins' in much the way that Canadians and Americans do. Under other circumstances, however, the Maguzawa would probably have gone on, eventually, to become a separate ethnic group.

CONCLUSIONS

Chapter 8 took the prestige/self-esteem goal from its origins in primate social dominance, to its neurophysiological underpinnings, to its complex and culturally ordered subgoal/plan derivatives. In this chapter we have seen how individuals, in seeking prestige, can generate social change, ranging from the resurgence of Islam to the generation of an ethnic boundary. These changes are emergents, sociological phenomena generated by the interaction of individuals, individuals seeking prestige because our species has been selected to do so. There may still be those who think a 'sociobiological' approach has to do with accounting for complex social phenomena as the direct effects of single genes. But, as we have seen, between genes and culture we need complex, multi-level, but mutually compatible, structures of explanation.

The distance between the genes and emergent sociocultural phenomena is very great. In chapter 12, we will see that it is sufficiently great to permit much in culture to actually be genetically maladaptive for at least some segments of the local population. First, however, let us take time to look at how several other theorists have viewed the relationship between genes and culture.

SUMMARY

1. Applying evolutionary theory to culture requires a series of multi-level, mutually compatible explanations that move from genes to neurophysiology to individual motivation to social interaction to sociology. The goal is to demonstrate not the reduction of complex sociocultural phenomena to evolutionary biology, but rather their compatibility with our evolved, fitness-enhancing, human psychology, itself the product of biological evolution: *the social sciences are not to be replaced by biology but made compatible with it.*

2. The 'need for achievement' (*n-ach*) concept was based on the work of Henry A. Murray, but was developed by David McClelland. It was applied in Nigeria by Robert A. LeVine, who tested students from the major Nigerian ethnic groups for their 'need to achieve.'

3. The tests showed the Ibo to be high in n-ach and the Hausa low. Ibo had been very quick to take advantage of the new educational and economic opportunities brought about by British conquest, while Hausa had been slow. Because the Hausa were the bearers of an ancient Islamic culture and believed themselves superior to the Ibo, they were especially resentful of Ibo economic success. This resentment culminated in massacres of Ibo in Hausa towns and in the secession of the Ibo region from Nigeria. The result was a civil war.

4. LeVine analysed the status-mobility systems of nineteenth-century Ibo and Hausa. In effect, he showed that the Ibo had only to change tactics but not their general prestige strategy, since the latter already

emphasized the accumulation of wealth. The Hausa strategy for prestige stressed loyalty to a patron. The McClelland scoring system scored traditional Ibo prestige strategy and tactics as reflecting a high need for achievement. But Hausa strategies were rated not as n-ach but as need for affiliation and obedience, a misinterpretation.

5. Ibo traditional prestige strategies lent themselves to the opportunities provided by a modernizing, capitalist economy. But Hausa prestige subgoals/plans, as it happened, were maladapted to the new opportunities. In effect, the Ibo had to change tactics but not strategy, the Hausa had to change both tactics and strategy.

6. The problem is that n-ach measures not the need for prestige, but a particular prestige strategy involving individualistic, entrepreneurial activity.

7. Though the city of Maradi was founded by those who fled from an Islamic jihad, early in the nineteenth century, I found many of its inhabitants to have a strong identification with Islam and to spend large portions of their time in studying this religion. Analysis suggested that the root cause was the monopolization of power and prestige by the French-educated, bureaucratic élite. One man, with neither French nor Koranic education, reacted by suffering from low self-esteem, presumably owing to his low status. But others, with Koranic but not French-language education, reacted by denying the legitimacy of the bureaucrats' claims to prestige on the grounds that only Islamic learning is worthy of respect. Such individuals would spend much time in Koranic study. Their behaviour may shed some light on the contemporary resurgence of Islam in much of the world.

8. Among rural Hausa, in Nigeria, a process of diffusion of high-prestige Moslem traits apparently has taken place during the centuries. Once widespread, such traits lose their ability to confer prestige but instead become symbolic of group identity. The Hausa now tend to define themselves as a Moslem people. The most rural and resistant to Islam Hausa, the Maguzawa, were therefore for a time perceived by Moslem Hausa as members of another ethnic group because the Maguzawa lacked these symbols of Hausa identity (for example, praying, keeping women in seclusion). Thus, differing prestige strategies generated, over time, an incipient ethnic split.

9. In this chapter we have seen how individuals, in seeking prestige, can generate social change, change ranging from the resurgence of Islam to the generation of an ethnic boundary. There may still be those who

think a 'sociobiological' approach has to do with accounting for complex social phenomena in terms of single-gene effects. But, as we have seen, a sociobiological approach means accounting for complex phenomena in complex ways, and the connection with genes is via a vertically integrated, hierarchically organized structure of processual explanations.

PART FOUR

Alternative Approaches and Maladaptation

10

Other Approaches to Gene-Culture Interrelationships

This book's general framework has finally been presented. It is one emphasizing multi-level but mutually compatible theories of processes, in which we continually find that higher levels of organization generate properties not predicted by the lower levels. In the last chapter, we accounted for sociocultural phenomena as products of the interaction of individuals, whose behaviour could in turn be explained in terms of the intra-individual system, which in turn was a product of natural selection. But no account was of the 'reduced to' or 'nothing but' variety. Sitting between genetic evolution and culture was always the intra-individual system, that complex filter that mediates and transforms the flow of information between the two processes.

This framework is only one way of thinking about the relationship between genes and culture. There have been many others, and this chapter and the one that follows it review and evaluate several of these.[1] While most of the attention will be on alternative sociobiological

---

1 This section could easily encompass every holistic approach in the social/behavioural-sciences literature and I have been forced to be quite selective. But the reader is referred to two important and integrative works that (in part) use sociobiology as a framework. These are Corning (1983) and, especially, Crook (1980). I have deliberately reversed the usual sequence of chapters in books presenting theoretical frameworks. Ordinarily, the first chapters are devoted to attacking existing theory, in order to justify building anew. In *Darwin, Sex, and Status* a new framework has been presented first, and only with the current chapter does the critique of rival efforts begin. This reversal is consistent with the book's emphasis on construction and integration, rather than on demolition.

approaches, by way of contrast we begin with more 'mainstream' anthropological views. The chapter concludes with an analysis of a recurring analogy in human sociobiology, that between genes and culture.

SIMILAR COMPONENTS, DIFFERENT EMPHASES

The approaches to be examined in this and the following chapter broadly share the intra-individual system's general purpose and components. That purpose is the provision of a framework for ordering and accounting for human social behaviour, particularly those behaviours usually considered 'cultural.' The shared components may be roughly referred to as: (1) genes (or genetic evolution in general); (2) mind (or, more precisely, processes within the individual); (3) culture; and (4) environment. Taken together, these four components provide a sort of grid for the comparison of different views.

Different theories emphasize different components. The component emphasized is usually the one for which the most detailed account is provided. (Of course, most theorists feel that they have presented all components with appropriate emphasis and detail.) We begin with the emphasis on culture, then move to cultural materialism and its focus on the environment.

EMPHASIZING CULTURE

Strong culture theories are rare in modern anthropology. If we want unambiguous theories of 'strong culture,' we have to go back either to A.L. Kroeber's (1917) argument for culture as 'superorganic' and not reducible to individual-level psychological or biological factors, or to Leslie White and his 'culturology.' For Kroeber (1963, originally published in 1948), 'the mass or body of culture, the institutions and practices and ideas constituting it, have a persistence and can be conceived as going on their slowly changing way above or "outside" the societies that support them.' Culture, for Kroeber, was a product reducible neither to 'mind' nor to individual psychology nor to biological evolution.

For Leslie White (1975: 6), echoing Emile Durkheim's dictum concerning social facts being explicable only in terms of other social facts, 'culture determines and causes culture; culture is to be explained in terms of culture.' White even equates Durkheim's 'social facts' with cultural traits, an equation that few modern sociologists would be quite prepared to make.[2] Unlike Kroeber, however, White also emphasizes the ecology, though he presents little in the way of a theory of mind or of genes.

But if culture as *explicitly* strong has become a relatively rare stance in modern anthropology, culture as *implicitly* strong remains common enough. Ethnography has a subtle tendency to convey the idea that it is somehow the *culture* that is determining the behaviour, though the writer may be well aware that culture is an observer's abstraction from the concrete behaviour of real individuals and not a 'cause' of anything.[3] An implicitly strong conception of culture is also apparent when ethnographers invoke the fuzzy notion of 'enculturation' to account for the complex process of culture transmission from generation to generation. 'Enculturation' seems to imply that culture is somehow strong enough to perpetuate itself unproblematically.

In its simplest form, enculturation 'is seen as an automatic process of absorption in which the child as tabula rasa acquires culture simply by exposure to it' (LeVine, 1982: 62). To use a hydraulic metaphor, wet-sponge parents are squeezed over their dry-sponge offspring and so the water of culture is transmitted from generation to generation. Even writers well aware of the limitations of the enculturation concept may still use it. Harris (1980: 110), for example, points out that 'replication of cultural patterns from one generation to the next is never complete,' while the 'rate of innovation and nonreplication' today has reached a very high level. In other words, the culture of the next generation is always somewhat and often very different from that of the previous generation. This fact does not lead Harris to abandon the strong-culture notion of enculturation entirely, however. Instead, he argues that there must have been 'a breakdown in the enculturation process.' Therefore, 'enculturation ... accounts only for the continuity of culture; it cannot account for the evolution of culture' (p. 111). So something else must account for culture change. Harris's implicit stance

---

2 It would be tempting to present the work of Clifford Geertz, discussed in chapter 7, as a contemporary example of 'emphasizing culture'; but his approach does not belong in the present framework, for his purposes appear to be other than the presentation of a unifying theory of social/cultural behaviour. This distinction is probably true of much of symbolic, structural, and cognitive anthropology as well, wherever they forsake the social sciences for the humanities.

3 Studies of sociocultural change are an exception to this generalization, since such change is generally ascribed to external political, economic, or technological causes.

here is common in much of anthropology: culture is strong and self-replicating except where it obviously is not. From this perspective, we need one theory for change and one for stability, rather than a single theory of culture transmission. The idea that stability is the norm and it is change that must be explained remains a common if waning notion in the social sciences. Notice, for example, that departments of sociology usually offer courses in 'deviance' rather than in 'social behaviour,' as if deviance were problematic but not conformity. From the intra-individual-system perspective, of course, both culture change and culture stability are generated by the interactions of actively strategizing individuals.

EMPHASIZING ENVIRONMENT: MARVIN HARRIS AND
CULTURAL MATERIALISM

Marvin Harris is not really a strong-culture theorist; nor does he stress genes or mind: Harris and his *cultural materialism* emphasize the environment.

In a widely used introductory textbook, Harris (1980) describes cultural materialism as seeking explanations of sociocultural processes 'by studying the material constraints to which human existence is subjected,' constraints involving 'the need to produce food, shelter, tools, and machines and to reproduce human populations within limits set by biology and the environment' (Harris, 1980: 5). The technology and material environment interact to produce the system of social relationships and of cultural beliefs and ideologies.

Why do not Hindus in India eat cows, for example? The answer (according to Harris, 1977, 1979, 1985) is that cows provide valuable dung for fuel and milk for drinking, pull the plows, and tend to live on land that is otherwise quite marginal. Moreover, the lowest castes and the non-Hindus do in fact eat beef. The general 'sacredness' of cows serves to restrict their consumption as meat because widespread beef-eating would interfere with these other, more vital functions. The religious ideology justifying strong restrictions on beef-consumption is a product of rather than a cause of the ways in which cows in India are exploited. Similarly, Hebrew and Islamic law forbid pork consumption not because the pig does not fit the logical categories defined in Leviticus (as we saw, in chapter 6, that Mary Douglas argues), but because the pig is an inefficient exploiter of the Middle Eastern environment and potentially quite destructive of it. To move away from food, 'primitive' warfare and preferential female infanticide serve to prevent overpopulation (Divale and Harris, 1976). Notice that, for Harris, explanation is not in terms of *processes* (that is, biological explanations involve the process of natural selection) but in terms of *functions* – what food prohibitions and other traits are *for*.

Cultural materialism sees culture as a response to material factors rather than as a cause. But it sees mind as another such response: as Harris (1979: 60) puts it, 'the human intuition concerning the priority of thought over behavior is worth just about as much as the human intuition that the earth is flat.' We do not do things such as abstaining from pork consumption because we think we should; we think we should because we do abstain from pork, and we abstain because doing so helps our society adapt to its material situation.

In this context, however, what Harris seems to have in mind by 'thought' is his distinction between *emic* and *etic*. Emic accounts are in the framework of the observed, while etic explanations are presented in terms of the observer's framework. Emically, I do not eat pork because my religion forbids me to do so, while etically I abstain from pork because doing so keeps my society adjusted to its environment. 'Emic' is not quite the equivalent of 'subjective,' for the observed is often unaware of his/her cognitive processes. 'Etic,' though, is rather similar to what we once would naïvely have called 'objective.' For Harris, 'etic' explanations have priority over 'emic' explanations. Thus, he is clearly a 'weak mind' theorist.

Harris believes that 'the test of the adequacy of emic analyses is their ability to generate statements the native accepts as real, meaningful, or appropriate' (1979: 32). By contrast, 'the test of the adequacy of etic accounts is simply their ability to generate scientifically productive theories about the causes of sociocultural differences and similarities' (ibid.). The emic systems – which usually deal with the 'mental' – do not get priority from Harris because they are not really causes of behaviour but reflections of the 'real' causes, the material factors in terms of which the cultural materialist provides an etic account. This reduction of thought and of emic analyses to a secondary role is not all that Harris has to say about mind, as we will shortly see.

While Harris is certainly hostile to what he considers to be sociobiology, he is comfortable with its close relative, the offshoot of Darwinism known as 'optimal foraging theory.' This theory derives from the idea that natural selection will favour those individuals who are most efficient in acquiring food. Thus, it predicts that 'hunters or collectors will pursue or harvest only those species which maximize the rate of caloric return for the time they spend foraging' (Harris, 1985: 165). Optimal-foraging theory permits Harris to account, for example, for why some cultures favour the eating of insects and why others do not. Insects are small and collecting enough of them to provide adequate protein is laborious; often it is more efficient to utilize other sources of high-quality protein. This tendency towards efficiency will cause societies with alternative protein sources to disregard insects as food, and quite likely (through unspecified processes) to develop a strong aversion against eating them. Thus, for Harris, what taboos against insect-eating are *for* is adaptation to the environment.

Criticisms of Cultural Materialism
A familiar anthropological criticism of cultural materialism involves the problems of origins. As Alland (1980: 531–2) explains, it 'cannot account for the *origin* of cultural traits, particularly such aspects of ideology as taboos' (italics in original). Moreover, says Alland, 'it cannot tell us why one solution is favored over another.'

Harris's mode of explanation cannot deal with origins or choices because its accounts are *functional* rather than *processual* in nature. For functionalists, to say what something 'is for' is to explain it. The question of how it came to have that function is not central and may even be ignored. We get neither laws of recurring processes nor predictions, just functions. Optimal-foraging theory, in Harris's hands, alters. For an ecologist, the optimal-foraging behaviour of a species is ultimately due to a well-understood process, natural selection. It is a product of that process. For Harris, optimal-foraging theory is a kind of functionalism in which foraging habits are 'for' adaptation of the group (rather than of the individual) to a particular set of environmental/technological circumstances. His focus is not on the product of a process but on function. Since any society available for analysis must be doing a great many things right or else it would not have long endured, Harris has little difficulty in finding ways in which cultural practices do indeed serve to perpetuate their society and adapt it to environment. Unfortunately, he provides little insight into the processes involved in the selection and integration of culture traits; we still do not know how individuals, interacting over time, generate their societies.

Harris's lack of attention to what makes one account or explanation acceptable and another inadequate is surprising, for he has some interest in the philosophy of science and is concerned with epistemology (Harris, 1979: 29–45). The only rule Harris provides for evaluation of the acceptability of explanations is his previously cited criterion of being 'scientifically productive': this idea is his test of the adequacy of etic accounts, but he fails to explain what he means by the term 'scientific.' If the productivity in question has to do with empirically verifiable hypotheses, then cultural materialism fails its own test.

Marvin Harris assumes that some variables in sociocultural systems (which he terms 'infrastructure') are much more important than others, are much better predictors. To the extent that he has correctly identified system constraints they may well be good predictors (that is, at times he may be right, even if for the wrong reasons). But he also believes that longevity is typical of human societies, and that aspects of culture that may contribute to that longevity can be accounted for by making a case for their so contributing. Thus, Harris 'explains' prohibitions against pork and beef in terms of their presumed role in perpetuating the societies in which these rules are found. This sort of functionalist argument has long been common in the social sciences.

FOCUS 10.1

SYSTEMS-THEORY APPROACHES

One test of adequacy I apply to multi-level theories is whether they take a systems or information theory type of approach, a perspective used not only in this work but shared by the natural and life sciences and, for some practitioners, the social sciences as well (for example, Barkow, 1967; Buckley, 1967). In this view, most processes studied are considered to be too complex for the term 'cause' to be particularly meaningful. Phenomena are seen as being generated by multi-factored, multi-layered processes that tend to be systemic in nature and that often include both positive and negative feedbacks. Phenomena emerge from these processes. Different explanations are expected to be compatible with one another and to be complementary. Climatologists, oceanographers, ecologists, and evolutionists take this approach. In such fields, explanation is often synonymous with modelling, usually mathematical modelling, of the key variables and their interrelationships. The models are always much simpler than the reality, and accuracy is generally evaluated in terms of predictive power. However, social-science models without numbers are quite feasible, too: chapter 9's discussion of the generation of an ethnic boundary among the Hausa, and the explanation for the spread of Islam in Niger, are systems-type, processual explanations that eschew single-factor ideas of causality.

It frequently happens, in many systems, that a single factor or a small set of factors (variables) may by themselves permit fairly accurate prediction. This is especially likely to be true of constraining factors, variables that affect the system but (at least in the short term) are not in turn affected by it. For example, in ecology, latitude is a reasonably good predictor of whether there is likely to be tropical rainforest, as opposed to permafrost. Latitude is therefore a powerful *constraint* on ecological systems, and it, along with mean annual rainfall, altitude, and temperature, forms a set of variables permitting powerful prediction. But latitude is neither a cause nor an explanation of an ecological system. To suggest that it might be is to reveal ignorance of ecological processes. Theorists such as Marvin Harris often mistake constraints for causes: their predictions may indeed be accurate even while their theories are overly simple.

Missing from cultural materialism is the idea of real people, with complex psychologies, interacting together in culturally patterned ways in a real physical environment, and so generating social phenomena.[4] Cultural materialism makes a priori assumptions about what is 'really' important, then seeks an interpretation consistent with that prejudice. By contrast, the intra-individual-system approach posits individuals interacting with each other over time, and generating cultural pools of information that include, among other things, the system-maintaining behaviour that Harris takes as causal. The intra-individual, generative perspective encourages empirical research into actual behaviour, impelling us to observe how and in what circumstances individuals will alter subgoals/plans.

Harris's Views of Mind, Genes, and Sociobiology
Harris's (1979) reactions to Wilson's (1975a) *Sociobiology: The New*

---

4 Harris (1985) may be moving towards a realization that theory requires interacting individuals making decisions. Thus, he now appears to be explaining the Hindu beef-taboo in terms of social conflict resulting from a changing environment. The Brahmans, he argues, were originally beef-eaters and the sacrificers of cows, back during a time when the Indian subcontinent boasted plentiful pasturage. As the pastures and forests were destroyed and replaced by fields, beef-eating became a Brahman privilege that incited the envy of the farming masses. In this context, religions that enjoined the killing of cattle became popular because they were in the self-interest of the great majority of the population. In order to maintain their power and position and in response to the competition from Buddhism, the Brahmans reversed roles and over time became cattle protectors rather than sacrificers.

Synthesis provide some understanding of his approach both to mind and to genes. Disarmingly, Harris is willing to concede that 'the theoretical principles of cultural materialism hinge on the existence of certain genetically defined pan-human psychobiological drives that mediate between the infrastructure and nature and that tend to make the selection of certain patterns of behavior more probable than others' (1979: 127). In short, he accepts that genes do indeed influence the human mind. Harris believes that his dispute with Wilson, whom he apparently takes as representing all who use the term 'sociobiology,' is over the *number* of 'psychobiological drives' (though this undefined and dated term is not used by Wilson). He accuses Wilson of the 'proliferation of hypothetical genes for human behavioral specialties' (p. 127), apparently equating these 'hypothetical genes' with 'psychobiological drives.'[5]

Harris feels that the preferability of cultural materialism's strategy of seeking 'to reduce the list of hypothetical drives, instincts, and genetically determined response alternatives to the smallest number of items compatible with the construction of an effective corpus of sociocultural theory' (p. 127) is axiomatic. If it is possible to explain even cross-cultural universals in terms of 'material' (technological/environmental) factors then that is what one should do. Genetic explanations apparently are to be relegated to the residual, the explanation-of-last-resort, category. Harris explicitly assumes that 'selection in the main has acted against genetically imposed limitations on human cultural repertoires' (p. 136), though he does not explain why this should have been so (and we will shortly see why it should *not* have been so). The 'bio-psychological principles' he is willing to begin with are four: human beings need to eat, be active, have sexual intercourse, have love and affection. Given the exciting advances in the cognitive sciences during the same period that Harris has been writing (see chapter 5's discussion of distributed parallel information-processing, for example), and given his prominence in contemporary anthropology, his ideas about human psychology are embarrassing; they are explicable, however, in terms of the condensation process of academic disciplines analysed in chapter 1. Harris's views on human psychology are quite similar to those of Bronislaw Malinowski (1944).

Notice that Harris's simplistic psychology settles by fiat a major

5 Wilson (1975a) does write, at times, as if there is a quite direct relationship between gene and behaviour. His more recent work, done in collaboration with Charles Lumsden and appearing only after Harris's criticisms, is considerably more sophisticated. It is discussed later in this chapter.

theoretical and empirical problem for human sociobiologists, ethologists, psychological anthropologists, and psychologists: the extent to which natural selection has or has not placed psychological constraints on 'human cultural repertoires.' For Harris, there apparently are no constraints except for his four needs or 'psychobiological drives.' However, for (among others) Lumsden and Wilson (1981), and Boyd and Richerson (1985), this crucial problem is by no means settled, and each of these sets of authors reviews a substantial body of empirical evidence for such restraints (for instance, the nature of certain phobias, data on the diffusion of innovation in other cultures, risk-taking behaviour). But there are strong theoretical reasons to believe that they and others have only scratched the service of these evolved constraints on human flexibility.

As we will see in more detail in chapter 11, selection for flexibility opens the door to fitness-reducing behaviours and therefore to selection limiting that very flexibility. This is because the greater the flexibility, the higher the probability of socially transmitted but genetically maladaptive behaviour. But such behaviour is, by definition, selected against. Assuming that the flexible behaviour has at least some genetic basis, then it must result in the evolution of limitations (perhaps subtle ones) to the very flexibility that permitted the maladaptive behaviour in the first place. This argument is especially cogent because culture itself tends to generate maladaptive traits (chapter 12), but here it is sufficient to note that to argue in favour of flexibility is to argue not for a limited number of 'biopsychological drives' but for a host of subtle psychological constraints on behaviour. In other words, selection is very unlikely to favour open-ended flexibility of behaviour without simultaneously placing important restrictions on it. Just as the rules of chess constrain the possibilities of that game while making the game itself possible, so too do the complexities of human psychology both constrain and enable culture (Lumsden, 1989; Barkow, 1989b). The more Harris and those who accept his position emphasize the flexibility of human behaviour, the more they are in effect arguing for genetic limits to that flexibility. The nature and extent of these limitations remain highly controversial but the controversy is scientific in nature, to be settled by theory and empirical research and not by arbitrary pronouncements.

We have seen that cultural materialists may at times identify the major constraints on a system correctly, even though they are likely to label them (at least implicitly) as 'causal.' Ironically, Harris (1979: 139) makes much the same comment about sociobiological models involving inclusive fitness and reproductive success: 'The reason for this predictability is that most of the factors which might promote reproductive success do so through the intermediation of bio-psychological benefits that enhance the economic, political, and sexual power and well-being of individuals and groups of individuals.' As we will see, sociobiologists would tend to agree with this statement but would add that the 'coincidence' of reproductive and political/economic success is not the product of chance but of natural and sexual selection.

LUMSDEN, WILSON, GENES, MIND, CULTURE

With Lumsden and Wilson we arrive at approaches that are broadly compatible with and even complementary to the intra-individual-system concept. At first glance, Lumsden and Wilson appear to emphasize genes, but more careful reading suggests that they give equal weight to genes, mind, and culture, slighting only the environment.

In 1981, Charles Lumsden and Edward O. Wilson published *Genes, Mind, and Culture*, their ambitious effort to integrate the social/behavioural sciences with evolutionary biology and population genetics. The ambition was evident in their scope, their level of neurophysiological detail, and their use of sophisticated mathematical models to explore various gene-culture interrelationships.[6] They begin in a manner that parallels that of an important earlier work by Charles Laughlin and Eugene d'Aquili (though Wilson, in a personal communication, states that he and Lumsden were not influenced by it). Let us begin therefore with the work of Laughlin and d'Aquili before going on to what Lumsden and Wilson have in effect added to their approach.

Biogenetic Structuralism
Laughlin and d'Aquili's (1974) *Biogenetic Structuralism* is concerned with culture, cognition, neuroanatomy, and neurological function. These authors argue that the deepest level of cognition, the level most proximately under genetic control, is a direct reflection of neurological processes. Though they sought to understand the interaction between the central nervous system and the environment without such intervening concepts as 'mind' and 'culture' (p. 11), perhaps in spite of themselves they develop a theory of 'mind.'

6 Lumsden and Wilson subsequently (1983) largely repeated these arguments but without the mathematical models.

Laughlin and d'Aquili were much influenced by Geschwind's (1965) theory of the 'inferior parietal lobule' (the supramarginal and angular gyri). Geschwind believed this region to be the site of *cross-modal transfers* that permit the brain to conceptualize and categorize (Laughlin and d'Aquili, 1974: 52–3). By 'cross-modal transfer' Geschwind meant that information originating from several sensory modalities (sight, sound, and so on) is cross-associated, permitting a highly complex internal representation. In most other species (the chimpanzee is an exception), there is no direct anatomical pathway among sensory modalities (p. 52).

Laughlin and d'Aquili argue that neuroanatomy directly influences learning, so that 'certain structures underlying cognition, certain models of reality, are genetically determined' (Laughlin and d'Aquili, 1974: 103). Hence, there are cross-cultural universals in cognition.

Lumsden and Wilson

Lumsden and Wilson would no doubt accept this last idea, for they cite much the same range of theory and data as do Laughlin and d'Aquili in seeking support for the existence of 'deep structures' or 'innate constraints' on cognition (Lumsden and Wilson, 1981: 35). This range embraces much of cognitive anthropology and includes theorists from Claude Lévi-Strauss to Jean Piaget and Noam Chomsky (Lumsden and Wilson, 1981: 35; Laughlin and d'Aquili, 1974: 103). Both sets of authors discuss Seligman's (1971) work on phobias, agreeing with him that these disorders have an evolutionary basis. For example, we seem to learn readily – or perhaps need not learn at all – to be afraid of the snake, a dangerous predator. Agoraphobia (fear of open space) may have been selected for because the avoidance of open space may in effect result in the avoidance of places in which there is no way to escape from either human enemy or predator.

There is also a marked similarity between Laughlin and d'Aquili's central concept of *neurognosis* and Lumsden and Wilson's closely related idea of *epigenetic rules*. 'Neurognosis' refers to 'biogenetically given rudimentary information about the world, embedded in various association areas in the brain, either by the time of birth, or by some later maturational stage' (Laughlin and d'Aquili, 1974: 83). Laughlin and d'Aquili subsequently (p. 101) distinguish between neurognosis as 'the informational content of models' (of the world) and neurognostic structure as 'the inferred neuroanatomical base for a neurognostic model.'

For Lumsden and Wilson (1981: 7): *'Epigenetic rules* ... are the genetically determined procedures that direct the assembly of the mind, including the screening of stimuli by peripheral sensory filters, the internuncial cellular organizing processes, and the deeper processes of directed cognition. The rules comprise the restraints that the genes place on development (hence the expression "epigenetic"), and they affect the probability of using one culturgen rather than another [italics in original].'

By 'culturgen' is meant an informational unit of culture, or as Lumsden and Wilson (1981: 7) put it, 'transmissible behaviors, mentifacts, and artifacts.'[7] Culturgens and other terms for units of culture will be discussed shortly. But it is important to note that with the concept of culturgen the parallels between Lumsden and Wilson and Laughlin and d'Aquili come to an end. Laughlin and d'Aquili do not discuss culture as made up of particles of any kind and eschew mathematics. Lumsden and Wilson are strongly interested in the interaction between these culturgens and genes, and present many mathematical models of that interaction.

Lumsden and Wilson speak of gene/culturgen interaction under the rubric of *gene-culture coevolution*, defined as 'any change in the epigenetic rules due to shifts in gene frequency, or in culturgen frequencies due to the epigenetic rules, or in both jointly' (Lumsden and Wilson, 1981: 11). For Lumsden and Wilson, both gene-pools and cultures are analogous in that both are particulate, the fundamental units of gene-pools being genes and the units of culture being culturgens. Just as gene frequencies in the gene-pool change in response to various processes, including natural selection, culturgen-usage frequencies within a culture also alter. However, the two sets of processes directly interact. Changing gene frequencies can lead to a change in culturgen frequencies, for Lumsden and Wilson. At the same time, changing culturgen frequen-

---

7 By 'mentifacts' the authors appear to mean what social scientists usually refer to as 'reifications,' that is, ideas or concepts that are treated as if they were real, tangible, physical items. Thus, in some religions the abstract concept of 'fate' may be reified – or (as in this case) personified – as an actual being or beings. To the extent that they are personifications of natural forces, for example, the Greek gods would be 'mentifacts.' Closer to home, anthropologists and others sometimes reify the concept of culture, thinking of it as something 'real' that can 'cause' or 'account for' phenomena. Presumably, Lumsden and Wilson would classify both the three fates of Greek myth and the naïve use of the concept of culture as 'mentifacts.' It is not clear that the term is needed but the right to neologism is a convention of academic writing, subject though it is to abuse.

cies can affect gene frequencies. Genetic evolution and culturgen evolution are not independent – they affect one another in lawful if complex ways, so that we can speak of a single process of *coevolution*.

Gene frequencies determine the epigenetic rules, which means that the individual acquiring his or her culture does not treat all culturgens equally but is biased towards accepting some rather than others. Lumsden and Wilson call this the 'leash' principle on the grounds that the genes restrict culture, that is, keep it 'on a leash' (p. 13). This term is original, though the concept is not (for example, Barkow, 1973). For Lumsden and Wilson, the 'central empirical problem of gene-culture coevolutionary theory' is 'the degrees of rigidity and specificity of the epigenetic rules created by the interaction of genetic and cultural evolution in human populations' (p. 19). In other words, they are asking what the nature is of the constraints that the genes (more proximately, the central nervous system) put on culture. What kind of culturgens are favoured and disfavoured and how rigid is the bias? Lumsden and Wilson are similarly concerned with the extent to which different cultures (or frequencies of culturgens) in effect exert selective pressures so altering gene frequencies that the epigenetic rules themselves change (a topic we will return to in chapter 11, in the context of the possibility of the genetic assimilation of culture).

What is the relationship between the brain and 'culturgens,' for Lumsden and Wilson? Here, they are much less influenced by Geschwind than were Laughlin and d'Aquili. Lumsden and Wilson's key concept is that of node: 'The human mind ... has a strong tendency to generalize episodic memory into concepts and higher-level entities, which then constitute the "nodes" or references points in long-term semantic memory' (p. 245). These nodes are organized into 'networks' that in turn are called 'schemata.' The brain refers to these schemata in organizing action. The schemata are 'meaning structures.' Learning new concepts has to do with 'a spreading search through the network that attempts to find links with previously established nodes.' Culturgens, it turns out, are represented in long-term memory as 'node-link structures.' In addition, information in the brain is 'chunked' (p. 62) or packaged. The nodes are 'elements of chunks, schemata, and plans' (p. 251). Epigenetic rules control the probability that particular nodes will form links with one another: 'Nodes and sets of closely linked nodes constitute chunks of schemata, and sets of schemata can be delimited from other parts of long-term memory. All of the culturally induced nodes and links stored in the memory of an individual constitute his received portion of the culture' (p. 253). A 'set of nodes and links in long-term memory' is a 'knowledge structure' (p. 253). These knowledge structures, composed as they are of interacting nodes, usually correspond to culturgens (p. 255).

The chain of processes between genetic fitness and culture operates in the following manner, according to Lumsden and Wilson (pp. 254–5): The individual is acculturated, that is, is 'exposed to the culturgens of other members of the society.' He or she then incorporates this information into long-term memory, under the influence of the epigenetic rules, and the resulting knowledge structures become the culturgens of the learning individual. Other epigenetic rules influence his recall, valuation, and decision-making. The resulting behavioural acts then determine his genetic fitness (pp. 254–5).

What of intentionality, purposiveness, goals? Lumsden and Wilson see cognition as the organizer of behaviour and rarely mention goal-oriented behaviour. Nodal ties to the limbic system and epigenetic rules explain the orderliness of behaviour: 'sequences of activities that are rewarded are linked to goal nodes and repeated at need' (pp. 246–7). Some links are 'hot,' meaning that they have connections to the limbic system and are therefore associated with emotion, while others are 'cold,' meaning that they lack such connections and are not involved with the brain's 'reward system' and are not associated with emotion (p. 249). There is no mention of specialized processors or global data banks. Lumsden and Wilson do devote a paragraph to 'will': 'Human will,' they write, 'might be nothing more than the resolution of competition among schemata' p. 89). However, the self, self-deception, and 'unconscious' behaviour are not mentioned by Lumsden and Wilson.

Criticisms

Lumsden and Wilson have gone considerably beyond the path blazed by Laughlin and d'Aquili and deserve much credit for attempting to detail the processes that intervene between genes and culture. Doing so, after all, meant synthesizing material from a wide range of disciplines. They emphasize genes, mind, and culture. Even ecology/environment enters into the theory, at least in terms of the speed with which it may alter, that is, the 'grain' of change (pp. 208–36). But both Lumsden and Wilson and Laughlin and d'Aquili were perhaps overly optimistic in thinking that we now understand the functioning of the brain and the manner in which it stores information. The neurosciences are rapidly moving fields and to use today's thinking is almost a guarantee of finding oneself out-of-date tomorrow. Serious criticisms of the mathematics used in their models have also been made (see Lumsden and Wilson, 1982).

The general framework of Lumsden and Wilson is that of gene-culture coevolution. The mind acts as a filter of culture, a filter whose properties have been determined by genetic evolution, and the resulting culture traits (culturgens) in turn affect the evolution of the mind. This approach is broadly compatible with that of the intra-individual system. But Lumsden and Wilson failed to divide their 'culturgens' into categories. This lack makes their theory extraordinarily complex, for in effect each and every culturgen is its own category, affected by evolved biases specific to it. Gene-culture coevolution is seen as involving a direct relationship between natural selection and (apparently) each and every possible culturgen. The result is that there seems to be little we can predict, empirically, about any particular culturgen: and we are left with a complex and abstract account that fails to lead to research because it fails to generate testable hypotheses.

Lumsden and Wilson's key concept, that of 'epigenetic rule,' is at so high a level of generality that it is difficult to work with. Presumably, different 'epigenetic rules' would apply to subcodes, subgoals, and subplans but, since Lumsden and Wilson themselves do not elaborate such distinctions, they cannot present hypotheses as to the nature of such 'rule' differences.

Lumsden and Wilson give us little insight into goal-oriented behaviour or into the plans or strategies by which goals are achieved. They have no theory of self-awareness. They devote little space to the problem of consciousness, though their brief remarks are at least compatible with the approach of chapter 4. Their framework does not appear to lead to empirical research into actual human behaviour (or, at least, I cannot see what research their work would lead to).

Additional, and powerful, criticisms of Lumsden and Wilson have been made by Robert Boyd and Peter Richerson (1985). We will discuss those criticisms in the following chapter, after we have become familiar with Boyd and Richerson's own framework. We will find that framework, as well as the other approaches to the gene-culture relationship presented in chapter 11, more clear if we first take time out to discuss a recurring analogy, the comparison between units of biological inheritance – genes – and units of cultural inheritance.

THE DIVISIBILITY OF CULTURE

The question of whether culture has units analogous to genes seems to have been introduced to human sociobiology by F.T. Cloak (1975), who termed his units 'instructions.' To what extent is it meaningful or useful to divide culture into some kind of discrete units or 'particles'? To what extent is culture 'divisible'? What is the relationship between cultural units and the information-processing/recording of the brain? These issues are of particular importance to those who wish to apply concepts born of the field of population genetics to culture. They are especially important for those who, like Lumsden and Wilson (1981) and Boyd and Richerson (1985), are attempting to model mathematically the relationship between genes and culture.

Early in this century, anthropologists took the particulate nature of culture for granted. One studied not so much cultures as culture traits: a pottery technique, the building of pyramids, when, where and how many times agriculture was invented, and so on. The notion of culture as holistic, as patterned and configured, came as something of a revolution (Harris, 1968). Anthropologists like A.L. Kroeber (discussed earlier), with his notions of the 'superorganic,' at first appeared to be visionaries. Nowadays the holistic nature of culture is the accepted wisdom in anthropology (which is not to say that it has been subject to much empirical evaluation, as Peter Richerson, in a 1987 personal communication, points out). Trait theory is of course alive and well and will probably always be useful in archaeology and in holocultural studies (cross-cultural correlational surveys), but anthropologists no longer tend to stress the particulateness of culture. Note, too, that when the anthropologist does discuss 'culture traits,' these are located somewhere 'out there' and are not considered to be information units of the brain.

Sociobiological views of culture as particulate do not stem from anthropological trait theory: they are based on an analogy with genes. Richard Dawkins (1976, 1982) carries the analogy close to its limits. His term for the 'particle' of culture, *meme*, even rhymes with 'gene'! By 'meme,' Dawkins originally (1976) seemed to mean almost any kind of idea at all: 'tunes, ideas, catch-phrases, clothes, fashions, ways of making pots or of building arches' (p. 206). Subsequently, he distinguished between a meme and its phenotype. The actual meme is information in a brain, while its phenotype or 'meme product' is its external effect (words, a carving, and so on) (Dawkins, 1982: 109).

Dawkins argues (1976: 206–14) that if the ultimate origin of the gene is the 'primordial soup' in which self-replicating molecules first came into existence, 'the new soup is the soup of human culture' (p. 206).

For Dawkins (1976: 208), both memes and genes must, as 'replicators,' share certain fundamental characteristics: 'longevity, fecundity, and copying-fidelity.' But, he explains, fecundity – the speed and frequency with which replicators replicate themselves in the gene-pool or culture soup – is more important than is longevity, the span of existence of any single copy. Copying-fidelity is more problematic, for memes. An idea is a meme but, unlike a gene, in moving from one individual to another it may be radically transformed. For example, I may not be replicating Dawkins's ideas about memes with total fidelity, here – perhaps my version of his ideas is a sort of meme mutation. After all, as Dawkins (1976: 209) warns us, memes may be 'subject to continuous mutation, and also to blending.' To avoid this problem, Dawkins resorts to what he himself terms 'a verbal trick' (p. 209). He suggests that 'an "idea-meme" might be defined as an entity which is capable of being transmitted from one brain to another ... The *differences* in the ways that people represent the theory are then, by definition, not part of the meme' (p. 210; emphasis Dawkins's). Dawkins does not explain how it might be possible for researchers to determine operationally when two memes are the same and when they are different.

Continuing his extended analogy, Dawkins finds another difficulty: 'Memes seem to have nothing equivalent to chromosomes, and nothing equivalent to alleles' (p. 211). They do, however, for Dawkins, compete with one another. They are competing not for chromosomal loci, argues Dawkins, but for storage space in the human brain and for time: 'If a meme is to dominate the attention of a human brain, it must do so at the expense of "rival" memes' (p. 211). Genes occur in systems of co-adapted gene complexes that give rise, for example, to functioning organ systems. This is because selection has ensured that almost all the allelic variants of a given gene can co-ordinate with the variants of the complex of other genes to produce that organ system. Memes, too, may occur in co-adapted complexes. Dawkins suggests that we might consider a social institution such as a church as 'a co-adapted stable set of mutually-assisting memes' (p. 212).[8]

8 Note that Dawkins has just moved his memes from the brain to 'out there.' Social institutions would presumably be analogous to phenotypes (or perhaps to phenotypic organ systems). Thus, it would be possible for different variants of memes to produce the same or similar institutions, since the memes are 'co-adapted.'

If Dawkins carried the meme idea 'close to its limits,' Ball (1984) reaches the limits and perhaps goes a bit beyond. Here is his typology of memes (p. 147):

1 A *symbiotic meme* promotes behavior that is adaptive for itself and adaptive also for its organism ... ('Sex is fun; pass it on.')
2 A *difficult meme* promotes behavior that is maladaptive for itself but adaptive for its organism ... ('I know how to do it but can't explain it.').
3 A *parasitic meme* promotes behavior that is adaptive for itself but maladaptive for its organism. ('Praise the Lord; send money; tell your friends.')
4 A *bad meme* promotes behavior that is maladaptive both for itself and for its organism. ('Get away from it all; be a hermit.')

I (1978c) provide an additional example of what Ball would term a 'parasitic meme,' one that is genetically maladaptive: the culture trait of military conquest. The resulting warfare is likely to be highly deleterious for the fighting soldiers, and the conqueror society's mortality rate would therefore be high. So long as the conquests are reasonably successful and the resulting conquest state continues to expand, the culture trait will nevertheless increase in frequency.

Durham (1982) provides an example of a 'bad meme,' a trait maladaptive both for itself and for its organism. This meme has to do with *kuru*, a degenerative disease of the nervous system. Kuru was found among the South Fore of New Guinea, and is now known to be caused by a 'slow virus' (a viral disease whose symptoms become evident only long after initial infection), but was originally believed to be hereditary. This was because it seemed to run in families, affecting only women and children. The women, however, would ritually consume the only partially cooked flesh (including the brains) of deceased and sometimes diseased relatives, occasionally feeding scraps to the children. The ingesting of infected, uncooked brain spread the disease (Gajdusek, 1977; Lindenbaum, 1974). The culture trait of mortuary cannibalism among the Fore was thus 'bad,' in Ball's terms: it was obviously maladaptive for its organism, the kuru victims, but was also maladaptive for itself, since if the Australians had not ended cannibalism the disease might have so sharply reduced the Fore population as to endanger its survival and thus Fore culture as a whole (the practice of eating the non-decomposed deceased had been adopted by the Fore only several decades before its forced cessation). (Durham himself describes the practice as an instance of gene-culture *opposition*, which would be the equivalent of Ball's 'parasitic meme,' but Ball's 'bad meme' category seems more applicable.)

Whereas Dawkins (1979) felt that memes have no equivalent of alleles, Ball (1984: 148) thinks that they do 'in the sense that a given environmental cue can release several different behaviors depending on which meme is present.' Also, memes can be dominant or recessive but 'a meme may be dominant in one brain, recessive in another, or dominant at one time, recessive at another' (Ball 1984: 148).

Ball (1984: 148) foreshadows some of the gene/culture interaction debate when he suggests that 'there is no mystery about the scarcity of bad memes. The relative scarcity of parasitic memes provides an argument in favor of tight genetic control over brains and against the blank-slate or tabula-rasa view that the mind is just a storage place for ideas without much selection.'

This notion is in agreement with the criticisms made earlier in this chapter of Marvin Harris's expectation of selection favouring maximum flexibility with regard to culture. For Ball, Lumsden and Wilson's 'epigenetic rules' are in part products of selection against 'parasitic' memes. However, it is not at all clear, as we will see in chapter 12, that 'parasitic' memes are indeed rare. (Are you smoking while reading this?) It may well be that our evolved filters against 'parasitic memes' are very general and very imperfect (as Boyd and Richerson argue), rather than quite strong and specific, as Lumsden and Wilson believe.

Ontology and Utility of Cultural Particles

Is culture 'really' particulate or not? This question may be of interest to philosophers concerned with the nature of existence, but for researchers, the fruitful problem is whether treating culture as particulate orders data, advances theory, or leads to testable hypotheses. As we have seen with Lumsden and Wilson, and as we will see in the next chapter with Boyd and Richerson (1985), the answer is 'sometimes.' Some categories or subcategories of cultural information do seem to lend themselves to a 'meme' or 'culturgen' approach; for example, whether I brush my teeth with a rotary motion or up-and-down and side-to-side. Others, such as my perception of the nature of the Holy Trinity, do not seem to lend themselves to particulate approaches.

Perhaps the question of whether culture is particulate or not is of much less importance than one might at first suppose. After all, it is difficult, in practice, to discuss the details of culture without discussing some kind of units, regardless of whether one terms them 'traits' or 'memes' or 'practices' or 'beliefs.' The important questions seem to involve the relationships between such cultural details and the processes – psychological and social-psychological – affecting their acceptance, rejection, transformation, and replacement.

In similar fashion, the important question is not the extent to which cultural evolution is analogous to genetic evolution, but rather the extent to which the analogy can fruitfully be applied to the complexities of actual history. The approach may at times be of use. As we will see in the next chapter, the analogy may help us to understand the origins of culture and perhaps even of some of the psychological mechanisms responsible for cultural transmission and revision. Moreover, thinking in terms of memes as at least somewhat independent of genes is good preparation for what will be a recurring theme of the next two chapters of this book, the theme of how culture may at times reduce genetic fitness.

With these remarks, we are ready for the next chapter and for the ideas of Robert Boyd and Peter Richerson.

SUMMARY

1. This chapter and the one that follows compare approaches that are either alternative or complementary to the intra-individual-system framework. These approaches share components and a goal: that of providing a framework for the understanding of human social behaviour; the components are genes, mind, culture, and ecology.

2. Modern theories rarely treat culture as explicitly causal in nature. Ethnography, however, tends to treat culture as implicitly causal.

3. Cultural materialism 'explains' in terms of material constraints involving food, shelter, tools, machines, and the need to limit population. It sees belief systems and ideologies as reflections of these material factors rather than as causes in their own right. In general, cultural materialism tends to take constraints on systems for causes, and to give us no processes involving the real decisions of real people.

4. Cultural materialism incorrectly views sociobiology as requiring a large number of 'psychobiological drives,' each of which is tightly linked to genes, while cultural materialism views the mind as extremely flexible. But minds so flexible could not have evolved, since cultures tend to move in fitness-reducing directions and only complex evolved restraints on mind can prevent this trend.

5. Laughlin and d'Aquili argue that the deepest level of cognition,

that most proximately under genetic control, is a direct reflection of neurological processes.

6. Lumsden and Wilson take a similar approach and present a conceptual, neurological model of human cognition. Their basic units of culture, the *culturgens*, are directly encoded in the mind. The mind reflects gene frequencies, so that changing gene frequencies can directly affect culturgen frequencies. Genetic evolution and culturgen evolution *coevolve* in lawful if complex ways.

7. Lumsden and Wilson have little to say about intentionality, goals, or plans. Their framework does not seem to lend itself to research (at least, not social-science research).

8. The analogy between genes and units of culture made by Lumsden and Wilson occurs often in human sociobiology. Richard Dawkins calls his units of culture *memes*, by which he means almost any idea at all. Memes, for Dawkins, are 'replicators' like genes. They compete with each other not for chromosomal loci but for storage space in the human brain. They occur in co-adapted systems, giving rise to institutions, such as churches.

9. Ball carries the analogy between cultural particles and genes even further. His typology includes symbiotic memes, difficult memes, parasitic memes, and bad memes.

10. Ball argues that the scarcity of 'parasitic' memes (memes that promote behaviour that increases their own frequency at the expense of the host's genetic fitness) is evidence against a *tabula rasa* approach to mind. I suggest that it is not at all clear that parasitic memes are particularly scarce.

11. The important question is not whether culture is 'really' particulate but whether treating culture as particulate orders data, advances theory, or leads to testable hypotheses. The answer to this question must be 'sometimes.' After all, it is difficult, in practice, to discuss the details of culture without discussing some kind of units, regardless of what term one applies to them.

11

Dual versus Unitary Evolution

This chapter continues the discussion of approaches that are comple-
ments of or alternatives to the intra-individual-system framework. It
will focus on two theories that deal with genes and culture. Both Robert
Boyd and Peter Richerson (1985) and Richard Alexander (1979) agree
that the genes are our first system of inheritance. While Boyd and
Richerson argue that culture is a second system of inheritance, Richard
Alexander holds that culture may not usefully be dissociated from the
inclusive-fitness strategies of individuals. We will be comparing both
sets of arguments with those of Lumsden and Wilson (1981), and with
the intra-individual-system framework presented in earlier chapters,
the framework of codes/goals/plans/mazeway.

BOYD AND RICHERSON AND DUAL INHERITANCE

Definitions of Sociobiology
We begin with the matter of labels. In *Culture and the Evolutionary Process*
(1985), Boyd and Richerson, who would certainly consider their
approach Darwinian, would prefer not to be considered human
sociobiologists. This is not a trivial matter, recalling chapter 1's
discussion of the sociological significance of disciplinary boundaries.
Boyd and Richerson feel that 'human sociobiologists make predictions
about patterns of human behavior by assuming that human behavior
tends to maximize inclusive fitness' (p. 13), and they themselves do not
make this assumption. They are concerned not primarily with genetic

fitness, as are many sociobiologists, but with the process of culture transmission within and across generations.

One must respect their right to categorize themselves as they wish, and 'human sociobiology' is often used in the manner they say: but not always. Neither D.G. Freedman (1979), in his important work *Human Sociobiology*, nor J.H. Crook (1980) in his major study *The Evolution of Human Consciousness*, for example, takes inclusive-fitness maximization as axiomatic, though both accept the 'sociobiology' label. *Darwin, Sex, and Status*, too, uses the term in this comprehensive manner, as including much of human ethology and other fields that take an evolutionary perspective but also take fitness-enhancement as something to be established empirically rather than axiomatically. For that matter, not even the prominent sociobiologist Richard Alexander would insist that all behaviour, cultural or otherwise, is either fitness-enhancing today or was yesterday for our ancestors (cf. Alexander, 1979: 93). I am afraid that, in the broad manner in which many of us use the term, Boyd and Richerson's own work is indeed 'human sociobiology.'

Boyd and Richerson's view of 'sociobiology' is particularly severe with regard to culture. Human sociobiologists, they argue, 'believe that it is not necessary to take the details of cultural transmission into account when predicting human behavior' (ibid.).[1] For Boyd and Richerson, culture and the details of cultural transmission must always be taken into account. This is because, for them, culture is *evolutionarily active*[2] and its properties can affect the results of coevolution with genes much as the properties of genes do.

1 By this definition, Richard Alexander (whose work we will discuss shortly) would be a 'sociobiologist.' Alexander (1987: 225), however, rejects the term on the grounds that it has entered the popular ('scientistic') mind as implying the use of biological arguments to support conservative political views.

2 Peter Richerson (in a personal communication) suggests this phrase as a substitute for the term 'semi-independent,' which I used in an earlier draft of this chapter. 'Semi-independent' overstated the case, he felt. The genes do influence the distribution of culture traits, but culture traits may themselves affect the frequency of genes, in the Boyd and Richerson framework. This is not to say that each affects the other equally. Elsewhere (1989b), I suggest that the Richerson and Boyd view of the relationship between genes and culture may be likened to the Earth-moon relationship. Strictly speaking, the moon does not revolve around the Earth: both Earth and moon revolve around a common centre of gravity. However, this common centre is so much closer to the centre of the Earth than it is to the moon that it is reasonably accurate to say that the moon does, more or less, revolve around the Earth. Similarly, the genes have far greater influence over culture than culture does over the genes.

Dual Inheritance
For Boyd and Richerson, culture is a system of inheritance in its own right, and they stress its partial separateness from genetic inheritance by speaking of human beings as having a 'dual inheritance.' This latter concept is subtly different from the coevolutionary approach of Lumsden and Wilson (1981), for the term 'dual' suggests the possibility of a considerable degree of active influence of cultural evolutionary processes on the final results of gene-culture coevolution. Boyd and Richerson present a range of mathematical models incorporating a variety of assumptions about the kinds of relationships that may obtain between genes and culture traits (they do not use the term 'culturgens'). One of their more interesting conclusions is that, since culture and the relative frequencies of culture traits may at times evolve in competition with genetic evolution, some culture traits may actually be genetically maladaptive, rather than, as most sociobiologists would expect, fitness-enhancing.

Particulateness of Culture
Boyd and Richerson deal with gene-culture interaction in mathematical terms, as do Lumsden and Wilson, but they differ from the latter in a number of important respects. Lumsden and Wilson think of their 'culturgens' as units of culture that correspond to units of neurological information-recording/processing. Boyd and Richerson do not even 'assume that culture is encoded as discrete "particles"' (p. 37). The point they are making in taking this stance is that we do not yet know precisely how the brain encodes information, or whether it encodes it as *indivisible* atoms. They assume, in certain of their models, that culture traits may blend with one another to form new units and (p. 75) are free to do so because of their lack of indivisibility.[3] Both Dawkins (1976) and Ball (1984), as we saw in the last chapter, discuss this possibility of 'blending' (as, for that matter, do Lumsden and Wilson).

Innate Structure
The culture trait of Boyd and Richerson is much less structured, neurologically, than the culturgen of Lumsden and Wilson, and is not

---

3 Of course, one could argue that culturgens are smaller units than are culture traits and the blending is simply a matter of the recombination of the former into new forms of the latter. Thus, the culture traits would be the equivalent of chromosomes. This possibility only underlines the fuzziness of both concepts.

linked to any particular conception of neuroanatomy. Boyd and Richerson here have been influenced not by theorists of deep codes like Chomsky or Laughlin and d'Aquili – codes that Boyd and Richerson would typify as 'innate structure' – but by the social learning theorists Bandura and Walters (1963; Bandura, 1977). For these psychologists, there is no need to posit that the brain possesses domain-specific information-processing 'mental organs.' They do not even accept that 'humans are innately predisposed in favor of certain grammatical rules' (Boyd and Richerson, 1981: 45). Instead, 'social learning theorists believe that the organic capacity to acquire culture is very general. Grammatical rules are held to be acquired through social learning' (ibid.).[4] Thus, for Boyd and Richerson, social transmission of information ('culture') can be accounted for by a rather undifferentiated social learning capacity.

Boyd and Richerson believe that this difference in approach between the 'innate structure theorists' (like Chomsky, 1980, or Lumsden and Wilson, or Laughlin and d'Aquili, 1974) and those influenced by Bandura and Walters has profound implications for how gene-culture coevolution is viewed: they argue that those who believe that informational units of culture have substantial structure necessarily hold views that 'require that innate biases influence which cultural dispositions are acquired' (p. 46). Such theorists are thus obliged to believe that cultural transmission involves fairly strong 'innate biases.' But those influenced by social learning theory – notably, Boyd and Richerson themselves – can view genetic evolution as having provided us with quite weak, general biases, as well as (in some cases) strong and specific biases in favour of certain culture traits rather than others. The mathematical models that Boyd and Richerson produce, some of which include the *costs* of strong and accurate biases, are quite consistent with a 'weak genes' approach.

Biases and Guided Learning
Social learning is, in Boyd and Richerson's terms, 'an inheritance system' (p. 79). For social scientists accustomed to speaking of 'social inheritance' and 'tradition,' this statement comes as no surprise, but Boyd and Richerson mean by it something rather specific: that culture is a system of inheritance comparable to genetic inheritance, and their

---

4 This position is becoming increasingly rare among psycholinguists. See, for example, Brown (1973) or Brown and Herrnstein (1975), or chapter 5's discussion of codes and subcodes.

mathematical models – largely derived from population genetics – reflect this view.

It is perhaps more surprising that they also argue that individual learning and social tradition are conceptually quite separate and distinct (p. 81), even if, in some of their models, strongly coupled. Boyd and Richerson identify the transmission of social tradition with observational learning and believe that the processes involved in it are quite distinct from what they term 'individual learning.' Though this distinction is obviously open to criticism, it permits them to make a mathematical point. In any system of natural selection, whether genetic or cultural, the rate of evolution will depend to a considerable extent on the amount of variability in the population. In genetic evolution, for example, if there are no alleles, no genetic variants, then evolution will not take place no matter how much selection pressure on phenotypes exists: there is nothing to select, the variation has already been used up. If our cultural system of inheritance depends entirely on social transmission, then the rate of cultural evolution, too, will depend on the amount of variability in the population. In this case, of course, we are talking about variability in cultural traits transmitted by observational learning. By contrast, if cultural transmission is dependent upon individual learning, then there is no way for variability to be exhausted because each individual continually produces variants. Individual learning, in short, has a sort of built-in high-culture-mutation rate, with the potential bonus that what is learned may be systematically advantageous instead of blind.

Guided Variation
Individuals do not learn at random – the variants learned presumably tend to favour the adaptive, usually owing to genetic evolution. 'If such learned variants are culturally transmitted, the result is a force that increases the frequency from one generation to the next of the same variants whose frequency is increased within a generation by learning' (p. 82). This 'force' is termed by Boyd and Richerson *guided variation*. It has to do with 'ordinary learning plus cultural transmission' (p. 9).

The proximate mechanisms of guided variation are diverse. For example, we may learn to prefer ripe to unripe fruit because the former is sweeter, and genetic evolution has resulted in our preferring the sweet to the sour or bitter, since that which is sweet is more likely to be nutritious. Individual learning to prefer ripe fruit would be the first step in the guided variation process. It might then happen that others will learn about the preferability of eating ripe fruit by observing us, in which case the eating of ripe fruit will be culturally transmitted. This would be guided variation. In each subsequent generation, then, the eating of ripe fruit will be more common in the pool of culture variants. This is because those individuals who have not acquired the trait through cultural inheritance (by observing others) will tend to learn it individually, and by doing so will increase the number of role models for the next generation (cf. p. 95).

Now, suppose that it is difficult for individuals to discover by individual learning what is genetically adaptive in the environment – perhaps some sweet tastes mask low nutrition or even poison, for example. Individual learning is thus costly. But suppose that the environment is also quite homogeneous and unvarying – once an adaptive trait has been acquired it will continue to be adaptive. In such a situation, genetic evolution will strongly favour observational learning (p. 110). The result will be a culture or protoculture in which individual learning plays a small role and observational learning – imitation – a very large one.

Let us change our suppositions. This time, suppose it is relatively easy for individuals to learn, through their personal experience, that which is adaptive. Suppose, too, that the environment is heterogeneous and varies considerably, so that what one observes another doing may turn out to be genetically maladaptive when one copies it oneself. In such a situation, we would expect a species to develop a high reliance on individual learning but relatively little in the way of culture or protoculture, of socially, observationally transmitted information. Boyd and Richerson provide mathematical models for these (and other) situations (pp. 94–115).

One conclusion that Boyd and Richerson (p. 116) eventually come to, on the basis of their models, is that 'natural selection will favor an increased reliance on culturally inherited beliefs whenever (1) the error rate of individual learning is substantially greater than that for social learning and (2) the environment is reasonably predictable.'

Biased Transmission

Boyd and Richerson distinguish among three types of biased transmission. *Direct bias* involves applying decision rules based on the property (or properties) of the trait itself. For example, a directly biased culture variant might be one that was the easiest to learn, or that worked better. Their example (p. 135) is a choice among ways to grip a ping-pong paddle. Lumsden and Wilson's models usually assume direct bias in favour of one culturgen variant rather than another. *Indirect bias* might involve choosing the grip favoured by successful ping-pong players. The bias is the result of a decision rule associated with a secondary trait carried by the bearers of the culture variant (the model). The secondary trait in effect indicates whom to imitate. Finally, there is *frequency-dependent bias*, which involves choosing a variant on the basis of how often it is 'used by most of the models' (p. 135). The rule might be to choose the variant most often used (conformism), but could also be to select the least common trait.

Direct bias is very similar to guided variation. In both cases, some external character is determining the choice of variant. In both cases, too, 'the guiding criteria that shape the direction of the ... transmission could be inherited genetically or culturally or learned independently' (p. 136). The only real difference seems to be that in direct bias the variants are modelled by actual individuals, while with guided variation the individual generates the variants him/herself ('learns' them). Moreover, the 'two processes are not mutually exclusive' (p. 136). Why, then, make the distinction? The answer (as was discussed previously) is that, in their equations, the source of variability can make a good deal of difference. Direct bias is heavily dependent upon existing variability – if the models present only a single variant then direct bias is irrelevant. But guided variation, since it involves self-generated variants, is not dependent upon the cultural repertoires of others (pp. 136–7). Moreover, presumably it is less costly to evaluate observed alternatives than to invent one's own.

Biased transmission may result from choices made by individuals from among alternative variants. It can also result from the particular range of choices (variants) to which parents expose their offspring (p. 144).

Direct Biases and Lumsden and Wilson

The most important criticism of Lumsden and Wilson made by Boyd and Richerson concerns the former's 'thousand year rule.' Under some circumstances, argue Lumsden and Wilson, the genetic assimilation of some cultural traits should take approximately one thousand years. Suppose we have two culturgens. In environment A, culturgen 1 tends to enhance genetic fitness. In environment B, it is culturgen 2 that is the more adaptive. In environment A, therefore, selection will favour individuals who have a learning bias (a 'direct bias,' in Boyd and

Richerson's vocabulary) in favour of culturgen 1. In environment B, selection will favour individuals who have a similar bias but in favour of culturgen 2. If the two environments each remain constant for fifty generations (one thousand years), argue Lumsden and Wilson, then there will be a genetically based psychological difference between the two populations. Individuals in population A will be more predisposed, genetically, towards learning culturgen 1; while in population B, individuals will be more genetically disposed towards the acquisition of culturgen 2. Thus, the psychic unity of humankind will have been violated. Lumsden and Wilson suspect that such genetically based differences in learning propensities may be common among human populations.[5]

Boyd and Richerson point out that the equations that suggest that genetic tracking of culture can occur within one thousand years assume that phenotypic selection is very strong and that the population is a genetic isolate – no migration, no gene flow. They also assume a constant environment, so that the selection pressure is unvarying. Boyd and Richerson suggest that, under these conditions, Lumsden and Wilson's conclusion is not at all surprising. Indeed, they wonder (p. 164) why, under such conditions, the behaviours being tracked would remain 'cultural' at all – would they not be assimilated to the point at which we need no longer speak of cultural transmission, so strong might selection for the propensities in question be? For Boyd and Richerson, then, the circumstances leading to the one-thousand-year rule would have been relatively rare, and the issue is not especially interesting.

Boyd and Richerson point out that Lumsden and Wilson are primarily concerned with direct biases, biases causing one variant (culturgen) to be acquired rather than another. But genetic selection will favour such direct bias only if there are alternative variants present. As Boyd and Richerson (p. 156) put it: 'For directly biased transmission to be strongly favored by selection, migration must maintain enough

5 Though it is presented in more mathematical form in Lumsden and Wilson (1981), Wilson (1971, 1975a, 1975b) has in the past discussed genetic tracking of culture in similar terms, and elsewhere (1980b) I have discussed at some length the problems of empirically investigating the genetic-assimilation-of-culture hypothesis. I also provide the only empirical analysis thus far available (admittedly, using not very high-quality data) of the possibility (Barkow, 1977a). My conclusion is that genetic tracking of culture may have been of some importance at various points during our evolutionary history but it is unlikely to have occurred in the recent past. In any event, it would be nearly impossible to demonstrate its occurrence empirically.

variability to create a significant probability that offspring will be exposed to maladaptive variants.' But the existence of migration means that immigrants are constantly arriving – gene flow is diluting the results of natural selection. In short, 'we should not expect alleles that code for the appropriate habitat-specific bias to become very much more common than the other biased allele' (p. 156).

The genetic evolution of the strong direct biases favoured by Lumsden and Wilson must automatically be weakened by the very situation that would result in their selection: if the selection pressure in favour of a direct bias is to be maintained then cultural heterogeneity must also be maintained, but its maintenance involves immigration and therefore gene flow, and a consequent weakening of the frequency in the gene-pool of the alleles coding for the direct bias! In this sort of situation, 'ordinary genetic adaptation works better without the existence of the intervening process of cultural transmission' (p. 157). Boyd and Richerson apparently do not envisage a situation in which the cultural variability is maintained not by migration but by taking outsiders as models.

Indirect Bias
Indirect bias means that human beings behave as if we have a certain built-in rule: acquire traits from individuals who are within a given range of values on a particular indicator trait (p. 243). The indicator trait that Boyd and Richerson usually appear to have in mind is prestige, so that 'indirect bias' is generally a formalization of the common observation that human beings tend to learn most readily from the high in prestige (though not from those perceived as radically different from themselves – see the discussion of 'encapsulation' in chapter 8 or in Barkow [1975a]). They find some empirical support for this observation in the diffusion of innovation literature (p. 245). We tend to imitate the prestigious, the successful, the respected. Indirect bias is important in the discussion of dual inheritance but since it is a relatively simple concept, and since we have dealt with prestige in detail in chapter 8, I will not devote more time to it here.

Frequency-Dependent Bias
Equally simple but still important is what Boyd and Richerson term 'frequency-dependent bias,' a concept that reduces to the rule of conformity: whatever others are doing, you do, without any evaluation of its effectiveness (p. 207). Though Boyd and Richerson do not point

this out, frequency-dependent bias seems to be a particularly important mode of trait acquisition for children, who presumably are not yet able to evaluate relative effectiveness.

In-group Co-operativeness

Boyd and Richerson are particularly interested in accounting for in-group co-operativeness. As we saw in chapter 6, they are unhappy with the autopredation-hypothesis approach to the evolution of co-operativeness. In place of it, they espouse a type of cultural group-selection model.

Boyd and Richerson here have been strongly influenced by D.T. Campbell's (1975) discussion of altruism and group selection. Campbell argues that co-operativeness and altruism can evolve culturally, as products of group selection among *cultures* (not *genetic* group selection). Back in chapter 2, we discussed how genetic group selection is generally considered to be much less powerful (at least for organisms other than social insects) than is individual selection. Campbell argues that this is not necessarily the case for cultural evolution, and that perhaps groups with values favouring internal co-operativeness have been more successful than have other groups, so that the culture trait of in-group co-operativeness has spread.

Boyd and Richerson's mathematical models support Campbell's approach, for they suggest that the various learning biases they postulate, frequency-dependent bias (conformity) in particular, can lead to a form of group selection in which culture traits for 'co-operation' or 'altruism' or 'self-sacrifice' may become established at high frequencies in spite of their tendency to reduce individual genetic fitness (pp. 227–40). They conclude that 'group selection can increase the frequency of cooperators' (p. 235), at least in small, 'culturally endogamous' groups. Moreover, it can do so without requiring the assumption of frequent extinction for the non-co-operating societies. Boyd and Richerson accept that their 'simple model of cultural group selection ... clearly is not verified by the data concerning ethnic cooperation' (p. 240), but they do not appear to believe that the data necessarily contradict their model either.

Weak Biases

One of the most important conclusions that Boyd and Richerson's models lead to is that 'relatively weak biases that would be difficult to detect empirically can lead to rapid change in the frequency of different variants in the population, particularly when transmission has an important horizontal component' (p. 146). Weak biases, in short, may be quite important in cultural transmission but at the same time be very difficult to demonstrate experimentally. ('Horizontal' transmission here refers to individuals within a generation learning from one another rather than a younger generation learning from its elders. The existence of horizontal transmission is one of the important ways in which cultural inheritance differs from genetic inheritance.)

Boyd and Richerson find that substantial bodies of social- and behavioural-science literature support their weak-bias position. Reviewing the diffusion of innovation literature (p. 167), for example, they find that non-industrial peoples adopt new practices quickly only when they confer rather obvious relative advantage, and that the first individuals to adopt them are those who can best afford the risk. They also find that existing cultural beliefs (for instance, whether drinking water has or has not been boiled is irrelevant to health) often interfere with innovation. They review behavioural decision theory (p. 168) and conclude that we human beings are demonstrably poor makers of decisions. We also form causal beliefs on slender evidence and take no account of sampling error and representativeness. Human beings as individuals, they conclude (p. 170), 'are not very good at solving novel problems, or ones requiring statistical evaluation,' and this fact 'suggests that complex cultural adaptations are unlikely to be the result of individual learning alone.' Moreover, cultural data are 'noisy' and much determined by chance, since we tend to hold to the first idea we happen to have. Finally (p. 170), 'the fact that beliefs are extremely resistant to change, even in the face of overwhelming evidence, also provides direct evidence that the forces due to direct bias and guided variation are weak.'

CRITICISMS OF BOYD AND RICHERSON

Boyd and Richerson's key points (at least for me) are the following: (1) Culture is itself a system of inheritance, not merely a direct reflection of the genes but evolutionarily active, capable of generating maladaptive as well as adaptive behaviours. (2) Weak and empirically difficult to detect biases are sufficient to account for culture tending, over the long run, to enhance inclusive fitness. We need not look for strong, direct biases, for hard-wired 'instincts' (though their theory in no way precludes the existence of such strong biases). (3) Culture does not simply reduce to enlarged inclusive-fitness-maximization strategies and may include fitness-neutral or even fitness-reducing traits. *None of the criticisms made below weakens these central conclusions*, and their implications will be discussed at length in the next chapter.

In-group Co-operation
The power of the autopredation hypothesis, rejected by Boyd and Richerson, comes from its ability to explain our species' immense capacity for in-group co-operation, as well as other aspects of the ethnocentrism syndrome. Though the autopredation process alone is probably insufficient to account for the evolution of in-group co-operation, it seems likely that it was one of the contributing processes. Cultural group selection, too, may have contributed to the evolution of in-group co-operation – the two accounts are logically compatible, and both are equally speculative. The mathematical model that Boyd and Richerson produce in support of their speculations is not entirely convincing: were they so inclined, no doubt they are capable of developing models inconsistent with the cultural-group selection account of co-operation. Might they not have assumed that 'uncooperativeness' also spreads by frequency-dependent bias and, since it gives a genetic advantage to its bearers, that natural selection would have favoured the evolution of a direct bias in favour of lacking co-operation? But just as the autopredation hypothesis is not so easily dismissed, neither is the argument in favour of cultural group selection for co-operativeness.

Recently (1989), Richerson and Boyd have presented a clearer and stronger case for cultural group selection in favour of co-operation. They even suggest that some aspects of religion may be both genetically and culturally adaptive by restraining some of our 'genetic selfishness' traits in favour of co-operation and other 'common good' behaviours. Richerson and Boyd present a mathematical model in which status becomes associated with collective good (such as co-operation), so that there is sexual selection for something other than individual-level genetic selfishness. They do not explain how status would have become associated with the collective good in the first place. (Focus 11.1 provides a rather speculative account of how the association may have arisen. There is some reason to believe that, as one ages, one becomes more altruistic. Should the aged for some reason have become numerically dominant, in an early hominid group, they might have used their influence to raise the status of 'co-operators' or even to cause their younger kin to mate preferentially with such co-operators.)

Building on the ideas of Richerson and Boyd, one could argue that cultural group selection would have spurred autopredation. Let us assume that a religion or moral code can be comparable to a technological advantage, in that it makes for more efficient in-group co-operation. Groups with this moral code would tend to have lower casualties than would other groups, in conflict situations, leading simultaneously to cultural group selection *and* to an autopredation effect. Unfortunately, fascinating as many of us find such speculations, it is difficult to imagine how they might be empirically evaluated.

Boyd and Richerson (p. 240) do not claim that theirs is 'a complete hypothesis to account for cooperative behavior in humans.' It will no doubt be very long before a consensus exists among evolutionists as to the origins of human co-operativeness. Just to underscore the speculative state of this controversy, Focus 11.1 provides an additional scenario for the development of co-operativeness in human groups.

Failure to Distinguish between Plans and Goals/Codes
Early in their book, Boyd and Richerson make clear their disagreement with the 'innate structuralists.' In part, this disagreement may stem from their shared (with Lumsden and Wilson [1981], among others) failure to distinguish between codes and plans/goals. Selection would have favoured processing different types of cultural information in different ways (discussed in chapter 7). Thus, Lumsden and Wilson's models tend to be appropriate for the apples of subcodes, while Boyd and Richerson appear primarily to have in mind the oranges of subplans. Boyd and Richerson would probably accept that different culture traits may be subject to different constellations of 'forces' but do not go on to develop a set of categories.

As was discussed in chapters 5 and 7, the arguments and evidence in favour of innate structures for linguistic encoding/decoding are very strong, and by extension it is at least reasonable to argue that cultural subncodes in general, where n is low, rely in some degree on innate structures. But subngoals and especially subnplans are quite flexible even when n is low (but above one or two), and arguing that they may in part be transmitted through simple observational learning can be in keeping with the intra-individual-system approach, provided one appreciates that the 'simple observation' is likely to involve evolved mechanisms (guiding attention, for example). The ideas of Lumsden and Wilson and Boyd and Richerson, too, may be more complementary than they imagine. The former appear to have codes and subcodes in mind, the latter plans and subplans.

FOCUS 11.1

TWO VIEWS OF THE EVOLUTION OF CO-OPERATIVENESS

Here are two conjectures regarding the evolution of co-operativeness. They are alternatives both to each other and to the culture-group selection approach of Boyd and Richerson. The first is demographic and developmental, the second involves the internalization of norms. All three approaches (including that of Boyd and Richerson), plus a fourth, that of autopredation, can be presented so as to be mutually compatible.

A Demographic Approach

This approach postulates that people become more co-operative as they grow older. Societies that either have a high proportion of older people, or else accord them more influence, will therefore develop cultures reflecting this possible increased tendency towards co-operativeness.

Do we really become more altruistic, more helpful towards others and less competitive, as we age? Though students of personality change during the life span have apparently not expressed this change in quite these terms, such a conclusion is consistent with the findings of Gutmann (1969, 1987) and of Levinson (1978). From an evolutionary perspective, it would have been in the fitness interests of our older ancestors to invest in kin rather than to compete for mates. Presumably, their tendency towards helpfulness and co-operativeness would have generalized beyond the circle of kin. Presumably, too, their status would tend to be relatively high, given their age, and so they would have influenced others towards co-operativeness (by being role models, by serving as mediators, and so on). If such a developmental trend towards altruism is a long-standing trait in our species, then a simple demographic change, or a political movement towards gerontocracy, would account for the growth of co-operativeness in human societies. A random demographic change might have triggered a growth in co-operativeness, which might then have spread through a Boyd-and-Richerson-type positive 'frequency-dependent bias' or even cultural-group selection.

The merit of this explanation is that it is, with some difficulty, empirically verifiable. The prediction is that societies with a higher proportion of older people will show more in-group co-operation than will other societies. Also, societies that accord higher status to the aged should demonstrate more in-group co-operation. Note that Boyd and Richerson themselves cite studies of changes during the life span and advocate 'models of age-structured cultural transmission' (p. 295).

The Internalization-of-Norms Approach

Here is a second hypothesis, one somewhat more complex. This has to do with selection for the internalization of norms. Elsewhere (1976a, 1977a), I have argued (at much length and in far more detail) that we may have been selected not merely to observe or imitate others but to internalize the rules for behaviour they have enforced, and that we are most likely to internalize those rules enforced by high-status individuals, particularly by those who have real power over us. This tendency is most evident in children but can manifest itself in adults as well.

The ultimate origins of norm acquisition, then, may have been selection in favour of children obeying parental admonitions even in the absence of the parents. Initially, such rules would have involved 'do not stray from camp' or 'keep away from predators.' Thus, there would have been strong selection in favour of this kind of norm-acquisition ability. But, more important for the evolution of co-operative behaviour, one rule parents then and now would no doubt have enforced would have been 'do not fight with your siblings.' This early norm would then have generalized, eventually resulting in a norm of in-group co-operativeness.

There is no way to demonstrate that such a norm-acquisition process was in fact partly responsible for the evolution of co-operativeness, but there is, at least, evidence for our having a powerful norm-acquisition mechanism consistent with it, one that can be activated even beyond childhood. As adults, when we find ourselves physically under the control of others we may, quite involuntarily, internalize the norms they exemplify. Hence, the phenomenon that Anna Freud (1946) termed 'turning against the self.' In this phenomenon, hostages in hijackings appear unaccountably favourable towards their kidnappers, and prisoners in situations such as concentration camps or the Siberian gulag ape their guards. This bizarre behaviour seems to closely resemble one of the ways in which children internalize norms.

It is instructive to compare the complexity of these two 'explanations' for the evolution of human in-group co-operativeness with the simplicity of the model presented by Boyd and Richerson. Note, too, that both explanations and Boyd and Richerson's account could all be true together. Finally, it may be that all three efforts are misguided. Both explanations assume that generalization from kin to non-kin occurs spontaneously.

No Sensitive Periods

A third criticism of Boyd and Richerson is their lack of any theory of sensitive periods, or of any other developmental phenomena. They are explicitly aware of this lack but preferred to keep their models as simple and manageable as possible. The price paid has been heavy, however, particularly when one notes that it includes omitting discussion of attention structure. While this last criticism, too, is equally applicable to Lumsden and Wilson, it is Boyd and Richerson, after all, who emphasize observational learning in cultural transmission: observation requires attention. The various 'biases' and 'guided learning' that they postulate may actually have to do with selection for attending to some sets of stimuli rather than to others, and to some categories of individuals rather than to others.

Boyd and Richerson do discuss the idea of 'cognitive style' but treat it purely as a culture trait, rather than what it is at the level of the individual, a developmental phenomenon or product of a sensitive period. 'Cognitive style' encompasses the notion of 'field dependence' and 'field independence.' H.A. Witkin and his collaborators noted that some individuals are able to perceive the upright even if the context is shifted, while others are context dependent. Field-independent people are those who tend to experience parts of the field 'as discrete from the field as a whole' (Witkin and Berry, 1975). Field-dependent people perceive a field globally, its parts fused to the whole. Field independence is associated with the ability to identify contextually hidden figures, individualism, and competitiveness. Cultural groups are usually typified by the predominance of one style or the other. Berry (1976) concludes, on the basis of the many studies he has conducted, that the varying cognitive styles of peoples reflect adaptation to ecology. Focus 11.2 discusses the relationships among the ideas of sensitive period, attention structure, and cognitive style.

The Distinction between Guided Variation and Direct Bias
Is the distinction between guided variation and direct bias meaningful? Is there really a substantial difference in information-processing between learning behaviour by individual effort and acquiring it by observing someone? On the one hand, Boyd and Richerson (1985: 136) do not appear to be arguing that distinct neurological mechanisms are involved; on the other, the two processes are seen as distinct in that they have different consequences for culture transmission.

Ethnography casts doubt on the individual learning/observational learning distinction. Studies of Northeastern Algonkian Indians show that their socialization techniques emphasize attention to small detail rather than to verbal explanation. Children who ask questions are rebuked or answered with sarcasm. The individual learns to infer highly complex, non-verbal rules (cf. Hallowell, 1955: 125–50).

FOCUS 11.2

COGNITIVE STYLE, ATTENTION, AND SENSITIVE PERIODS

I propose here that field independence and hedonic attention structure are closely related cognitive styles, and that they may both result from a predominantly hedonic attention structure towards parents and other authority figures during a sensitive period in childhood (probably one ending by puberty but this is an empirical and unstudied question). Similarly, field dependence may be a product of a predominantly agonistic relationship with authority figures during the sensitive period. Agonistic attention and field dependence both represent greatly constricted perception. I will also argue that while field independence/hedonic attention structure may well be ecologically adaptive among the hunter-gatherer societies in which they are the norm, there is no particular reason to believe that field dependence and agonistic attention structure are or have ever been ecologically adaptive.

I am assuming here that parental warmth and nurturance are associated with hedonic attention. That parental warmth and nurturance and emphasis on independence and self-reliance generally occur together is not an assumption but a research finding (Kohn, 1963; Werner, 1979). These traits are also typical of the American middle class and of the élites of developing nations. By contrast, among American lower classes, who tend to be field dependent, parents are more likely to emphasize obedience and responsiveness to *external* authority than they are to emphasize warmth and self-reliance (Kohn, 1963). Similarly, agricultural peoples, who also tend to be field dependent, are relatively harsh in child discipline.

Witkin and Berry (1975) argue that cognitive style is generally ecologically adaptive (they are not considering genetic adaptation here). For example, élite middle-class executives require field independence for positions that involve much decision-making. Members of fairly authoritarian, hierarchical societies – who tend to be field dependent – benefit from the tendency to co-operate and to defer to authority that is associated with that cognitive style.

In similar fashion, relatively stern, authority-oriented child-rearing practices among agricultural and other groups have been interpreted as adaptation to the physical and social environment. Barry, Child, and Bacon (1959) concluded from their pioneering cross-cultural survey that food-accumulating peoples (such as farmers) required reliability in subsistence activities more than they did independence and self-reliance, and therefore socialized their children accordingly.

Boyd and Richerson (1985: 180) largely accept the 'adaptive' explanations of field independence/dependence (they do not deal with attention structure), but provide an alternative to the sensitive-period hypothesis. They suggest that field independence is typical of the middle class and of élites in developing nations because, in these cases, 'field-independent individuals are more likely to do well in school and subsequently to become teachers, business owners or managers, bureaucrats, and so on ... The new field-independent élites transmit their values and skills to some extent horizontally and obliquely to their employees and pupils.' Boyd and Richerson thus see field independence as an aspect of culture that is being socially transmitted. This possibility is not incompatible with field dependence/ independence also being a sensitive-period phenomenon. Note, however, that their approach would not explain why parental warmth should encourage field independence.

I would propose that horizontal transmission of the high-hedonic-attention structure/high-field-independence cognitive style combination is at best a minor contributor to a sensitive period phenomenon that occurs wherever children are raised in a warm, relatively-free-from-social-fear environment. Middle-class and élite peoples are more hedonic and field independent because they are economically more secure and of higher status, and are thus less constricted and angry in dealing with their own children. If anything is being socially transmitted from parents to children directly, it is not hedonic attention structure/high field independence but economic security and a particular set of child-rearing practices.

Field independence/hedonic attention are also typical of hunter-gatherer peoples, who are notably warm and indulgent in their child-rearing. The resulting cognitive style is indeed ecologically adaptive. (Note, for example, the description of the Cree goose hunt that follows this focus.)

But agonistic attention and field dependence are unlikely ever to be adaptive. Were there such a thing as independent and self-reliant, hedonically oriented peasants and lower-class workers, they might well transform their economies. Agricultural peoples and lower-class workers are agonistic in attention as children and field dependent as adults because they are more fearful and angry than are élites and the middle class. In the case of lower-class workers, this state of mind is probably the result of low power and status. In the case of agriculturalists, the harsh discipline and resulting agonistic attention is probably a product of living in an environment far from that to which we are adapted. Hunter-gatherers need not discipline their children harshly because, thanks to natural selection, the children find the activities of collecting and hunting so pleasurable as to constitute play. But agriculturalists must force their children – and themselves – to practise heavy, prolonged, unenjoyable physical labour at a schedule not of their own choosing. This state produces the constriction of agonistic attention and field dependence.*

If agonistic attention/field dependence are never ecologically adaptive then why should there be a sensitive developmental period that may produce them? The answer is that they may be *genetically* adaptive. Low-ranking individuals from low-ranking kin-groups may have had a selective advantage in focusing their attention, in a fear-constricted manner, on the activities and desires of the high-ranking. Note that one aspect of field dependence is the tendency to defer to authority. This constriction may very well have hampered hunting and gathering activities, but such a cost may have been more than compensated for by the benefit of avoidance of punishment from the high-ranking.

*Zelniker and Jeffrey (1979) provide an interesting discussion of 'attention and cognitive style in childen' that is not, however, particularly relevant to this discussion. The problem is that they appear to be unaware of Chance's work on hedonic vs. agonistic attention structure and seem primarily concerned to demonstrate that differences in attention between field-dependent and field-independent children amount to something more than a matter of developmental lag.

For example, during a Cree goose hunt there are myriad complex factors to be taken into account, yet these factors are never discussed (Craik, 1975). No one is 'taught' to hunt and verbal explanations are not provided. All that is seen is some very quiet men following the lead of a 'goose boss' who himself speaks almost not at all. They arise before dawn and go to a particular spot at a lakeshore, position themselves, and wait. The choice of site and position is crucial, but young Cree must infer for themselves the bases of the choice. The complex calculations involving wind direction, behaviour of other birds, weather, sounds made by the hunters themselves, past experiences at the site – these cannot in any case be observed. In this type of context, is it really possible to distinguish between 'observational' learning and 'individual' learning? This possibility seems rather implausible. The fact that Boyd and Richerson can develop models based on the postulate that the two processes are distinct does not render their distinction meaningful.

Reliance on Social Learning Theory
Boyd and Richerson accept a generalized learning ability that seems very unlikely to have ever evolved, or to reflect the neurological bases of learning (cf. Symons, 1989). The problem here is that they have followed the wrong psychological mentors. Current approaches to the human mind were discussed back in chapter 5, approaches in which the brain is seen as having a substantial number of specialized processors or subsystems. No mention was made of a 'global learning processor.' As Tooby and Cosmides (1989) convincingly argue, learning cannot be a

unitary process because, in each domain, different 'error rules' are required. For example, the first test for whether you have learned to shape stone correctly involves whether it fractures before your tool is fashioned. This is one error rule. The test for whether or not food is nutritious involves our chemical senses of taste and smell – here, the rule is that what smells 'good' (that is, contains certain marker chemicals) is nutritious. The test for whether a cave is safe involves whether it contains fresh bear or other large animal dung. Now, imagine we were writing an 'expert' computer program capable of determining whether our tool-making techniques are adequate, whether food is nutritious, or whether a cave is safe. Could we write a single 'learning subroutine' for all three cases? The answer is no, we would need a different error rule or test in each case. We would have to write three different subroutines. Human learning, whether 'individual' or 'observational,' is no doubt similar, if far more complex. 'General learning' involves the simultaneous use of a multitude of what Staddon (1981: 135) terms 'computational elements' and Tooby and Cosmides (1989) call 'mental organs.' Whatever our scenario for the beginnings of selection for the capacity for culture, it is clear that it would have begun only with domain-specific learning, as with other species. We might initially have been selected for individual recognition of conspecifics, for communication about the location of food sources (as Kurland and Beckerman [1985] argue), or for imitating food-acquisition techniques. However we began, selection would have favoured the acquisition of specific attentional biases and information-processing abilities. After all, selection for some sort of global learning ability, even if possible, would have been far more costly, energetically, than selection for the very specific abilities we actually needed.

We saw in chapter 10 (and will discuss at greater length in chapter 12) that, were our psychology as simple as some anthropologists have imagined it to be, culture would inevitably move in fitness-reducing directions and we would be selected against, rather than for, the capacity for culture. Similarly, Lumsden (1989) and Symons (1989) have cogently argued that only complex psychologies can account for cultural transmission and cultural variability. The self-esteem/prestige behaviour discussed in chapter 8 is one example of such a complex psychological trait. Other examples include the sensitive-period hypothesis for the determination of courtship strategies (Draper and Harpending, 1982, discussed in chapter 13); sexual jealousy (discussed in chapter 14); the male courtship patterns of deceitful seduction, honest co-operation, and forcible rape (chapter 14); and the hypothesis that co-rearing leads to future sexual aversion, thereby generating the 'incest taboo' (chapter 14). Similarly, Cosmides and Tooby (1989) analyse the psychological bases of reciprocal altruism as another 'mental organ.'[6]

But when Boyd and Richerson posit mechanisms such as 'indirect bias' or 'frequency dependent' bias, they, too, are postulating complex psychologies. If their mechanisms seem simpler than those developed by others, it is in part because, as was suggested previously, they are more interested in subgoals and subplans than they are in subcodes, and the mechanisms involving the latter are more complex than those pertaining to the former. The dichotomy that Boyd and Richerson posit between 'structuralists' and 'non-structuralists' such as themselves is not fruitful: the meaningful question involves the kind of psychological mechanisms needed to account for the diversity of human behaviour.

Boyd and Richerson deliberately chose to use simple models whose simplifications are clear, rather than highly complex models whose errors might not be. The simplicity creates problems. Perhaps the single most important question they are asking is: Under what circumstances will natural selection favour cultural transmission, and what kind of psychological mechanisms would be likely to evolve, in such cases? One of their answers, as we have seen, is that when individual learning is expensive and the environment fairly predictable, the mechanism selected for will result in heavy reliance on social transmission. This is a good preliminary answer. There is little doubt that Boyd and Richerson have demonstrated the power of their approach.

It is unfortunate that they chose to use a version of psychological theory – 'social learning theory' – that (in my opinion) cannot bear the burden they place on it: but this decision hardly invalidates their general approach. Boyd and Richerson simply need to posit more complex psychological mechanisms, limited to specified domains, in place of global mechanisms somehow processing diverse kinds of information. In the case of frequency-dependent bias or imitate-the-high-in-status biases, for example, they are clearly on the right track – we no doubt do have specialized processors leading us to attend to sexual and resource-related behaviour on the part of the high-in-status, and to monitor the frequency with which specific prestige strategies are used by those around us. While we do not yet understand the algorithms used by

6 For discussion of evolved psychological mechanisms, see Barkow, Cosmides, and Tooby, eds, *The Adapted Mind: Evolutionary Psychology and the Generation of Culture* (New York: Oxford University Press; in preparation).

these processors, for Boyd and Richerson the next step would be to specify the circumstances in which their postulated biases should operate and then examine empirically whether the resulting model predicts actual behaviour. Their models do imply the operation of different mechanisms in different circumstances, but these implications need to be made explicit and detailed.

If Boyd and Richerson want models that begin to approach the actual complexity of cultural transmission, they need to ask questions such as these: In what kinds of environments, for what kinds of information, for what life stages of individuals, will selection favour what kinds of information-acquisition mechanisms, with what algorithms? Thus far, they have not dealt with the problem of kinds or categories of information, or of life-stage differences in selection pressures for information acquisition. Pointing out this lack is not meant as criticism but as an indication of how much work remains for them and others to do.

Since Boyd and Richerson's approach permits varying assumptions to be made in each model, they can deal with geographic and temporal variation in environment (though they have not yet done so in any systematic manner). We evolved not in a single environment but, both at any one point in time and across the millennia, in a wide variety of them. Probably all their assumptions about the environment have been, for some times and places, accurate, and for other times and places, inaccurate. There may well have been a time and place, during the long history of the hominids, when each model presented both by Lumsden and Wilson and by Boyd and Richerson was for a time correct.

Daly (1982) and Daly and Wilson (1989) have pointed out that culture-transmission models based on analogies with population genetics, such as those of Richerson and Boyd, omit people. Human beings are acting, strategizing, goal-seeking creatures: but in models dealing with 'biases' and the relative frequencies of alternative 'culture traits,' people seem to be lacking, especially goal-oriented people. Whatever the unit of selection is, for transmission theorists, it clearly is not the individual. This is perhaps not so damning a defect as Daly and Wilson believe. There is something to be said for a population genetics that ignores phenotypes in favour of allele frequencies, and there may well be a place for theories of culture traits coupled to disembodied learning biases. After all, Boyd and Richerson would certainly agree that biases and guided variation are the products of individuals acting in a strategizing, fitness-enhancing manner. Their approach, and that of transmission models in general, is simply at too high a level of abstraction for discussion to focus on the individual. As was made clear in chapter 1, no discipline or approach has a monopoly on truth, and our goal is for a variety of compatible theories. Ultimately, the kinds of mathematical models that Boyd and Richerson create must first be judged by their compatibility and consistency with other theory, and secondarily by whether they produce empirically verifiable hypotheses.

Boyd and Richerson do go a way towards bridging the gap between sociobiological approaches to culture, on the one hand, and most anthropological views, on the other. They provide us with a respectable middle ground. Their general approach can be made broadly compatible with, and complementary to, that of the intra-individual system. Culture is a system of social inheritance, as 'mainstream' anthropologists have all along assumed. It is tied to genetic evolution, as sociobiologists have argued: but the tie is complex and some maladaptive cultural traits are to be expected (as will be illustrated in chapter 12), given the potential costs associated with acquiring information of a very high degree of accuracy. Boyd and Richerson deal with mind, genes, and culture, but no one of these is elevated to the status of a main determinant. These theorists make it clear that their efforts are preliminary, not definitive: eventually, one hopes, they will produce models of specific times and habitats, and populations.

Boyd and Richerson, like Richard Alexander, believe that human beings tend to enhance their inclusive fitness. However, the models Richerson and Boyd produce indicate that it would be too costly for us to rely exclusively on individual learning, so that selection has favoured a capacity for culture that, at times, may permit us to accept maladaptive culture traits. For Richard Alexander, culture is not a second system of inheritance and so he is not concerned with the details of culture transmission. For Alexander, it is inclusive-fitness optimization alone that lies centre-stage.

RICHARD ALEXANDER

Richard Alexander (1974, 1975, 1979; Flinn and Alexander, 1982) has set out to challenge the discipline of anthropology by repeatedly demonstrating that, hostile though many anthropologists may be to sociobiology, the data of anthropology nevertheless support sociobiology. Alexander does not provide a sociobiological theory of the origins of culture, as Boyd and Richerson in effect do (by explaining under what circumstances social transmission should be favoured by selection). Nor does he attempt to link culture to neurological function, as do Lumsden and Wilson. What he does is to argue, with considerable success, that many recurring aspects of culture enhance the inclusive fitness of the individuals who participate in them. For Alexander, such a functionalist (as opposed to processual) account constitutes explanation.

While Boyd and Richerson see cultural transmission as evolutionarily active, Alexander tends to see culture as the amplification of individual fitness strategies, the accumulation of such strategies, and the result of compromises and alliances among individuals. He offers no theory of mind save the notion that we are genetically self-interested and that our behaviour should be enhancing our inclusive fitness; when given a choice, we should usually choose the more fitness-enhancing course.

The differences between Alexander and Boyd and Richerson are as much matters of emphasis as substance. Boyd and Richerson would expect some culture traits to be genetically maladaptive. From their point of view – and my own – the burden of proof is on those who claim any particular culture trait to be fitness-enhancing. Alexander and those who follow him (for instance, Irons, 1979) would expect the great majority of cultural institutions to be fitness-enhancing. For them, the burden of proof is on those claiming maladaptation.

Chapter 12 will be devoted to theory and data explaining precisely why we should expect much of culture to be genetically maladaptive for at least some people. Let us therefore spend the remainder of this chapter seeing how Alexander can make non-intuitive cases for it being adaptive. First, we will see how his approach can lead him to error, then we will see how it often leads to accurate interpretation.

Not All Cousins Are Equal

The English language reflects our 'Eskimo'-type kinship system: for us, all cousins are equal. That is, both in terms of terminology and in behaviour, we tend to make no distinctions among first-degree cousins. This seems to make sociobiological sense, since cousins have a coefficient of relatedness of one-eighth. But for many of the world's societies all cousins are *not* equal. In particular, distinctions between *cross* and *parallel* cousins are very common. A parallel cousin is father's brother's child or mother's sister's child. That is, a parallel cousin is the offspring of a parent's same-sex sibling. A cross-cousin is the offspring of a parent's opposite-sex sibling, that is, father's sister's child or mother's brother's child. Alexander (1979: 180), citing Murdock (1967), finds that approximately half of the world's peoples distinguish between cross and parallel cousins.

The distinction is not just terminological, for it is common for cross-cousins to be preferred marital partners, but for parallel cousins to be forbidden marriage to one another. Parallel cousins, in fact, are frequently treated as siblings, in terms of marriage rules. This distinction seems to violate sociobiological expectation and suggests that in this case cultural evolution has been quite independent of its genetic forbear. After all, the coefficient of consanguinity between first degree cousins, whether parallel or cross, is one-eighth. Alexander (pp. 176–83), however, explains that one-eighth is not always one-eighth.

Again making use of Murdock's world sample of societies, Alexander reports that, for approximately two-thirds of those of the world's peoples for whom data are available, under some circumstances a man may have intercourse with his brother's wife, or a woman with her sister's husband. This means that it is apparently fairly common for socially defined parallel cousins to be genetic half-siblings. Thus, rules forbidding parallel-cousin marriage boil down to *incest avoidance*. But no such problem arises between cross-cousins: a man can hardly have fruitful sexual intercourse with his wife's *husband*, after all, or a woman with her brother's wife; so a cross-cousin can never be a half-sibling. The distinction between cross and parallel cousins therefore *is* of considerable genetic significance. Cross-cousins may be related to each other by one-eighth but parallel cousins vary between one-quarter (when they are biological half-siblings) and one-eighth (when they are not).

To further strengthen his case, Alexander takes a close look at the seventy-nine societies in which sororal polygyny is practised. In these societies, a man may marry sisters. In seventy-five of the seventy-nine such societies in Murdock's survey of the world's cultures, parallel cousins are treated as siblings while cross-cousins are not. The data clearly support Alexander's incest-avoidance explanation of cousin asymmetry.

Note that Alexander has not provided us with any theory of 'proximate' mechanism – any idea of the actual human psychological traits or of the nature of the social interaction processes that generate, in some societies, the distinction between cross and parallel cousins. For Alexander, making a case for a culture trait's consistency with the maximization-of-inclusive-fitness axiom of sociobiology is sufficient –

he is content with functional explanations. But what happens when we seek the proximate mechanism involved?

We have considerable understanding, as Alexander himself points out, of the proximate mechanisms underlying incest avoidance *per se*. It is now well established that children raised as siblings will not find each other appealing as potential marriage partners, once puberty arrives (see Shepher [1983] for discussion and references). The tendency for familiarity not to breed seems to be a social-psychological mechanism that tends to prevent inbreeding in our species. Close inbreeding tends to reduce genetic fitness (Charlesworth and Charlesworth, 1987), and so selection has favoured those who find siblings sexually uninteresting.

But selection has provided us with no special sense of degree-of-kinship detection (as was discussed in chapter 3). Instead, it reliably achieved incest avoidance by the evolution of the algorithmic rule that those with whom one is reared hold much less sexual interest for one than do more novel individuals. This particular proximate mechanism presumably evolved during a time when those reared together had a very high probability of being either siblings or other close kin. The mechanism is still there and, when we rear genetically unrelated children together, as in the Israeli kibbutz, once they reach puberty they tend not to find each other suitable for marriage.

Now, let us apply that rule to Alexander's findings. If we look at his sororal-polygyny data, we find that in most cases the parallel cousins are raised together, the cross-cousins are not. Though I have not recalculated his data in detail, residence pattern is probably at least as good a predictor of cousin asymmetry as is genetic relatedness. Moreover, co-residence predicts *which* set of parallel cousins will be classified as siblings.

Most matrilineal societies are also matrilocal or uxorilocal, meaning that after marriage the new family lives with or near the kin of the bride. Matrilateral parallel cousins would therefore grow up living together or near to one another. Thus, I would predict that, in societies with matrilocal/uxorilocal residence rules, matrilateral parallel cousins (mother's sisters' children) should be classified as siblings, but not father's brother's children. This is precisely what we usually find in matrilineal systems (for example, Crow-type kinship systems). Similarly, in patrilineal societies the residence rule is usually patrilocal/virilocal (with the groom's father or in his vicinity). This time, it should be the patrilateral parallel cousins (father's brother's children) who are classified as siblings. This is what we find when we look at, for example, Iroquois-type systems, which are patrilineal and almost always patrilocal.[7]

Alexander may be correct in hypothesizing that parallel cousins are somewhat more closely related to each other than cross-cousins are to each other. But this possibility, even if it were empirically established, might well be an irrelevant epiphenomenon, since as Alexander himself (p. 181) admits, the great majority of the world's peoples, regardless of kinship system, forbid marriage between first-degree cousins of any kind.

Note that the residence-pattern explanation of cousin asymmetry is quite as 'sociobiological' as is that of Alexander, since it is based on a trait – co-rearing reduces sexual attraction – that presumably evolved because it tended to enhance genetic fitness. But I do not explain current kinship systems (or even cousin asymmetry alone) in terms of that trait. Rather, I argue that the kinship systems evolved in response to the interaction of human beings with this particular trait over many generations. Presumably, people who tended to feel towards parallel cousins much as they felt towards siblings, but towards cross-cousins in quite a different way, would have been more comfortable finding terms and marriage rules that reflected their feelings. Note, too, that this supposition leads to an empirically verifiable hypothesis: if the analysis is accurate then, historically, residence pattern should tend to change first and kinship behaviour and terminology only later. Finally, the predictions concerning residence pattern and whether and which parallel cousins will be defined as siblings are also empirically verifiable.

As I have repeatedly argued, we need levels of explanation and must not limit ourselves to a sociobiology of selection pressures. By slighting the proximate, Alexander does damage to his own case.

The Avunculate

Alexander (1974, 1979) and Kurland (1979) have striven to account for the fact that, in some societies, a man appears to invest substantially in his sisters' offspring rather than in those of his wife. In these societies (which are matrilineal), children belong to the lineage of the wife rather than the father, and they inherit not from father but from their male

---

7 Thornhill and Thornhill (1987: 392–3) discuss Alexander's conclusion that parallel cousins are less likely to be permitted to marry one another than are cross-cousins. They agree that the crucial factor here is co-rearing, and that parallel cousins are more likely to have been reared together than are cross-cousins.

lineage members, mother's brothers. At first glance this pattern – which is known as the *avunculate* – would appear to violate the sociobiological inclusive-fitness-enhancement axiom. After all, a man's children share one-half of his genes, but his sister's children – his nephews – share only one-quarter of his genes if the sister is a full sister, and only one-eighth if, as is often the case, he and the sister have only their mother in common.

But how closely *is* a man related to his wife's children? Marriage, in these societies, tends to be unstable. A man usually resides with his wife but his real interests – and his heirs – are back home, where his sisters are. Moreover, even if a marriage is of long duration, surrounded as he is by his wife's relatives and far from his own, a man is in a very poor position to control his wife's sexuality. And, in fact, in these matrilineal, avunculate societies, there tend to be relatively few restrictions on female sexuality (compared, at least, to non-avunculate, patrilineal, and bilateral-descent societies). So there is a very real possibility that the children of a man's wife are not, in fact, his genetic children at all. Therefore, goes the Alexander/Kurland reasoning, it may well be in a man's genetic interest to invest in his sister's children – who are somewhere between one-quarter and one-eighth related to him – rather than in those of his wife, who may be no kin to him at all.

Let us assume that empirical research shows that Alexander's controversial suppositions about coefficients of relatedness between men and their nieces and nephews in avunculate and non-avunculate societies are correct. Is his account therefore an explanation? Once again, without knowledge of the proximate mechanisms the answer is, 'no'; it is a functionalist interpretation. The only proximate explanation I have been able to invent (Barkow, 1984) is a hypothetical and hitherto-unknown psychological trait: human males must apparently monitor the sexual activities of their wives and automatically calculate their paternity confidence. When their confidence of paternity falls, they should become increasingly interested in their sisters' children. Such a trait would presumably, in societies in which paternity certainty was consistently low, give rise to the avunculate. Alternatively, perhaps there is some emotional quality in a marital relationship that either enhances or suppresses, in a man, interest in a sisters' children. These hypotheses are empirically verifiable (though not without some difficulty). If neither of them is valid, and if no functionally equivalent hypothesis is, either, then Alexander's interpretation of the avunculate must fall (Barkow, 1984). Genes cannot influence behaviour or culture without proximate mechanisms. If there are no such mechanisms then, however one is to account for the avunculate, Alexander's 'explanation' is impossible.

Alexander Is Often Right
These two examples notwithstanding, Alexander provides too many accounts in which cultural patterns are indeed consistent with the inclusive-fitness-maximizing axiom for it to be plausible that all – or even most – are irrelevant epiphenomena. Alexandrian genetic-fitness interpretations of culture traits provide valuable opportunities to generate testable psychological hypotheses, hypotheses concerning his missing proximate mechanisms (Barkow, 1984). They also provide an interpretation of culture that seems to anger many anthropologists.

Marshall Sahlins (1976) was one of sociobiology's earliest and most severe anthropological critics. Nevertheless, Alexander convincingly argues that Sahlins's own (1965) work in economic anthropology includes theories of reciprocity that are entirely consistent with socio-biological expectation.

Sahlins distinguishes among three kinds of reciprocity. *Negative reciprocity* refers to coerced or forced exchange. One side gives a good deal more than the other under real or implicit compulsion. In a sense, negative reciprocity is not really reciprocity at all. One side exacts resources from the other unequally. Just as a sociobiologist would predict, negative reciprocity involves relationships *outside* the local group, that is, outside what was, until quite recently in human history, the kin group. Negative reciprocity means one group or individual using power to enhance its or his/her genetic fitness at the expense of another.

Sahlins's *generalized reciprocity* involves an ethic of everyone receiving their share, even when this sharing involves sustained unequal transactions. Returning the benefit is not required, even if the imbalance is of long duration. Generalized reciprocity is typical of hunting-gathering (foraging) societies, where it in effect makes for a single standard of living and automatically protects the infirm, injured, and aged. The unit of generalized reciprocity is the local group, the band. Since this would have been in effect a band of kin (or, at least, it would have been so earlier in our evolutionary history), generalized reciprocity is a good approximation of nepotistic altruism.

Balanced reciprocity is virtually identical to Trivers's (1971) concept of 'reciprocal altruism.' The partners keep track of how much each is given, and each partner is expected to return to the other the equivalent of what he or she has received, if the relationship is to continue. For example, Nigeria's Migili (Koro) engaged in work-bees, during the 1970s (Barkow, 1982), and each participant was expected to donate to the others as many days of labour as were donated to him, a typical example of balanced reciprocity. Where labour aid was donated, the recipients tended to be kin. The average coefficient of relatedness was considerably lower among the members of work-bee groups then it was between givers and recipients of donated labour aid (p. 43). That is, just as Alexander would predict, nepotistic altruism was directed towards kin, reciprocal altruism towards non-kin (or at least towards those with whom one was less closely related).

As usual, Alexander in discussing reciprocity does not find it necessary to analyse the proximate mechanisms involved. In this instance, at least, however, the fields of human ethology, and developmental and cognitive psychology, as well as behaviour genetics, provide him with some help. Rushton et al. (1986), in a study comparing monozygotic and dizygotic (identical and fraternal) twins, concluded that the former were more similar in degree of altruism than the latter, with approximately one-half of the variance being due to genetic differences. This high heritability of altruism suggests that individual differences in that trait, at least for the particular population studied, are associated with allele differences. Hoffman (1982) concludes that studies of pro-social behaviour in young children confirm that there is indeed a strong and spontaneous tendency towards altruism in the young. Cosmides and Tooby (1989) have attempted to specify the algorithms used by a hypothetical specialized processor regulating altruism, and have found experimental evidence for its existence. Thus, while the specific evolved mechanisms underlying altruism are still not fully understood, there is strong evidence that such mechanisms do exist, and we are beginning to analyse them.

Culture is not, for Alexander, a system of inheritance, and he accepts neither that culture is particulate nor that the complexities of the processes of cultural transmission are of special importance. He specifically disagrees with an earlier presentation of their thinking by Richerson and Boyd (1978), writing (1979: 78–9): 'To whatever extent the use of culture by individuals is learned ... *regularity of learning situations or environmental consistency is the link between genetic instructions and cultural instructions which makes the latter not a replicator at all but, in historical terms, a vehicle of the genetic replicators* [emphasis in original].'

But Alexander also writes of 'cultural inertia' (p. 77), which results from 'conflicts of interest among individuals and subgroups, from power distributions that result in stalemates, and from the incidental long-term persistence of some cultural institutions. This means that culture will not be seen as maximizing group interests.' Alexander is at once saying that culture is not a replicator but a 'vehicle for the genetic replicators' (p. 79), while arguing that, because of 'cultural inertia' (p. 77), these vehicles may in fact not be optimizing anyone's fitness. Presumably, for at least some individuals, culture may well be reducing fitness from what it would be were the culture somewhat different. If this is so then Alexander's entire enterprise of interpreting culture as enlarged inclusive-fitness-optimization strategies must fall. He accepts that 'cultural inertia' means that there is a decoupling of culture from genes. Having come this far, it is surprising that he is not willing to consider that culture, too, may be a system of inheritance.

Evaluation of Alexander's Approach to Culture
Alexander, who strongly rejects gene-culture coevolution and any other 'dual inheritance' approach, may be confusing the *use* of culture with *culture*, a theory of culture with one of how we human beings manipulate it in the service of inclusive fitness. As individuals, we do manipulate, edit, distort, and reinvent our cultures in response to goals and plans and biases that evolved as a result of genetic evolution. Thus, culture tends to be fitness-enhancing. But once we understand 'culture' to refer to a pool of socially transmitted information and accept that the transmission process is complex and, as Boyd and Richerson (1985) argue, has properties not reducible to a calculus of inclusive fitness, then it becomes apparent that some culture traits may, at times, be genetically maladaptive; and the relationship between genes and culture must be one of coevolution.

William Durham (1982), who argues powerfully for a coevolutionary view, makes a compatible point: Flinn and Alexander (1982) reject coevolution partly on the grounds that the approach makes cultural evolution autonomous, separate from genetic evolution. Durham's reply is that culture tends to be genetically adaptive because 'the *products* of natural selection in human evolution ... the structures and functions of human neurophysiology, do influence the course of cultural evolution in substantial ways' (p. 319, emphasis in original). Most of the time, argues Durham, the result is genetically adaptive cultural information. The occasional neutral or genetically maladaptive trait, for Durham, is 'transitory.' He does not argue, as I do, that the strongest support for the coevolutionary view – the view that cultural and genetic evolution, while intricately interwoven, nevertheless have a certain degree of mutual independence – comes from the existence of genetically maladaptive cultural traits. Much of the next chapter is devoted to that topic. Some cultural traits, we will see, are likely to be fitness-reducing, perhaps in spite of our individual efforts; and Durham notwithstanding, such traits are not necessarily transitory but under some circumstances may endure.

Alexander's great strength is in the simplicity of the data required to evaluate his hypotheses: data on inclusive fitness, or at least on reproductive success. Though I have argued above that these data are often quite misleading and even entirely irrelevant, at least he is indicating what class of data should be collected. This simplicity makes his ideas attractive for anthropological field-workers and other researchers. No doubt, too, anthropology's long tradition of functionalism has made some anthropologists particularly receptive to Alexander's brand of genetic functionalism. At the same time, the anti-psychological bias of anthropology may also have made some anthropologists comfortable with Alexander's habitual slighting of psychological processes (Barkow, 1984). The far more complex and abstract approaches of Lumsden and Wilson or of Boyd and Richerson do not readily yield simple research designs with an emphasis on a single type of hypothesis and data, and do require some scholarly understanding of psychology. As for vertically integrated approaches, these require a wide variety of types of data and theory, and a rather unusual degree of sensitivity to and respect for other disciplines.

Alexander's mode of reasoning has similarities with that of Marvin Harris, whose ideas were discussed in chapter 10. Both are functionalists, that is, they believe that culture traits are to be explained in terms of what they are *for*. Harris and Alexander differ, however, in the kinds of functions they find acceptable as explanations. For Harris, as we have seen, the function of a culture trait has to do with group (not individual) adaptation to a particular set of environmental circumstances at a particular level of technology. A trait is 'for' group adaptation to environment. For Alexander, the function of a culture trait ultimately has to do with enhancing the genetic fitness of those who participate in it; it is 'for' the enhancement of genetic fitness.

Such functionalist accounts are inherently incomplete and unsatisfactory because, even if the trait does indeed serve the function attributed to it, we do not understand the processes whereby it came to have that function. In the case of Alexander's provocative work, the processes involve history and social psychology, that is, people with particular, evolved psychological traits interacting over historical time, in a given (and often changing) environment, generating culture. Alexander's inclusive-fitness accounts are often brilliant and insightful, but they need to be fleshed out with potential proximate mechanisms and then to be recast in terms of hypotheses that can be empirically verified.

Within anthropology, Alexander's work has (in part, at least) inspired a school of sociobiological functionalism, the flagship volume of which is *Evolutionary Biology and Human Social Behavior* (edited by Napoleon Chagnon and William Irons, 1979). Members of this school tend to 'explain' cultural traits in terms of their effects on inclusive fitness. Donald Symons (1987, 1989), who labels this approach 'Darwinian anthropology,' suggests that despite its weaknesses it may be more powerful than other anthropological theoretical approaches. Certainly, it is stronger than competing functionalisms (structural functionalism, ecological functionalism). It is not, however, a substitute for processual, vertically integrated explanation.

FOCUS 11.3

ALEXANDER'S *THE BIOLOGY OF MORAL SYSTEMS*

In his more recent (1987) work, Alexander maintains his theoretical perspective but shifts targets: this time he is concerned with an evolutionary critique not of sociocultural anthropology but of moral philosophy. His chapter 3 is a sustained attack on moral philosphers – at least on those who have failed to see human beings as inherently selfish and moral systems as having to do with conflicts of interest. For Alexander, 'true' altruism is unlikely because such altruists would surely have had lower genetic fitness, in past generations, than those who were genetically selfish. Because they have failed to understand this biological fact, argues Alexander, philosophers have often built elaborate moral systems on a base of biological sand, the sand of the mistaken assumption that 'genuine altruism' can exist.

For Alexander, we adhere to moral codes because doing so is in our fitness interests: given the ubiquity of conflicts of interest among individuals, 'moral' behaviour yields the dividends of indirect reciprocity, that is, our behaving 'morally' makes it more likely that others will do so, so that we all benefit. Of course, we seek to encourage others to follow the codes more rigidly than we ourselves do, since morality is about self-interest. Thus, we hold up as exemplars worthy of emulation (by others) celibate saints and the self-sacrificing heroes of battles, while we ourselves let our genetic fitness interests guide our behaviour.

Alexander is adamant that we must not 'biologize' ethics. The study of biology, he explains, only reveals how we do behave and not how we should. His book none the less has a strong tone of moral exhortation: if we do not understand our 'true' biological motives, teaches (preaches?) Alexander, we will continue to be trapped in endless conflict, conflict that may well end in nuclear war! Though an understanding of biology is no guarantee of a peaceful resolution of our conflicts, it would appear (to Alexander) to be our only hope. However, excessive optimism is not called for, since Alexander also believes that we have been selected to self-deceive about our true, selfish motives, so that most of us unthinkingly reject the wisdom to be found in Darwin and Alexander. (Disagreeing with Richard Alexander is very much like disagreeing with one's psychoanalyst. The analysand's resistance itself may be taken as evidence for the correctness of the interpretation, just as rejection of a genetic-selfishness perspective, for Alexander, illustrates its accuracy: why else would we reject such obvious truth, had we not been selected to do so?)

Vertically Integrated Explanation and Alexander

The evolutionary theory that Alexander adheres to is the core of both his book and the one you are now reading. The differences in approach largely stem from the presence of the vertically-integrated-explanation perspective in the one case and its absence in the other. The perspective makes a difference. For example, is it true that genuine altruism is an evolutionary impossibility?

It is certainly true that genetically altruistic individuals would have been selected against in the course of evolution. But it is also probably true that selection pressures involving nepotistic and reciprocal altruism led to specialized 'mental organs' the algorithms of which are extremely complex (Cosmides and Tooby, 1989). We are now in an environment dramatically different from that of our ancestors: since we do not yet fully understand the psychological mechanisms underlying altruism, we cannot say how these mechanisms operate in this altered environment. In the absence of a well-developed psychological theory of altruism, it is premature to conclude that genuinely selfless behaviour is unlikely.

I have used the word 'psychological' twice in the preceding paragraph, while Alexander uses it not once in his entire book. Searching for compatible, multi-level explanations is not the way in whch Alexander proceeds. Since he fails to appreciate the need for a theory of psychology, he makes biology his psychology and equates *genetic selfishness* with *selfishness*. As we saw in chapter 3, this is not a minor error.

Nor is it only in connection with psychology that he makes it. For Alexander, the assumption that human beings are selfish is a 'biological' insight and its application a biological view. Thus, he presents his discussion of the nuclear arms race and balance-of-power theories of political science as a 'biologist's view,' and implies that it derives its authority from his disciplinary affiliation. He writes as if the various social-science schools of thought that begin with the premiss that human beings are self-interested and therefore have conflicts of interest (much of legal theory, conflict theory in sociology and political science, much of sociology's symbolic interactionism, Adam Smith's *Wealth of Nations*, 1986 Nobel Prize—winner James Buchanan's work on public choice theory, James Madison in the *Federalist Papers*, and so forth) required reinvention as extensions of biology. What is actually needed is an eventual winnowing for *compatibility*: psychological theories incompatible with our understanding of evolution must be discarded, as must social-science theories incompatible with a Darwinian psychology. No doubt our psychological theories will show human beings to be 'selfish' in complex and predictable ways, and no doubt our social-science theories will reflect this 'selfishness,' so that some of Alexander's assertions may well be verified. In the meantime, however, he is presenting not a biological or any other kind of scientific perspective but his personal view of human society. That (unlike James Buchanan) he claims to have arrived at this view from the study of evolutionary biology is a fact that may be of interest to his future biographer but is not otherwise relevant. Alexander has had considerable influence on some social and behavioural scientists, but the flow of influence appears to have been one way.

As Kaye (1986) has pointed out, biologists who have deduced 'far-ranging implications from their scientific work' (p. 6) include Darwin, Spencer, Monod, Crick, Konrad Lorenz, and E.O. Wilson. These implications derive not from the science itself but from 'the guiding presence of metaphysical, moral, and social assumptions embedded' in their work (p. 6), assumptions of which they are unaware. There is no reason to believe any of us – not Alexander, not myself – are exempt from this tendency.

Alexander's work is often rich and provocative: it should be inspiring not one more functionalism but a program of empirical evaluation of the likely proximate mechanisms implied by sociobiological functionalist interpretations of culturally ordered behaviour.

CONCLUSIONS

We have come a long way from Marvin Harris's simplistic approach to explanation. Whatever one may think of the ideas of Laughlin and d'Aquili, Lumsden and Wilson, Boyd and Richerson, and Alexander, it is clear that the brain is not neutral with respect to information. There is widespread consensus that at a number of levels, from the perceptual to the purposive, the brain includes structures that bias its information-processing in particular ways, and these ways, ultimately, reflect gene frequencies determined by natural selection. In short, the algorithms of the brain's mechanisms favour genetic fitness (or at least, behaviours that would have meant fitness for our ancestors).

The question is, how effective are those mechanisms, particularly in contemporary environments? If they are sufficiently effective, then an Alexandrian approach to culture will usually be correct. But perhaps that statement should be phrased, 'where they are sufficiently effective ...'

The next generation of models and arguments concerning genes and culture must deal with delimited categories of cultural information, regardless of whether these follow the plans/goals/codes/mazeway model or some other analytic system. Assumptions about psychological, information-processing mechanisms must be age-specific. Finally, models must specify environment. The usefulness of current arguments has been limited by their generality and their global approach to cultural information.

I have a field-worker's bias with regard to theory: I need theory that tells me what to look at in naturalistic settings. The intra-individual-system approach is designed to do just that. I can readily relate ideas of goals, strategies, and communicative structures to what I find in the field. But I do not quite know what to do with highly abstract ideas of node and culturgen, or of guided variation and direct bias, in understanding actual people. Lumsden and Wilson, who lament the lack of empirical data in the social/behavioural sciences, present us with a framework that I find difficult to transform into a research program. Perhaps this is simply a matter of my own lack of grasp. But, thus far, it is not clear that current efforts at building mathematical models lead to research, though perhaps the next generation of models will. At the same time, the inclusive-fitness oversimplification of Alexander's approach, while seductive, is of genuine use only when it is tied to a commitment to a multi-level explanation of just *why* a given trait is or is not enhancing someone's fitness (Barkow, 1984).

For those of us concerned with collecting data rather than with constructing mathematical and verbal models, I would suggest that we next focus on longitudinal behavioural data, life-history data in terms of subcodes, subplans, and subgoals (cf. Boyd and Richerson, 1985: 298). We need to understand how people actually make choices and what the alternatives are from which they choose.

SUMMARY

1. Boyd and Richerson argue that culture is a second system of inheritance, distinct from the first system, that of the genes. That cultural and genetic transmission are distinct implies that some culture traits may be genetically maladaptive. The relationship between genes and culture is at once indirect and highly complex.

2. Boyd and Richerson prefer not to consider themselves 'human sociobiologists' because they do not take inclusive-fitness maximization as axiomatic. However, by a broader definition of that field they are, indeed, human sociobiologists.

3. Unlike Lumsden and Wilson, Boyd and Richerson assume that units of culture (which they refer to as 'culture traits') may blend together. They argue that Lumsden and Wilson's 'culturgens' are so structured that they require assumptions about neurological functioning and strong learning biases, while the culture-trait notion remains agnostic on this point. But Boyd and Richerson's concepts and models may actually be applicable to subgoals/plans, while the approach of Lumsden and Wilson may best fit codes and subcodes.

4. In 'guided variation,' a culture variant is learned by an individual through means other than observing the behaviour of another. The variant is, subsequently, socially transmitted. Guided variation has the implication for mathematical models that the amount of variation can never be exhausted.

5. When individual learning is inexpensive and the environment unpredictable, then selection will favour it. But when individual learning is expensive (that is, often inaccurate or energy-demanding)

and the environment predictable, then selection will favour social transmission of information through observational learning, that is, cultural transmission.

6. *Biased transmission* refers to natural selection having made one culture variant easier or more desirable to learn than another culture variant.

7. *Indirect bias* is the result of a decision rule associated with a secondary trait carried by the bearers of the culture variant. For example, 'learn preferentially from the high in status' is indirect bias, status being the 'secondary trait.'

8. *Direct bias* involves our tendency to acquire specific culture traits more readily than we acquire others, as a result of natural selection. Lumsden and Wilson are primarily concerned with direct-bias transmission. Unlike guided variation, with direct bias there is no automatic supply of new variants, so that variability may eventually be exhausted.

9. For Lumsden and Wilson, genetic assimilation of a culture trait could take place within one thousand years. Boyd and Richerson argue that this conclusion is consistent only with unlikely assumptions, including that of very strong selection pressure in favour of a direct bias involving the trait, coupled with the population in question being essentially a genetic isolate, but open to a flow of foreign culture.

10. *Frequency-dependent bias* reduces to the rule of conformity: Do what others are doing. Selection will favour it when individuals are in a poor position to evaluate the relative effectiveness of alternative cultural variants. This type of bias is likely to be particularly strong in children.

11. Boyd and Richerson argue that in-group co-operativeness may be the result of cultural (not genetic) group selection and present mathematical models to support this position. They are sceptical of the autopredation/genetic-population-structure explanation advanced in chapter 6. Focus 11.1 provides two alternative explanations for in-group co-operativeness.

12. One of the most important conclusions that Boyd and Richerson's models lead to is that 'relatively weak biases that would be difficult to detect empirically can lead to rapid change in the frequency of different variants in the population' (p. 146). Weak biases, in short, may be quite important in cultural transmission, but at the same time be very difficult to demonstrate experimentally.

13. Two criticisms of Boyd and Richerson are that they do not divide cultural information into categories and that they choose to ignore sensitive-period and other age-related aspects of cultural transmission.

Thus, they see cognitive style exclusively as a culture trait rather than as a sensitive-period phenomenon. Focus 11.2 links cognitive style and attention structure and interprets these phenomena in a manner very different from the approach of Boyd and Richerson.

14. The distinction that Boyd and Richerson make between guided variation and direct bias, though necessary for their equations, is of questionable meaningfulness. The Cree goose hunt is described in order to illustrate the practical identity of the 'two' processes. Boyd and Richerson would argue that the behavioural differences are sufficient, for their models, and that they have no need to assume neurological differences.

15. We need Boyd and Richerson–type models that ask more complex questions, including: In what kinds of environments, for what kinds of information, for what life stages of individuals, will selection favour what kinds of information-acquisition mechanisms?

16. Boyd and Richerson's work goes a long way towards bridging the gap between culture-is-everything anthropologists and genes-are-everything sociobiologists. They see culture as tied to genetic evolution, but tied in complex ways that may be weak or strong and that require detailed examination before any predictions may be made. Their stance is broadly compatible with the intra-individual-system approach.

17. Richard Alexander sees culture as the amplification of individual fitness strategies, the accumulation of such strategies, and the result of compromises and alliances among individuals. He is not concerned with the details of cultural transmission and would be very reluctant to accept that some culture traits may be genetically maladaptive.

18. Alexander has interpreted much ethnological data as consistent with sociobiological expectation. For example, many peoples of the world distinguish between parallel cousins (parent's same-sex siblings' children) and cross-cousins (parent's cross-sex siblings' children). For both types of cousins, the coefficient of relatedness is ordinarily one-eighth. However, Alexander finds that, for many societies, sexual intercourse with one's spouse's same-sex sibling is permitted, so that parallel cousins in fact may actually be genetic half-siblings. Thus, he explains cousin asymmetry in terms of an extension of the incest taboo.

19. Alexander weakens his case by ignoring the question of proximate mechanism. The mechanism underlying the incest taboo in our species is that co-rearing breeds sexual disinterest, as on the Israeli kibbutz. Parallel cousins are much more likely to share a residence, cross-culturally, then are cross-cousins. Thus, the possible genetic distinction

between cross and parallel cousins is likely to be an irrelevant epiphenomenon. Residence is probably a better predictor of which cousins will be treated as siblings and which will not, with regard to marriage.

20. Similarly, Alexander analyses the avunculate sociobiologically. In this practice, a man invests more in his sisters' offspring than in those of his wife, and it is his sororal nieces and nephews who inherit from him. Alexander argues that the paternity certainty is so low in these matrilineal, weak-restrictions-on-female-sexuality societies, that in fact a man may be on the average as closely related to his sisters' children as to his wife's (since the latter's offspring may be no kin at all to him). Once again, Alexander provides no proximate mechanism. His case depends on psychologists finding that, when a man's paternity confidence lowers, he automatically grows increasingly interested in his sisters' children. Thus far this possibility has not been studied. But genes cannot affect behaviour without a proximate mechanism.

21. By contrast, Alexander successfully and convincingly reinterprets Marshall Sahlins's three types of economic reciprocity in terms of sociobiological concepts of reciprocity.

22. More often than not, Alexander is probably correct in showing that cultural patterns do tend to be consistent with sociobiological expectation. This is valuable in itself, but the main value of his approach is that the implicit proximate mechanisms constitute empirically verifiable psychological/ethological hypotheses about human behaviour.

23. Alexander's approach has the virtue of specifying what kind of data are to be collected: measures of genetic fitness. It has the vice of permitting the collection of such data to take the place of genuine understanding of the complex relationships between genes and culture. Lumsden and Wilson and Boyd and Richerson, while providing richly mathematical models, present us theory at a much higher level of abstraction and which is therefore much more difficult for researchers to apply to real behaviour. The intra-individual-system approach, with its subplans and subgoals and codes, is designed to be directly applicable to field settings. Its data are life histories and the evidence they provide of choices, plans, and strategies.

12

Maladaptation in
Mind and Culture

Maladaptation is a crucial issue in the debate over the distance between 'genes' and 'culture' (that is, between theories of biological-evolution biology and theories of culturally patterned individual behaviour). If culture traits often are genetically maladaptive then there is obviously much distance between genes and culture; and the approach of Richard Alexander in particular (discussed in chapter 11) and those who, like him, seek to 'explain' cultural institutions by matching them with fitness-optimization models of individual behaviour, is often likely to be in error. Evidence of maladaptive cultural traits is thus evidence for the need for theories of culture and of the social-psychological processes of culture transmission that, while compatible with modern evolutionary thought, are nevertheless quite distinct from it. Similarly, evidence for frequent maladaptive individual decisions implies that simple 'human beings optimize fitness' models of behaviour are inadequate, and must be replaced with more complex, psychological-level theories.

A chapter on the maladaptive may nevertheless seem unexpected in a work so strongly influenced by evolutionary theory: but maladaptation is as much a part of evolution as is adaptation and does not challenge the evolutionary paradigm. Almost every adaptive (fitness-enhancing) trait is likely to carry with it a maladaptive (fitness-reducing) consequence. Monkeys are arboreally adapted, but sometimes they fall from trees, and this is a genetically maladaptive consequence of arboreal adapta-

---

1 This chapter is in part based upon Barkow, 1989a.

tion. The falls are no mere epiphenomena, either, but constitute a strong selection pressure in favour of better co-ordination, depth perception, and equilibrium. Human culture traits and individual decisions that reduce fitness may be comparable to the monkey's falls.

Whether or not we use the label 'maladaptive' (or its synonym, 'fitness-reducing') often depends on the scale at which we are working. This is because even the most fitness-enhancing trait has costs as well as benefits: natural selection has to do with net effects, and an adaptive or fitness-enhancing trait is simply one in which the benefits *on balance* are greater than the costs (Sober, 1984). What is merely a cost of an adaptive trait at coarse grain, at fine grain may be considered a distinct and maladaptive trait in its own right. Thus, one person's 'maladaptive trait' may be another's 'cost of an adaptive trait.' Let us return to the monkey's tendency to fall from trees. From a coarse-grained perspective, the salient trait here is that of arboreal adaptation, and the monkey's tendency to fall occasionally is simply a cost of this trait that, on balance, is (presumably) highly adaptive. But if we approach the problem from a fine-grained perspective, the relevant trait *is* the monkey's tendency to fall from trees, and that is clearly maladaptive. The advantage of the finer grain and the 'maladaptive' label is that they force us to pay attention to the consequences for selection of the costs of what are on balance fitness-enhancing traits.

Human culture and psychology, like arboreal adaptation in monkeys, are clearly fitness-enhancing when considered from a coarse-grained perspective. On balance, they are presumably fitness-enhancing. But in this chapter I will focus on the finer grain and consider some aspects of culture and of human psychology that appear to be fitness-reducing, genetically maladaptive, *traits*. We will see that the fineness of the focus is justified in part because, as with the falls of the monkeys, the maladaptiveness of such traits may have been important selection pressures in the evolution of our species.[2]

Human sociobiologists have paid scant attention to the maladaptive and to its evolutionary implications. Just as the training of physicians often leaves them so oriented towards the prolongation of life that they may deal badly with the irremediably dying, so the bias of evolutionists has been so strongly towards the adaptive that they may offer little

---

2 To be more precise, a maladaptive culture trait is socially transmitted information likely to lead to fitness-reducing behaviour on the part of individuals accepting it, the reduced fitness being relative to that which would have resulted from rejection of the information. For example, the ancient medical belief that cupping (deliberate bleeding) improves health is presumably a maladaptive culture trait.

theory of the maladaptive. Only the transmission theorists (Boyd and Richerson, 1985; Pulliam and Dunford, 1980; Richerson and Boyd, 1989), as we saw in the last chapter, are much concerned with the possibilities of genetically maladaptive culture traits and of individuals making maladaptive choices. In this chapter we will discover that the capacity to make fitness-reducing choices is a major cost of the intra-individual system, just as the existence of maladaptive cultural practices is a cost of culture. These costs, in turn, have constituted important selection pressures, shaping our evolution.

OUTLINE OF THE ARGUMENT

Both our shared culture traits and our individual decisions may reduce our genetic fitness. Let us begin by looking at cultural maladaptation.

'Culture,' it will be recalled from chapter 6, is a pool of at least somewhat organized information, socially transmitted both within and between generations. In this chapter, I will be arguing that any particular culture is likely to include information that has genetically maladaptive consequences for some or all of that culture's participants. The tendency for cultures to come to include fitness-reducing information I will term 'stretch,' while any particular item of socially transmitted information I will term a 'culture trait.' In addition to the hypothetical stretch-producing processes Boyd and Richerson believe result from the 'evolutionarily active' nature of culture transmission are the four kinds of processes the present chapter is concerned with: (1) First, environments alter, so that culture traits genetically adaptive in the past are likely to become maladaptive if unchanged when climates, soils, insects, and disease organisms alter. (2) Second, expenses emerge, as when techniques that were genetically adaptive in the short term reveal maladaptive long-term consequences. Keeping goats may be adaptive initially but, if they lead to desertification and your descendants starve, the practice may eventually prove maladaptive. (3) Errors accumulate. We make mistakes and we may teach these errors to our children. As we will see, some peoples of the world deny the infant the first milk, the immunity-conferring colostrum, and are probably increasing their infant mortality rates as a result. (4) Elites appropriate. The powerful are likely to favour culture traits that are in their own fitness interests but not necessarily in the interests of other elements of the population. It is no coincidence that religion the world over tends to support whatever is the current distribution of political power.

The tendency for culture to stretch in fitness-reducing directions has apparently resulted in selection in favour of psychological traits that, whatever their other functions, tend to reduce stretch by causing us to challenge and revise our cultures with each generation. Thus, culture 'transmission' is a problematic process, involving much testing, editing, revision and innovation.

Aside from the genetically maladaptive culture traits we may participate in, most of us also make some *individual* decisions that are likely to reduce our genetic fitness. Perhaps we simply ignore our health, as when we fail to exercise regularly, or choose to eat too much sugar and saturated fat. The most striking example of a decision to reduce individual fitness is that of making love while practising contraception. The fact that this is a common and rather easily made decision suggests that neither pregnancy nor parturition is a goal-state of the intra-individual system. Human beings have apparently been selected to seek copulations with partners with particular characteristics, rather than to seek pregnancy *per se* (Barkow and Burley, 1980). In the past, given the absence of contraception, the close connection between sex and reproduction was sufficient to ensure that selection in favour of our enjoying courtship and copulation was sufficient to ensure frequent pregnancy; but today that tie has been broken. So we seek not evolution's end of reproductive success but evolution's means, love-making. The point of this example is that some human psychological traits may, at least in our current environment, be fitness-reducing.

This, then, is the very bare outline of the chapter's argument. Now, let us look more closely at culture traits that reduce genetic fitness.[3]

CULTURE STRETCHES IN FITNESS-REDUCING DIRECTIONS

Four processes lead to culture traits being genetically maladaptive.

1. *Environments Alter*

Imagine a static culture. Each generation hunts with the same techniques for the same species, gathers the same plants in the same

---

3 The reader who does not recall chapter 6's discussion of culture may mistakenly take the phrase 'culture's tendency to reduce genetic fitness' for a reification (or even a personification) of 'culture.' 'Culture' is not a thing and can do nothing. The phrase is an abbreviated way of expressing the idea that 'culture, defined as a body of somewhat organized information socially transmitted between generations and within each generation, often incorporates specific informational items ('culture traits') that are likely to lead those accepting them to behave in a manner tending to reduce their genetic fitness.'

manner, grows the same crops in the same way. Sooner or later, this unchanging culture will stretch to reduce the genetic fitness of its participants. New game animals may be ignored, or perhaps the old techniques will be ineffective with them. Perhaps the climate slowly dries so that the old cultivars no longer grow well. If each generation fails to revise and refashion its culture then the average genetic success of the population will fall.

2. Expenses Emerge

Why wait for the environment to alter by itself? Many cultural traits have clear short-term advantages but entail long-term ecological disaster. Such traits may involve what Hardin (1968) terms the 'tragedy of the commons.' For example, there is some archaeological evidence for a long-term, progressive growth of malnutrition among Maya commoners. Maya civilization was supported by slash-and-burn cultivation, which requires lengthy fallow periods for the restoration of soil fertility. A growing population may have forced the progressive shortening of the vital fallow period, until poor nutrition contributed to the collapse of that civilization (Wood, 1979: 180–6).

Many resource-acquisition strategies are *frequency-dependent*, that is, their effectiveness depends on the number of people following them. Often, the more common they become, the more they wax ineffective. Thus, when university graduates were in short supply, a degree was almost a guarantee of lucrative employment; but when a large proportion of high-school graduates began to go on to post-secondary education, the economic value of the university degree diminished (and in the process, devalued the worth of the secondary-school diploma). Fisheries are of the same nature. In the short term, a culture that encourages its young people to fish may prosper; but if the population continues to grow and overfishing results then, eventually, the fishery must fail. A previously fitness-enhancing culture trait, fishing, has stretched. Culture traits frequently alter environments in such stretch-producing ways.

Culture traits may also have other kinds of unanticipated fitness-reducing consequences. For example, Brothwell and Brothwell (1969: 181) discuss the advent of scurvy, the vitamin C–deficiency disease associated with ready bruising, bleeding gums, and loss of teeth. Our forager ancestors probably never suffered from scurvy, argue the Brothwells, for their diets would have included a wide variety of fruits and vegetables, and vitamin C (ascorbic acid) is actually a quite common nutrient. But the Neolithic, which involved cultivation and livestock, also meant a more limited range of foodstuffs. Then as now, the more narrow the variety of foods consumed, the greater the risk of deficiency disease. True enough, the Neolithic revolution probably enhanced genetic fitness as a whole, but it may have meant a narrowed diet and increased risk of deficiency diseases such as scurvy.

The introduction of maize from the New World to the Old, during the sixteenth century, may also have had unanticipated, genetically maladaptive consequences. In Mesoamerica, maize was consumed as a part of a dietary complex that included both beans and squash. Readily grown as well as eaten together, the complex contains complementary amino acids and thus provides high-quality protein, as well as a wide range of other nutrients. In Europe, however, maize was introduced alone as a dietary staple, without its companions. One result was pellagra, caused by niacin deficiency. As Grivetti (1978: 172) puts it: 'Once maize was "plucked" from the maize-bean-squash complex and introduced as a single food, pellagra emerged as a serious medical-nutritional problem in the Old World, one that probably did not previously exist.'

More contemporary examples of adaptive culture traits entailing some genetically maladaptive consequences are unfortunately common. Cockburn (1971), for example, argues that widespread malaria and schistosomiasis (bilharzia) are products of the clearing of forest and of irrigation. Irrigation trenches create breeding grounds for the snail that serves as the vector of schistosomiasis, while stagnant irrigation ponds permit the anopheles mosquito, the vector of malaria, to propagate.

3. Errors Accumulate
Any information-transmission system is subject to error and there is no reason to suppose that culture is an exception. Most socially transmitted errors probably have little direct effect on fitness, particularly when they deal with cosmology or eschatology. Some errors, however, may have fitness-reducing consequences.

The ethnographic record includes surprisingly little discussion of potentially maladaptive traits. This omission presumably reflects the enduring strength of the various forms of functionalism in anthropological theory, so that ethnographers have tended to emphasize those culture traits they could 'explain' in terms of some kind of utility (see, for example, the discussion of cultural materialism in chapter 10). However, the linked fields of medical and nutritional anthropology provide ample evidence of culture traits likely to have been genetically maladaptive. As does our own history.

The Millennial Church, usually known as the Shakers, originated in England in the mid-eighteenth century and came to the United States in 1874. The shaking dance ritual of this church gave it its name, but its relevance to the present discussion stems from its having enjoined strict celibacy on its adherents. When their recruitment rate fell below their mortality rate, the Shakers gradually disappeared (Alexander, 1977). They left behind them a heritage of lovely music and furniture, but not a heritage of genes. Shakerism led to genetic extinction, the most extreme form of maladaptation.

Medicine, both in our own and in many of the world's cultures, yields similarly genetically maladaptive culture traits. Restoring health by letting blood is a practice found throughout European history and wherever Islamic medicine has had influence. For example, the Hausa frequently suffer from backache, a condition presumably related to their spending long hours stooped over their short-handled hoes. In the standard treatment, the barber pricks the area of a pain with a razor, wets it, then presses a cow's horn against the skin. The barber sucks the air from the tip of the horn and stoppers it. Since the horn with its reduced air pressure is now sealed to the pricked skin, as much as an inch of purplish, jelled, venous blood gradually accumulates in it. When the horn is unstoppered the dark, congealed blood is taken as evidence for it having been the 'bad blood' that caused the back pain. Far more copious letting of blood, including the application of leeches, was for many centuries a standard part of Western medical practice, as was the application of powerful purgatives and emetics (Haggard, 1929). It is difficult to see how such practices were in the fitness interests of the ill.

Non-Western pharmacopoeias yield traditional drugs of undoubted curative value but also some of dubious safety and efficacy. Taylor et al. (1973: 208), for example, explain the dangerousness of the mercury and other heavy-metal compounds used in Indian Ayurvedic and also in Islamic medicine. The Yoruba of Nigeria, MacLean (1971: 84) points out, treat convulsions with so strong a solution of nicotine that children are often brought to the hospital in a state of 'deep unconsciousness,' their brain activity dangerously depressed.

Nutrition, too, is an area in which traditional cultural knowledge is often very weak. In 1968, while living in a small, Hausa village, I was entreated by the sixty-seven-year-old village head for my 'medicine' (Hausa, *magani*). I eventually grasped that he wanted to know the secret of my being overweight! I explained to him that I ate too much, and he grew very cool to me. He knew perfectly well that eating had little to do with health or weight. He himself was quite slender and, as was common at that time, perceived obesity as a sign of health and wealth. As I eventually learned, the rural villagers among whom I was living had no identifiable concept of nutrition. Food was about hunger, not health. Signs of protein and iron deficiency were everywhere but people would grow low-protein cassava and sell their relatively high-protein guinea corn for cash. They would do the same with the eggs their hens laid. But scientific concepts of nutrition are new to Western cultural tradition, too.

Until 1820, in North America, a potentially important source of vitamin C was considered poisonous. In that year, a man of great courage, Robert G. Johnston, dramatically ate a tomato on the steps of the courthouse in Salem, New Jersey (Sebrell et al., 1967: 149). In doing so he revised his culture, redefining the tomato as 'edible.' Americans and Canadians continue to resist consuming insect protein, however, and will eat snails only if imported from Europe, ignoring the identical species from their own gardens (Simoons, 1978: 178), and expressing revulsion at the notion of consuming the related gastropod, the common garden slug.[4]

Whether these examples actually involve the reduction of genetic fitness is unknown. Colostrum-denial, however, provides a less ambiguous case of a maladaptive culture trait. Before the 'true milk' comes in, a new mother's breasts secrete a yellowish fluid, the colostrum. Colostrum has important nutritional and immunological components but in many of the world's cultures is denied the newborn. Angela Hallett and I, in Focus 12.1, review the biomedical and ethnographic literature concerning colostrum's utility and denial. Our conclusion is that colostrum-denial raises infant mortality rates and is thus an example of a genetically maladaptive cultural trait. Here are two illustrations of colostrum-denial, the first from Berland's (1982: 115) study of rural Pakistan:

4 Marvin Harris (1985), as we saw in chapter 10, would probably argue that we do not eat such 'small things' because it would be inefficient to do so, given our other, relatively plentiful, sources of high-quality protein. That explanation would not account for our consuming imported but not domestic snails.

A mother's breast milk is believed to be safra ['hot'] for seven days following birth, so the baby is fed a mixture of water and brown sugar by dipping a twisted cloth into an open cup of the *gurpani* (sweet water or *sherbet*). Because the cup is exposed to flies, newborn babies frequently develop intestinal infections, and many die of marasmus and dehydration within two to three weeks. Between 60 and 65 percent of all babies die within the first month to six weeks of life. Because of the high infant mortality rate, babies are often not given a name until they are a year or more old ...

The second account is taken from a study of infant feeding practices in urban Central America. This particular example comes from the city of Tegucigalpa, in Honduras:

Colostrum is a special case of bad milk in the worldview of more than half the mothers of Tegucigalpa. Only three percent of mothers are aware that it contains protein and antibodies; almost 40 percent profess ignorance of its existence. Colostrum is described as dirty, thin, thick, sticky, ruined, old, agitated, hot, stored, yellow, brown, or simply, bad. Any milk which is old or has been stored is considered bad for infants. Colostrum is especially damaging because the heat of the mother's body and blood as she exerts herself physically and emotionally during birth affects the milk stored in her breasts. (O'Gara and Kendall, 1985: 112)

FOCUS 12.1

THE DENIAL OF COLOSTRUM

Jerome H. Barkow and Angela L. Hallett*

Anthropologists do not usually claim that *no* cultural trait can be in some sense maladaptive — that is, that no trait reduces physical health, or lowers genetic fitness, or damages the local environment. But perhaps as a reaction against the racist ethnocentrism of our earliest generation, our ethos has been to emphasize the adaptive. From Malinowski (1954) to Radcliffe-Brown (1952) to Vayda and

* Angela Hallett is a family physician in Nova Scotia. She was a student at the time this focus was originally written. The authors gratefully wish to acknowledge the support of Dalhousie University's Research Development Fund.

Rappaport (1968) and Harris (1979), anthropologists have tended to assume that most cultural traits are in some way adaptive or functional; our disagreements are usually limited to just *how* cultural traits are beneficial.

Exceptions to this generalization exist, of course, the most apparent being workers concerned with the effects of social inequality (especially age and gender differences) on diet and nutrition, and those concerned with ritual genital operations and mutilations (for example, Katona-Apte, 1975; Hoffer, 1975; Wood, 1979: 111). The exceptions notwithstanding, our ethos is such that a first reaction to any assertion that a particular trait is 'maladaptive' is probably to question the adequacy of the analysis. Much of this focus will therefore deal with evidence that the trait in question is indeed maladaptive.

The cultural trait we focus on is that of colostrum-denial. Colostrum is the 'pre-milk,' the yellowish or bluish fluid secreted by the breasts for the first few days after delivery, when it is replaced by the 'true milk.' As we will see, in some cultures the infant is not placed at the breast to nurse until the true milk comes in. Various fluids may be given the neonate until then, but not the colostrum. However, the neonate's immune system is immature at birth, and colostrum in effect permits the infant to share important aspects of the mother's immune system. Denying the infant the colostrum thus would appear to be a clear example of a maladaptive cultural trait.

In keeping with the 'adaptive until proven otherwise' ethos discussed above, the goals of this focus are modest. First, we seek to establish that a particular cultural trait, the denial to the infant of the colostrum, is indeed maladaptive in the sense that it is harmful to the newborn's health. Presumably, that which is harmful to health is also likely, ultimately, to be harmful to inclusive fitness. The first half of this discussion reviews the appropriate biomedical literature for evidence of the effects of colostrum-denial. The second half examines the prevalence of colostrum-denial cross-culturally in order to establish that it is not a unique or even a particularly uncommon phenomenon. For this purpose, we will be relying on the Human Relations Area Files for ethnographic data.

The Value of Colostrum

The importance of colostrum to newborn mammals has been known since the 1920s. Even by that period, it had been shown that deprivation of colostrum was lethal. In one study, three-quarters of the calves deprived of colostrum died of septicemia, while a single feed of colostrum proved enough to protect them (McClelland, 1982). We now know that *human* colostrum and milk contain viable cells, cell fragments, immunoglobulins, and a wide variety of other non-immunoglobin proteins. Recent studies have suggested that human colostrum and milk transfer specific immunity to the external mucosal surfaces of the intestine, and possibly to the respiratory tract, of the newborn infant. The acquisition of such passive immunity may be particularly important in the early neonatal period, when the secretory immune system is poorly developed (Ogra and Ogra, 1978a).

When IgM immunoglobulin concentrations were compared for colostrum and true milk, the highest IgM levels were in the colostrum on the first post-partum day. Initially, the mean level of IgM in colostrum was approximately 29 mg/g protein. Subsequently, the IgM activity declined and the concentrations observed in milk ranged from 3.5 to 4.1 mg/g protein (Ogra and Ogra, 1978a).

The IgA immunoglobulin concentrations in the colostrum during the first four to five days post-partum exceeded those in the mother's serum four- to eight-fold. The mean IgA concentration in the colostrum and milk ranged from 158 mg/g protein on the first day to 113 mg/g protein two days post-partum, and the concentration 80 days post-partum ranged from 20 to 27 mg/g protein (Ogra and Ogra, 1978a). Secretory IgA immunoglobulin is relatively resistant to pH changes and proteolytic enzyme digestion, suiting it to a protective role on mucous membranes. The resistance of colostral and milk antibodies is attested by their presence in high titres in the stool of breast-fed infants (Chandra, 1978).

Although the immune system of the neonate is well differentiated and functionally competent shortly after birth, the development of the secretory IgA system at the external mucosal surfaces is a relatively late phenomenon. Apparently by way of compensation, human colostrum and milk are rich sources of resistant immunoglobulins, particularly of the secretory IgA class.

The cells found in colostrum are for the most part leucocytes, including macrophages (3000 per mm^3) that can ingest and kill bacteria and fungi and seem to mediate protection against invariably fatal necrotizing enterocolitis. Lymphocytes of T, B, and null type also occur in large numbers (500-2500 per mm^3). These cells are capable of synthesizing immunoglobulins and antibodies, interferon, secretory piece, complement, and transfer factor (Chandra, 1978).

A comparison of the distribution of cells in colostrum and milk found the highest number of cells on the first post-partum day. The total cell and lymphocyte counts decreased to about one-fifth by the fifth post-partum day. The highest T-lymphocyte activity in the colostrum was seen immediately after the onset of lactation (Ogra and Ogra, 1978a).

For these reasons, Ogra and Ogra (1978a, 1978b) suggest that breast-feeding during the first week may be crucial in providing the infant with high concentrations of a wide variety of antibodies at a time when the mucosal immune system has a poor level of function.

Aside from the immune system, colostrum also plays a role in regulating the bacterial population of the new-born's intestines and in clearing the meconium from them (Montagu, 1979). Breast-fed infants are rapidly colonized by *Lacto-bacillus bifidus*, whereas infants fed cow's milk develop a mixed intestinal flora. This ability of the breast-fed infant to promote the growth of *Lactobacillus* is attributed to a specific growth-promoting *bifidus* factor. It has been characterized as a nitrogen-containing polysaccharide and is present in substantial amounts in human milk, whereas its content in cow's milk is extremely small. *Lactobacilli* produce acetic and lactic acids, thereby resulting in a low pH of fecal contents and inhibition of the growth of many gram-negative bacilli and fungi (Montagu, 1979).

A recent study indicates that colostrum from women in India contains anti-bodies against cholera, while this is not the case among Swedish women. The Indian mothers showed no history of either having had cholera previously or of having been vaccinated against it in recent years. The results may therefore reflect differences between these two groups of women in the degree of exposure to these antigens (Majundar and Ghose, 1982). It would seem that 'nature has equipped the lactating mother with a system for producing in her milk [and in her colostrum] specific IgA antibodies directed against microorganisms which she encounters in her environment and which are therefore likely to pose a threat to the infant' (McClelland, 1982).

McClelland seems to be suggesting that, in the course of mammalian evolution, natural selection favoured individuals whose mother's colostrum and milk provided them with antibodies against local pathogenic antigens until their own immune systems could begin to take hold. Selection would also have favoured the individual whose mother's milk varied in composition over time, thereby matching changing metabolic needs. Thus, for our own species, breast colostrum and milk change from day to day, adjusting to the infant's requirements. Chemical and cellular composition of the milk continues to alter throughout the lactation period (Montagu, 1979).

Ojofeitimi and Elegbe (1982) give us some indication of the consequences of colostrum-denial. These authors examined the proliferation of intestinal bacteria in the infants of new Nigerian mothers. The women, whose new-borns are exposed to a plethora of bacteria, fed their offspring glucose water instead of colostrum during their three-day stay in a maternity ward in one of two maternity centres in Ile-Ife, Oyo State, Nigeria. The maternity centre involved has an open ward with twelve beds in which newly delivered mothers stay for a maximum of three days after delivery. The centre's water supply is usually brought by truck and stored in tanks, but when water shortages occur, relatives are requested to bring water from home for the use of the mothers and infants.

In the Ojofeitimi and Elegbe (1982) study, babies born between October 1980 and January 1981 were randomly assigned at birth to two groups, one receiving glucose-water feedings and the other colostrum. Bacterial counts for the glucose-water infants were significantly higher than for those receiving colostrum. More important, so were counts for fecal specimens from the glucose-water infants, as compared to specimens from those fed colostrum. The source of bacterial contamination for the former group was the water brought from the homes of the new mothers by relatives; the lower counts for the colostrum regime may have been due to the immunologic and antimicrobial factors in the colostrum, discussed previously.

Colostrum Denial in Cross-Cultural Perspective

When breast-feeding does not begin until three or more days after birth, the infant is denied the mother's immunity-conferring colostrum. Surprisingly, this practice is (or at least has been) not uncommon among the peoples of the world.

Raphael (1966: 145), in a pioneering cross-cultural study of breast-feeding that utilized the Human Relations Area Files, reports that, in most societies, women clearly recognize the difference between colostrum and true milk. Of the fifty-seven societies for which information was available (of a total of 168 HRAF cultures surveyed) concerning initial breast-feeding, the largest group (19 societies) begin breast-feeding three days after birth, or approximately when the 'true milk' appears. Her breakdown is given in table 3.*

Note that even if the infant is suckled during this period by a lactating neighbour or relative, the milk – though it will at least be sterile – will not closely match the infant's metabolic and immunological needs.

The Nature of the Ethnographic Illustrations
The ethnographic illustrations provided below are largely taken from the HRAF microfiches of some of the colostrum-denial cultures identified by Raphael (listed above). But some caveats are in order. Since Raphael's study (therefore these illustrations as well) relies on the HRAF, it suffers from certain drawbacks (as Raphael acknowledges).

First, many of the HRAF societies were studied long ago (though we have taken advantage of more recent material, in some cases, in providing the examples below). The present tense used in some of the accounts is the 'ethnographic present': it should not be mistaken for current information and in some cases is more than a half-century out-of-date. This dated quality in no way invalidates the use of these data for present purposes, though it can be taken for granted that most of the

---

* These data were supplied in a personal communication from Dr Dana Raphael, to whom the authors wish to express their appreciation for aid and advice.

TABLE 3
Day breast-feeding begins

Immediately (9)	First day (7)	Second day (7)
Southeast Salish	Nahane	Northeast Paiute
Araucanians	Aymara	Plateau Yuman
Mosquitos	Buka	Siwans
Siriono	Fang	Bambara
Alor	Gusii	Pukapukans
Kwoma	Jordan	Tarasco
Ifugao	China	Mixtecan
Mossi		
Lepcha		
Third day (19)	Hottentott	Manus
Pomo	Punjab	Hausa
Tarahumara	Gujarati	Iran
Tubatulabal	India	Nupe
Goajito	Okinawa	
Jivaro	Manchuria	Seventh day (3)
Carib		Twi
Manus	Fourth day (10)	Burosho
Marquesas	Creek	Dard
Marshallese	Navaho	
Samoa	Tewa	After seventh day (1)
Tarong	River Yuman	Yurok
Mongo	Ojibwa	
Tuareg	Gros Ventres	

Adapted from Raphael (1966)

world's peoples today are likely to rely on prepared formulas and tinned or powdered milk when substitutes for breast milk are desired. A potential drawback of the HRAF for present purposes, however, is (as Raphael points out) the fact that most of the data were collected by men. Thus, where the ethnographies surveyed usually say that 'the ... do such-and-such,' they should be read as if they stated that 'male informants among the ... say that their women do such-and-such.' Again, there is no reason to believe that this circumstance introduces any systematic biases into the data. More likely, any error it might create would be of the nature of random 'noise.'

The ethnographic material provided below is intended to be illustrative only. Neither Raphael's nor the present study constitutes a modern holocultural survey. A representative world sample has not been used and the data have not been rated for quality. Most important, no attempt has been made to correlate colostrum-

denial with any other variables, such as climate, food source, and child socialization techniques. The illustrations are intended only to establish that colostrum-
denial is a real and not even unusual phenomenon. A cross-cultural survey linking
colostrum-denial to other aspects of culture and ecology remains to be done.

The Illustrations
The San hunters ('Bushmen') studied by Schapera (1930) are among those peoples
who deny the infant the colostrum until the third day after birth. The San group
studied believes that if a child is placed too soon at its mother's breast both will die.
However, should there be another nursing mother available in the small band,
then she will suckle the neonate during the first days of its life. Konner (1972: 287),
working with a different San group several decades later, confirms that, for
Zhun/twa women, 'the infant is not put to the breast until the colostrum has run
out, and he may be nursed by another lactating woman or simply wait for two or
three days until his mother's breasts engorge with milk.'
    Similarly, among the Tarahumara Indians of northwest Mexico, a neighbour or
relative may nurse the child during the first three days but the mother herself will
not. Should no mother surrogate be available, the child is fed with warm goat's
milk (Lumholtz, 1894). Among the Manus of the Admiralty Islands (north of New
Guinea), the child is not fed at all until twenty or twenty-four hours after birth,
when it is given milk by other nursing mothers and a bit of taro that its own
mother has chewed fine. But not for three to four days will it be permitted to nurse
from its mother's breasts (Mead, 1930).
    The mother's milk is considered 'too hot' among the Mongo, and for the first few
days of its life an infant will therefore be nursed by another woman, usually a
relative. In similar fashion, among the people of the Marshall Islands a wet nurse is
employed for the first two or three days. She is ordinarily a member of the clan
of either of the infant's parents, but no attention is paid to the age of her own child
(Wedgwood, 1943).
    According to Schultze (1907), the Hottentots believe that the mother's milk
would not be healthy for the new-born infant until the third day. Until then, the
child would be fed thinned goat's or cow's milk, unless another woman weaning
her own infant and so with spare milk happened to be available (Schapera,
1930). In similar fashion, in Manchuria a clan woman would suckle the newborn
for the first three days (Shirokogoroff, 1924–5).
    In some cultures, no attempt to find a surrogate mother to feed the infant during
its first few days of life is made. Among Colombia's Goajiro, the newborn is not
fed at all until three days after birth (Gutierrez de Pineda, 1950). The Tuareg of the
Sahara feed the infant goat's milk with a small spoon for three days (Blanguernon,

1955). In the Punjab, the child is given drops of goat's milk with a cloth wick until it is nursed on the third day (Gideon, 1962). Okinawan custom permits the new-born to be fed warm water with small amounts of white sugar for the first three days, after which the mother breast-feeds it (Glacken, 1953).

In some societies, more elaborate preparations to feed the new-born during the colostrum-denial period are made. Samoans fed the infant with the juice of the chewed kernel of the coconut or of the sugar-cane, pressed through a piece of native cloth and dropped in the mouth (Turner, 1884). The Tubatulabal of the southern Sierra Nevada foothill region of California fed the new-born a thin gruel made of water and acorn or pinyon meal (Wheeler-Voegelin, 1938).

Marquesan custom prescribes a purgative for the new-born. It is made by pounding shrimps with a stone pounder and mixing them with coconut milk. After the mixture is cooked, it has the appearance of curry sauce. The mixture was said to make the *tutai putona* (juices) come out from the child's intestinal system (Handy, 1923). The Marquesans may also feed the new-born a little gruel of thinned bread-fruit paste. More recently, Suggs (1963) reports many Marquesan parents using tinned milk in place of gruel and even using sugared water as a substitute. One of Handy's (1923) informants explained that if a mother nurses her infant immediately, the child will be difficult to raise.

In India, Stevenson (1920) reported as very widespread the practice of feeding a child for the first three days on *galasodi*, a mixture of molasses and water. In some parts of India the child, before being given the breast for the first time, was given a drink made by boiling certain roots in calf's urine (Briggs, 1920).

Occasionally, in some societies, the infant is not breast-fed until the fourth day after birth, rather than the third. This was the practice of the Algonkian-speaking Gros Ventre Indians of Montana, who would have someone other than the new-born draw out the colostrum. No water or oil was given the infant before its first nursing (Flannery, 1953). Among the River Yumans, a baby is given only drops of warm water for the first four days of life (Spier, 1933). The Hausa feed a new-born only water until the mother's milk comes in. If the child is a boy, he drinks only water for the first three days; if a girl, for four days (Smith, 1954).

Among the Creek, before the child is allowed to suckle it is taken to a spring and water is thrown upon its tongue several times. Some children are kept from nursing for the first four days of life while being given certain small roots to swallow. The belief is that this practice ensures long life, though it is also believed that the same effect may be achieved by keeping the infant indoors for four months so that no one can see it (Swanton, 1924–5).

In Iran, a new-born is given a few small spoonfuls of hot, sugared water. During his first three days he is made to swallow butter mixed with pilaret seeds, believed to condition and refresh the intestines before the child can be given milk (Masse, 1938). Among the Tewa Indians of New Mexico, where the mother does not breast-feed until the fourth day, a female relative may give the infant a small amount of water and cow's milk (Whitman, 1947).

Among the peoples who deny the infant the breast until the fourth day, Nigeria's Nupe feed the infant a boiled infusion of herbs collected by the father (Nadel, 1954). Temple (1922) describes this preparation as water in which the leaves of the *aduruku* (*Newbouldia laevis*), or of some seven to ten different kinds of trees, have been boiled for three to seven days. The liquid is poured into the infant's mouth.

The Navaho formerly would feed the infant only corn pollen suspended in water during the first four days of life. Some families would purge the new-born by giving it a liquid brewed from the inner bark of the juniper and pinyon, producing vomiting. More recently, mothers provide the infant with heated goat's milk and water for the first few days of life, since the colostrum continues to be distrusted (Leighton and Kluckhohn, 1947).

A few cultures may deny the infant the mother's breast for seven days or longer. Erikson (1943) reports that the Yurok Indians of northwestern California consider the post-natal period to be ten days in length and the infant is not permitted the mother's breast until the end of this time. Instead, the new-born receives a sort of nut soup, served in a small shell. The colostrum is considered to be unhealthful for the infant. Kroeber (1925) writes that the Yurok believe that the colostrum would injure the infant's jaws and cause it to starve. Thompson (1916) describes the Yurok as pounding hazel-nuts into a flour that, mixed with warm water, is given to the infant. Milk taken from the mother's breasts may be given to the infant, but he is not permitted direct access himself until the tenth day.

Conclusion

The costs of colostrum-denial are clear. If there are any benefits then they remain unknown. Thus, colostrum-denial, at least until new data are available, must be considered a maladaptive culture trait.

The case of colostrum-denial tells us that we do not understand how such harmful health practices enter cultures. We do not know how or whether they are eliminated. We do know that they exist, and that there is little in anthropological theory concerning them. Their existence is a challenge to that theory, which whether functionalist or cultural-materialist or ecological presupposes some kind of adaptiveness for most culture traits.

Notice how simple it would appear to be to lower infant mortality by nursing the infant within hours rather than days of birth. There is no evidence for any other species denying the infant the colostrum, strongly suggesting that here we are dealing with a consequence of our capacity for culture: a maladaptive consequence.

4. Elites Appropriate

Like Marxism, a sociobiological view of society yields conflict theory. As we saw in chapter 8, the conflict is about power, prestige, and the control of resources: the victor was presumably rewarded with greater reproductive success during evolutionary times, and is rewarded today with greater copulatory opportunity. The weapons in the conflict often involve culture traits and the relative frequency of cultural variants in the pool of information of which culture is composed. Each faction, in these conflicts, makes use of publicity, propaganda, religion, and education. Each faction claims that the gods, ancestors, spirits, public opinion, morality, and common sense support it (Alexander, 1974; van den Berghe, 1979; Lumsden and Wilson, 1985). This behaviour is of course in keeping with the sociobiological lesson that communication is ultimately about manipulating the behaviour of others (as was discussed in chapter 3). As Wallace (1966: 26) points out 'It is not surprising ... to find that religion is frequently a way of asserting an ethnic or class or racial identity in a situation of intergroup conflict.' For each faction, the teachings of the opposition represent culture stretch, its own claims, culture revision.

Many religions preach forbearance in this life in order to gain a reward in another existence. Such belief systems include most forms of Christianity and Islam, as well as Hinduism. The effect, of course, is support for the existing order. Some religions invite martyrdom, as when Iranian Shi'ite Moslems went to their deaths in the war with Iraq, firmly convinced that they would awaken in Paradise. Christianity, of course, has had its own 'Children's Crusade,' and in neither Christianity nor Islam is the concept of 'holy war' considered an oxymoron. In all instances, it can be argued that the battles are in the political interests of those justifying them on supernatural grounds, and only rarely in the interests, political or genetic, of those most likely to be killed.

The ethologist Eibl-Eibesfeldt (1982) offers an alternative interpretation. For him, such fitness-reducing behaviour on the part of some elements of a society is evidence for group selection, and he criticizes sociobiologists for paying little attention to this level of evolution.

Eibl-Eibesfeldt cites Robert Murphy's (1957, 1960) account of the Mundurucú, among whom a successful head-hunter must abstain from sexual intercourse for three years. His conclusion is that 'in non-literate tribal cultures, indoctrination of heroic virtues creates a readiness for self-sacrifice for the group' (p. 193). So, too, does 'training for obedience.' Aside from that fact that neither Murphy nor Eibl-Eibesfeldt offers any evidence that this norm is actually adhered to (ethnographies tend to be biased towards the culturally ideal rather than the real), a group-selectionist account of such behaviour would fail to explain the phenomenon of *culture revision*. A particular group or faction in a particular society may indeed succeed in promulgating culture traits in its own interest, but this situation is not necessarily permanent: it may lead to the revision of the culture, as we will see shortly.

It could be argued that the information-distortion caused by social inequality and factional conflict is in effect a special case of the accumulation of error. In this case, however, the error is deliberately introduced (though, given our cognitive distortion abilities, self-deception as well as plain-vanilla deceit may be involved). Note that since factions are quite capable of promulgating beliefs that are not actually in their fitness interests – error is always a possibility, as in chapter 7's discussion of revitalization movements – some propaganda and religion may actually be in no one's fitness interests at all.

REVISION: THE PROCESS OF CULTURE-STRETCH CORRECTION

If culture did nothing but stretch then it would no longer be adaptive and selection would gradually reduce our capacity for culture. But culture is never stable – it is always altering (though the rate at which change occurs is highly variable). At least some of this culture change involves the opposite of stretch, *revision*, the processes whereby culture traits return to fitness-enhancing pathways.

The mechanisms of revision are varied and are discussed in some detail below. The nature of the revision process depends in part on the type of cultural information that has been stretched. As we recall from chapter 8, codes and low-n subcodes are unlikely to stretch, since their doing so would impede communication. General mazeway background information, by contrast, seems to stretch quite readily – the examples of stretch from the medical and nutrition fields discussed earlier involve mazeway data. So, too, do the examples of factional manipulation of ideological and supernatural material. Once stretched, such data are very resistant to revision and it may require the kind of widespread mazeway resynthesis discussed in chapter 7 for revision to take place.

Sub^{n}goals and subplans seem to be revised fairly often, particularly when they are in the service of the prestige/self-esteem goal. Our (related) tendency to imitate the high in status and power, too, accounts for considerable revision. The adolescent, in rejecting parental example and admonition in favour of imitating a powerful popular figure, is revising his or her culture. Prestige-seeking and imitation are important mechanisms of revision. (Of course, if the 'wrong' person is imitated, the result can be stretch rather than revision.)

Notice that, in the last analysis, the mechanisms of culture revision and the plan/goal behaviours of the intra-individual system are probably identical. Recall that the use of particular subplans is governed in part by corrective feedback. When a sub^{n}goal is not reached, then alternative subplans may be activated. When numerous subplans fail, basic mazeway data may be questioned. Human beings are cognitively active and we try out alternatives, model reality mentally, and weigh the degrees of success and failure of subplans. In the process, we simultaneously may both enhance our individual fitness and revise some culture traits. If my family has always fished but now the fishery is failing, I may seek to farm, or to find a factory job – I am not forced to sit and starve. If a more wealthy and powerful group worships a different set of gods, then I may expand the range of deities to whom I make offerings. If earning a bachelor's degree no longer seems a guarantee of employment, then perhaps I will seek an MBA. Finally, as we have seen, I may deliberately socialize my children to meet a predicted future, attempting to prepare them with skills I myself do not possess. As I and others do these things, we may be revising our culture.

Genetic Response to Culture Stretch

Our general goal/plan behaviour probably revises away many stretched culture traits: but suppose a particular genetically maladaptive culture trait lingers for a lengthy period. It is theoretically possible that natural selection, acting on the relative frequency of the alleles underlying our acquiring the behaviour in question, may eventually do the revision. As was discussed in chapter 11, we are here talking about selection for what Boyd and Richerson term a 'direct bias' against a culture trait, a psychological predisposition to not acquire a particular piece of socially transmitted information. However, Boyd and Richerson convincingly argue that such specific genetic responses would be rare. It seems quite unlikely that any modern culture has been revised through the evolution of learning biases against specific culture traits.

Lag Times
How long does it take for revision to eliminate a stretched culture trait? The answer obviously depends on many complex factors. Here are four of these.

1. The first factor affecting the lag time for revision of a stretched (genetically maladaptive) trait is its evolutionary novelty. If the fitness-reducing culture trait is of a type that has frequently recurred during human evolutionary history, then selection has probably already equipped us with a revision mechanism. For example, suppose that our close kin model prestige subplans for us that are failing. As adolescents, we are quite likely to reject these kin as role models and instead imitate non-kin who are high in prestige and power. The lag time for revision will be very short. By contrast, suppose the trait in question is novel – the invention of non-nutritive sweeteners, for example. Here, the lag time will be very long, for we have no psychological mechanism in place to eliminate this novel cultural trait, even if the artificial sweeteners turn out to have strongly deleterious effects on our genetic fitness.

2. The second factor affecting lag time has to do with the ownership of the gored ox, that is, with the power of the negatively affected group. For example, in the young nations of modern Africa, the culture trait of 'nationalism' is generally not in the interests of traditional rulers. It is, however, in the interests of the new but powerful Western-educated élites. Thus, it is unlikely that this trait will be revised away in the foreseeable future.

3. A third factor affecting the 'lag time' required for revision of a stretched culture trait involves its gravity. For example, if the trait involves the classification of a potential food as inedible, but if the nutrients included in this potential food are already plentiful in the diet, then the lag time may be very long. Few of us eat the nutritious dandelion greens from our lawns, for example, and there is no reason to believe that either our health or our genetic fitness suffers from the lack.

4. The final factor in determining lag is applicable only to possible genetic responses to culture stretch (discussed above). If no existing mechanisms are able to eliminate it and if it has a persistent negative effect on genetic fitness, then selection may eventually produce a 'direct bias' against the trait; provided that this particular trait has alleles underlying it such that a change in their relative frequency would alter

the behaviour in question; and provided that the local population was sufficiently small and genetically isolated for a sufficiently lengthy period of time. As we saw in chapter 11's discussion of this possibility, Lumsden and Wilson's (1981) highly controversial estimate was that one thousand years might be necessary for the evolution of such a genetically mediated bias, under such conditions.

MAXIMIZING THE WRONG THINGS

Now let us move from maladaptive cultural traits to maladaptive psychological ones. Just as cultures can stretch, we as individuals can make decisions that reduce our inclusive fitness. Such decisions resemble evolutionarily novel culture stretches. They are often caused by an altered environment leading us to maximize what, evolutionarily, are now the 'wrong things.'

Recall from chapter 5's discussion of the intra-individual system that the environmentally stable goals of the major plans are linked to the limbic system. They have the subjective experience of pleasure or reward. Sub^nplans that succeed do so by achieving sub^ngoals, and pleasure is the product. Failure means pain and the probability of alternative sub^nplans being followed. Ordinarily, the success of sub ^{n}plans – gaining in relative standing, copulating, eating, drinking, practising skills in play, cementing reciprocity partnerships, aiding kin – directly or indirectly enhances inclusive fitness.

Now let us enter a novel environment in which the achievement of a sub^ngoal no longer enhances inclusive fitness. For example, a sweet taste once meant needed calories, the ripeness of fruit. In our new environment, sweetness may mean refined sugar and a risk of obesity and dental caries. But we are still adapted to the old environment, and thus we seek sweetness. The sensation of sweetness remains a sub^ngoal wired into the intra-individual system, and sub^nplans that achieve it result in pleasure. Selection has equipped us with the sub^ngoal of achieving a sweet taste because that sensation once was linked to enhanced fitness. In our novel environment it no longer is, but this new fact cannot instantly alter our evolved intra-individual system.

What of sex? In the old environment, copulation was a major goal and selection ensured that we would ordinarily find it highly rewarding. Intercourse was, after all, intimately related to reproductive success. In the new environment of contraception, that relationship is far weaker. Many of us now pursue sexual intimacy but seek strenuously to minimize reproduction. Such behaviour is fitness-reducing. For both sex and sweetness, we maximize not evolution's goal, inclusive fitness, but the intra-individual system's goal, pleasure (Barkow and Burley, 1980). An altered environment means that pleasure and fitness are no longer necessarily linked. Moreover, it may be that this is not the first time that this link has been broken.

Concealed Ovulation
Burley (1979) has argued that, in the distant past, too, members of our species sought to maximize copulation while minimizing reproduction. Why else, she asks, are human females not aware of their ovulations? Our closest ancestors experience a dramatic, reddish perineal swelling around the time of ovulation, a visible signal that is coupled with greatly enhanced sexual receptivity, leading to frequent coupling. In the human female, selection has eliminated any trace of this phenomenon. Even more remarkably, despite the massive hormonal changes attendant upon ovulation, human females have almost no internal cues to this state. It is as if selection had favoured the suppression of both external and internal cues to ovulation. Why should this be?

Burley suggests that early hominid females used their intelligence to do precisely what modern, contraceptive-using women do today: they recognized the link between ovulation, copulation, and pregnancy, and sought to control their own fertility. Early hominid females would have recognized that copulation leads to pregnancy. While courtship and sexual activity are highly pleasurable, evolution has not made pregnancy and parturition pleasurable goal-states. There had never been a selection pressure favouring their being pleasurable, since copulation inevitably led to pregnancy. But the newly intelligent hominid females were capable of restricting their sexual activity to periods when they were not ovulating, thus minimizing pregnancy and childbirth while maintaining the pleasures of courtship and sex. In the process, they were lowering their fertility.

One might argue that since only the more intelligent females could so act, they in effect selected themselves out of the population, resulting in human females having lower intelligence than do human males. Ms Burley demonstrates the implausibility of this hypothesis by having been wise enough not to mention it. Selection pressure for intelligence/culture capacity was extremely strong (as we discussed in chapter 7 and elsewhere), so that evolution eliminated not female intelligence but the internal and external cues to ovulation. As a result, hominid females are ordinarily unaware of their periods of fertility. If Burley is correct, then concealed ovulation was the product of a genetic response to the fitness-reducing tendency of early hominid females to separate court-ship and copulation from reproduction. Contemporary women may be acting much as did their ancestresses, producing, in most of the Western industrial nations, zero or even negative population growth. (However, as we will see in chapters 13 and 14, several other scenarios present plausible alternatives to Burley's account.)

Zero Population Growth and the Demographic Transition
Low-technology societies tend to have high rates of fertility and of mor-tality. Many children are born, many die, and population remains fairly stable. The *demographic transition* begins when, through industrializa-tion and public health measures, mortality falls. The result is an exploding population. But then, at least in the Western industrial nations, fertility, too, falls. When a society's fertility and mortality rates are both low, then population again tends to stabilize and the demo-graphic transition is complete.

As Barkow and Burley (1980) explain, the demographic transition appears to contradict sociobiology's inclusive-fitness-maximization tenet. Surely, upper classes in post–demographic transition societies could readily have more offspring than they do. Vining (1986) believes that their failure to do so is *the* challenge to sociobiology. We saw in chapter 8 that in small-scale, low-technology societies, reproductive success is well correlated with power, prestige, and wealth. Should the correlation not hold in industrial, post–demographic transition societies as well?

Vining thoroughly reviews a very confused demographic landscape. He argues, on the basis of considerable analysis of demographic data, that the apparent lower genetic fitness of élites in Western industrial nations is a phenomenon associated with lowering overall fertility levels, and that when the fertility rates of the population as a whole are increasing then those of élites are, if anything, likely to rise faster than the average. He does find, using American data, that 'the available data would appear to show higher fitness among the nation's economic, political, social and technocratic elite' (p. 7). However, since we now seem to be entering the 'unknown territory' of long-term low fertility, Vining's (p. 10) rather tentative conclusion is that 'until evidence is presented to the contrary, I think we can take it as one of the universals characterizing modern culture that social and reproductive success are inversely related.' Similarly, Hill (1984) finds that the British upper classes have failed to match the fertility rates of other British social strata.

Barkow and Burley (1980) suggest that Burley's account of the evolution of concealed ovulation applies to the current situation. Hominid females, conceivably for the second time, are using their restored control over their own fertility to lower it. If upper-class females have relatively few children, and if women in general in wealthy, industrialized nations make the same choice, it is because they are in a position to so choose. That is, the real social determinant of fertility is *autonomy*, the independence of the fertile woman to make her own choices, rather than have her fertility controlled by older women or by her husband.

From this perspective, the demographic trends Vining reviews reflect the growth of female autonomy. If this hypothesis is accurate, then the fertility decline of the post-demographic transition is a product of the growth of female control over her own fertility in these modernizing societies (a testable hypothesis). Prestige structures for women in pre–demographic transition societies overwhelmingly emphasize fertility. In Hausa society, for example, a young married woman is not really considered an adult until she has given birth, and (as in Chinese and other societies in which the extended family is the norm), until then, she remains under the authority of her mother-in-law. The demographic transition may be related to the freeing of women from the control of kin, providing both more autonomy and alternative strategies of prestige acquisition.

In similar fashion, fluctuations in the fertility of élite Western women, who presumably already have considerable autonomy, is best explained not by economic indicators or sociobiology but by the intellectual currents, ideas, aspirations, and alternative opportunities affecting these women. Their fertility behavior is to be understood in terms of social psychology, not inclusive fitness. The industrial society demographic data presented by Vining are confused because they include no variables dealing with the availability of alternative prestige structures, or with the social pressures of élite friendship and kinship circles.

One sociobiologist, William Irons (1979, 1983), rejects the Barkow and Burley autonomy hypothesis in favour of 'quality over quantity.' In brief, he believes that human beings react to resource abundance by limiting the number of their offspring but investing more heavily in each. In biological terminology, we react to resources by becoming more K- and less r-selected. A K-selected species is marked by few and relatively infrequent offspring but by low infant mortality rates and by heavy investment in each offspring. Elephants are K-selected, as are human beings. Rabbits are relatively r-selected, as are (to take an extreme example) frogs. Irons argues that the fertility of élites in post–demographic transition societies reflects a psychological tendency to reduce fertility, a tendency that has been triggered by their relatively wealthy situation. While this concentration of investment in a small number of offspring no longer enhances the fitness of those in whom the mechanism is triggered, it would presumably have done so for our ancestors.

Unfortunately, as Barkow and Burley (1980) and Vining (1986) point out, Irons's explanation does not account for the widespread tendency for women in modern societies to elect to have *no* offspring (see Vining for references to the tendency for women to choose not to reproduce). Unless one assumes that the decision to have no offspring is strongly correlated with massive help towards nieces and nephews, it is difficult to argue that zero fertility enhances one's fitness! Even the suggestion that we react to resource availability by narrowing our investment is dubious – one could just as easily argue that it is when resources are scarce, not plentiful, that we should lower our fertility and focus our investment on a reduced number of offspring.

Will the maladaptiveness of current fertility trends lead to a genetic response? The answer here must be affirmative, provided two conditions are met: (1) the trend must endure for a sufficient number of generations; and (2) there must be some kind of genetic basis for a disposition to want children. Konrad Lorenz (1965) long ago pointed out that the contours of the young – the roundedness, oversized head and eyes, gawky gait – release in human beings (and apparently in other mammals as well) protective behaviour and emotions usually signalled by coos, 'ahhhs,' and 'isn't it cute?' The sight of an attractive member of the opposite sex may elicit a desire for copulation; does the sight of a young child elicit the desire to have one? This is an empirical question, of course, but we have only anecdotal evidence that it does so. Still, if current fertility trends are indeed resulting in a genetic response, it may be that the form it will take will be an amplification of the current 'cuteness' response to infants. Perhaps, in future generations, the sight of an infant will elicit in women a strong desire for pregnancy. Of course, the evolution of such an 'instinct for pregnancy' would take many generations (particularly since the size of our local breeding population is immense), and the zero-population-growth tendency is a very recent and not necessarily enduring trend.

CONCLUSIONS

In a sense, adaptation is a product of maladaptation. Only through phenotypic maladaptation – through the presence of traits that reduce genetic fitness or at least enhance it less efficiently than do alternative traits – can the genotypes be culled, with each generation, and genes producing better-adapted phenotypes be thereby increased in frequency in the gene pool. But maladaptation has been somewhat neglected in sociobiology, perhaps because some have made the error of believing that the existence of fitness-reducing traits somehow damages the evolutionary paradigm. On the contrary, without a certain, small amount of maladaptation there can be no evolution.

Natural selection has to do with the ratio of costs to benefits, for any given trait. Even when the benefits far outweigh the costs, the latter remain, generating selection pressures. The intra-individual system permits us to make fitness-reducing choices. Culture often stretches, encouraging us to act against our own fitness interests. But human psychology and, if all else fails, selection itself gradually pull both culture and individual choice back towards fitness-enhancing pathways. There is an elastic between genes and culture and individual choice.

This elastic has an interesting implication for research strategies in sociobiology. If traits may often be genetically maladaptive, determining whether or not a given culture trait enhances inclusive fitness is in itself of limited utility. Such analysis becomes meaningful only when combined with a study of the underlying 'proximate,' psychological-level mechanisms mediating between the genes and the culture trait. Otherwise, all we can discover is the current degree of stretch, with no means to interpret it.[5]

SUMMARY

1. Maladaptation is as much a part of evolution as is adaptation and does not challenge the evolutionary paradigm. Almost every adaptive

---

5 Richerson and Boyd (1989) criticize the stretch metaphor on the basis of mathematical models showing the possibility of cultural group selection. For them, existing culture traits may affect which behaviours are or are not fitness-enhancing. Therefore, it is not meaningful to speak of genes returning culture to fitness-enhancing pathways, because these pathways are not predetermined but are in part determined by the culture itself. For example, in a culture in which co-operativeness is considered prestigious and sexually attractive, the preference for co-operative mates might result in a genetic advantage for those who bear that trait, an advantage that would be absent in another culture. See footnote 2 of chapter 11 for further discussion, or see Barkow (1989b).

trait is likely to carry with it a maladaptive consequence (which is just another way of saying that traits have costs as well as benefits).

2. Human cultures include genetically maladaptive traits and human beings frequently make fitness-reducing decisions as individuals. These maladaptive tendencies have been and continue to be important selection pressures in shaping the evolution of our species.

3. Culture's tendency to reduce genetic fitness – a tendency I term 'stretch' – is fourfold in nature. First, environments alter, so that culture traits genetically adaptive in the past are likely to become maladaptive when climates, soils, insects, and disease organisms alter.

4. Second, expenses emerge, as when techniques that were genetically adaptive in the short term reveal maladaptive long-term consequences. Keeping goats may be adaptive initially but, if they lead to desertification, they will eventually prove maladaptive.

5. Third, errors accumulate. We make mistakes and we may teach these errors to our children. For example, Focus 12.1 documents how some peoples of the world deny the infant the first milk, the immunity-conferring colostrum, and are probably increasing their infant mortality rates as a result. Traditional ideas of nutrition are often maladaptive, and traditional medical practices, such as blood-letting, dangerous and ineffective.

6. Fourth, élites appropriate. The powerful are likely to favor culture traits that are in their fitness interests but not necessarily in the interests of other elements of the population. Culture is an arena for conflict in which each faction emphasizes culture traits and beliefs in its own interests. Hence, religion and ideology are often associated with political conflict. Religions that preach reward in another existence in effect support the existing political élite, since they discourage active challenging of the status quo.

7. Aside from the genetically maladaptive culture traits we may participate in, most of us also make some *individual* decisions that are likely to reduce our genetic fitness. We may ignore our health, as when we fail to exercise regularly, or choose to eat too much sugar and saturated fat.

8. The most striking example of a decision to reduce individual fitness is that of making love while practising contraception. Human beings have apparently been selected to seek copulatory opportunity rather than to seek pregnancy. In the past, given the absence of contraception, the close connection between sex and reproduction was sufficient to ensure that selection in favour of our enjoying courtship and copulation

was sufficient to ensure frequent pregnancy; but today that tie has been broken. So we strive not for evolution's end of reproductive success but for evolution's means, love-making.

9. Fitness-reducing culture stretch gives rise to culture *revision*, the processes whereby culture traits return to fitness-enhancing pathways.

10. The prestige goal, coupled with our tendency to imitate the high in status and power, results in considerable culture revision.

11. Equally important for revision is the fact that sub^{n}plans work by corrective feedback. When a sub^{n}goal is not reached then alternative sub^{n}plans may be activated. When numerous sub^{n}plans fail then basic mazeway data may be questioned.

12. If our existing psychological characteristics fail to revise away a genetically maladaptive culture trait then, presumably, natural selection will do so, acting at the level of the allele frequencies underlying our acquiring the behaviour in question. But the trait must endure a sufficient number of generations for this revision to occur, and the behaviour in question must be readily affected by changes in allele frequencies. It seems unlikely that natural selection has revised culture since the end of the Pleistocene.

13. How long does it take for revision to eliminate a stretched culture trait? Four factors are involved. The first of these has to do with whether there is a powerful faction promulgating the trait in question and, if so, how powerful it is.

14. The second factor affecting the 'lag time' required for revision of a stretched culture trait involves its gravity. If the maladaptive consequences of the trait are trivial or non-existent then revision may never occur.

15. The third factor affecting the lag time for revision of a stretched trait is its evolutionary novelty. If the culture trait is a recurring one then selection has probably already equipped us with a revision mechanism. But if the trait is novel, as with the development of nuclear weapons, then revision may take a long while or never occur at all.

16. The fourth factor in determining lag is the duration of the stretched culture trait. If it does not endure for a sufficient length of time, then no revision mechanisms will come into play. A genetic response requires the longest duration of a maladaptive trait if revision is to occur.

17. Demographic data suggest that people often fail to have nearly as many offspring as they could afford to have, particularly in the industrialized nations, which frequently have zero or even negative

population growth. One sociobiological explanation, presented by Irons, is that such people are having fewer but higher-quality offspring, rather than more but lower-quality offspring.

18. Barkow and Burley, however, argue that this account cannot possibly explain why many people choose to have no children at all. They argue that human beings were selected to seek courtship and copulation but not pregnancy and childbirth. The combination of a growth in the ease of contraception and (more important) the increase in female autonomy that comes with industrialization has led many women to choose to restrict their fertility.

19. Burley has argued that human concealed ovulation may have evolved much the same way, when early hominid females might have noted the connection between ovulation and copulation and used this insight to restrict their fertility. The result then (she suggests) was selection for the inability to detect one's own ovulation, but it is unclear what the result of the current female self-restriction of fertility will be.

PART FIVE

The Evolution of Human Sexuality

13

Sexuality and Scenarios

Earlier chapters presented a theory of mind and of culture, and of how it is that both have aspects that at times may reduce rather than enhance genetic fitness. The present chapter and the one that follows it discuss how it was that our particular species may have evolved the capacity for culture in the first place. We will be discussing evolutionary scenarios – reconstructions of the selection pressures likely to have led to our species – and we will find that sex and the relationship between the sexes may have been central in human evolution.

Why emphasize sexuality in discussing human evolutionary scenarios? Our sexuality and the sexual selection processes that produced it were intimately involved with the evolution of our intelligence and capacity for culture. We differ from our closest relative, the chimpanzee, in only three major respects: sexuality, intelligence/cultural capacity, and bipedal locomotion. This chapter will present scenarios that depict all three differences as having evolved together.

OUTLINE OF THIS CHAPTER

The chapter begins by briefly reviewing the 'standard sociobiological portrait' of human sex differences (first discussed in chapter 3). Then it summarizes the changes to that portrait made in chapters 6 and 8, when we saw that sexual selection may have played a major role in the evolution of the capacity for culture. Next, we analyse two different evolutionary scenarios in order to see how assumptions about selection pressures affect our expectations about the nature of human sexuality. The focus then shifts to one of understanding individual and cross-cultural variability in sexual behaviour. We review Draper and Harpending's (1982) important work on human reproductive strategies and the evidence for there being a childhood 'sensitive period' in the determination of the courtship pattern the individual will later follow.

REVIEW OF SEXUAL SELECTION AND THE 'STANDARD PORTRAIT'

Relations between the sexes were crucial in our evolution. We saw in chapter 3 that selection favours males competing with one another for females, simply because females risk so much of their reproductive potential with each copulation while males risk little. Human males tend to take advantage of the minimal cost of copulation by seeking as many sexual partners (and therefore as many offspring) as possible, while females tend to follow the common mammalian pattern of being discriminating ('coy') in choosing or permitting males to copulate. Males should prefer younger females (who are of greater reproductive value and more likely to be fertile and healthy) and females whose reputation suggests confidence in paternity is warranted. Females should prefer males who give evidence of being able to provide resources for future parental investment (that is, males who are high in status and/or highly skilled), being willing to provide those resources to the female and her offspring, and who show phenotypic evidence of 'good genes.'

In chapter 6 it was argued that females, in choosing males best able to invest in offspring, were in effect selecting for males high in 'cultural capacity.' Then, in chapter 8, it was suggested that the standard sociobiological portrait of human sexuality needed to be modified in the case of males seeking longer-term relationships with females, females in whose offspring they would be likely to invest parentally. The greater the total parental investment available (one assumes), the higher the number of surviving offspring likely to result. Thus, for longer-term relationships, males should prefer females whose above-average ability to produce or control resources permits them to provide more parental investment than do other females. Female prestige systems should therefore in many ways resemble those of males, and male-female mate selection strategies should be more similar to each other in long-term than in short-term relationships. In the former case, human males, too, should tend to be fairly discriminating, seeking mates who not only appear likely to be fertile and provide paternity certainty but who also show evidence of being able themselves to produce and control resources.

Having reviewed this background, we are now ready to discuss evolutionary scenarios.

THE NATURE OF EVOLUTIONARY SCENARIOS

An evolutionary scenario (some prefer the terms 'narrative,' 'story,' or 'account') is a somewhat speculative theory in which the usual requirements for empirical verifiability are relaxed in favour of an emphasis on completeness, internal logic, and plausibility. Back in chapter 1, for example, various scenarios leading to our species' loss of fur were discussed. Scenarios provide a sense of closure, but they must be consonant with known data and logically consistent. For human evolutionary scenarios, these 'known data' include the fossil record of human evolution, non-human primate behaviour, and the present behavioural and morphological characteristics of our species. Scenarios should never be taken too seriously, given their unverifiable nature. For aficionados, they are fun.

SCENARIO 1: LOVEJOY'S ACCOUNT

Lovejoy's (1981) scenario, 'The Origin of Man,' appeared in the highly prestigious journal *Science* and is still frequently cited. Though flawed, it represents an advance over its predecessors.

Lovejoy begins, in standard fashion, by seeking to demonstrate the inadequacy of earlier accounts of how the hominid line separated from that of the apes. These efforts variously emphasized selection for weapon and other tool use, climate change, and especially, an assumed early hunting adaptation. The climate change – the drying trend of the late Miocene/early Pliocene (the Miocene was twenty-five to five million years ago) – is not in dispute. The notion of our reacting to it by developing a hunting ecology based on weapons and other tools (argued specifically by, for example, Laughlin, 1968; Washburn and Avis, 1958; Washburn, 1959; Washburn and Lancaster, 1968) is.

Lovejoy points out that we have had tools for only about two million years (since his writing the date has been pushed back an additional half-million years), and the hominid line must be far older than that. If tool use was the key adaptation, writes Lovejoy, the tools must have remained 'primitive and unchanged for at least five million years' (p.

341). Since this presumed stasis seems unlikely, tool use was probably not the critical factor in originating the hominid line. Lovejoy cites comparable problems with other single-factor scenarios.

In their place, Lovejoy emphasizes that the Old World monkeys and apes have moved in the direction of increasing 'K selection.' That is, they have moved in the direction of providing increasingly heavy parental investment to each of fewer, more dependent, but longer-lived offspring. At the extremes of this movement are the chimpanzee and ourselves. We know that the first hominids evolved during the late Miocene: Lovejoy argues that the ecological conditions of this period meant that the major problem in getting food was the time it took to find it, rather than the time needed to process and consume it.[1] Under these circumstances, selection would have favoured males who did not compete directly for food with their females and offspring. The result would have been males ranging more widely in search of food than did females and young.

Any male who tended to range widely from the females would have obviously lowered his genetic fitness. However, by bonding with a female to form a monogamous pair, a male could ensure his paternity certainty while still foraging more widely than did his mate.[2] At the same time, the female would be assured of his not competing with her and their offspring for food. The bond would be monogamous rather than polygynous because the benefits of lack of competition would be sharply reduced if the female had to share her more limited range with other females and their offspring. Moreover, given assurance of biological paternity, selection would favour the male investing parentally by bringing food back to the female and to their (joint) offspring.

This provisioning (of scavenged meat, fruit, and so on) would have provided vital nutrients to the female during pregnancy and lactation. The provisioning males would therefore have had more surviving offspring than did other males, so that selection for such behaviour

1 Compare with chapter 6's summary of Kurland and Beckerman (1985), who suggest that this environment of 'patchily' distributed, hard-to-find food would have resulted in selection for communication. Compare, too, with chapter 11's discussion of Boyd and Richerson (1985) and of their approach to the 'initial kick.'

2 Lovejoy does not mention the increased exposure to predator pressure entailed in such consortships, given that they involve forfeiting the protection of the rest of the band. This danger is particularly important when one recalls that Lovejoy is assuming that monogamy developed prior to weaponry and at a time when hominids were physically much smaller than we are today.

would be strong. But how is the male to bring food back to the home base? The hand is more efficient than the mouth, argues Lovejoy, and selection would therefore have favoured bipedality in order to free up the hands for carrying foodstuffs back to the female and young. Thus Lovejoy accounts for our walking on two legs.

Having disposed of bipedality, Lovejoy goes on to apply his provisioning/monogamy scenario to human sexuality. As we discussed in chapter 12 (in connection with Burley's overly-intelligent-female explanation for the evolution of concealed ovulation), human females lack the periodic sexual receptivity and perineal sexual swellings typical of other primates.[3] Rather than an estrous cycle, human females have a menstrual cycle and may accept or elicit copulation throughout that cycle. Lovejoy accounts for this difference by arguing that the continual copulation would reinforce what he terms a 'pair bond' between the male and female. Perhaps more important, a bonded male who copulates throughout his mate's cycle has the same probability of producing offspring as does a male who practises 'complete promiscuity' (p. 211).

In support of his scenario, Lovejoy emphasizes the relatively low degree of sexual dimorphism of our species.[4] As was discussed in chapter 3, in species in which there is strong male-male competition for females the males tend to be larger in general and also to have specialized agonistic equipment, such as antlers, horns, or canines, that females either lack or have in much reduced form. But monogamous species have relatively little male-male competition and thus have relatively little dimorphism. The relative lack of sexual dimorphism in human beings, argues Lovejoy, supports his scenario. The sexual dimorphism we do have strongly suggests epigamic (mate choice) sexual selection in that display rather than functional traits predominates. Here, Lovejoy (p. 211) mentions 'the body and facial hair, distinctive somatotype, the conspicuous penis of human males, and the prominent and permanently enlarged mammae of human females.' These

3 Some authors have described the human female as 'continuously sexually receptive.' This seems a bit of an overstatement. I would prefer to think of human females as 'continuously facultatively receptive.'

4 Lovejoy (1981: 211) passes over the real possibility that our earliest probable ancestor, Australopithecus afarensis, was highly sexually dimorphic. Instead, he chooses to emphasize that this dimorphism is less than that of other terrestrial primates, such as baboons, even though much greater than that of modern human beings. An alternative explanation for the reduction in human dimorphism is the development of weaponry, which would have greatly reduced selection pressure for large physical size and large canines, while increasing that for weapon making/using capability.

traits, he argues, help to maintain the pair bond, as does our individuated body odour (we each have a distinctive personal scent) (p. 212).

Criticisms of the Lovejoy Scenario

Lovejoy's scenario is consistent with the fossil record, and by moving away from earlier, single-factor accounts, it advances the debate. But there are serious flaws in Lovejoy's application of evolutionary theory, while his account is in part inconsistent with current knowledge of human behaviour.

To begin with the latter, the evolution of monogamy is central to Lovejoy's scenario. Unfortunately, human beings are only facultatively monogamous and do not 'pair bond' in a manner at all comparable to that of gibbons or ducks (Symons, 1979). As we saw in chapter 8, the late G.P. Murdock (1967) established some time ago that most human cultures have permitted polygyny. Gibbons and ducks are invariably and exclusively monogamous: men and women vary enormously in the nature of their ties to one another, even within a single culture (Symons, 1979). Lovejoy, in short, 'explained' a non-fact, human monogamy. Possibly what he had in mind was the idea of an enduring relationship between a male and a particular female, regardless of whether that male had similar relationships with additional females. The question arises, then, as to whether a single male would have been able to provide much investment for more than one female and her offspring.

Lovejoy's error of theory has to do with the need for intermediate steps between the earlier, estrous-cycle/obvious ovulation stage and the later menstrual-cycle/concealed-ovulation pattern. Lovejoy fails to tell us how we got from the one to the other without a disastrously maladaptive step between. In effect, he gives us a bridge with a hole in the middle.

Smith (1984) has analysed this particular 'hole' in some detail. Reviewing the non-human primate behaviour literature, Smith concludes that, in a polygynous or communal mating situation, females at the peak of ovulation tend to get the most attention from the highest-ranking (the 'best genes') males. Generally, the sign of this ovulatory peak is a swelling peak – the sexual swelling is a reliable indicator of ovulatory status: 'Therefore any female variant that de-emphasized swelling, as a first move towards concealed ovulation, would have had diminished attractiveness to the best males, and would therefore have been selected against' (p. 639). In other words, 'you can't get there from here' if 'here' is obvious ovulation with communal or promiscuous mating and 'there' is concealed ovulation with monogamy. (Smith is among those who argue that concealed ovulation could have been selected for only after our species no longer practised communal or promiscuous mating.)

Smith (1984: 638) also points out a more minor problem: Lovejoy (along with eight other theorists cited) apparently believes that copulation enhances the 'pair bond,' that is, 'that diminution of or loss in signals about a female's reproductive condition and the extension of sexual receptivity have somehow trapped promiscuous males into monogamy, which is maintained by conjugal sexual contentment for the ultimate benefit of altricial offspring.'

But as Smith (citing Symons, 1979) indicates, this belief is incompatible with the 'Coolidge Effect.' In male mammals, including our own species, the post-ejaculatory refractory period is appreciably shortened when a novel female is presented. In other words, the male will be ready for a new copulation much faster if he is presented with a new female. It is well documented that, for species ranging from rats to human beings, novelty is, for males, a strong sexual stimulus. This finding – and perhaps the stereotyped male complaint that marital sex grows dull (Symons, 1979) – would seem to be inconsistent with Lovejoy's assumption that repeated copulation results in bonding. This is just as well. Were continuous sexual receptivity the cement that bonds the pair, we would expect pregnancy to tend to dissolve that bond; but there is no evidence that it does so. The attachment between men and women, though perhaps often initiated through sexual attraction, would appear to be somewhat more complex. Theorists have no need to invoke sexuality in order to account for intra-sexual bonds of reciprocity and alliance: no doubt people of different sexes, too, can remain associated without the continual reinforcement of sexuality.

We have now seen (1) that the 'diminution of ... signals about a female's reproductive condition' could not have been selected for in the manner Lovejoy posits; (2) that Lovejoy is in error about our being monogamous as a species (though many of us are as individuals, at least intermittently); and (3) that it is unlikely that male-female ties depend upon copulation for their perpetuation. Lovejoy's scenario is clearly flawed, though it did carry the debate about the origins of the hominid line forward.

S.T. Parker (1987) provides a more recent scenario that, however, does not avoid all problems. The discussion below is by no means a complete summary of Parker's important paper, in which she also thoroughly reviews sexual-selection theory and (at various points) follows Parker and Gibson (1979) in making use of a Piagetian framework to deal with the evolution of human intelligence and language. Our concern here, however, is with her scenario.

SCENARIO 2: PARKER'S NARRATIVE

Parker's (1987) scenario begins at some point earlier than three and a half million years ago (late Miocene/early Pliocene), when it is likely that 'the earliest hominids were a small, ape-like species that arose in a mosaic habitat in the Rift valley in East Africa' (1987: 241). She assumes that these early ancestors of ours rather resembled chimpanzees in social organization and behaviour. Thus, we begin as group-living foragers who probably mated communally and promiscuously. Judging from the fossils usually classified as *Australopithecus afarensis*, males would have been considerably larger than females.

Because this was a period during which the African climate was slowly becoming drier, selection emphasized foraging by the extraction of 'energy-rich embedded foods such as nuts, roots, tubers, fungus, ants, termites, grubs and eggs,' using tools (p. 242). As in the chimpanzee, males may have supplemented their extracting with hunting or trapping and scavenging.

Extracting food, even with tools, requires some skill and strength and so would have been difficult for the young. Thus, suggests Parker, selection would have favoured sharing food with offspring. Because the presence of the kinds of foods that require extracting is not at all obvious, selection would have also favoured learning and communicating.

Food supply would have fluctuated seasonally, suggests Parker, and so we would expect a fission-fusion type of social organization (comparable to that of the common chimpanzee) in which groups form and disperse depending upon the degree to which the food supply is concentrated or dispersed. In such a setting, selection would have favoured the often-promiscuous mating patterns similar to those of some groups of the modern chimpanzee. Sexual selection would have taken the form of sperm competition in males (discussed in chapter 14), as evidenced by the large testes and long penis of chimpanzees and modern human beings. For females, sexual selection involved advertising estrus through perineal swellings around the time of ovulation, combined with prolonged estrus so as to lengthen the period during which nuptial gifts could be obtained.

But consort pairs would also have formed, as males, being larger and more powerful than females, in effect offered females aid in the labour of extracting foodstuffs in return for going off with them, away from the group. The offering of food by a male to a female during or just prior to mating is common among animals and insects and is known as 'nuptial feeding' (discussed in chapter 2 in the context of scorpionflies and deceit). Parker even suggests that, for our ancestors, a frequent nuptial gift may have been scavenged brain, a calorie- and protein-rich prize whose extraction requires the difficult task of opening the cranium (p. 244). Males would have come to compete with each other in the size and quality of their nuptial gifts, that is, in terms of their resource-acquisition abilities. Females would have competed for the gifts of the most productive males. As Parker (pp. 245–6) puts it: 'Sexual selection then would have favoured intellectual abilities relevant to hunting/scavenging, division and transport of food in males, and those relevant to social manipulation through referential communication in both sexes ... As male parental investment increased in importance, female competition for resource contributions would increase along with male efforts to increase their confidence of paternity.'

Important to Parker's argument is a recent reinterpretation by Potts (1984, 1986) of accumulations of fossils at some two-million-year-old sites at Olduvai, in Kenya. Previously, these sites had been interpreted as evidence of home bases, similar to those of modern hunter-gatherers. Potts argues that these locations were more likely to have been butchery sites selected for proximity to sources of stone for tool-making. Parker suggests that males would leave butchery tools (or at least their makings) at a specific site to which they would then bring scavenged or hunted carcasses. More important, she argues that these males would have benefited by attracting females to the sites, using the lure of meat gifts. This would have been the beginning of male control of females. Eventually, males would have begun to hunt co-operatively and to form alliances together to control females.

Back in the earlier situation of communal mating, selection had favoured females who advertised their ovulations. But now, argues Parker, since estrus females were benefiting from the meat gifts of males, selection would have favoured a shift 'from estrus advertising to estrus concealment.' Citing Short (1980), Parker believes that 'display of permanently enlarged breasts and hips may have been favored as substitutes for swollen and colored genital displays.' Females 'who traded the increased confidence of paternity (or the appearance of it) for increased male parental investment' would have been able to rear infants whose larger brains and concomitant increased dependency would otherwise have made them unlikely to survive. This change in courtship pattern may have led to the 'rapid divergence' of the hominids from the ancestors of the modern chimpanzee.

FOCUS 13.1

ON THE ORIGINS OF LANDSCAPE

Human communication abilities probably did not evolve in a straight line. Hockett and Ascher (1964) distinguish between the call system of animals and the language of human beings. Call systems consist of a limited number of vocal signals, each of which is appropriate to a specific type of situation. They give the example of the gibbon, whose system includes a vocalization for the discovery of food, a signal that means 'danger,' one that may indicate desire for company, one that apparently permits individuals to keep track of one another's location, and several other situation-specific signals. While calls may vary in their loudness and in how many times they are repeated, they are always mutually exclusive: an individual either makes the call appropriate to a particular situation or does not, but never merges or blends calls. The linguist's term for this type of system is *closed*, that is, new types of vocalizations cannot be generated.

In contrast, explain Hockett and Ascher, human language systems are *open* or *productive*, in that we can generate an infinite number of meanings. Human language also differs from a call system in that it exhibits *displacement*, meaning that the signal can be emitted apart from the actual situation. A gibbon may emit a 'here is food' vocalization in the presence of food, but cannot use the call to discuss food in its absence. Human beings, in contrast, can discuss food at any time (and some of us certainly do). We can talk about anything anywhere, thanks to this displacement feature of language. Language also exhibits *duality of pattern*. A gibbon's call cannot be broken into separate components: it is a discrete whole. Language, in contrast, may be broken into elementary signalling units called 'phonemes.' (The chimpanzee communicational system appears to be neither language nor a call system but somewhere in-between. See de Waal [1982] for examples of the subtlety of chimpanzee communication.)

Hockett and Ascher assume that our early ancestors must have had a call system similar to that of other primates. As they left off arboreal existence for life on the savannah, however, our ancestors developed a more complex social organization and faced many novel situations for which their existing calls were inadequate.

Selection would have therefore favoured a more flexible system of communication. Hockett and Ascher suggest (with tongue in cheek) that a system of communicative, controlled flatulence might have evolved. Instead, selection favoured the *blending* of calls, components of calls being put together to create novel vocalizations for novel situations. They use a sort of 'grinding down' metaphor to explain the origins of duality of pattern. Pre-language became increasingly flexible and complex as numerous calls were blended together. At the same time, different groups with different pre-languages would meet and thus enlarge their mutual stock of meaningful minimum-signal elements. Eventually, these elements became the phonemes of genuine languages. Hockett and Ascher argue that this was the only way in which our original closed system could have evolved into an open one.

Gordon Hewes (1973) offers a different approach, one that implies that obscene gestures, for example, would have evolved prior to the development of obscene words. For Hewes, our first language would have been composed of *gestures* rather than vocalizations. Non-human primates show great non-verbal communicational ability, an ability our ancestors would presumably have shared. Moreover, even today, human children if deprived of the experience of hearing speech spontaneously develop gestural languages; while children learn sophisticated sign languages (such as American Sign Language) with the same alacrity with which they acquire spoken language. The latter, Hewes suggests, would have evolved only long after its gestural ancestors. Human beings often emit spontaneous sounds in response to physical effort (as when one grunts while trying to thread a needle). Sounds produced in the effort to communicate gesturally, perhaps in the dark or with the hands full, would have been the 'initial kick' for selection for speech. Such sounds would have gradually come to supplement, and then to replace, gesture. The adaptive advantage of a system of communication that could be used in caverns and other shelters, and in the night and while carrying burdens, is obvious.

Hewes's theory is only one of the many concerned with language origins. For example, Steklis and Harnad (1976), who take a view somewhat similar to that of Hewes, emphasize the importance of brain lateralization. Philip Lieberman (1984: 323–6) rejects the 'gestural hypothesis' entirely and believes that our ancestral communication system must have been at least in part vocal. Mary LeCron Foster (1980) introduces the idea of symbolism to speech. The actions of mouth and tongue and breath would have initially represented physical action, for LeCron Foster, as when pressing the lips together came to symbolize pressing or grasping. Ultimately, this process would have given rise to such 'mmm-words' as the Latin *manus* ('hand').

The work of Philip Lieberman (1975, 1984) and his colleagues provides some data, as opposed to speculation, on the origins of language. Lieberman has used careful measurements of hominid fossils in order to reconstruct the pharyngeal tracts of our ancestors, and so discover the extent to which they would have been able to form the sounds of which modern languages are composed. Lieberman (1975, 1984; Lieberman, Crelin, and Klatt, 1972) concludes that our ancestors would probably have communicated at a much slower rate than do modern human beings. Even ancestors as recent as *Homo sapiens neandertalensis*, who very likely did have language, would not have been able to communicate as efficiently as do we, his successor.

Even the neurophysiological basis of speech is subject to controversy, with the pendulum swinging between those who posit specialized structures in the cerebral cortex underlying speech behaviour (for instance, a 'speech centre' in the dominant hemisphere, consisting largely of Broca's and Wernicke's areas) and those who argue, as does Lieberman (1984), in favour of speech being mediated by a more distributed system. The data at present appear to support the latter approach (Ojemann, 1983; Wallesch et al., 1985).

The selection pressures that gave rise to human communicational abilities no doubt varied over time. Parker and Gibson (1979) suggest that, initially, selection would have favoured the ability to communicate to close kin the identity and location of foodstuffs. Later on, the selective advantage of communication might have involved the ability to co-ordinate hunts (Parker, 1985). Finally, 'language must have been used for encoding predictions and complex rules and for ritual transformations of status' (Parker, 1987). Sexual selection surely would have played a major role, at least during the later stages of our evolution, for both men and women often compete verbally, and the verbal derogation of sexual rivals in particular is, in many cultures, almost an art form (cf. Buss and Dedden, n.d.). We know that, in evolutionary terms, communication is about the manipulation of others: selection pressures in favour of human language may have had much to do with the capacity to successfully alter the actions of those around us. Much of impression management, after all, has to do with what we say and how we say it.

The origins of language remain a topic on which a clear consensus has not yet emerged. Steklis and Harnad (1976), and the volume which they edited, as well as Lieberman (1984), are good sources of bibliography for those who wish to pursue the subject. A recent approach to language origins is that of Wallace (1989), who argues that the 'deep structure' of language and the brain's ability to form geographic cognitive maps both are functions of the hippocampus. For Wallace (who has been strongly influenced by O'Keefe and Nadel [1978, 1979], the hippocampus of the dominant hemisphere was selected to convert its geographic mapping abilities to the mapping of the structure of language.

Since the males were carrying the nuptial gifts, bipedality probably began first with males, argues Parker. Females preferred males who could and would bring such gifts. Parker agrees with Lovejoy that bipedalism arose first among males because it freed their hands for carrying. While Lovejoy (1981) saw this carrying as a form of parental investment (carrying foodstuffs to offspring at a home base), Parker (p. 248) sees it as the product of males competing with one another to provide nuptial gifts to females (mate-choice sexual selection). Only later, she suggests, as females were selected for the ability to carry their increasingly dependent infants, would bipedalism have become a trait of both sexes.

Some anthropologists, Claude Lévi-Strauss (1969) in particular, have argued that kinship has to do with male exchange of rights over females. Parker argues (as does Fox, 1972) that males would have made alliances with one another in order to exchange women. By restricting the sexual activities of their sisters and daughters, men increase the value of these women to their potential mates, whose confidence in paternity would thereby have been enhanced. Such high-value kinswomen could either be exchanged for equally high-value mates or could be married to prestigious (high resource–controlling) men. By the advent of modern *Homo sapiens*, language would have been used to encode rules regarding sexuality, marriage, and the control and distribution of resources (Parker, 1987: 247). Thus, Parker accounts for the origins of the kinship systems that anthropologists have studied among the cultures of the world. Note that, where Lovejoy emphasized monogamy, Parker emphasizes male efforts to control females.

Parker also emphasizes females' efforts to control and manipulate males. Given the importance of sexual selection, suggests Parker, it is in the female's interest to incite competition so as to choose the 'best genes' male. Thus, females would have been selected for 'the considerable analytic and tactical skill involved ... in setting up the appropriate conditions and audiences for inciting male competition by using one male as a foil to get the attention of another. Other female strategies for social manipulation involve controlling social networks through which she can display herself and her kin to advantage, and build powerful alliances' (p. 247).

Though males would have been selected to control female sexuality, females would have been selected for ways of overcoming that control. The result, as mentioned by Parker and discussed at length by Smith

(1984, whom Parker cites in this context), is relentless inter-sexual conflict. The conflict is not so much direct challenge as it is a sowing of confusion: confusion about ovulatory status. Thus, female countermeasures to male control include concealed ovulation, continuous (facultative) sexual receptivity, and large breasts. Gone is the obviousness of the perineal swellings of estrus. Gone, too, is its periodic but intense receptivity, replaced by a much weaker and more situationally dependent sexuality. The enlarged breasts of pregnancy are now permanently in evidence (presumably because, Smith suggests, males were less likely to guard the sexual activities of pregnant females).

It would have been in the fitness interests of females to have had multiple sexual partners. Smith's account (1984: 610–14) of why this should be so merits summarizing here, in the interests of disturbing male complacency. Multiple males can benefit a female thusly: First, her offspring may inherit half of a 'better' set of genes than those possessed by her regular mate. The 'better' may include not just ability to provide resources but also the capacity to charm or seduce – after all, to the extent that variability in charm and seduction reflects genetic variability, a woman increases her chances of herself having a 'charming' son or grandson by copulating with a successful 'charmer.' Second, the non-usual or secondary mate provides for additional genetic diversity – in a varying environment, a female's having all her offspring with one male is the equivalent of putting all her eggs in one basket. Genetically varied offspring increase the probability that at least some will be able to cope with environmental fluctuations. Third, the secondary mate provides assurance that, should her regular mate happen to be infertile, her own reproductive success will not be affected. Fourth, the secondary mate may provide resources in exchange for copulation: prostitution is cross-culturally ubiquitous and 'probably has its origin in courtship gifting' (Smith, 1984: 613).[5] Fifth, Smith believes that the secondary mate may also provide a sort of 'back up' of physical protection in the absence of the regular mate and that in some cases his high standing may enhance the social position of the female. I would suggest that a more important (and sixth) reason for a secondary mate is as a potential

5 For example, among the Hausa the distinction between a 'prostitute' and an ordinary woman between marriages has more to do with whether or not she lives with a father or brother than it does with her sexual or economic activities. See Barkow (1971) for an analysis of courtesanship among the Hausa.

replacement for the regular mate should he die, desert (in favour of another female), or become ill or injured.

Adding Breasts and Concealed Ovulation to Parker's Model
Parker's scenario is (in my opinion) one of the more powerful of those presented in recent years to account for the hominid separation from the chimpanzee and our development into modern human beings. Parker's scenario is also fully consistent with the theory, discussed in chapter 8, of how primate social dominance may have evolved into human self-esteem. But let us add and amend it a bit.

Breasts. It may have been Desmond Morris (1967: 62) who originated the idea that the human permanently enlarged breast evolved as a sexual attractant (as a replacement for the no-longer-quite-so-visible buttocks of our quadrupedal ancestors, actually). Smith (1984), however, makes the point that large breasts could not have evolved back during our hypothetical period of communal mating. Selection would have favoured males who were not attracted but repulsed by large breasts, since they would have been a sign of pregnancy or lactation – and therefore of the female's not ovulating. Smith (p. 641) suggests that they evolved later.

But even after we no longer mated communally, why should large breasts have evolved? Smith believes they were selected for as a means of confusing males about a female's lactatory and therefore ovulatory status, in order to circumvent male control over female sexual activities. To the extent large breasts are now a sexual attractant, he argues, this development would have occurred only after they had already become firmly established. Smith does not, however, explain why the swollen abdomen of pregnancy, like the enlarged breasts, did not also become a permanent female secondary sexual characteristic. Nor does he account for breasts becoming sexually attractive.

Smith does not discuss the argument made by Cant (1981), Gallup (1986), and Mascia-Lees, Relethford, and Sorger (1986) that the breasts enlarged initially because they were storage areas for fat. Presumably (though this is not part of Cant's argument), storage in this region could have been selected for only after the ending of communal mating. Since pregnancy and lactation make heavy physiological demands upon the body, large breasts would have been reliable indicators of female ability to bear young successfully. Males would therefore have been selected to prefer females with enlarged breasts. Such a preference would in turn have resulted in the sexual selection of females who tended to have (deceitfully) large breasts even when their fat reserve levels were low. We might then add the following to Parker's scenario: large breasts evolved only after the ending of communal mating and because (a) they were a site at which to deposit adipose tissue (that is, to store fat); (b) males were selected to prefer large breasts because these indicated a nutritional reserve; (c) females were then selected for relatively large breasts even when this reserve was low; and (arguably) also (d) the enlarged breasts confused males about ovulatory status and so weakened male control over female sexual activity.[6]

What of the shift from 'estrus advertising to estrus concealment'? Smith (1984) criticizes the treatment of estrus concealment by Lovejoy and others on the following grounds: a female who began to conceal her estrus, reducing the prominence of her perineal swellings and perhaps retaining the enlarged breasts characteristic of pregnancy, would have been signalling 'no ovulation' to the males. Such females would presumably have been the least likely to receive nuptial gifts. Males would presumably have been selected to favour females who showed prolonged visible signs of estrus, rather than their lack. As Parker points out, we find prolonged estrus among chimpanzees (pygmy chimpanzees in particular [Susman, 1987]). How, however, would we have moved from estrus concealment to no estrus at all and a menstrual period instead? Unfortunately, we have at least three answers to this question.

1. We could posit two stages for the evolution of concealed ovulation. Initially, there would be strong selection for prolonged signs – both behavioural and visible – of estrus, as females competed for male nuptial gifts. For a time, all early hominid females may have had

---

6 Low, Alexander, and Noonan (1987) come to fairly similar conclusions concerning the enlarged breast and concealed ovulation (discussed below). Anderson (1988) disagrees completely with them, attacking the very notion that sexual selection was responsible for the female form. Low, Alexander, and Noonan (1988) rebut strongly and effectively. Mascia-Lees, Relethford, and Sorger (1986) accept Cant's (1981) arguments concerning breasts as storage areas for fat but deliberately avoid any consideration of sexual selection, in the mistaken belief that the theory is somehow 'ethnocentric' and that reliance on natural selection is more 'parsimonious.' Instead, they emphasize seasonal variability in food supply resulting in strong selection pressure on females for pregnancy and ovulation, and also discuss the hormonal bases for the deposition of adipose tissue in the breasts. For a balanced discussion of sexual selection with particular emphasis on female choice, see Majerus (1986) or Kirkpatrick (1987).

permanently engorged perineal regions. Once this former sign of ovulation became unreliable, however, selection on males to attend to it would have relaxed. Now, during the second stage, selection would have favoured males who chose the recipients of their nuptial gifts on other grounds entirely, the most likely grounds presumably involving readiness to form sexually exclusive, high-paternity-confidence consort relationships. Since males were now ignoring sexual swellings, selection on females to produce them would in turn have relaxed. Instead, selection would have favoured females who did not waste energy on such swellings each month. Unfortunately, since perineal swellings do not fossilize, direct evidence for early hominid females having had prolonged apparent estrus is unlikely to be found. One would predict, however, that for any estrous-cycle primate species the more frequently males provide food to females the more enduring the sexual swellings will be.

Only after consort relations became the norm would selection have begun to favour females who confused males as to when they were ovulating (Benshoof and Thornhill, 1979). Large breasts and the modern menstrual cycle would date from this point. However, selection on females for these devices to confuse males about ovulation would have generated counterselection on males in favour of reliable detection of ovulation. The result would have been a sort of arms race (reciprocal positive-feedback relation) between selection for female concealment and selection for male detection. The end product is presumably our modern species, in which most women apparently do not even themselves know when they are ovulating.

2. Burley's (1979) overly-intelligent-female explanation for concealed ovulation provides a second alternative. We recall from chapter 12 that the intelligence of early hominid females may have enabled them to avoid copulating during the height of estrus, thus in effect selecting against external and internal cues to ovulation. If we assume that this process occurred when males were attracting females to their butchering sites, then Burley's account neatly amends that of Parker. Burley's scenario, however, would require a separate and independent explanation for the evolution of enlarged breasts.

3. The third possible amendment involves assuming that Parker's scenario, while largely accurate, was occurring in the context of frequent raiding and aggression among hominid bands. Smith may be correct in his assessment of concealed ovulation and large breasts as having evolved to confuse males about female ovulatory status, but the males

involved may have been members of rival groups. Concealed ovulation and large breasts may have served to reduce the frequency of raids from neighbouring bands, who might be attracted by estrus females and, through infanticide and the killing of brothers and other close kin, reduce the females' inclusive fitness. Females who appeared to be lactating (swollen breasts) and anestrous (no perineal swelling) may have in effect discouraged raids. (Parker herself, however, in a 1986 personal communication, indicates that she does not accept the autopredation hypothesis.)

Autopredation as a Context for Parker's Account
Note that this addition of the autopredation hypothesis to Parker's account has the virtue of strengthening an additional portion of her argument, her reasoning that male co-operation evolved in order to better control female sexuality. Positing external enemies provides a more plausible explanation for intra-group co-operation, and not just among males but among males and females together. Autopredation, I would suggest, is the appropriate context for Parker's scenario. In particular, it strengthens her account of the evolution of intelligence.

Parker argues that growth in intelligence resulted in greater infant dependency, since larger brains can pass through the birth canal only if the infant is born at an earlier stage of physical maturity. However, she further argues, females nevertheless (sexually) selected males for intelligence, since they preferred those males best able to provide nuptial gifts. Here, she and I are entirely in agreement, but I would add that competition from rival bands could have been a powerful, complementary selection pressure for intelligence and culture capacity. Otherwise the penalty of greater infant dependency might have prevented selection for large brains.

A Digression on Tools
With Parker's scenario (and with the earlier discussion in Parker and Gibson, 1979), tools return to respectability. Parker mentions tool use first in connection with extraction, and subsequently in the context of butchering scavenged or hunted meat. Earlier writers (such as Spuhler, 1959) emphasized tools, but usually had weapons and hunting in mind. Perhaps because an emphasis on hunting as the key adaptation is no longer widely accepted among anthropologists, or perhaps because we now know that tool use, rather than being a uniquely human trait, is shared by the chimpanzee, the importance of tool use is not always

emphasized in modern evolutionary thinking and, as in Lovejoy's account, may be denigrated.

Recent research, however, suggests that tool use, while certainly not the key adaptation leading to the capacity for culture, may have been of considerable importance. We now know that use of stone tools is definitely at least two and a half million years old and possibly much older (Campbell, 1985: 206–7). Toth (1985) has shown that handedness, which is related to hemispherical dominance and (probably) the ability to make stone tools, appears to be at least two million years old. Presumably, it evolved only after a long period of tool use.

Given the perishability of organic materials, the only clear evidence of use of a non-lithic material, wood, is the characteristic marks wood-working leaves on the edges of stone tools (visible under a microscope; see Pfeiffer [1985: 74] for references and discussion). Thus, we know that we worked with wood by one and one-half million years ago. It is likely that use of perishable, organic tools is far older than that. Chimpanzee tools, after all, are not made of stone. Our ancestors may have used tools of twigs, bark, wood, grass, and reed for millions of years. Lovejoy probably overstates the case against tool use having been instrumental in selection for human cultural capacity, and even Parker may not have given it sufficient emphasis. Information about how, when, and where to make and use tools may have been among the first contents of culture (or protoculture). Tool use was undoubtedly one of the major factors in hominid evolution, even if not the sole such factor.

THE NON-EXCLUSIVITY OF SCENARIOS

Parker's work has brought us a long step forward. I predict that the next generation of scenarios will incorporate many of her ideas, along with additional thinking about the process of autopredation. But there will likely always be a next generation of scenarios. We can hope that some kind of consensus eventually emerges as to the most likely scenario for the evolution of human cultural capacity, but the issue will never close because we can only achieve plausibility, not provability. Perhaps male-female pairs evolved as the result of a pandemic of a sexually transmitted disease, so that only those who formed exclusive consort pairs tended to survive: how could we ever know this? Perhaps bipedal locomotion came first and it resulted in the termination of sexual swellings because these impeded walking (though that would not result in the loss of periodic sexual receptivity, merely in the loss of its

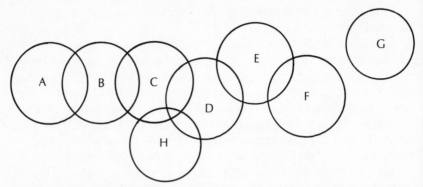

Figure 1. Hypothetical population distribution at a single point in time. Each circle represents a local breeding population (deme) and the extent of overlap the degree of gene flow between them.

advertisement). Perhaps some of the crucial steps in the scenario were not the result of selection at all, but were epiphenomenal products of developmental constraints associated with selection for some other trait entirely. Even given the constraint that scenarios must be consistent with what we know, it is difficult to evaluate scenarios in any objective, empirical manner. Many a scenario remains to be written, and the writing itself will remain a pleasurable but frustrating intellectual challenge, as certainty is forever impossible. Worse, however: competing scenarios may each be correct, or have been correct, at some point and place in our evolutionary history. Differing scenarios are not only possible but necessary. We did not evolve on a single stage.

Let us return to Sewall Wright's 'island model' of human evolution (discussed in chapter 6). We probably evolved in terms of a number of somewhat overlapping but partially genetically isolated populations (demes). Figure 1 is a hypothetical 'snapshot' of the population structure of early hominids at a single point in time. The extent of overlap indicates the degree of gene flow among these groups. Perhaps systematists would classify populations A and F as subspecies, and perhaps B and C would be considered as minor variants within a single population. What is important here is that each population has a somewhat different habitat, yet there is gene flow among them. Ultimately, genes can move from A to F, and only G is separated, perhaps on its way to speciation or extinction. At any given point in time, each local group (deme) may have a distinct evolutionary scenario, perhaps with a different predominant reproductive strategy.

The boundaries of these demes are not fixed. Some demes may merge with others, some may be cut off and suffer extinction. Even deme G, isolated though it is, may earlier have had some of its genes enter the overall gene pool, owing to gene flow. Over long periods of time, even if a given local population is stable geographically, its environment may alter, and so may its evolutionary scenario. Thus, we have a sequential diversity of possible scenarios, as well as the likelihood of a simultaneous diversity.[7] In short, scenarios may vary both over time and, at any given point in time, geographically.

This possibility of synchronous and asynchronous diversity of scenarios has two major implications. First, many quite different scenarios may have been valid either for some place or for some time. Debates over the correct scenario cannot be resolved. The best we can hope for is to eliminate scenarios that violate either theory or fact. Thus, the three explanations for the evolution of concealed ovulation provided above (as part of the comments on Parker's model) may, in fact, all have been valid.

The second implication of this diversity of scenarios is that we should expect considerable genetic variability to underlie our sexual behaviour.[8]

7 See Tooby and DeVore (1987: 202) for a compatible view, as well as for an excellent discussion of the scenario-building effort as a whole. Tooby and DeVore emphasize the need for a multi-stage approach, 'hominization' undoubtedly having consisted 'of a large number of discrete stages characterized by sharply differentiated selective forces and adaptive complexes.' They criticize existing scenarios for focusing on a 'single process.' See King (1980) for a discussion of primate vs. carnivore models of early hominid behaviour.

8 Some of this supposed genetic diversity resulting from gene flow among partial genetic isolates with distinctive evolutionary scenarios could have been lost through a genetic 'bottleneck.' It has been suggested (Brown, 1980), on the basis of studies of mitochondrial DNA, that our ancestors passed through such a bottleneck, perhaps 200,000 years ago, and that it could be that all of modern *Homo sapiens* stems from a single mother 'Eve.' If so, then the genetic variability underlying human behaviour may be less than that for which I have been arguing. The importance of a bottleneck, for present purposes, would depend not just on when it occurred but on subsequent population structure and natural selection. It is not at all clear, however, that such a bottleneck ever actually occurred, and very unlikely that there was ever a single 'Eve.' Avise, Neigel, and Arnold (1984) conclude that the human mitochondrial DNA data can be explained without invoking 'a dramatic population reduction' (p. 104). See Wainscoat (1987), Cann, Stoneking, and Wilson (1987), and Lewin (1987) for discussion of the controversy over the bottleneck hypothesis. For a popular account, see the article in the *Newsweek* of 11 January 1988, 'The Search for Adam and Eve.' Though the bottleneck hypothesis is unlikely to be accurate, there is considerable support for (as well as controversy about) the view that modern human beings first evolved in Africa around 200,000 years ago, then dispersed around the globe, replacing other early human populations (Stringer and Andrews, 1988).

There is no reason to believe that selection ever favoured a single set of reproductive strategies in our species. Our immense individual and cross-cultural variability in sexual behaviour is consistent with that expectation. The discussion of institutionalized homosexuality in Melanesia, in the following chapter, illustrates the extent to which the cross-cultural patterning of sexuality can vary. None the less, individual variability in sexual behaviour is not necessarily random: Draper and Harpending's (1982) sensitive-period hypothesis for human reproductive strategies suggests that these may be in part determined by early experience.

SENSITIVE PERIODS AND REPRODUCTIVE STRATEGIES

If scenarios were as mutable as I have suggested, then selection would have favoured those who could alter their reproductive strategies in response to changing conditions. One means by which an organism may track a changing environment is through a 'critical' or 'sensitive' period.

Draper and Harpending (1982) hypothesize that from birth to approximately age five is a 'sensitive' period for the development of an individual's reproductive strategies. Early family structure may 'set' the kinds of sexual relationships that the child, once matured, will seek. This 'setting' also determines the developmental pathways to be emphasized. It is as if the low-father-involvement child (a broader term than 'father-absent child') were assuming that its early family structure indicated the kind of society within which, at puberty, it would have to compete with others for reproductive success. The theory argues that the low-father-involvement child is in effect preparing to live in a society in which males compete frequently for sexual access to a number of females and in which no female can count on an enduring bond with (and substantial 'parental investment' from) any single male. Hence, the child should follow a developmental path emphasizing those abilities and attitudes that, given his society, would tend to enhance its later reproductive success.

What qualities would enhance reproductive success, in these (presumed to be) low-father-involvement, high male-male sexual competition societies? Male competition in such cultures, argue Draper and Harpending, often takes the form of verbal contests, sometimes to the point of physical violence: hence, low-father-involvement boys should show a developmental emphasis on verbal (at the expense of other) abilities, resulting in what some have interpreted as a 'feminization' of the boys' cognitive profile. Hence, too, the association of low-father-involvement with aggressiveness and delinquency. The reproductive strategy of low-father-involvement boys involves seeking not a long-term bond with a single female but competition with other males for sexual access to as many females as possible. In Dawkins's (1976) deliberately outrageous vocabulary, low-father-involvement boys would be 'choosing' to emphasize a 'philanderer' strategy.

Reproductive Strategy theory predicts complementary but different strategies for low-father-involvement females. Such girls should emphasize developmental pathways making not just for competitiveness but for early sexuality so as to maximize fertility in compensation for the lack of male parental investment. They should also be expected to show a relative lack of selectivity in choosing sexual partners (since no male could be expected to bond in an enduring fashion). In Dawkins's term, they follow a 'fast' strategy. They seek to obtain whatever male investment they may during the period of potential conception rather than (necessarily) during subsequent years.

High-father-involvement societies, by contrast, dictate very different reproductive strategies. For males, these would favour not verbal or physically violent competition, but skills relevant to subsistence activities. They would (in terms of evolution if not their conscious motives) be striving to impress females with their ability to invest parentally. Thus, rather than verbal ability, spatial and quantitative abilities are emphasized developmentally. At the same time, the male will be prepared to form enduring partnerships with females, rather than seeking a series of brief encounters. In Dawkins's terms, high-father-involvement males should follow a 'faithful' strategy, since it would be the most likely to result in their relative reproductive success.

For females in these high-father-involvement societies, the reproductive strategy should emphasize 'coyness,' that is, sexual discrimination and delay in reproduction until a male ready to invest in the resulting offspring in long-term fashion has been located (Harpending, 1980). Dawkins terms this the 'domestic bliss' strategy.

This Reproductive Strategies approach implies that it is unnecessary to postulate 'feminization' or later 'protest masculinity' in boys from low-father-involvement societies. Draper and Harpending follow modern biological thinking in assuming that all human beings have been selected to strive unwittingly to enhance their biological fitness. A male child raised in a predominantly female environment should act (according to Reproductive Strategies theory) as if he has discovered that male investment in offspring – bonding to a single female and investing in their joint offspring – is unlikely to be the most effective strategy for reproductive success. Instead, he competes strongly with other males for (relatively non-exclusive) sexual access to a number of females. He therefore follows a developmental path that emphasizes the skills that will eventually be necessary for male-male contests: the skills of verbal and of physical contests.

The female child in a similar low-father-involvement situation should 'discover' that males are unreliable as sources of parental investment, and that the appropriate strategy is a series of short-term bonds with males.

The Reproductive Strategies approach also suggests that mother's attitude towards males may be more important than her formal marital status in pointing a child along a particular developmental pathway. Hetherington's (1972) findings support such a position. Hetherington found behavioural differences between the adolescent daughters of widows and those of divorcees. In the households of widows but not of divorcees, father tended to be 'psychologically' present (pictures of him displayed, laudatory discussion of him, and so forth). Hetherington found that the daughters of divorcees but not of widows displayed interest in males, flirtatiousness, early sexual behaviour, and initiative in approaching boys, all in excess of that considered normative. Daughters of widows behaved in an opposite manner, tending to be even more circumspect with young men and boys than were girls from intact marriages. These differences were greater when separation of parents occurred in the first years of the daughter's life. The daughters of widows seem to be following the courtship strategies associated with high father-involvement, while those of divorcees follow the strategies associated with low father-involvement.

The Reproductive Strategies approach leads to some testable predictions. Low father-involvement in child-rearing should be associated with violence and aggression in males, who should also have high verbal ability. Females from low-father-involvement families should tend to be more sexually assertive, take more partners, and have lower expectations of long-term male commitment than females from high-father-involvement families. They should also tend to begin sexual activity and to reach menarche earlier.[9]

9 This discussion has drawn in part on Blain and Barkow (1988). Blain and Barkow also find, in a cross-cultural survey testing hypotheses drawn from Reproductive Strategies theory, that high father-involvement with infants is negatively correlated with an ideology of male 'toughness.' Assuming that father-involvement is a valid indicator

SUMMARY

1. An evolutionary scenario (some prefer the term 'narrative,' 'story,' or 'account') is a somewhat speculative theory in which the usual requirements for empirical verifiability are relaxed in favour of an emphasis on completeness and plausibility.

2. Lovejoy's (1981) account emphasizes monogamy. Males would have provisioned females and then invested in the jointly produced offspring. Bipedal locomotion would have initially evolved as a means of freeing the male's hands so he could carry provisions back to the female. Concealed ovulation would have evolved as a means of protecting the male's paternity confidence.

3. But human beings are not strictly monogamous, while concealed ovulation would have lowered female fitness in the early stages of its development. Thus, Lovejoy's scenario has serious flaws.

4. Parker's (1987) scenario begins more than three and a half million years ago and assumes that our ancestors began with a fission-fusion type of social organization similar to that of the chimpanzee. It also assumes that extractive techniques were important in food-getting. Males would have come to compete with one another in providing nuptial gifts to females in what was initially a system of promiscuous mating. Males would have attracted females to butchering sites. Ovulatory concealment would have evolved because it permitted females to maximize the meat gifts they received from males. Males would have begun to seek to control females and their sexuality, in order to enhance the value of the females when used in exchanges. Such control is not in the fitness interests of the females, who benefit from having secondary males available.

5. Selection for concealed ovulation and permanently enlarged breasts is difficult to explain because, given our likely initial mating pattern, these traits would have tended to lower rather than to enhance fitness. Several explanations for breast enlargement and concealed ovulation are possible. For example, females may have first passed through a stage in which the external appearance of estrus was universal, since in this way females would gain more 'nuptial gifts' from males; followed by a second stage, in which selection would have favoured the disappearance of the external signs of ovulation. Breasts

of male parental investment and 'toughness' of male aggressivity, then these data support Reproductive Strategies theory. Draper (1989) has recently altered her emphasis, arguing that reproductive strategies have to do primarily with perception of resource availability.

may have enlarged initially because of fat storage and secondarily as a (deceptive) signal to males of adequate energy reserves for pregnancy. Finally, adding the autopredation hypothesis to Parker's scenario strengthens it considerably.

6. Parker's scenario, unlike that of Lovejoy, gives tool use adequate attention. Parker and Lovejoy agree that bipedalism would have arisen first among males to permit them to carry foodstuffs. While Lovejoy (1981) saw this carrying as a form of parental investment, Parker sees it as the product of males competing with one another to provide nuptial gifts (sexual selection). Later, as females were selected for the ability to carry their increasingly dependent infants, it would have become a trait of both sexes.

7. Males have evolved to seek to control female sexuality and females have responded with the evolution of confusing signals about their ovulatory status. These female countermeasures to male control include concealed ovulation, continuous sexual receptivity, and (some argue) large breasts. Females hide their ovulations and retain permanently the enlarged breasts of pregnancy, Smith (1984) suggests, because males were less likely to guard the sexual activities of pregnant females. Females were selected to incite male-male competition so as to be better able to choose the 'best genes' male.

8. Sequential alternations in scenarios and gene flow among geographically separated and scenario-distinct groups have important implications. First, many quite different scenarios may have been valid either for some place or for some time. Second, we should expect considerable genetic variability underlying our sexual behaviour, and therefore great individual and cross-cultural variability.

9. Draper and Harpending's (1982) reproductive-strategies theory is consistent with this last point. They argue that early family structure determines the strategies the child will use early in life. Children from high-father-involvement households should emphasize developmentally the behaviours and abilities consistent with reproducing such a household themselves later in life. Children from low-father-involvement households should be characterized by different abilities and behaviour patterns, that is, by those consistent with high male-male competition and low male parental investment. In general, males from low-father-involvement families should be high in aggressiveness and verbal ability; girls from such families should be sexually active at an earlier age and less sexually selective than girls from high-father-involvement families.

14

Aspects of Sexuality

If sexual selection was as important in human evolution as the preceding chapter argued, then the nature of our sexuality has much relevance for our theories and scenarios. Compatibility between scenarios and sexuality is the theme of this chapter. We begin with a topic often neglected in human sociobiology, sperm competition, and then move to subjects for which ample human literatures do exist: sexual jealousy, rape, incest, and homosexuality. The discussion of homosexuality will be limited to male homosexuality, and then further limited to the institutionalized form it takes in some societies in Melanesia. We will see that even when we deal with a subject as closely linked to fitness as sexuality, culturally patterned behaviour cannot be explained simply in terms of selection pressures involving genes: explanations having to do with evolved human psychology and with history and sociology are essential.

SPERM COMPETITION AND SEXUAL SELECTION

Sexual selection, as we saw in chapter 13's analysis of Parker's scenario, was probably crucial in the evolution of our species. We will recall that there are different forms of sexual selection.[1] For example, we have discussed males competing to acquire or control resources, and competing in terms of threat and violence. Males can also compete by guarding

1 Parker (1987) neatly summarizes the forms of sexual selection in a series of figures. Borgia (1979) presents similar information in a somewhat more technical manner.

the female to prevent her from copulating with others. Females should in theory compete for the 'best genes' males and for those males most likely to be able and willing to invest parentally. Their competition should involve their apparent ability to provide male paternity confidence, their reproductive value (youth and 'good genes'), and their ability to invest parentally (skills and abilities).

But sexual competition can also involve *sperm competition*, competition among the sperm of different males within the female's vaginal tract. R.L. Smith (1984) has helped to overcome the usual neglect of this topic in discussions of human evolution. Though rather Panglossian – he reaches energetically, if imaginatively, for fitness interpretations – his approach (as we will see) is justified in that it leads to some testable hypotheses.

Human sperm, Smith informs us (1984: 603), remain motile (though not necessarily viable) for seven to nine days in the female's reproductive tract. Should the female copulate with another male while viable sperm remain from the prior mating, the two males' sperm will be in direct competition with each other to fertilize the female's ovum. The long life of human sperm suggests that sperm competition was an important factor in the evolution of our species. Smith explains that the circumstances leading to sperm competition include communal sex, rape, prostitution, courtship (since during courtship a woman may copulate with more than one lover), and 'facultative polyandry' (by which he apparently means all forms of secondary marriage and adultery).

Smith suggests that sperm competition explains a number of sexual attributes of our species. The long penis means that the sperm have had their journey towards the ovum somewhat shortened. The forceful ejaculation has the same effect. The large testes permit frequent copulation with high sperm count in the ejaculate.[2] The scrotum,

2 Here we have another two testable hypotheses. Sperm competition would have been strongest in populations marked by females with multiple mates. Penis length and testes size are products of sperm competition. Therefore, in those human populations which have had a history of fairly frequent communal mating (for instance, the Melanesian group described by Serpenti [1984]), penis length and testes size should be greater than for populations with no history of communal mating, assuming that the populations in question are relative genetic isolates. The same prediction may be made of populations with low levels of paternity certainty relative to those with higher levels. Males from low-paternity-certainty societies should have longer penises and larger testes than do males from high-paternity-certainty societies (again, assuming that the low-paternity societies are relative genetic isolates).

usually interpreted as a means of maintaining the sperm at lower than body temperature, may actually be more related to selection for sperm storage (pp. 628–9). It is even possible that the prostaglandins present in the semen cause 'uterine contractions that move the sperm in an ejaculate toward the ovum' (p. 632). Male masturbation may serve to replace stored sperm with fresh sperm of greater viability and motility. (Presumably, female masturbation would not be explained among similar lines, but Smith does not address this question.)

The Female Orgasm

Male sperm competition leads to counterselection for female control of fertilization, argues Smith, and thence to the female orgasm. Donald Symons (1979), in a major sociobiological study of human sexuality, asserts that the female orgasm is non-adaptive, but Smith (p. 643) rejects this view. Smith interprets the research literature as supporting his contention that the orgasm creates uterine suction that moves the sperm towards the ovum. Females, he argues, are more likely to have orgasms with partners whom they prefer than they are with other partners. Female orgasm was therefore selected for in response to male sperm competition because it gives the female some control over who fertilizes her ova. Smith notes that the frequency of orgasm varies sharply across both cultures and individuals, so that it is best described as a facultative ability of human females.

Smith criticizes Symons's view that the female orgasm is an epiphenomenon resulting from the fact that *males* were selected to have orgasm. For Symons, the female orgasm is the equivalent of the male nipple, present only because it is adaptive when it occurs in the opposite sex, and because it is apparently more efficient, developmentally, for evolution to minimize embryological sex differentiation. Symons believes that the innervation of the female reproductive tract is sufficiently similar to that of the male to permit the female to have orgasms, particularly when the homologue of the male penis, the clitoris, is directly stimulated. The inconsequentiality of female orgasm for natural selection, Symons argues, is shown by the extent to which it is variable across both individuals and societies, and by the fact that the relevant innervation is not in the vaginal walls, which are directly stimulated during intercourse, but in the clitoris, which is not.

It is difficult to envisage empirically investigating Symons's position, while that of Smith does lead to a number of testable hypotheses (there are already some pertinent data available, as in the research he cites on 'uterine suction' during orgasm). Smith's argument seems to imply (1) that women are more likely to experience orgasm with preferred partners; (2) that the 'uterine suction' of orgasm does help to move the semen along; and that (3) female orgasms (and therefore any resulting suction) usually occur either together with or following male ejaculation. Smith also seems to imply, unwittingly, (4) that the uterine suction is somehow *selective*. After all, it is Smith who has previously argued that females must frequently have the still viable sperm of multiple partners in their vaginas: uterine suction must be (rather implausibly) selective if it is to have the function Smith ascribes to it. Otherwise, would not its chief beneficiary be the sperm likely (according to Smith) to already be present in the vagina, sperm presumably deposited by a non-preferred male? Symons's non-adaptationist account of female orgasm may in fact be accurate, but at present there seem to be no empirical grounds for accepting either his or Smith's position.

The Hymen
Smith interprets the hymen as the result of males selecting females for virginity, in an effort to avoid sperm competition and enjoy high paternity confidence. A physical sign of no prior sexual experience, Smith believes, would have been preferred by the 'best' males, so that sexual selection would have favoured females with partially obstructed vaginas. Families would guard the hymen of a daughter in order to improve her value when (in effect) exchanging her for the daughter of another family. As evidence, Smith points out that no other primate has a hymen. This account is consistent with Parker's (1987) argument that selection favoured males' exchanging females and restricting their sexual activities so as to enhance their exchange value. But Smith's case would be greatly strengthened by cross-cultural data indicating that, among most of the world's peoples, the presence of a hymen at marriage actually is valued. (My own reading of the ethnographic record suggests that this hypothesis would not be supported, but the research remains to be done.)

Smith argues that alternative evolutionary interpretations of the hymen are thus far lacking, making his own conjecture worthy of debate. He does not consider the possibility that the hymen has no adaptive function at all but is epiphenomenal. Even if one assumes that it is adaptive, it might be that the hymen serves a protective function. Very young girls seem prone to introduce foreign objects into their vaginas, with a resultant risk of injury or infection. Females of our own species may be more at risk here than are other primates because, as hand-using tool-makers, we appear to have been selected for what amounts to a developmental obsession with manual manipulation of objects. Our species may therefore require more vaginal protection when young than do other primates, so that it is our species and no other that has been selected for the hymen.[3]

Of course, Smith may be partly correct in that, once a hymen had evolved, in some cultures men learned to use its presence as a sign of virginity and therefore suggestive of future paternity certainty.

MALE SEXUAL JEALOUSY

Jealousy is a feeling of anger or resentment associated with heightened vigilance towards a possession we fear may be claimed by another. ('Envy' would be the resentment we feel over the accomplishments of a rival.) Sexual jealousy is a special type of jealousy, one in which an individual attempts to restrict intimate contact between potential rivals and his or her actual or intended mate. Sexual jealousy is therefore associated with a type of guarding behaviour. It is unclear what the relationship is between sexual and other forms of jealousy, such as sibling rivalry, and this discussion will be limited to sexual jealousy. Selection pressure in favour of sexual jealousy must have been quite strong, since it is one of the 'limbic-system overrides' discussed in chapter 5.

An evolutionist would expect male sexual jealousy to be quite different from female sexual jealousy. Let us assume that we have a mated couple. If the female copulates with another her mate risks investing in that other's offspring. Selection for traits that would increase his confidence in paternity will be very strong, and jealousy is presumably one of those traits.

Now let us take the perspective of a female. Suppose her mate copulates with another female. She cannot possibly be deceived into investing parentally in another's offspring. Moreover, the amount her

3 The preceding discussion of the female orgasm, as well as the analysis of the hymen, owes much to the students in my seminar in 'Human Nature and Anthropology,' during August 1986. I particularly want to thank pediatric nurse Catherine O'Shea Lewin (BN, RN), who responded to the question 'why should human females have hymens?' with the instant expostulation, 'Beans!' What she had in mind, as she eventually explained to the rest of us, was the propensity for young girls to put inappropriate objects into their vaginas. The seminar also noted that neither Smith (1984) nor I had seen fit to discuss the evolution of foreskins (possibly similar to the hymen in serving to prevent infection and injury).

mate can invest in her offspring has not been appreciably diminished by the loss of an energetically very inexpensive copulation. His copulation could, however, be the beginning of a relationship with another female that *would* diminish his investment in her (his mate's) offspring. Therefore, selection will indeed favour her experiencing at least some sexual jealousy even over copulation. But only when her fitness is clearly threatened by her mate actually investing in the other female – with the possibility that he may desert, or force her to share his limited parental investment with another female's offspring – should selection favour her experiencing very strong sexual jealousy. Thus, selection should favour strong male sexual jealousy being evoked by female copulation with a rival, but should favour strong female sexual jealousy not primarily over copulation but over a male's actual or potential investment in rivals (and in the rivals' offspring). Selection favours the female who is only somewhat jealous when her male copulates with others. Specifically, the extent of her jealousy should correspond to the risk that her rivals will succeed in drawing away the male's (by definition limited) parental investment to themselves and to their offspring (Barkow, 1981; Symons, 1979; Daly et al., 1982).

Human sexual jealousy has been thoroughly analysed by Symons (1979, 1987b) and male sexual jealousy in particular by Daly et al. (1982). The latter reanalyse ethnographic accounts to demonstrate convincingly that attempts to argue that jealousy is lacking in some societies are simply distortions of the ethnographic record. Nevertheless, there is immense cultural variability in the expression of jealousy, male jealousy in particular. In some societies, it is expected that the jealous male will commit homicide, while in other societies the cuckold will be mocked but is not expected to react with violence. Often a violation of sexual restrictions on a female is treated as a violation by one male of the property rights of another (Daly et al., 1982). In our own society, jealousy is disvalued and some consider it shameful.

Frequently, it is not just her husband but her male and female kin as well who seek to keep the female from sexual contact with other men, or from men in general if she is unmarried. Since a female's attractiveness to high-status, resource-controlling males is often in part determined by her reputation for chastity (in sociobiological terms, whether she is likely to offer a high degree of confidence in paternity), by protecting her reputation kin may be enhancing her fitness and therefore their own inclusive fitness. Moreover, since marital arrangements often involve a degree of exchange, the greater the paternity confidence associated with the daughters and sisters of a given kin group, the greater the confidence associated with the potential wives offered to the males of that kin group.

It is possible that male sexual jealousy is mitigated when the female produces or controls resources that may be invested parentally. Back in chapter 8, it was predicted that, for long-term relationships, all things being equal males should prefer females who may provide above-average parental investment. Selection favours males who, in contemplating a long-term relationship, act as if they were calculating the various weights of (1) the female's youth and health (reproductive potential); (2) the quality of her genes (judged phenotypically); (3) the confidence in future paternity she inspires (her reputation); and (4) her ability to produce and control resources for parental investment.[4] Where the weighting on the last factor is high, the weightings on the other factors presumably could be lower. Sexual jealousy is a mechanism evolved to enhance paternity confidence. Since males courting or mated to a high-investment-providing female would accord paternity confidence a lower relative weight, sexual jealousy in such cases should be somewhat reduced. Thus, one would predict that males should experience lower jealousy in a relationship with a high-status female than in a relationship with a lower-status female, all other factors being equal. This hypothesis has the virtue of being testable.

Jealousy and Culture
Some indirect support for this last hypothesis comes from Barry and Schlegel (1984), who in a cross-cultural survey find that restrictions on female sexuality tend to be lower in societies in which female contribution to subsistence is higher. Female status, too, tends to reflect female subsistence contribution. However, these findings are not necessarily related to reduced male sexual jealousy: higher female power, or a residence pattern in which the female may count on the support of her consanguineal kin against her affines (her own family against her husband and in-laws), may be more parsimonious interpretations of Barry and Schlegel's findings.

Male sexual jealousy and the desire of families to marry their daughters to high-status grooms no doubt are the psychological predispositions that gave rise to the various restrictions on female

---

4 Presumably, we have evolved specialized processors or systems that in effect make use of algorithms that take account of these four factors.

sexuality and behaviour one finds cross-culturally. But these restrictions now are often aspects of complex social and cultural patterns and are not to be reduced to nothing but sexual jealousy; or worse, be reduced to male guarding behaviour. Customs that arise as the result of one set of psychological mechanisms or systems may often be maintained by another set.

Female Genital Operations and Jealousy

For example, the origin of female genital operations presumably is linked to male sexual jealousy, but their current meaning and maintenance may be quite different. Infibulation is an operation in which the labia majora are joined, with only a small opening remaining to permit the passage of urine and menstrual fluid. Following infibulation, the female requires additional surgery to permit sexual intercourse. A connection with male guarding behaviour seems apparent, and Daly et al. (1982: 19) cite Hosken (1979) in arguing that the operation is a product of male sexual jealousy. But the extent to which male jealousy is the current major determinant of the practice is unclear.

Reports from Somalia (Grassivaro Gallo, 1986) and from the Sudan, where infibulation is widespread, indicate that the strongest support for the operation comes from the women themselves, particularly from older women, and has much to do with infibulation having become symbolic of the sphere of authority of these women. Boddy (1985) reports that in Hofriyati, in the Sudan, men returning from having worked in Saudi Arabia have attempted to alter the nature of the female genital operation and move it towards what they believe is the Saudi norm. Though they are at times confused as to exactly what this entails, the genital operations they advocate are definitely less severe than what has been the usual practice in Hofriyati. Their efforts have been strongly resisted by the older women (that is, by women with children). For the men, a lesser operation has apparently become associated with higher status, while for women the men's efforts are interpreted as males encroaching upon a female preserve (Boddy, 1985; personal communication, 1986). In Somalia, a recent survey (Grassivaro Gallo, 1986) showed that the great majority of nursing students (who were all female) supported infibulation and were likely to replace the traditional midwives not just in delivering infants but in performing the genital operation. The general consensus among anthropologists who have studied female genital operations seems to be that they have relatively little to do with males and much to do with older females controlling younger females (Hayes, 1975).[5]

Claustration

Claustration of females, like infibulation, may at first glance also appear to be a product of male sexual jealousy, and no doubt that emotion often plays a role in this institution. But, according to Mildred Dickemann, the practice is primarily about the desire of families to procure high-status grooms for their daughters. Female claustration or 'purdah' refers to the seclusion of women away from the eyes of non-kin males. Dickemann (1981: 427) explains why 'claustration and veiling are universally status-graded. The higher the groom's status, the greater the degree of paternal investment of effort into his offspring, the greater the groom's demand for probability of paternity, the greater the competition between bridal families to demonstrate and assure confidence of paternity to future grooms.' Bridal families may therefore sequester their women in order to increase their value to high-status males. Claustration also serves, Dickemann adds, to guard them from the eyes of possibly rape-prone males (to be discussed shortly). She provides a wealth of empirical data consistent with her argument. Her data come from history and ethnography but not from psychology.

Note that Dickemann, who seems to write almost as if individuals were consciously attempting to maximize their inclusive fitness (that would certainly not be her explicit position), is actually making an assumption about an evolved psychological mechanism: the more parental investment a male provides or intends to provide, the more he should attempt to guard his paternity certainty and the more he should seek females likely to provide a high degree of paternity certainty. This assumption is a potentially testable hypothesis. Had Dickemann made it explicit rather than implicit, it might by now have been tested using not social classes and societies but individuals and families as the units of analysis. Do men who invest more heavily than do others strive to procure higher-paternity-certainty wives? If eventual empirical data support this hypothesis, then Dickemann's interpretation of seclusion will be sustained; but if the data fail to be consistent with it, then her interpretation falls. Genes can hardly generate social patterns by themselves: there must be processes first between the genes and the

5 For discussion of female genital operations, see Dareer (1982) and Hayes (1975).

individual behaviour, then between the behaviour of individuals and social forms (Barkow, 1984). Regrettably, Dickemann shows little interest in the processes (psychological mechanisms) between genes and individual behaviour (in this respect being similar to Richard Alexander, whose work was discussed in chapter 11). This disinterest leaves her psychological assumptions implicit and unexamined.

Dickemann does not claim that female claustration is in all cases a matter of families attempting to raise the value of daughters so that they can be married off to high-status males, and this is wise: the nature of female claustration varies from society to society and in some cases may have vanishingly little to do with male sexual jealousy, or with sociobiology at all. Rural Hausa in northern Nigeria, for example, practise a form of wife-seclusion in which women may move relatively freely in the evening but not during the day, and are rarely prevented from making frequent visits to kin. The emphasis on seclusion during the day rather than the night is indicative of the relative power of Hausa women. Non-secluded rural women provide much of the labour for their husbands' farms and may work on their own plots – whose produce they control – only when their work on the husband's is finished. Seclusion means that the women leave farm labour and substitute craft and trade activities (conducted with children, particularly girls, as intermediaries). The earnings from these activities are entirely their own. Hausa women, as of the late sixties, were anxious to be secluded and understood the attendant advantages perfectly well. Their husbands were equally aware of the fact that seclusion denied them labour but saw the practice as associated with Islam and as highly prestigious (Barkow, 1972, 1978b). Girls are not secluded until they marry. Interpreting Hausa wife seclusion as stemming from male jealousy and the desire of families for high-status marriages for their daughters would be a leap to an unwarranted conclusion.

CULTURE AND HOMOSEXUALITY IN MELANESIA

Sexual behaviour is so tightly and obviously bound to genetic fitness that it provides a test case for demonstrating the extent to which the processes of cultural evolution can constrain and pattern evolved goals and subgoals, plans and subplans. In order to emphasize the extent to which our fitness-enhancing filters of culturally transmitted information are imperfect, and the extent to which cultures can evolve in ways that could never be predicted from sociobiology alone, I have chosen to discuss Melanesian homosexuality. I am not here arguing that Melanesian homosexuality is genetically maladaptive, only that it exemplifies the limits of evolutionary thought and the extent to which we need theories of culture and of history. Note that I will not deal with why some individuals should prefer partners of the same sex in societies that penalize such a preference. This question is an important one but I am unaware of any special insight into it that an evolutionary perspective provides.[6] Melanesian homosexuality is discussed here in order to learn about evolved constraints (and their lack) on human sexuality, rather than to learn about homosexuality per se.

Melanesia consists of New Guinea, the New Hebrides (or Vanuatu), Fiji, and other island groups of the western South Pacific, northeast of Australia. Institutionalized, ritualized homosexuality was found among 10% to 20% of Melanesian peoples studied (Herdt, 1984: 8), prior to European control and missionization, and was centred in southwestern coastal New Guinea, where it was 'universal' (Herdt, 1984: 50). Melanesian homosexuality may have diffused from a common source (Herdt, 1984: 50–3).

As Herdt (1980, 1984) points out, this homosexuality had little in common with Western folk notions of homosexuality as a 'social problem' or a form of 'deviance,' and bears no relationship to our idea of an association between homosexuality and effeminacy. Rather, the association is between mother's milk and semen.

In many Melanesian societies, semen was believed necessary for proper development of both boys and girls, if they were to grow into healthy adulthood. It might be supplied to boys through anal or oral sex, massaged into the skin, or rubbed into shallow incisions. Every male would pass through life stages when he would be first the passive and later the active partner in homosexual relationships. Homosexual acts thus had symbolic meaning and were rule-bound. They also tended to be associated with male initiation ceremonies, and to involve sex between males of different age grades (Herdt, 1984: 6).

Serpenti (1984) describes institutionalized homosexuality among the Kimam-Papuans of South Irian Jaya. Young boys would pass through a series of ceremonies (shaving of the hair, piercing of the ears, piercing of the septum) during which they were believed to grow progressively away from the mother. At some time prior to puberty, they would move

---

6 A thorough if inconclusive treatment of sociobiology and homosexuality is to be found in Ruse (1981). See also Ross (1984) and Seaborg (1984).

away from her altogether, into the *burawa* or 'bachelors' house.' Here, they would be adopted by an older boy, already pubescent, who would serve as (in Serpenti's term) 'mentor.' The semen the mentor supplied through anal intercourse would make the boy grow strong.

The boy would have been betrothed when still very young. During the ceremony in which he entered the bachelors' house, adult men would have had some form of sexual intercourse with this fiancée (Serpenti is not sure what kind of intercourse), and the semen then collected. It would be rubbed on the boy's body and, in some villages, into small incisions on his skin. In some cases, the men might have anal intercourse with the boy. In other cases, the semen of especially prestigious men, such as the best hunters, would be collected to rub on him. After a year or more, the boy would be promoted (with much ceremony) to the next stage, and would himself be eligible to become a mentor. Eventually, he would be an adult male, able to marry and to have sexual intercourse with women.

Symbolic anthropologists are of course tempted to interpret this set of customs as ritually moving the boy away from his mother and helping him to become a man. Sociobiologists are tempted to interpret it as a clever means, devised by older males, of preventing young men from competing with them for young women by turning the young men's sexuality towards younger boys.[7] Both of these interpretations may be valid. But we are interpreting not just cultural practice here, but history. One might speculate that, in a very early Melanesian culture, it was noticed that semen bore a superficial resemblance to breast milk. Perhaps then some creative soul reasoned that if milk was necessary for the baby, perhaps semen was necessary for the child. Perhaps the equation was born in part of envy of men for the ability of women to bear young. Perhaps, some time later, other men had an additional creative idea, that of having adolescent males supply the needed semen to the boys. Perhaps this idea was born in part of a desire to lessen competition for young females. Perhaps. This is conjecture.

We may be certain that these possible past conspiracies are not what for many centuries maintained the complex of traits involving homosexuality. Rather, these practices would have been transmitted to children during socialization and were sufficiently novel for there to be no evolved 'filter' to revise the information. As was discussed in chapter

7 This would be an example of the 'élites appropriate' type of misinformation discussed in chapter 12.

12, our culture-revision mechanisms are not particularly efficient. Children do rebel and test information in some domains, but are apparently unable to test whether semen is 'really' good for you, or whether we need accept an older youth as mentor. Indeed, any single individual who protested these ideas and practices would have been labelled deviant. Once such ideas and practices are established they are self-perpetuating. No individual is in a position to change them; or particularly to want to.

Theoretically, a genetic response might have revised this complex of traits away, provided it was sufficiently genetically maladaptive and endured for a sufficient number of generations. However, there is no reason to believe the complex was genetically maladaptive, since the reproductive success lost in youth was regained in adulthood. Thus, only when the massive might of Europeans and their (by local standards) immense wealth came, and when the missionaries, identified with this wealth and power, strongly attacked traditional customs and beliefs and reshaped local prestige-allocation criteria, particularly those regarding homosexuality, did the institution of ritualized homosexuality weaken and collapse.

We thus see that there have been societies in which young male sexuality systematically has been turned towards younger males. We also see the limits to biological interpretations of culture. The processes of cultural evolution may shape even sexuality, tied tightly though it is to fitness, in ways that, from a purely biological perspective, are, to say the least, rather unlikely. As I have argued elsewhere (1984), one can be a good evolutionist and still conclude that there is considerable distance between the genes and culture.

RAPE

Rape provides an additional example of how human culture and sexuality interact. Rape in our own species has been extensively analysed by Symons (1979), Shields and Shields (1983), and Thornhill and Thornhill (1983), while Crawford and Galdikas (1986) have thoroughly reviewed analogous behaviours in other animals. The account below will rely on these sources, and on Shields and Shields (1983) in particular. Note that, in order to avoid the powerful emotional associations of the term 'rape,' some writers substitute phrases such as 'forced (or forcible) copulation.' They are especially likely to do so when speaking of non-human behaviour. Thornhill and Thornhill (1983) define forced copulation as copulation in which the female's fitness is lower than it would be if she were able to make her own choice. This lowering results from her being unable to choose the 'best genes' male or to choose the male readiest to provide investment (for example, by provision of a nuptial gift).

Rape and Other Male Reproductive Strategies

Shields and Shields (1983: 117–19) point out that for species (including our own) in which females are more selective than are males, and in which females favour males likely to provide parental investment, a given male may follow one (or more) of three reproductive strategies. The first of these is 'honest courtship' or 'cooperative bonding.' The male communicates accurate indications of his high-quality genes and equally valid signs of his readiness to invest parentally in the potential offspring. Here, male and female fitness interests may coincide and the result is monogamy (one male, one female) or polygyny (one male, more than one female).

The second strategy is that of 'deceitful or manipulative courtship.' Here, the male communicates falsely about the quality of his genes and about his ability and intention to invest parentally. This approach is labelled by Shields and Shields that of the 'deceitful seducer.'

The third strategy is that of 'forcible rape,' a possibility in any species in which the male is physically and anatomically capable of a forced copulation and in which the female has at least some probability of rearing any resultant offspring without investment from the rapist. For example, a male mallard duck may forcibly mate with a female already bonded to another male (Barash, 1982). (Interestingly, the 'cuckolded' male's response is to himself immediately force a copulation on his mate, apparently in the 'hope' of regaining through sperm competition what he has lost through forced copulation.)

Each of these three strategies depends on the costs and benefits associated with them. Thornhill and Thornhill (1983: 137–8), for example, argue that 'rape is employed by men who are unable to compete for resources and status necessary to attract and reproduce successfully with desirable mates.' For such men, the relative benefit of rape is high, the cost (risk) acceptable. For men of power and position, however, sexual access to desirable mates is not likely to be a problem, so that rape's benefits are relatively low. Its costs, however, are very high in that such men risk losing their high status and thus their ability to attract mates and to invest in offspring. Thornhill and Thornhill's analyses of American data indicate that 'poor men seem to be the rapists' (p. 150).

In similar fashion, rape's potential fitness benefit for the rapist will vary with the reproductive value of his victim. The reproductive value of young females is greater than that of older females, so that the former should be the preferential victims of a rapist. Thornhill and Thornhill's analyses indicate that this is so, and also that 'young women are at a relatively higher risk of rape than murder' (p. 147), unlike older women. The two crimes are apparently of a different nature.

Rape is obviously not in the fitness interests of a female or her kin, since it removes from her the opportunity to choose the 'best genes' and/or 'most likely to invest parentally' male. Thus, selection will favour the resistance of the female and of her kin, and this resistance – or retribution – is a cost to the rapist. The sociobiological prediction here is not novel: the more costly the rape is likely to be, the less likely it is to occur. Shields and Shields argue that it is during wartime that females are most vulnerable and rape therefore least costly, and they join Symons (1979) in pointing out that rape, often on a very large scale, seems to be a universal fact of war. Shields and Shields believe that the relatively high rate of rape in the United States is due to the infrequency with which rapists are caught and the even greater infrequency with which they receive substantial prison sentences. Their policy recommendations are to make rape more costly, and they suggest that training women in self-defence may be the most realistic way to go about this policy.

Rape and Feminism

For both Symons (1979) and Shields and Shields (1983), the context for any discussion of human rape is not just sociobiology but also feminism. Susan Brownmiller (1975), in an often-cited study of rape, concludes that the act is not primarily sexual at all: it is about power and violence,[8] about sexism, and about men learning that it is legitimate to assault women. Feminists have attacked traditional 'strong sex drive' interpretations of rape and instead have insisted that it has more to do with male hostility and ideology than with lust. But for Donald Symons, arguing that rape is something other than a sexual act is error, and both he and Thornhill and Thornhill (1983) present (largely u.s.) data in support of the conclusion that rapists are typically attacking women of high

8 For additional references to feminist approaches to rape, see Shields and Shields (1983: 121).

reproductive value to whom they would otherwise have no sexual access.

Shields and Shields (1983: 123–4) find merit in both feminist and sociobiological interpretations. They argue that evolution has equipped human males with not one but two sexual behavioural programs that control rape behaviour. They write: 'We assume the existence of a polygenic substrate that generates a *closed* behavioral program linking hostility and female vulnerabilty with forced copulation. We perceive this connection as "hard-wired" and the genetic substrate encoding it as essentially *fixed* in the human population' (p. 123, italics in original).

But human males also have an 'open' behavioural program for 'assessing female quality and vulnerability.' Presumably, its content is culturally and situationally determined. However, they emphasize that 'conscious considerations of *fitness* do *not* enter into a male's decisions about rape' (p. 123, italics in original). Note that Shields and Shields appear to mean by the rather vague term 'program' much what I mean by the equally vague terms 'modules' and 'specialized processors.' In my vocabulary, these processors would make use of algorithms that include data as to the age and degree of vulnerability of a female.

Shields and Shields thus accept the feminist contention that rape is indeed an act of hostility perpetrated by men actively feeling hostile towards women; but they also accept the sociobiological contention that rape is about sex and fitness. In support of the latter argument, they cite evidence that rape often does indeed lead to conception.

We must not, however, lose sight of the fact that human males have two other reproductive strategies, in addition to forcible rape. For the strategy Shields and Shields label 'cooperative bonding,' male sexuality is associated not with hostility towards the partner but with feelings of love and tenderness. If men are potential rapists, they are also potential loving and honest partners.[9]

9 Perhaps, just as forcible rape is associated with psychological mechanisms involving hostility and aggressivity, 'cooperative bonding' is associated with the caring for and protectiveness associated with parental behaviour. Where the individual calculates that the female is highly vulnerable and the cost of assault low, the lust + aggressivity link activates. Where the female is not perceived as vulnerable and the cost of assault is high, the lust + protectiveness response activates. Under what circumstances, however, should the 'deceitful seducer' mode of male sexual activity activate? One might also hypothesize that males in whom the same female alternately invokes the lust + protectiveness and lust + violence responses are likely to be spouse abusers. Finally, one could conjecture that pedophilia may result from the sexual response mechanisms occasionally getting 'crossed' so that, for some males, instead of women eliciting the protectiveness response that is ordinarily made to children, children elicit the sexual response ordinarily made to women.

INCEST[10]

Incest may be defined either biologically or sociologically. Biological incest usually refers to mating between close consanguineal kin, that is, either between parents and offspring or between siblings. Sociologically, incest may be expanded to include almost any set of relatives with little regard to their degree of consanguinity. Thus, the term is at times applied to mating between stepparents and children, or between first cousins. As used by ethnographers, 'incest' may mean any mating and/or marital relationship said to be proscribed by reason of kinship regardless of biological relationship. ('Proscribed marriage/mating' would be a less confusing term than incest, in this context.) In many of the world's societies, marriage to one relative may be defined as incestuous (proscribed) while marriage to another, with whom one shares the identical coefficient of consanguinity, is acceptable and perhaps even preferred (cf. chapter 11's discussion of Richard Alexander and cousin asymmetry). Even more confusing, rules for marriage and for mating are often not identical.

Let us begin with biological incest and its avoidance. From this perspective, incest has to do with avoiding inbreeding. Inbreeding reduces fitness. This reduction in fitness caused by mating between close kin is known as 'inbreeding depression.'[11] Note that the extent to which inbreeding depression occurs drops sharply when one moves from full siblings or parent-child matings ($r = 0.50$) to first cousins ($r = 0.125$) (see van den Berghe, 1983: 93, for references). For species in

10 The discussion of incest in this chapter constitutes a brief and personal synthesis rather than an overview of the incest literature. The latter is vast and the reader wishing to sample it might begin with the article by Pierre van den Berghe (1983). Van den Berghe's paper is particularly valuable because it appears in the journal *The Behavioral and Brain Sciences*, and is therefore followed by the comments and criticisms of (in this case) some twenty experts, in addition to van den Berghe's own response to their evaluations. For a hostile critique of sociobiological interpretations of incest, see Kitcher (1985: 270–80).

11 There is a good deal of theory and research as to why inbreeding depression should occur. Charlesworth and Charlesworth (1987) summarize that literature. The two classical theories of inbreeding depression and *heterosis* ('hybrid vigor,' the opposite of inbreeding depression) are the overdominance and partial-dominance hypotheses. According to the former, 'inbreeding depression is due to the superiority of heterozygotes at individual loci affecting the trait in question' (Charlesworth and Charlesworth, 1987: 238). According to the latter, inbreeding depression and heterosis are due to 'the fact that inbred lines become fixed for recessive or partially deleterious alleles; crosses between inbred lines fixed for deleterious alleless at different loci produce genotypes which are superior to the parents becuse the deleterious affects are partly covered up in the F1s [the first generation of hybrid offspring]' (ibid.)

which dispersal of offspring is not automatic, mechanisms typically evolve to lower the probability of inbreeding (Trivers, 1985). The proximate mechanism by which human beings avoid incest and its attendant inbreeding is usually referred to as the 'Westermarck hypothesis' (Westermarck, 1891).

The Westermarck hypothesis holds that those who are closely associated in early childhood will not, upon reaching puberty, find one another sexually attractive. The hypothesis is generally accepted by those who analyse incest avoidance from a Darwinian perspective (for example, Bischof, 1975; Shepher, 1983; van den Berghe, 1983). Two sources of data are widely cited in support of the Westermarck hypothesis. The first of these comes from work in Taiwan. Here, *sim pua* marriages are sometimes arranged in early childhood, the 'bride' being raised by her future husband's parents. Until puberty, the relationship between the pair is similar to that between siblings. Though the couple is expected to marry upon reaching puberty, there is a strong tendency for the couple to resist the marriage; when married in spite of their wishes, they are likely to have considerably lower-than-average fertility (Wolf and Huang, 1980).

The second source of support for the Westermarck hypothesis comes from the Israeli kibbutz. For a time, on many kibbutzim, children were reared communally with no modesty taboos observed, very much as if all were siblings. Though there were no restrictions on marriage between members of the same kibbutz, those reared together would marry one another only very rarely and clearly did not find one another sexually attractive (Spiro, 1958, 1979; Shepher, 1983). Cross-culturally, marriage between close kin who have been reared together is unusual and generally involves royalty.

Pastner (1986) has argued that the Westermarck hypothesis does not always hold. Among the Zikri Baluch fisher-folk of coastal Pakistan, explains Pastner, first-cousin marriage is both preferred and normative (64% of her sample of 171 marriages were between first cousins). Moreover, cousins play together until the girls reach puberty, so that future spouses frequently have been child playmates. Surprisingly, Pastner's data reveal neither aversion between first-cousin spouses nor depression in fertility.

Pastner suggests that several specific cultural practices apparently serve to prevent or mitigate the effects that sociobiologists such as Shepher and van den Berghe would predict. First, males marry at an older age than do females, so that even if a bride is the groom's former playmate, she would have been a much younger playmate (Pastner, 1986: 578). Then, too, young people have relatively little power to choose their own mates, this being the responsibility of parents. The young people are aware that their future spouse is likely to be a first cousin but, unlike the Taiwan case, such marriages are preferred rather than being a mark of low status. Perhaps the most important factor mitigating against a Westermarck effect is socialization into 'a sense of sexual shame' (Pastner, 1986: 577). The young are taught 'prudery' and 'are increasingly exposed to the norms of adult sexual segregation and a concern with modest demeanor for both sexes' (p. 578) as they grow older. With betrothal, this modesty and sexual restraint becomes 'strict premarital avoidance.' Pastner's conclusion is not that the Westermarck hypothesis is in error, but that her data suggest that it may be an oversimplification of a complex process in which culture plays an important role. After all, the processes by which the Westermarck hypotheses operates are not well understood.[12] Perhaps the Westermarck hypothesis should be restated as follows: co-rearing ordinarily produces future sexual aversion, except under certain conditions.

Even as restated, the Westermarck hypothesis deals only with sex and marriage between those who in effect have been reared as siblings: what of relationships between parents and children? Westermarck's is a sensitive-period hypothesis (some use the term 'critical period' or even 'negative imprinting'). Since children are within their sensitive period, argues van den Berghe (1983), they should not later find their parents or others who foster them sexually attractive. However, since the parents are well past their own sensitive periods they may find their children to be of sexual interest. Van den Berghe believes that this lack of symmetry accounts for the fact that parent-child incest does in fact at times occur, even if at very low rates. Mother-son incest is much more unusual than is father-daughter incest. Van den Berghe explains that males are more sexually aggressive than are females. Since sons are not sexually interested in their mothers, the more sexually aggressive individual in the potential sexual relationship is here inactive, so that mother-son incest is extremely rare. But since fathers may be interested in their daughters and as males are presumably high both in power and in sexual aggressiveness, father-daughter incest is not uncommon. However, observes van den Berghe, the daughters flee the relationship as soon as they are able.

12 Spain (1987), for example, suggests that Freudian theories of repression and penis envy are consistent with the hypothesis.

Van den Berghe may be overstating the case. It is not at all clear that the only thing that keeps most mothers from copulating with their male offspring is a lack of interest on the part of the sons; or that fathers automatically feel lust towards their daughters. Other mechanisms may be involved here, including those of the 'obligate norms' discussed in chapter 11. Parents may experience revulsion at the very thought of sex with their own children.

Cultural 'Incest Taboos'
What, however, of the myriad cultural 'incest taboos' (marriage proscriptions) found in the ethnographic literature, proscriptions that seem to have little to do with degree of consanguinity? I would suggest that we are here dealing with a phenomenon only tangentially related to incest avoidance. Lévi-Strauss (1969) and others have argued that marriage proscriptions force groups to exchange women and thereby to have relationships with one another, and as we saw in the previous chapter, Parker (1987) and Smith (1984) argue that men would have tried to control the sexuality of their consanguineal female kin in order to have higher-value females for exchange (higher in the sense of appearing to be likely to provide higher paternity certainty). The Westermarck hypothesis accounts for why men needed to exchange women rather than simply to mate with their own daughters and sisters. The complexities of cultural marriage rules, however, are probably products of cultural evolution, of history, and once beyond the level of the nuclear family have scant relationship to inbreeding depression. Any attempt to account for the marriage rules of various cultures in terms of inbreeding avoidance would be unwise (as we saw in the case of Richard Alexander's attempt to do so, back in chapter 11).

SUMMARY

1. Sperm competition is a form of sexual selection that occurs when females copulate with more than one male during a relatively brief period of time. Such copulation, whether in the form of communal mating, adultery, or secondary marriage, has apparently been typical of our species. As a result of sperm competition, we have evolved long penises, long-lived sperm, forceful ejaculation, and possibly the scrotum and male masturbation. Female orgasm and its accompanying uterine contractions may have evolved in response to male sperm competition in order to provide the female with some control over who fertilizes her.

2. The hymen may have evolved, according to Smith (1984), as a result of males seeking evidence that a female would provide high paternity confidence. But it seems more likely that it evolved to prevent very young girls from risking infection and injury by inserting inappropriate objects into the vagina. It is always possible, of course, that the hymen has no adaptive value.

3. Male and female sexual jealousy are theoretically distinct. When it comes to copulation, selection in favour of jealousy and other guarding mechanisms will be strong when it is the male who has the adulterous mate; but when the female has an adulterous mate, it will be strong only to the extent that her male invests (or appears likely to invest) in the other female and *her* offspring.

4. Wife seclusion and female genital operations at first glance appear to be evidence of male 'guarding' behaviour and sexual jealousy. However, though jealousy may have played a role in their ultimate origins, in extant societies the perpetuation of these social institutions may also be explained in sociological terms. Female genital operations may often receive more support from females than from males. Female claustration, it has been argued, may have to do with families attempting to enhance the paternity confidence associated with their daughters, so as to obtain high-status grooms. Here, too, in at least the Hausa case, the claustration may be initiated and maintained at the urging of the women, since it turns out that seclusion is to their economic advantage.

5. Institutionalized homosexuality was common in Melanesia. In some societies, all boys would play the passive role in homosexual relationships, and when older the active role; but eventually they would have heterosexual relations. Institutionalized homosexuality illustrates the extent to which culture (or, more properly, history) may shape even so fitness-related a trait as sexuality in ways that would not be predicted from evolutionary theory alone.

6. Human males appear to have several sexual strategies available to them. According to Shields and Shields (1983), 'cooperative bonding' is associated with subjective feelings of love and tenderness. 'Forcible rape' is associated with feelings of hostility. Feminists are correct in arguing that rape is a hostile act against women but sociobiologists are also correct in considering it a sexual one. Rape may be construed as a matter of costs and benefits. During wartime, females are very vulnerable so that the cost of rape to a soldier is very low, resulting in a very high rape rate. Ordinarily, however, higher-status males, at least, have much to lose in attempting rape. Lower-status males, who may otherwise

have little sexual access to females of high reproductive value, have relatively more to gain, from a fitness perspective. As expected, lower-status males are disproportionately represented among rapists. According to sociobiologists, raising the costs associated with rape by, for example, training females in self-defence should reduce the rate at which rape occurs.

7. From a biological perspective, incest taboos are a means of avoiding the fitness depression associated with close inbreeding. In our own species the 'Westermarck hypothesis' accounts for incest avoidance by theorizing that rearing opposite-sex children together from an early age will result in their finding one another sexually uninteresting upon reaching puberty. Data from Taiwan and from the Israeli kibbutzim support the Westermarck hypothesis. However, culturally elaborated incest taboos (marriage proscriptions) often have little to do with fitness depression and are best explained in other terms.

15

Social Engineering

The final chapter is where, by tradition, the author attempts to demonstrate how all that went before can solve social problems, improve morality, make one a more effective competitor, or in some other manner contribute to making life better for us all. Now that we have a framework for understanding the evolution of the human mind and of culture, are we better off? Do we have the basis for a science of social engineering?

'Social engineering' is a presumptuous goal, with a whiff of the totalitarian about it; but we all want to tinker and some of us want revolution. We wish to shape the behaviour of individuals and the structures of our societies. We *need* to do so, given Third World poverty, urban ghettos in the West, ethnic and religious conflict, ecological destruction, and always, the unthinkable reality of thousands of nuclear weapons awaiting a word to destroy our civilization and perhaps even our species.

These values in terms of which I am discussing the need for social engineering are those of conventional Western morality. They are personal but presumably are shared by anyone likely to read this book. These values are *not* especially biological and they do not somehow flow from evolutionary theory. I am not convinced that the social/behavioural and biological sciences have anything to tell us about what *should* be, though they have much to tell us about what *is*.[1]

1 Kaye (1986), in a discussion of biological theory and morality, finds that many biologists read their personal values and perspectives into what they consider to an objective view of human nature and culture. Thus, Kaye (1986: 128) writes of E.O. Wilson,

LEVELS OF CHANGE

There are (at least) two levels of problem, in social engineering. Of course we need to know how to change the behaviour of individuals (level 1), but this is not enough. We also need to know (level 2) how to change the behaviour of various categories of individuals in such a way that, in interacting with one another over time, they (and the groups they form) will generate the desired social and cultural changes. In other words, we need not only a psychology of behaviour but a sociology of the generation of social forms through social interaction, as well as a notion of what kind of society we want to have when we are, for the moment at least, done with changes.

The first level, that of individual behaviour, is the province of the intra-individual system and has to do with plans and goals, and sub^{n}plans and sub^{n}goals. When we talk about altering individual behaviour we mean (given the framework developed in chapter 5) feeding data into the intra-individual system. The new information may involve alternative subplans and subgoals, or it may alter background mazeway data, so that existing subplans and subgoals get different priorities because the assessment of their probable outcomes has changed. For example, feeding into the intra-individual system of a potential rapist the information that he is likely to be caught and severely punished may cause him to change his reproductive strategy. (Interestingly, there is no requirement that the new information be accurate; nor will the individual necessarily ever have been aware that he was a potential rapist.)

The second level at which the social engineer must work is that of social interaction creating, modifying, and maintaining social structures. At the first level we have individuals following the sub^{n}plans of their respective intra-individual systems. But the interaction of these people, in their daily lives, *generates* social structure and organization. This was the lesson of chapter 9, in which we saw ethnic conflict, ethnic boundaries, and even the spread of Islam being generated by the social

---

who would 'biologize' ethics and derive morality from biology, that his work reflects 'his residual, Protestant belief in the value of a life of passionate, ascetic commitment to a harmoniously organized community from which the individual draws identity and purpose.' No doubt my own world-view has similarly and inevitably influenced my choice of topics, emphases, and interpretation of data: but I explicitly deny that my academic specializations have given me any special insight into how we should, as opposed to how we do, live our lives.

interaction of individuals following various subplans (in this case, subplans related to prestige). Assuming we have somehow solved level one's problems of knowing how to alter people's behaviour as individuals, we still have to solve level two's problem of determining which individual-level behaviours will result in the interaction that generates the social forms we desire.

This is not necessarily a matter of having everyone follow the same subplan and strive for the same subgoal. The generation of social structure usually involves different groups following different strategies, in interaction with one another. We need to know which faction (social group or category) should have which subplan/goal 'inputted,' and when. The processes of interaction of groups and other such collectivities (such as social classes and nations) need to be understood, and not just the results of interaction among individuals.

Finally, we need to decide what kinds of societies we want: before one asks 'How do we get there?' it is necessary to know where 'there' is. A number of thinkers have suggested that the human species will do best if organized in societies in some ways similar to those in which we evolved and in which we lived for most of our corporate existence: small-scale, reasonably self-sufficient communities of approximately five hundred in size and which, unlike contemporary societies, are ecologically stable in the long term.[2]

To simplify the discussion, let us slight all problems other than those of level one. We shall put aside the details of the societies we wish to design, ignore the task of getting individuals to interact in such a way as to generate desired sociocultural change, and leave the complexities of interaction among collectivities to the political scientists. Level-one problems alone are, as we shall see, sufficiently daunting. If they cannot be solved then it makes no difference where we think we want to go: we cannot get there.

PROBLEMS OF LEVEL ONE: THE WRONG LIMBIC-SYSTEM
OVERRIDES AND OTHER ADAPTATIONS TO PAST ENVIRONMENTS

We deal best with short-term, local crises: a fire, a predator, a rival, a threat to our own family, clan, or community. Presumably, these are the kinds of problems our ancestors faced, and selection has therefore

2 For interesting and anthropologically informed discussions of what kinds of society we might consider aiming for, see Tax (1977), Taylor (1972), Ehrlich and Harriman (1971), Ehrlich (1974), and, especially, Goldsmith et al. (1972).

equipped us to meet them. We cope with them either with the kind of limbic-system overrides discussed in chapter 5, or else by assigning a high priority to the appropriate subgoals/plans. You will react immediately if your child is drowning and will give a high priority to the (sub)goal of preventing such accidents in the future. Drownings, a charging bear, a sexual rival: these are the kind of local, short-term difficulties that we manage reasonably well.

Unfortunately, many of today's threats to genetic fitness are neither local problems nor short-term emergencies. Today's grave menaces may come from the long-term problems of soil depletion, destruction of the ozone layer, and an increasing 'greenhouse effect' from added atmospheric carbon dioxide; or perhaps from a fishery being exhausted by over-exploitation. They come from the threat of nuclear war, or from the long-term possibility of a health risk from poor diet or from a food additive. These, today, are more likely to kill us than are charging bears. But when we learn that too much sodium may increase our risk of hypertension and therefore of cardiovascular disease, do we jump up in automatic, emotional response, ready to fight or flee? When we learn of the dangers of soil depletion through erosion, of ground-water contamination, of a growing greenhouse effect, or of the disaster of acid rain, do we panic with fear, as if a bear were chasing us? Do we seek some immediate action to take? Well, a few of us do. But most of us turn the pages of our newspaper, or shake our head, and do nothing.

The problem is not that we are morally weak and foolish, or too stupid to understand our peril. We understand intellectually but fail to react emotionally because this is not the kind of danger our ancestors faced. They dealt with short-term crises; we face long-term, probabilistic risks. They and their close relations were under immediate threat, we face longer-term threats, and not just to kin but to continents. Unfortunately, evolutionary wisdom is always past wisdom. Selection has never favoured a danger response to long-term and collective (though nevertheless deadly) perils.

Our limbic-system overrides are still adapted to a past environment. They are occasionally useful, even today, since short-term danger remains; but they are lacking for those situations for which we now most need them.[3] If our reactions to the statistics on automobile fatalities were

3 Often, of course, these limbic-system overrides are maladaptive in the modern context. Fleeing in panic may once have been somewhat effective in the case of forest fire but is much less so when caught in a crowded, burning building. Freezing motionlessly in fear may have been somewhat adaptive when the danger was a predator or human enemy but is much less so when one is endangered by an approaching car.

10% as strong as our reactions to sexual rivals, we would insist on both air bags and seat belts in our vehicles, fill them with padding and enclose them in thick bumpers. One way to think of this problem is in terms of priorities among subgoals. The subgoals of avoiding injury in an automobile accident – or avoiding nuclear war – are genuine subgoals of the intra-individual system, but neither has a priority nearly as high as the subgoal of getting a date for Saturday night.

More Problems of Level One: Ethnocentrism
The ethnocentrism syndrome was cited, back in chapter 6, as evidence for the autopredation hypothesis. Unfortunately, it is also the root cause of sectarian conflict. We automatically fall into in-groups and out-groups, their size ranging from 'we Africans' to 'we members of a high-school clique who do (or do not) wear designer jeans.' Ethnocentric-like behaviour encompasses many 'isms' – nationalism, racism, sectarianism, factionalism, and the various forms of chauvinism. One of the many strategies of political leaders everywhere is to foment ethnocentrism in order to benefit from the solidarity thereby engendered. It takes only a little encouragement for us to fall into factions each of which considers itself 'in the right,' that is, morally superior to other factions and acting in the common good. Organized anti-Semitic, anti-abortion, and anti-nuclear-war groups all present themselves as acting for the good of all.

Because of the paucity of gods associated with monotheism, in wartime all sides are forced to claim the support of the same deity. Thanks to our capacity for *self-deception*, this absurdity in no way lessens claims to moral superiority.

Still More Problems of Level One: Self-Deception
Self-deception, whatever contribution to fitness it may make in some circumstances, is today often maladaptive in several senses of the term. Return to nuclear war as a threat to our fitness. Nuclear war represents a possible long-term consequence of subplans that, for a very large number of people, result in the attainment of important subgoals. Perhaps I work in a munitions factory, or perhaps I receive dividend income from a corporation that manufactures weapons; or perhaps I have a military career that would be damaged by my opposing current political trends; or I may be a political leader – or hope to be one – and the more I can portray outsiders as 'enemies' and emphasize the threat they represent, the more able I am to garner political support and thus prestige and position. Thanks to the cognitive-distortion capabilities of

the intra-individual system, I have no difficulty in convincing myself that the risks involved in current military policy are absolutely necessary. Granted, some subsystem of my intra-individual system may hold contradictory information, but it is out-of-awareness and unlikely to affect my behaviour.

Level One Problems and Bureaucracy
Bureaucracy is one of the great inventions of our species, along with the wheel and fire. There is no other way to organize large-scale society than division of responsibility and a hierarchical, pyramidal structure of authority. We evolved, however, in the context of small, not large-scale, societies, and bureaucracy is not our natural habitat. Our behavioural strategies, evolved in former times, subvert bureaucracy.

Bureaucracy, whether corporate or governmental, is created to perform specific functions. Campbell (1982) laments that bureaucracies are blithely designed as if the setting of procedures and purposes will cause individuals to take the formal goals of the bureaucracy as more important than their own, personal goals. Everywhere, this fails to happen, and everywhere, bureaucracies are accused of 'inefficiency.'

Different units of large bureaucracies readily become ethnocentric. For example, the chief priority of bureaucratic units of large corporations may involve not the economic well-being of the company as a whole but, rather, the increase of the prestige and power of own unit over that of rival units. Beyond a certain size, factional and divisional ethnocentrism may cost a firm its 'economies of scale,' sometimes leading frustrated senior executives to divide the corporation into semi-autonomous units.

As Campbell indicates, those who design bureaucracies often appear to believe that individuals readily give collective goals priority over personal ends. To some extent they may, provided the unit is perceived at the level of the intra-individual system as familial, so that strategies of nepotistic altruism may be aroused. The Japanese are frequently described as being unusually successful in making the corporation the emotional family. In the West, firms that succeed in arousing familial emotions are often described as 'paternalistic.' (Note, however, that not even nepotistic altruism necessarily means that all self-interest is forgone.)

In general, bureaucrats and other workers usually attend more to personal than to corporate rewards. In poorly designed bureaucracies, the reward system may militate against the very purposes for which the unit was created. Very often, these systems reward those who 'stay out of trouble,' and attaining this enviable status is likely to involve taking no risks and as little responsibility as possible. Similarly, they may reward those who support their superiors politically, no matter how ineffective the latter are in achieving the organization's ends.

Only for the most senior executives may the bureaucracy's formal goals also be personal goals, since these individuals are likely to be rewarded with increased wealth and prestige when the 'official' goals are met. Thus, their task must be to strive to oppose the self-interest of others, and also to convince these others that their self-interest and that of the company are indeed identical (through persuasion, profit-sharing plans, and so forth). Even senior executives may be interested only in meeting the company's short-term goals (for instance, profit for the next quarter). There may be no corporate employees at all with a personal interest in the company's long-term goals. (Hopefully, but not necessarily, members of the corporate board and the shareholders are concerned with long-term goals.)

When corporate bureaucracies spend much of their time in internecine warfare, the company's profitability is likely to suffer and the 'discipline of the market-place' may force reorganization. But what of governmental bureaucracies? Here, external feedback may be entirely lacking for very long periods. Thus, governments can and do tolerate inefficiencies that would bankrupt private corporations (just as large, monopolistic companies may tolerate inefficiencies that would bankrupt smaller firms fighting for profitability and market share). This inefficiency is, of course, a powerful argument against any form of centralized control (of the type that has existed, for example, in the USSR), because such control entails immense bureaucracies. However, were the designers of both state and corporate bureaucracies to take account of evolved human nature, they might well succeed in overcoming the auto-subversion tendency. Carefully structured bureaucracies can reward individuals for system goals, so that personal and collective interest coincide. Biology is not destiny unless one ignores it. (Is it in the interest of the planners of bureaucracies to take account of human nature, when by doing so they may offend powerful others?)

One of the factors in bureaucratic subversion, particularly when it occurs not between but within bureaucratic units, is envy.

Envy
We may enhance our relative standing in two ways: by seeking prestige for ourselves, or by striving to reduce that of a rival. The emotion

associated with the subgoal of reducing the standing of rivals is known as *envy*.

Envy is something of a taboo subject in our society, much as homosexuality once was. To display envy is to risk losing status, and we enjoin losing politicians and athletes not to display this feeling. In Hausa society, in contrast, it is a frequently discussed topic, and *jin kishi*, 'feeling envy,' is acknowledged, even if more readily attributed to others than to self.

It is possible to argue that envy breeds egalitarianism and even socialism. Egalitarianism is an ideology (that is, a set of rules for self-presentation and rhetoric) in which few claims of higher relative standing than others are treated as legitimate, and in which any such claims invite others to unite against one. Socialism is the economic equivalent (and is usually allied with it) – economic disparities are considered illegitimate.[4] What is considered legitimate is envious action against those who would appear to claim either higher social or higher economic status than others. As we have already seen (in chapter 8), George Foster (1972) has argued that envy is typical of peasant societies, in which individuals often seem more concerned with preventing others from improving their standing than in advancing their own. (Foster had previously gone so far as to argue that peasants tend to view life as a 'zero sum game' in which the advance of one is believed to automatically entail the expense of another.)

Envy is the bane of all social structures and interferes with more than peasant productivity. It is, as we have seen, rife in bureaucracies, where it subverts their goals. Egalitarianism and encapsulation, however, can (as we will see), provide some hope for the social control of envy.

SOME GROUNDS FOR OPTIMISM[5]

Some of us do stop smoking and drinking, some of us do lose weight. I know at least one former high-level executive in a munitions firm who

---

4 Cf. MacDonald (1983). Both socialism and egalitarianism resemble evolutionarily stable strategies. It could be argued that, in the long run, if a majority of the population adopts egalitarianism, perhaps no individual would enhance his or her relative fitness by overtly claiming particularly high relative standing. Similarly, if a majority of the population adopts socialism, perhaps no individual would better his or her economic well-being by overtly adopting an entrepreneurial prestige strategy. Of course, both egalitarian and socialist societies have many people who covertly violate, or attempt to covertly violate, the official ideology.

5 Testable hypotheses are also a ground for optimism, if not about social engineering then at least about future research. Focus 15.1 gathers together most of the various

quit his position to accept one offering considerably less income and prestige but which was unrelated to military production. Sometimes, in other words, information does enter the intra-individual system to produce behaviour that gives collective-good subgoals higher priority than individual good subgoals.[6]

How do we engineer society so as to raise the priority of collective-good goals in the intra-individual system? Richard Alexander (1979, 1987) notwithstanding, it will take more than some knowledge of human sociobiology (as was discussed in chapter 3). A course in human sociobiology is no more likely to make us less genetically selfish than a course in personality theory is to make us more sane. Education is not a panacea for social problems, fashionable though it has long been to call on the schools to cure every abuse from alcoholism to automobile accidents.

But it *is* possible to alter the relative priorities of subgoals by taking advantage of the attention gates of the intra-individual system: the problem is understanding how to 'input' appropriate information. True, two of the fields with the aim of altering individual-level behaviour, psychotherapy and criminology, seem to have had rather limited success (the latter in particular). But a third field, advertising, has a much better record.

The success of commercial advertising probably reflects the empirical approach of its practitioners, who naturally do more of whatever increases sales and less of whatever does not. Criminology and psychotherapy lack so well-defined a feedback channel as to the effects of their interventions, and are not necessarily responsive to what feedback they do receive. But advertisers have developed techniques that (not surprisingly) are consistent with what we now understand of the attention mechanisms of the intra-individual system. For example, advertisements routinely associate products with the high in status and with sexual attractiveness, so as to get our attention. Announcers and

---

hypotheses discussed in this and previous chapters. These hypotheses do not form a coherent whole – this book is hardly so tightly organized – but researchers are encouraged to help themselves. Note that in all cases it is necessary to return to the chapters from which the hypotheses were drawn in order to understand their theoretical context. The focus on testable hypotheses is not meant as the 'pop Popperism' some deride, but as a counterbalance to the emphasis on vertically integrated theory.

6 Of course, one could argue that ceasing to work in military production entailed an increase in status, given this individual's membership and reference groups, and was only apparently a subplan in the service of a collective-good subgoal. Let us resist such cynicism.

celebrities speak directly and personally to the audience, conveying the message that the speaker is a high-status member of the listener's social group, thereby eliciting imitation. Such techniques are often very effective.

Note that these techniques can be equally effective when used in campaigns believed to be in the 'public good.' Merely telling people to use seat belts or to engage in regular physical activity is usually ineffective because the information does not get into the modules concerned with plans and goals, even if the listener readily agrees that he or she 'should' do what is being advised. In contrast, the Canadian government's 'Participaction' physical-activity campaign has been quite successful because it has bombarded the television-watching, magazine-reading public with images of highly attractive role models exercising. Comparable campaigns for seat belts, to take another example, have been similarly successful. Advertisements in which high-school students who smoke or drink are portrayed as being scorned by others (that is, are portrayed as being of low relative standing) do appear to have some effect. We know how to modify mass behaviour in a fairly reliable manner.

The conclusion here is somewhat unexpected: if we dislike aspects of human nature (such as insincerity in sexual relations, or other behaviours that violate the ethics most of us wish to present ourselves as espousing), we should advertise against them. Perhaps research specifically into the structure of human attention and of how information is 'inputted' into the intra-individual system will eventually provide more effective means of altering behaviour, but commercial advertising shows at least one way of doing this.[7] (Of course, the goals of those using such techniques may be different from our own. It is salutary to recall that the seminal genius in the field of advertising/propaganda was named Goebbels. Politicians and political propagandists are often expert in inputting information into what might be termed the 'ethno-centrism' module, triggering a behaviour pattern that causes us to rally around a leader in defence of our group and against an external enemy. Would-be leaders are adept at inventing external enemies.)

Finally, education *can* work to transmit knowledge to the intra-individual system, *if* the educational system has been properly designed. The problem remains that of getting data into the intra-

---

7 No doubt there are other ways to alter behaviour, such as coercive persuasion or 'brainwashing.' The recruitment techniques of certain religious groups, in which initially unconditional love later becomes increasingly conditional, may also be effective, however distasteful some of us may find them.

individual system. The purveyor of the information has to get our attention, with its evolved gates. A low-status teacher whom all know is paid little (and therefore valued little, in our society), and who 'teaches' us to behave in ways likely to lower our relative standing in our membership group, is rarely effective. An authoritarian, feared teacher is likely to be attended to agonistically, and the resulting constricted receipt of information will be narrow. High-status but warm (or at least, not feared) teachers should be the most effective.

Moral Solutions

Can systems of morality develop that may restrain individual selfishness? D.T. Campbell (1975) argues that the ethics of the major world religions are much the same, and that this is no coincidence. As societies have grown in scope and complexity, moral codes restraining individual self-seeking and promoting the common good have spread because the societies that have prospered and propagated themselves are precisely those that have developed such moralities. Not even Campbell claims that this process continues today, however.

Can we develop a system of morality and status in which those who espouse long-term collective interests and fail to give priority to their own short-term, individual concerns are given honour and respect? Would a new religion accomplish this goal? Or would a subtle advertising campaign, in which status and sex are associated with those who think in terms of the long-term benefit of the entire society, be effective? The existence of voluntary, non-governmental organizations that lobby for public-interest goals (for instance, an end to war, freeing political prisoners, preserving the environment, stopping child abuse) suggests that it is possible for some of us, at least, to give some priority to the common good.[8]

Optimism over Self-Esteem

There seems to be universal consensus, in the mental-health community, that we need to maintain self-esteem if we are to be happy, productive,

8 It may be that in some cases the pursuit of public interest is primarily a strategy for obtaining a selfish interest, for example, that of status within the group that espouses the public-interest goal. This possibility in no way obviates the fact that a public-interest goal is indeed being pursued. A much more serious problem is that groups often differ in what they consider a public-interest goal. The Canadian Inuit (Eskimos) and Newfoundland fishermen whose livelihood was wiped out by the Greenpeace Foundation's successful campaign against the purchase of seal pelts by the European Economic Community nations would not agree that Greenpeace had acted for the common good.

functioning members of society. Any social engineer will therefore wish to design his/her society in a manner permitting everyone to maintain self-esteem – to have pride and self-respect. Here, at last, we can be optimistic, for this goal is in principle possible.

As we saw in chapters 8 and 9, self-esteem means evaluating oneself as being higher in relative standing than are others, the evaluating being done in terms of a set of criteria associated with a real or imaginary, present or absent group in which we claim membership. At first, this appears to be a paradox: How can everyone be higher than some? Must not someone be at the bottom? Here, our capacity for cognitive distortion comes into play. Suppose I base my self-esteem on my illustrious family background, my nine-hundred-year-old name or whatever. Smith, with whom I play golf, bases his (her) self-esteem on his (her) having risen to a vice-presidency of a large corporation. Each of us feels superior to the other. But each of us also utilizes a set of shared culture traits called 'manners,' 'graciousness,' and 'etiquette' to avoid acting out our felt superiority. On this basis, we can play golf; though, to be sure, we may do so rather competitively. If ever our self-presentation slips and one of us reveals his (her) true self-assessment then we will probably have to find new golf partners.

Note, by the way, that since in North American society (or at least in major segments of it) evaluation criteria *include* social skills and manners, and since it is considered unmannerly for one individual blatantly to act as if he or she were more important than another, we will strive not to slip. If we do detect that the other considers himself or herself superior we will probably not argue over relative standing but over some symbolic issue (such as, showing up late for the game). Thus, wherever the egalitarian ideology reigns, self-presentation tends to involve an elaborate, Goffmanesque dance, each partner moving to his or her own music, the theme of which is '*I* am really higher in relative standing but will refrain from overtly claiming to be so.'

Of course, many relationships are not egalitarian at all, even in North America. Moreover, in societies lacking an egalitarian ethos, hierarchical relations are the norm. Where the gaps in relative standing are openly accepted, we have recourse to encapsulation (discussed in chapter 8). When encapsulation is effective, the lower groups consider those with demonstrably high power and control of resources as being non-comparables, as members of a different species.

But encapsulation is always potentially unstable, since we are, in fact, members of the same species. When encapsulation fails then envy, that emotion associated with the desire to reduce the relative standing of others *vis-à-vis* ourselves, is likely to result. The envy of the lower-standing groups may lead to the strategy of revolution, which if successful may end in the restructuring of the society. (Note that where the lower-status groups are physically deprived – actually suffering from hunger or cold, for example – then the subplan called 'revolution' is likely to be in the service primarily of subsistence or physiological maintenance goals, and the envy of the prestige goal may play a distinctly secondary role. People fight angrily when envious, but they also fight when hungry or otherwise oppressed.)

This discussion suggests that it is indeed possible, at least in principle, to engineer a society in which self-esteem is available for all. The requirement is for the society to have numerous groups and therefore a plenitude of sets of criteria for prestige and self-esteem. Thus, all of us can be 'higher,' provided we share an etiquette of dissimulation in which one risks losing relative standing by overtly claiming superiority. Such an etiquette would permit our covert self-assessment of 'higher than others' to remain covert, so that we would avoid directly challenging others. Of course, if the society we have in mind is not egalitarian, then we need to foster encapsulation. In such cases, we should plan for maximum social distance between classes or castes.

Encapsulation, in modern industrial nations at least, may be waning. The ideology of communism obviously directly contradicts it. Less obviously, the commercial advertising of free-enterprise economies does so as well. Advertisements seem to be saying that the secret to high status is the possession of consumer goods, and that such possession is the only meaningful criterion for the evaluation of relative standing. Pay for a gold card, buy the proper car, shop at the appropriate market, and you, too, can be royalty! An emphasis on wealth and the possession of goods as the primary determinants of relative standing attacks encapsulation because these are potentially open to all. Relative standing becomes a matter of relative success in acquiring money, the key to the symbols of status. Those of higher status than oneself are not perceived as a different species but merely as one's more successful competitors, one's rivals. For those who are handicapped by the nature of their background or abilities, there is always the career of crime, the most equal-opportunity employer of all! *If encapsulation is untenable, in modern society, then only egalitarianism can produce social stability in the long term.*

Optimism over the Self

Can we solve all the level-one problems by one fell swoop, by enlarging the self? We saw in chapter 4 that the self – the internal representation of the organism itself – is 'culturally constituted.' One implication of this fact is that the extent to which it receives information from other subsystems of the intra-individual system must vary across cultures and across individuals. Is it possible to expand the self to the point at which it becomes coterminous with the entire intra-individual system? I do not know how this might be done. But were it to happen, so integrated a person might, by appreciating his or her own enlightened self-interest, give the highest of priorities to common-good goals.[9]

Hints of Happiness

Let us assume that the goal of the social engineer is human happiness. Here are a few optimistic hints as to how we might learn something about it.

There is a sort of ethnographic mystique in which the returned field-worker prefaces his or her writings with remarks about feeling deep gratitude and affection for his 'many friends' among the So-and-so. Only rarely does the anthropologist clearly indicate that he or she did not like the people so painstakingly described (though see Hallpike [1977] for one of those exceptions, and see Turnbull [1974] for an extreme example of how badly some field-workers have actually been treated by their 'good friends').

Ethnographers do tend to be frank within the fold of their fellow field-workers: and it is my own (unscientific) experience that those who have worked among hunter-gatherers and, to a lesser extent, those who have worked among pastoral nomads, really do mean the admiring things they publicly say. They like the peoples they have studied. But those who return from work among rural cultivators, especially when these are peasants (that is, cultivators who are not autonomous but beholden in a major way to members of another social class), may return with affection for a few individuals but with only grudging respect, if any, for the peoples they have studied. A typical complaint, for example, is that the peasants assumed that anything the field-worker said was a lie and of course felt free to lie to the field-worker.

It is my suggestion that field-workers here are really responding to whether or not the people they have studied tend to be *happy*. It may be that the closer people are to the kind of environments in which we evolved, the happier they are likely to be (Barkow, 1973). But which

9 One could argue that religions such as Buddhism, which seek the destruction of the self, may actually (through ritual and meditation) be expanding the self to include the entire intra-individual system.

aspects of those early environments would have been crucial? Perhaps hunting and gathering activities themselves, perhaps the small scale of society, perhaps ... Since we can never go back in time, what we need is a cross-cultural epidemiology of happiness, a study of its prevalence and incidence and the factors that affect these. In this way, we might learn how we should be engineering our societies.

Perhaps child-rearing practices are an indication of unhappiness. Let us assume that people are more likely to discipline their children harshly when they themselves are unhappy. Let us also assume that they discipline harshly when the tasks the children must perform are so resisted that only harshness is effective in controlling the children's behaviour, and that the necessity for this severity makes the parents unhappy. Finally, let us assume that children harshly disciplined tend to be unhappy as a direct result of the discipline. If these assumptions are valid, then the severity of child-training is an indicator of unhappiness. Child-rearing therefore permits a test of this hypothesis: (1) hunter-gatherers should be the happiest of peoples, since they presumably (and it is a presumption) live in a manner closer to our environment of evolutionary adaptedness than do others, and since the tasks they must learn are (by no coincidence) similar to the ordinary play of children; (2) but cultivators, particularly peasantries, should be the least happy, for their routine, arduous labour, and lack of autonomy seem furthest from the hunting-gathering life of our ancestors; (3) pastoral nomads and members of modern industrial societies should rank somewhere between hunter-gatherers and peasants in happiness. A cursory look at cross-cultural studies of child socialization and of child abuse (for example, Rohner, 1975; and Barry, Bacon, and Child, 1959) suggests that this hypothesis is likely to be supported. What will be needed next is a detailed examination of the severity of child disciplines and of their correlates, not just on a cross-cultural but on a cross-family, within-culture basis. We just might be able to learn something about what makes for human happiness, surely the ultimate goal of any social engineer.

GENETIC SOLUTIONS ARE UNLIKELY

Of course, if natural selection is going to solve our problems, perhaps we do not need any social engineering. Since many of our intra-individual-system traits are probably maladaptive in our contemporary environment, will not ongoing genetic evolution eventually alter them?

Probably not, since these 'maladaptive' traits are not necessarily *genetically* maladaptive. There is no evidence whatsoever that those who respond to long-term or common-good risks have higher inclusive fitness than do others. Indeed, since one of those common-good risks, for much of the world, is overpopulation, one could argue quite the opposite. Moreover, given the size of our population units, a genetic response of any kind would be extremely slow, on the order of thousands and perhaps hundreds of thousands of years. If we rely on natural selection, we may have destroyed ourselves long before meaningful shifts in gene frequencies have taken place (even assuming that genetic differences account for much of the variance in responsiveness to long-term hazards, and that selection favouring 'long-term thinkers' is actually occurring, both of these assumptions being dubious).

Of course, we could hurry things along by mounting our own eugenics program. But how would we know what to breed for? In any event, any society sufficiently totalitarian to undertake such an experiment would probably be most interested in selecting in favour of some of our most dangerous traits (such as, ethnocentrism).

Social engineering – deliberately altering our societies – is the only choice we have. Reliance on natural selection could leave us like the great majority of past species: extinct.

CONCLUSIONS AND DREAM-WALKING

Compared to our folk-psychology notions of will and self-control, the reality is that we are all walking in our sleep. Evolution did not design us to be awake. Our conscious experience is the tip of the iceberg of our neurophysiological processes. Now we feel anger, now we feel envy, now joy, now fear, now attraction. With each new emotion, subplans and subgoals change in priority, but we are unaware of these changes. The emotions themselves reflect the selection pressures on our ancestors and, as we have seen, may be quite inappropriate, given the dangers – and perhaps the potential pleasures – of our modern environment. Our prized self-awareness is little more than the surface of a sea beneath which much lurks; from the depths, from time to time, bits bob up.

Can we change all this? Can we enlarge the scope of self-awareness until it encompasses the entire intra-individual system, and our evolved, compartmentalized subsystems share all information with one another? Can we awaken? It is possible.

Can we engineer our societies so that few suffer pain and many happiness? Can we control cultural evolution? Can we at least keep ourselves from self-destruction? That, too, is possible.

SUMMARY

1. We must engage in social engineering, given Third World poverty, urban ghettos in the West, ethnic and religious conflict, ecological destruction, and, always, the unthinkable reality of thousands of nuclear weapons awaiting a word to destroy our civilization and perhaps even our species.

2. There are (at least) two levels of problem in social engineering. First, we need to know how to change the behaviour of individuals. This boils down to the question of how to get the appropriate information into the appropriate subsystem of the intra-individual system. Second, we need to know how to change the behaviour of various categories of individuals in such a way that, in interacting with one another over time, they (and the groups they form) will generate the desired social and cultural changes. This second problem will be slighted here, the first one already being sufficiently daunting.

3. We deal best with short-term, local crises: a fire, a predator, a rival, a threat to our own family, clan, or community. Presumably, these are the kinds of problems our ancestors faced, and our limbic system either gives them a high priority or overrides present activity completely. Unfortunately, today's threats to inclusive fitness are neither local nor short-term emergencies and come from such problems as soil depletion, the exhaustion of fisheries, the threat of nuclear war, or the possibility of a health risk from poor nutrition or from a food additive.

4. The problem is not that we are morally weak and foolish, or too stupid to understand our peril. We understand intellectually but fail to react emotionally because these are not the kind of dangers our ancestors faced. They dealt with short-term crises; we face long-term, probabilistic risks. They and their close relations were under immediate threat; we face longer-term threats not just to kin but to continents.

5. Ethnocentric-like behaviour encompasses many 'isms' – nationalism, racism, sectarianism, factionalism, and the various forms of chauvinism. Politicians routinely foment ethnocentrism in order to benefit personally from the resultant in-group solidarity.

6. Thanks to self-deception, I can ignore my own contribution to long-term perils if doing so is in my short-term interest (for instance, I can work for a munitions factory).

7. Bureaucracies are often subverted by the tendency for their segments to become ethnocentric and compete with one another; and for the tendency for rivalry and envy within components to lessen efficiency.

8. Bureaucracies are seldom designed to control these tendencies. As a result, large bureaucracies are notoriously inefficient. In addition, their reward systems seldom reward those who contribute to the formal bureaucratic goals, but do reward those who 'stay out of trouble' or who provide political support to their superiors.

9. The 'discipline of the market-place' combats the natural tendency for corporate bureaucracies to automatically subvert themselves. But for government bureaucracies and for corporate bureaucracies in monopolistic settings, no such corrective external feedback exists, and gross inefficiencies may be tolerated for long periods.

10. The emotion associated with the subgoal of reducing the standing of rivals is known as *envy*. It is possible to argue that envy breeds egalitarianism and even socialism. In egalitarian ideologies and in socialist economies, envious action against those who would appear to claim either higher social or higher economic status than do others is considered legitimate. Since hierarchically ordered societies require encapsulation, and since encapsulation is incompatible with modern society, only egalitarian ideologies are likely to promote social stability in the long run.

11. The success of advertising techniques in taking advantage of the evolved 'gates' to 'input' information into the intra-individual system provides grounds for optimism. Similar techniques can permit behavioural change in the service of the common good. Education, too, can be effective, provided the teacher is perceived as being of high status and attracts hedonic rather than agonistic attention.

12. The existence of voluntary, non-governmental organizations that lobby for public-interest goals (such as, ending war, freeing political prisoners, preserving the environment, or stopping child abuse) suggests that it is possible for some of us, at least, to give some priority to the common good.

13. Self-esteem is essential for happiness. Paradoxically, given the concept's definition, our capacity for cognitive distortion permits each of us to feel superior to others since (a) we are unaware of others' self-ranking and (b) we each use the criteria in terms of which we ourselves do best. Even in a hierarchical society, self-esteem for all is possible, given the possibility of encapsulation.

14. If we assume that severity of child discipline is related to happiness, then it is possible to study happiness cross-culturally by examining child-rearing practices. It is unlikely to be coincidence that hunter-gatherer societies have the least severe socialization practices.

15. Natural selection will not adapt our 'human nature' to modern societies, given the absence of any relevant selection pressures. Deliberate breeding programs to accomplish the same end are probably impossible and would be very ill-advised.

16. Our conscious experience is the tip of the iceberg of our neurophysiological processes. The normal human state is not so very different from sleep-walking. Can we enlarge the scope of self-awareness until it encompasses the entire intra-individual system and our evolved, compartmentalized subsystems share all information with one another? It is possible.

17. Can we engineer our societies so that few suffer pain and many happiness? Can we control cultural evolution? Can we at least keep ourselves from self-destruction? These things are possible.

FOCUS 15.1

TESTABLE HYPOTHESES

Scattered through this book are various testable* hypotheses. This focus brings them together in one place, for the convenience of researchers. No claim is made that these hypotheses form a coherent whole, but their existence at least suggests that the framework developed in these chapters leads readily to empirical research. No doubt many of these hypotheses have occurred to others, and in some cases relevant bodies of literature may already exist. As was pointed out in the preface, the Greeks must have invented sociobiology.

1 (from chapter 3) Selection should favour an infant permitting weaning at an earlier age if the next sibling is likely to share the father than it would if the next sibling is likely to have a different father. Thus, one might predict that a nursing infant exposed regularly to more than one adult male should be more resistant to weaning than one exposed only to a single adult male.

*Some prefer to speak of 'falsifiable' hypotheses, following Karl Popper's reasoning that, since it is in principle impossible to prove a hypothesis true, what we want are hypotheses that may be proved false.

2 (from chapter 3) Occasionally, in Western societies, women's clothing styles feature padded shoulders. One would hypothesize that men should find this style either unattractive or non-attractive, but definitely should not prefer it.

3 (from chapter 4) Language ability is associated with the hippocampus (O'Keefe and Nadel, 1978, 1979; Wallace, 1989). Self-awareness is closely related to cognitive mapping, which is also (it has been argued) associated with the hippocampus. Both self-awareness and deception are intimately tied to cognitive mapping. The possibility arises that the hippocampus is the region of the brain associated with deception and self-deception. If so, then *individuals with lesions in this area should be unable to lie.*

4 (from chapter 6) If youth and physical condition are held constant, then males should prefer the more intelligent, skilled (including socially skilled), resourceful, confident females when choosing partners for long-term relationships.

5 (from chapter 7) Some cultural domains should change more rapidly than others. In particular, domains clearly linked to subgoals/plans – domains such as prestige and status, economics, sexual behaviour, even marital and kinship patterns – should tend to be quite malleable. Code-derived cultural domains, however – language grammar, rituals of etiquette, pottery design, myth – these should be much less labile, except when utilizing one subcode rather than another becomes a tactic in a prestige strategy (for instance, speaking a higher-status language) or during the formation of a new social group. While this hypothesis is in principle empirically verifiable, those who would attempt the verification should be aware of an apples-and-oranges comparison problem: how do we compare rates of change in dialect usage, say, or in cognitive classificatory systems, with rates of change in prestige strategies or subsistence techniques? Obviously, some equivalencies will first have to be established.

6 (from chapter 7) Subplans capable of serving more than one goal should be preferred to subplans limited to serving only one goal. A subplan that yields both income and prestige, for example, should be preferred over a subplan yielding either alone. (This hypothesis may seem too obvious for testing but it does follow from the theory presented.)

7 (from chapter 7) It is possible to distinguish between obligate and facultative norms. Some norms seem to be obligatory – their violation results in a feeling of physical revulsion, even if the transgression is unknown to others. Other norms are facultative – we follow them or fail to follow them more or less opportunistically, depending upon our assessment of the consequences. Facultative norms are the type discussed in chapter 3 in connection with 'deception.' We may manipulate or violate them, at times, when our self-interest so dictates, but we nevertheless uphold them for others. Obligate norms are not manipulable. They are identifi-

able readily because the thought of their violation carries with it a physical revulsion. (The research needed here is an empirical demonstration that it is indeed possible to classify norms in this manner.)

8 (from chapter 8) Adults should tend to rank their own social-identity/skill areas as higher in relative standing than others would rank them.

9 (from chapter 8) In few or no societies are men or women who combine lack of productivity with lack of control of existing resources respected. (Note that the warrior or soldier is an exception here, because prestige criteria related to agonism rather than to production are dominant.)

10 (from chapter 8) Individuals who tend to rank low in dominance (as a human ethologist would measure it) should compensate by seeking to be competitive in an ability sphere. (This prediction fits the stereotype of the socially maladroit child becoming the expert computer 'hacker' or artist or writer.)

11 (from chapter 8; related to the above item) The general level of self-esteem with which the adult will be comfortable may be 'set' by social rank in childhood or early adolescence. Former high-ranking individuals may later use their self-esteem for people-type, personnel skills, utilizing the high self-esteem presumably generated by their past rank to convey to others non-verbally that they are indeed alpha. These may be the individuals who become our politicians, the 'big men' of both large- and small-scale societies, the individuals with 'charisma.'

12 (from chapter 8) In any given society, self-esteem should correlate with sexual access to high-self-esteem partners (and would presumably have correlated, back in the Pleistocene and possibly in extant hunting-gathering societies today, with high reproductive success).

13 (from chapter 8) Given the work of Raleigh et al. on serotonin and status, are the neurophysiological bases of 'self-confidence' and 'self-esteem' influenced not only by current events but also by knowledge of one's family standing? Is social-class transmission more than a simple matter of 'learning'?

14 (from chapter 11) Residence pattern should be at least as good a predictor of cousin asymmetry as is genetic relatedness. Moreover, co-residence should predict *which* set of parallel cousins will be classified as siblings. Where matrilateral kin tend to co-reside, matrilateral parallel cousins should be classified as siblings and marriage between them be forbidden. Where patrilateral parallel cousins tend to co-reside, patrilateral parallel cousins should be classified as siblings and marriage between them be forbidden. (A cross-cultural survey or 'holocultural' study would be needed to test this hypothesis. Murdock [1967] provides information about marriage rules and cousins but does not differentiate between matrilateral and patrilateral parallel cousins. Only this one variable need be added to the existing data on the world culture's study sample to test this hypothesis. The

most efficient way to undertake such a study would be to utilize the data base of the *World Cultures Electronic Journal* which provides in electronic form the sample, bibliography, and coded data.)

15 (from chapter 11, supplementary to the above hypothesis) Historically, residence pattern should tend to change first and kinship behaviour and terminology only later.

16 (from chapter 11) Human males may monitor the sexual activities of their wives and automatically calculate their paternity confidence. When their confidence of paternity falls, they should become increasingly interested in their sisters' children. (The challenge in testing this hypothesis is developing an ethically acceptable and valid measure of a husband's perception of the fidelity of his spouse. The other variable, interest in sisters' children, could be operationalized in terms of frequency of contacts, exchange of gifts, and so on.)

17 (from chapter 11, Focus 11.1) Societies with a higher proportion of older people will show more in-group co-operation than will other societies. Also, societies that accord higher status to the aged should demonstrate more in-group co-operation. (The difficulty here will be in operationalizing 'in-group co-operation.' One way to go about it would be to rate the severity of sanctions against lack of in-group co-operation, (such as punishment for homicide, adultery, theft) within the unit of co-operation. It might also be that the higher the status of older people, the more powerful their influence for co-operativeness. Thus, the relative status and power of older people should be rated, as well, and used both as a control variable and as a separate independent variable.)

18 (from chapter 12) The fertility decline of the post-demographic transition is a product of the growth of female control over own fertility in modernizing societies. The greater the extent of personal control over own fertility (as opposed to control by older women, husbands, or any others) both within and across societies, the lower that fertility should be.

19 (from chapter 12, Focus 12.1) Colostrum-denial should be associated with high rates of infant mortality.

20 (from chapter 13) The reproductive strategy of boys from low-father-involvement families and societies should involve seeking not a long-term bond with a single female but competition with other males for sexual access to as many females as possible. Since such competition is both verbal and physical, low-father-involvement boys should tend to be more verbal and more aggressive than boys from high-father-involvement families or societies. In physique, they should tend to be more powerfully built than other boys.

21 (from chapter 13) Low-father-involvement girls should demonstrate early sexuality so as to maximize fertility in compensation for the lack of male parental investment. They should reach menarche sooner and be sexually active at an

earlier age and less sexually selective than girls from high-father-involvement families.

22 (from chapter 13) Boys from high-father-involvement families or societies should favour not verbal or physically violent competition but skills relevant to subsistence activities. Thus, spatial and quantitative abilities should be emphasized developmentally. At the same time, the male will be prepared to form enduring partnerships with females, rather than seeking a series of brief encounters.

23 (from chapter 14) Sperm competition would have been strongest in populations marked by females with multiple mates. Penis length and testes size are products of sperm competition. Therefore, in those human populations that have had a history of fairly frequent communal mating (for example, the Melanesian group described by Serpenti [1984]), penis length and testes size should be greater than for populations with no history of communal mating, assuming that the populations in question are relative genetic isolates.

24 (from chapter 14) The same prediction may be made of populations with low levels of paternity certainty relative to those with higher levels. Males from low-paternity-certainty societies should have longer penises and larger testes than do males from high-paternity-certainty societies (again, assuming that the low-paternity societies are relative genetic isolates).

25 (from chapter 14) Smith (1984) interprets the hymen as the result of males selecting females for virginity, in an effort to avoid sperm competition and enjoy high paternity confidence. Smith's interpretation of the hymen would be strengthened by a cross-cultural survey that supported the hypothesis that, in most of the world's peoples, the presence of a hymen at marriage is valued.

26 (from chapter 14) Smith's interpretation of the female orgasm having resulted from selection for female control of whose sperm reaches the ovum first rests on a number of testable assumptions that merit conversion to hypotheses. If Smith is to strengthen his case, he requires undisputed evidence (1) that women are more likely to experience orgasm with preferred partners; (2) that the 'uterine suction' does help move the semen along; and (3) that female orgasms and therefore any resulting suction usually occur either together with or following male ejaculation, since prior suction would otherwise have no effect on the partner's semen. Smith also seems to assume (4) that the uterine suction is somehow selective, so that it benefits the new sperm but not that likely (according to Smith) to be already present in the vagina, sperm presumably deposited by a non-preferred male.

27 (from chapter 14) Selection will favour strong male sexual jealousy being evoked by female copulation with a rival; but it will favour strong female sexual jealousy not primarily over copulation but over male actual or potential investment in a rival (and in the rival's offspring).

28 (from chapter 14) Dickemann (1981) is making an implicit assumption about

an evolved psychological mechanism: the more parental investment a male provides or intends to provide, the more he will attempt to guard his paternity certainty. Dickemann is in effect testing this hypothesis using social classes and societies; but it requires testing using individuals and families as the units of analysis.

29 (from chapter 15) Males should experience lower sexual jealousy in a relationship with a high-status female than in a relationship with a low-status female, all other factors being equal.

30 (from chapter 15) Let us assume that the severity of child-training may be taken as an indicator of general unhappiness in human populations. This assumption permits the testing of the following hypotheses: (1) hunter-gatherers should be the happiest of peoples, since they presumably live in a manner closer to that in which we evolved than do others, and since the tasks they must learn are (by no coincidence) similar to the ordinary play of children; (2) but cultivators, particularly peasantries, should be the least happy, for the routine, arduous labour and lack of autonomy seem furthest from the hunting-gathering life of our ancestors; (3) while pastoral nomads and members of modern industrial societies should be somewhere between. Note that there is already a substantial body of literature dealing with the cross-cultural study of child-training practices (cited in the text). However, these studies tend to utilize a very global, independent-variable, subsistence economy. What is needed is more micro-analysis of precisely what about the various ways of life affects the severity of child-training.

References

Aberle, D.F. 1966. *The Peyote Religion among the Navaho.* Viking Fund Publications in Anthropology no. 42. New York: Wenner-Gren Foundation for Anthropological Research

Alexander, R.D. 1971. The search for an evolutionary philosophy of man. *Proceedings of the Royal Society of Victoria, Melbourne* 84: 99–120
– 1974. The evolution of social behavior. *Annual Review of Systematics* 5: 325–83
– 1975. The search for a general theory of behavior. *Behavioral Science* 20: 77–100
– 1977. Natural selection and the analysis of human sociality. In *Changing Scenes in the Natural Sciences: 1776–1976,* C.E. Goulden, ed., pp. 283–337. Bicentennial Symposium Monograph, Philadelphia Academy of the Natural Sciences, Special Publication 12
– 1979. *Darwinism and Human Affairs.* Seattle: University of Washington Press
– 1987. *The Biology of Moral Systems.* New York: Aldine de Gruyter

Alexander, R.D., and G. Borgia. 1979. On the origin and basis of the male-female phenomenon. In *Sexual Selection and Reproductive Competition in Insects,* M.S. Blum and N.A. Blum, eds, pp. 19–80. New York: Academic Press

Alexander, R., and K.M. Noonan. 1979. Concealment of ovulation, parental care, and human social evolution. In *Evolutionary Biology and Human Social Behavior: An Anthropological Perspective,* N.A. Chagnon and W. Irons, eds. North Scituate, MA: Duxbury

Alland, A., Jr. 1980. *To Be Human. An Introduction to Anthropology.* New York: John Wiley

Anderson, J.L. 1988. Comment. Breasts, hips and buttocks revisited. Honest fatness for honest fitness. *Ethology and Sociobiology* 8: 319–24

Anderson, J.R. 1983. *The Architecture of Cognition*. Cambridge, MA: Harvard University Press

Anderson, M. 1986. Cultural concatenation of deceit and secrecy. In *Deception: Perspectives on Human and Nonhuman Deceit*, R.W. Mitchell and N.S. Thompson, eds, pp. 323–48. Albany: State University of New York Press

Arnold, S.J. 1983. Sexual selection: The interface of theory and empiricism. In *Mate Choice*, P. Bateson, ed., pp. 67–107. New York: Cambridge University Press

Averill, J. 1982. *Anger and Aggression: An Essay on Emotion*. New York: Springer-Verlag

Avise, J.C., J.E. Neigel, and J. Arnold. 1984. Demographic influences on mitochondrial DNA lineage survivorship in animal populations. *Journal of Molecular Evolution* 20: 99–105

Axelrod, R., and W.D. Hamilton. 1981. The evolution of cooperation. *Science* 211: 1390–6

Axelrod, R., and D. Dion. 1988. The further evolution of cooperation. *Science* 242: 1385–90

Baars, B.J. 1983. Conscious contents provide the nervous system with coherent, global information. In *Consciousness and Self-Regulation. Advances in Research and Theory*, vol. 3, R.J. Davidson, G.E. Schwartz, and D. Shapiro, eds. New York and London: Plenum

Ball, J.A. 1984. Memes as replicators. *Ethology and Sociobiology* 5: 145–61

Ballard, D.H. 1986. Cortical connections and parallel processing: Structure and function. *Behavioral and Brain Sciences* 9: 67–165

Bandura, A. 1977. *Social Learning Theory*. Englewood Cliffs, NJ: Prentice-Hall

Bandura, A., and R. Walters. 1963. *Social Learning and Personality Development*. New York: Holt, Rinehart & Winston

Barash, D.P. 1982. *Sociobiology and Behavior*. 2nd ed. New York: Elsevier

Barkow, J.H. 1967. Causal interpretation of correlation in cross-cultural studies. *American Anthropologist* 69: 506–10

- 1971. The institution of courtesanship in the northern states of Nigeria. *Geneva-Africa* 10: 58–73

- 1972. Hausa women and Islam. *Canadian Journal of African Studies* 6: 317–28

- 1973. Darwinian psychological anthropology: A biosocial approach. *Current Anthropology* 14: 373–88

- 1975a. Prestige and culture: A biosocial approach. *Current Anthropology* 16: 553–72

- 1975b. Strategies for self-esteem and prestige in Maradi, Niger Republic. In *Psychological Anthropology*, T.R. Williams, ed., pp. 373–88. The Hague and Paris: Mouton Publishers

399 References

- 1976a. Attention structure and the evolution of human psychological characteristics. In *The Social Structure of Attention*, M.R.A. Chance and R.R. Larsen, eds, pp. 203–20. London and New York: Wiley
- 1976b. The generation of an incipient ethnic split: A Hausa case. *Anthropos* 71: 857–67
- 1977a. Conformity to ethos and reproductive success in two Hausa communities: An empirical evaluation. *Ethos* 5: 409–25
- 1977b. Human ethology and intra-individual systems. *Social Science Information* 16: 133–45
- 1978a. Social norms, the self, and sociobiology: Building on the ideas of A.I. Hallowell. *Current Anthropology* 19: 99–118
- 1978b. The Hausa. In *Muslim Peoples: World Ethnographic Survey*, R. Weekes, ed., pp. 151–63. Westport, CT: Green-Wood Press
- 1978c. Culture and sociobiology. *American Anthropologist* 80: 5–20
- 1980a. Sociobiology: Is this the new theory of human nature? In *Sociobiology Examined*, A. Montagu, ed., pp. 171–92. New York and London: Oxford University Press
- 1980b. Biological evolution of culturally patterned behavior. In *The Evolution of Human Social Behavior*, J. Lockard, ed., pp. 227–96. New York: Elsevier
- 1980c. Prestige and self-esteem: A biosocial interpretation. In *Dominance Relations: An Ethological View of Human Conflict and Social Interaction*, D.R. Omark, F.F. Strayer, and D.G. Freedman, eds, pp. 319–32. New York: Garland
- 1981. Evolution et sexualité humaine. In *Sexologie contemporaine*, C. Crépault, J. Lévy, and H. Gratton, eds, pp. 103–18. Quebec: Les Presses de l'Université du Québec
- 1982. Return to nepotism: The collapse of a Nigerian gerontocracy. *International Journal of Political Science Review* 3: 33–49
- 1983. Begged questions in behavior and evolution. In *Animal Models of Human Behavior*, G. Davey, ed., pp. 205–22. Chichester and New York: John Wiley
- 1984. The distance between genes and culture. *Journal of Anthropological Research* 37: 367–79
- 1989a. The elastic between genes and culture. *Ethology and Sociobiology* 10: 111–29
- 1989b. Overview. *Ethology and Sociobiology* 10: 1–10

Barkow, J.H., and N. Burley. 1980. Human fertility, evolutionary biology, and the demographic transition. *Ethology and Sociobiology* 1: 163–80

Barkow, J.H., L. Cosmides, and J. Tooby, eds. In preparation. *The Adapted*

Mind: Evolutionary Psychology and the Generation of Culture. New York: Oxford University Press.

Barry, H., III, M.K. Bacon, and I.L. Child. 1959. Relation of child training to subsistence economy. *American Anthropologist* 61: 51–63

Barry, H. III, and A. Schlegel. 1984. Measurements of adolescent sexual behavior in the standard sample of societies. *Ethnology* 23: 315–29

Barth, F. 1969. *Ethnic Groups and Boundaries*. Boston: Little, Brown

Bastock, M., D. Morris, and M. Moynihan. 1953. Some comments on conflict and thwarting in animals. *Behaviour* 6: 66–84

Benshoof, L., and R. Thornhill. 1979. The evolution of monogamy and concealed ovulation. *Journal Social Biological Structure* 2: 95–106

Berenstain, L., and T.D. Wade. 1983. Intrasexual selection and male mating strategies in baboons and macaques. *International Journal of Primatology* 4: 201–35

Berland, J.C. 1982. *No Five Fingers Are Alike. Cognitive Amplifiers in Social Context*. Cambridge, MA: Harvard University Press

Berlin, B., and P. Kay. 1969. *Basic Color Terms: Their Universality and Evolution*. Berkeley: University of California Press

Bernstein, I.S. 1981. Dominance: The baby and the bathwater. *Behavior and Brain Sciences* 3: 419–58

Berry, J.W. 1976. *Human Ecology and Cognitive Style*. New York: Wiley

Betzig, L.L. 1986. *Despotism and Differential Reproduction. A Darwinian View of History*. New York: Aldine

Bigelow, R.S. 1969. *The Dawn Warriors: Man's Evolution toward Peace*. Boston, MA: Little, Brown

– 1973. The evolution of cooperation, aggression, and self-control. In *Nebraska Symposium on Motivation 1972*, J.K. Cole and D.D. Jensen, eds. Lincoln: University of Nebraska Press

Birdsall, J.B. 1968. Some predictions for the Pleistocene based on equilibrium systems among recent hunter-gatherers. In *Man the Hunter*, R.B. Lee and I. DeVore, eds, pp. 229–40. Chicago: Aldine-Atherton

Bischof, N. 1975. Comparative ethology of incest avoidance. In *Biosocial Anthropology*, R. Fox, ed. New York: Wiley and Sons

Blain, J., and J.H. Barkow. 1988. Father-involvement, reproductive strategies, and the sensitive period. In *Sociobiology and Human Development*, K.B. MacDonald, ed., pp. 373–96. New York: Garland

Blakemore, C. 1976. *Mechanics of the Mind*. Cambridge: Cambridge University Press

Blanguernon, C. 1955. *Le Hoggar*. Grenoble: Arthaud.

Blurton Jones, N.G. 1982. Origins, functions, development, and motivation:

Unity and disunity in the study of behavior. *Journal of Anthropological Research* 38: 333–49

Bock, P.K. 1980. *Continuities in Psychological Anthropology: A Historical Introduction*. San Francisco: W.H. Freeman

Boddy, J. 1985. Saudi Islam, Egyptian dramas, and northern Sudanese women. Unpublished paper presented at the 1985 Annual Meeting of the American Anthropological Association, Washington, DC

Bolles, R.C. 1975. *Theory of Motivation*. 2nd ed. New York: Harper & Row

Bond, C.E., K.N. Kahler, and L.M. Paolicelli. 1985. The miscommunication of deception: An adaptive perspective. *Journal of Experimental and Social Psychology* 21: 341

Bonner, J.T. 1980. *The Evolution of Culture in Animals*. Princeton, NJ: Princeton University Press

Borgerhoff Mulder, M. 1987. Adaptation and evolutionary approaches to anthropology. *Man* 22: 25–41

Borgia, G. 1979. Sexual selection and the evolution of mating systems. In *Sexual Selection and Reproductive Competition in Insects*, M.S. Blum and N.A. Blum, eds, pp. 19–80. New York: Academic Press

Bowlby, J.A. 1969. *Attachment and Loss. Vol. I: Attachment*. New York: Basic Books

Boyd, R. 1988. Is the repeated prisoner's dilemma a good model of reciprocal altruism? *Ethology and Sociobiology* 9: 211–22

Boyd, R., and P.J. Richerson. 1985. *Culture and the Evolutionary Process*. Chicago: University of Chicago Press

Brace, C.L. 1979. Biological parameters and Pleistocene hominid life-ways. In *Primate Ecology and Human Origins: Ecological Influences on Social Organization*, I.S. Bernstein and E.O. Smith, eds, pp. 263–89. New York: Garland

Brandon, R.N., and R.M. Burian, eds, 1984. *Genes, Organisms, Populations. Controversies over the Units of Selection*. Boston: Bradford/MIT Press

Breden, F., and M.J. Wade. 1981. Inbreeding and evolution by kin selection. *Ethology and Sociobiology* 2: 3–16

Briggs, G.W. 1920. *The Chamars*. London, New York, Calcutta: Association Press, Oxford University Press

Brothwell, D., and P. Brothwell. 1969. *Food in Antiquity. A Survey of the Diet of Early Peoples*. London: Thames and Hudson

Brown, R. 1973. *A First Language: The Early Stages*. Cambridge, MA: Harvard University Press

Brown, R., and R.J. Herrnstein. 1975. *Psychology*. Boston: Little, Brown & Co.

Brown, W.M. 1980. Polymorphism in mitochondrial DNA of humans as revealed by restriction endonuclease analysis. *Proceedings of the National Academy of Sciences (USA)* 77: 3605–9

Brownmiller, S. 1975. *Against Our Will: Men, Women, and Rape.* New York: Simon and Shuster

Brownmiller, S. 1975. *Against Our Will: Men, Women, and Rape.* New York: Simon and Shuster

Buckley, W. 1967. *Sociology and Modern Systems Theory.* Englewood Cliffs, NJ: Prentice-Hall

Burd, M. 1986. Sexual selection and human evolution: All or none adaptation? *American Anthropologist* 88: 167–72

Burley, N. 1977. Parental investment, mate choice, and mate quality. *Proceedings of the National Academy of Sciences* 74: 3476–9

– 1979. The evolution of concealed ovulation. *American Naturalist* 114: 835–8

Buss, D., and L.A. Dedden. Derogation of competitors. Manuscript submitted for publication.

Campbell, B.G. 1985. *Humankind Emerging.* 4th ed. Boston and Toronto: Little, Brown

Campbell, D.T. 1960. Blind variation and selective retention in creative thought as in other knowledge processes. *Psychological Review* 67: 380–400

– 1965. Variation and selective retention in sociocultural evolution. In *Social Change in Underdeveloped Areas: A Reinterpretation of Evolutionary Theory,* R.W. Mack, G.I. Blanksten, and H.R. Barringer, eds. Cambridge, MA: Schenkman

– 1969. Ethnocentrism of disciplines and the fish-scale model of omniscience. In *Interdisciplinary Relationships in the Social Sciences,* M. Sherif and C.W. Sherif, eds, pp. 328–48. Chicago: Aldine

– 1975. On the conflicts between biological and social evolution and between psychology and moral tradition. *American Psychologist* 30: 1103–26

– 1982. Legal and primary-group social controls. *Journal of Social and Biological Structures* 5: 431–8

Cann, R.L., M. Stoneking, and A.C. Wilson. 1987. Mitochondrial DNA and human evolution. *Nature* 325: 31–6

Cant, J. 1981. Hypothesis for the evolution of human breasts and buttocks. *American Naturalist* 117: 199–204

Caro, T.M., and P. Bateson. 1986. Organization and ontogeny of alternative tactics. *Animal Behavior* 34: 1483–99

Caro, T.M., and M. Borgerhoff Mulder. 1987. The problem of adaptation in the study of human behavior. *Ethology and Sociobiology* 8: 61–72

Case, R. 1985. *Intellectual Development. Birth to Adulthood.* Orlando, FL: Academic Press

Chagnon, N.A. 1974. *Studying the Yanomamö.* New York: Holt, Rinehart and Winston

– 1983. *Yanomamö: The Fierce People.* New York: Holt, Rinehart and Winston

– 1988. Life histories, blood revenge, and warfare in a tribal population. *Science* 239: 985–92

Chagnon, N.A., and W. Irons, eds. 1979. *Evolutionary Biology and Human Social Behavior: An Anthropological Perspective.* North Scituate, MA: Duxbury

Chance, M.R.A. 1967. Attention structure as the basis of primate rank order. *Man* 2: 503–18

Chance, M., and C. Jolly. 1970. *Social Groups of Monkeys, Apes and Men.* New York: E.P. Dutton

Chandra, R.K. 1978. Immunological aspects of human milk. *Nutrition Reviews* 36: 265–72

Changeux, J. 1985. *Neuronal Man: The Biology of Mind.* New York: Pantheon

Charlesworth, D., and B. Charlesworth. 1987. Inbreeding depression and its evolutionary consequences. *Annual Review of Ecology and Systematics* 18: 237–68

Cheney, D.L. 1983. Extra-familial alliances among vervet monkeys. In *Primate Social Relationships: An Integrated Approach*, R.A. Hinde, ed., pp. 278–86. Sunderland, MA: Sinauer Associates

Cheney, D.L., T. Seyfarth, and B. Smuts. 1986. Social relationships and social cognition in nonhuman primates. *Science* 234: 1361–6

Chomsky, N. 1972. *Language and Mind.* New York: Harcourt, Brace, Jovanovich

– 1980. *Rules and Representations.* New York: Columbia University Press

Churchland, P.M. 1979. *Scientific Realism and the Plasticity of Mind.* Cambridge: Cambridge University Press

Churchland, P.S. 1986. *Towards a Unified Science of the Mind-Brain.* Cambridge, MA: Bradford/MIT Press

Cloak, F.T. 1975. Is a cultural ethology possible? *Human Ecology* 3: 161–82

Cockburn, T.A. 1971. Infectious diseases in ancient populations. *Current Anthropology* 12: 45–62

Corning, P.A., 1983. *The Synergism Hypothesis: A Theory of Progressive Evolution.* New York: McGraw-Hill

Cosmides, L., and J. Tooby. 1987. From evolution to behavior: evolutionary psychology as the missing link. In *The Latest on the Best: Essays on Evolution and Optimality*, J. Dupré, ed., pp. 277–306. Cambridge, MA: The MIT Press

– 1989. Evolutionary psychology and the generation of culture, II. Case study: A computational theory of social exchange. *Ethology and Sociobiology* 10: 51–97

Craik, B. 1975. The formation of a goose hunting strategy and the politics of the hunting group. In *Proceedings of the Second Congress, Canadian Ethnology Society*, J. Freedman and J.H. Barkow, eds, pp. 450–65. National Museum of Man Mercury Series. Canadian Ethnology Service Paper no. 28. Ottawa: National Museums of Canada

Crawford, M.H., and V.B. Encisco. 1982. Population structure of circumpolar groups of Siberia, Alaska, Canada and Greenland. In *Current Developments in Anthropological Genetics*, M.H. Crawford and J.H. Mielke, eds. New York: Plenum

Crawford, C., and Galdikas, B.M.F. 1986. Rape in nonhuman animals: An evolutionary perspective. *Canadian Psychology* 27: 215–30

Crook, J.H. 1980. *The Evolution of Consciousness*. Oxford: Clarendon Press

Dahlberg, F., ed. 1981. *Woman the Gatherer*. New Haven: Yale University Press

Daly, M. 1982. Some caveats about cultural transmission models. *Human Ecology* 10: 401–8

Daly, M., and M.I. Wilson. 1978. *Sex, Evolution and Behavior*. North Scituate, MA: Duxbury

– 1981. Abuse and neglect of children in evolutionary perspective. In *Natural Selection and Social Behavior*, R.D. Alexander and D.T. Tinkler, eds, pp. 405–16. New York and Concord: Chiron Press

– 1985. Child abuse and other risks of not living with both parents. *Ethology and Sociobiology* 6: 197–210

– *Homicide*. New York: Aldine de Gruyter

– 1989. Homicide and cultural evolution. *Ethology and Sociobiology* 10: 99–110

Daly, M., M.I. Wilson, and S.J. Weghorst. 1982. Male sexual jealousy. *Ethology and Sociobiology* 3: 11–27

D'Aquili, E. 1972. *The Biopsychological Determinants of Culture*. Reading, MA: Addison-Wesley Modular Publications

Dareer, A. El-. 1982. *Woman, Why Do You Weep?* London: Zed Press

Darwin, C. 1871. *The Descent of Man, and Selection in Relation to Sex*. 2nd ed., Revised and Augmented. New York: Appleton & Co. (1930)

– 1872. *The Expression of the Emotions in Man and Animals*. London: John Murray. Reprinted Chicago: University of Chicago Press 1965

Dawkins, R. 1976. *The Selfish Gene*. Oxford: Oxford University Press

– 1982. *The Extended Phenotype: The Gene as the Unit of Selection*. Oxford and San Francisco: W.H. Freeman

Dennett, D.C. 1983. Intentional systems in cognitive ethology: the 'panglossian paradigm' defended. *Behavioral and Brain Sciences* 6: 343–90

De Vos, G.A. 1968. Achievement and innovation in culture and personality. In *The Study of Personality*, E. Norbeck, D. Price-Williams, and W.M. McCord, eds. New York: Holt, Rinehart and Winston

de Waal, F. 1982. *Chimpanzee Politics*. New York: Harper & Row

Dickemann, M. 1981. Paternal confidence and dowry competition: A biocultural analysis of purdah. In *Natural Selection and Social Behavior: Recent Research and New Theory*, R.D. Alexander and D.W. Tinkle, eds, pp. 417–38. New York: Chiron Press

Divale, W.T., and M. Harris. 1976. Population, warfare, and the male supremacist complex. *American Anthropologist* 78: 521–38

Dobzhansky, T. 1963. Cultural direction of human evolution. *Human Biology* 35: 311–16

Douglas, M. 1966. *Purity and Danger*. New York: Frederick A. Praeger

Draper, P. 1989. African marriage systems: Perspectives from evolutionary ecology. *Ethology and Sociobiology* 10: 145–69

Draper, P., and H. Harpending. 1982. Father absence and reproductive strategy: An evolutionary perspective. *Journal of Anthropological Research* 38: 255–73

Durham, W.H. 1982. Interactions of genetic and cultural evolution: Models and examples. *Human Ecology* 10: 289–323

Ehrlich, P. 1974. *The End of Affluence*. New York: Ballantine

Ehrlich, P., and R.L. Harriman. 1971. *How to Be a Survivor. A Plan to Save Spaceship Earth*. New York: Ballantine

Eibl-Eibesfeldt, I. 1972. *Love and Hate. The Natural History of Behavior Patterns*. New York: Holt, Rinehart and Winston

– 1975. *Ethology: The Biology of Behavior*. 2nd ed. New York: Holt, Rinehart and Winston

– 1982. Warfare, man's indoctrinability and group selection. *Zeitschrift für Tierpsychologie* 60: 177–98

Erikson, E.H. 1943. *Observations on the Yurok: Childhood and World Image*, Berkeley: University of California Press

– 1959. Identity and the life cycle. *Psychological Issues* 1: 1–171

Etkin, W. 1954. Social behavior and the evolution of man's mental faculties. *American Naturalist* 88: 129–42

– 1963. Social behavioral factors in the emergence of man. *Human Biology* 25: 299–310

– 1964. Co-operation and competition in social behavior. In *Social Behavior and Organization among Vertebrates*, W. Etkin, ed., pp. 1–34. Chicago: University of Chicago Press

Fagan, B.M. 1985. *People of the Earth. An Introduction to World Prehistory*. 5th ed. Boston and Toronto: Little, Brown

Fedigan, L.M., 1983. Dominance and reproductive success. *Yearbook of Physical Anthropology* 26: 91–129

Fisher, R.A. 1930. *The Genetic Theory of Natural Selection*. Oxford: Clarendon Press

Flannery, K.V. 1968. Archaeological systems theory and early Mesoamerica. In *Anthropological Archaeology in the Americas*, B. Meggers, ed., pp. 67–87. Washington, DC: Anthropological Society of Washington

Flannery, R. 1953. *The Gros Ventres of Montana: Part 1, Social Life*. Washington, DC: Catholic University of America

Flinn, M.V., and R. Alexander. 1982. Culture theory: The developing synthesis from biology. *Human Ecology* 10: 383–400

Fodor, J.A. 1980. Reply to Putnam. In *Language and Learning*, M. Piatelli-Palmarini, ed., pp. 325–34. Cambridge, MA: Harvard University Press

– 1983. *The Modularity of Mind*. Boston: MIT Press

– 1985. Multiple book review of *The Modularity of Mind* in *Behavioral and Brain Sciences* 8: 1–42

Foster, G.M. 1972. The anatomy of envy: A study in symbolic behavior. *Current Anthropology* 13: 165–201

Foster, M. LeCron. 1980. The growth of symbolism in culture. In *Symbol as Sense*, M. LeCron Foster and S.H. Brandes, eds. New York: Academic Press

Fox, R. 1972. Alliance and constraint: Sexual selection in the evolution of human kinship systems. In *Sexual Selection and Human Evolution*, B.G. Campbell, ed., pp. 282–331. Chicago: Aldine

Freedman, D.G. 1979. *Human Sociobiology: A Holistic Approach*. New York: The Free Press

Frese, M., and J. Sabini, eds. 1985. *Goal Directed Behavior: The Concept of Action in Psychology*. Hillsdale, NJ: Lawrence Erlbaum Associates

Freud, A. 1946. *The Ego and Mechanisms of Defense*. New York: International University Press

Freud, S. 1950. *Totem and Taboo*. Trans. by James Strachey. London: Routledge & Kegan Paul

– 1961. *Civilization and Its Discontents*. Trans. and ed. by James Strachey. New York: W.W. Norton & Co

Gajdusek, D.C. 1977. Unconventional viruses and the origin and disappearance of kuru. *Science* 197: 943–60

Gallup, G.G., Jr. 1975. Toward an operational definition of self-awareness. In *Socioecology and Psychology of Primates*, R.H. Tuttle, ed. The Hague: Mouton

– 1979. Self-awareness in primates. *American Scientist* 4: 307–16

– 1986. Unique features of human sexuality in the context of evolution. In *Alternative Appproaches to the Study of Sexual Behavior*, D. Byrne and K. Kelley, eds, pp. 13–42. Hillsdale, NJ: Erlbaum

Gazzaniga, M.S. 1985. *The Social Brain*. New York: Basic Books

Geertz, C. 1962. The growth of culture and the evolution of mind. In *Theories of Mind*, J.M. Scher, ed. Glencoe, IL: Free Press

– 1973. *The Interpretation of Cultures. Selected Essays*. New York: Basic Books

Geschwind, N. 1965. Disconnexion syndromes in animals and man. *Brain* 88: 237–94, 585–644

Gideon, H. 1962. A baby is born in the Punjab. *American Anthropologist* 64: 1220–34

Giglioni, P.P. 1972. *Language and Social Context*. London: Nichols

Glacken, C. 1953. *Studies of Okinawan Village Life*. Washington, DC: Pacific Science Board, National Research Council

Gluckman, M. 1963. Gossip and scandal. *Current Anthropology* 4: 307–16

Goffman, E. 1959. *The Presentation of Self in Everyday Life*. Garden City, NY: Doubleday/Anchor

– 1967. The nature of deference and demeanor. In *Interaction Ritual*. New York: Anchor Books

Goldsmith, E., et al. 1972. *Blueprint for Survival*. Boston: Houghton Mifflin

Goodall, J. 1986. *The Chimpanzees of Gombe*. Cambridge, MA: Belknap Press/Harvard University Press

Goodenough, W.H. 1970. *Description and Comparison in Cultural Anthropology*. Chicago: Aldine

Gould, S.J. 1980. Sociobiology and human nature: A postpanglossian vision. In *Sociobiology Examined*, A. Montagu, ed., pp. 283–90. New York and London: Oxford University Press

Gould, S.J., and N. Eldredge. 1977. Punctuated equilibria: The tempo and mode of evolution reconsidered. *Paleobiology* 3: 115–51

Gould, S.J., and R.C. Lewontin. 1979. The spandrels of San Marco and the panglossian paradigm: A critique of the adaptationist programme. *Proceedings of the Royal Society, London* 205: 581–98

Granit, R. 1977. *The Purposive Brain*. Cambridge, MA: MIT Press

Grassivaro Gallo, P. 1986. Views of future health care workers in Somalia on female circumcision. *Medical Anthropology Quarterly* 17: 71–3

Gray, J.P. 1985. *Primate Sociobiology*. New Haven, CT: HRAF Press

Griffin, D.R. 1976. *The Question of Animal Awareness: Evolutionary Continuity of Mental Experience*. New York: Rockefeller University Press

– 1978. Prospects for a cognitive ethology. *Behavioral and Brain Sciences* 1: 527–38

Grivetti, L.E. 1979. Culture, diet, and nutrition. *BioScience* 28: 171–7

Gur, C.R., and H.A. Sackheim. 1979. Self-deception: A concept in search of a phenomenon. *Journal of Personality and Social Psychology* 37: 147–69

Gutierrez de Pineda, V. 1950. *Organización Social en La Guajira*. Bogota

Gutmann, D. 1969. The country of old men: Cross-cultural studies in the psychology of later life. In *Occasional Papers in Gerontology*, W. Donahue, ed. Ann Arbor: Institute of Gerontology, University of Michigan

– 1987. *Reclaimed Powers: Toward a New Psychology of Men and Women in Later Life*. New York: Basic

Haggard, H.W., 1929. *Devils, Drugs, and Doctors. The Story of Healing from Medicine-Man to Doctor*. New York: Blue Ribbon Books

408 References

Haldane, J.B.S. 1955. Population genetics. *New Biology* 18: 34–51

Hall, C.S., and G. Lindzey. 1970. *Theories of Personality*. 2nd ed. New York: Wiley

Hallowell, A.I. 1955. *Culture and Experience*. Philadelphia: University of Pennsylvania Press

– 1959. Behavioral evolution and the emergence of the self. In *Evolution and Anthropology: A Centennial Appraisal*, B.J. Meggers, ed. Washington, DC: Anthropological Society of Washington

– 1960. Self, society and culture in phylogenetic perspective. In *Evolution after Darwin*, vol. 2, *The Evolution of Man*, Sol Tax, ed., pp. 309–71. Chicago: University of Chicago Press

– 1961. The protocultural foundations of human adaptation. In *Social Life of Early Man*, S.L. Washburn, ed., pp. 429–509. New York: Viking Fund Publications

– 1965. Hominid evolution, cultural adaptation and mental dysfunctioning. In *CIBA Foundation Symposium on Transcultural Psychiatry*, A.V.S. de Reuck and R. Porter, eds, pp. 26–54. London: Churchill

Hallpike, C.R. 1977. *Bloodshed and Vengeance in the Papuan Mountains*. Oxford: Clarendon Press

Hamilton, W.D. 1964. The evolution of social behavior. *Journal of Theoretical Biology* 7: 1–52

– 1970. Selfish and spiteful behavior in an evolutionary model. *Nature* 228: 1218–20

– 1975. Innate social aptitudes of man: An approach from evolutionary genetics. In *Biosocial Anthropology*, R. Fox, ed., pp. 133–55. New York: Wiley

Hampshire, S. 1978. The illusion of sociobiology. Review of E.O. Wilson, *On Human Nature*, in *New York Review* 25 (12 October): 64–9

Handy, E.S.C. 1923. *The Native Culture of the Marquesas*. Honolulu: Bernice P. Bishop Museum

Hanna, J., and D.E. Brown. 1983. Human heat tolerance: An anthropological perspective. In *Annual Review of Anthropology*, vol. 12, B.J. Siegel, A.R. Beals and S.A. Tyler, eds, pp. 259–84. Palo Alto: Annual Reviews

Hardin, G. 1968. The tragedy of the Commons. *Science* 162: 1243

Harkness, C. n.d. An interpretation of developmental changes in verbal communication within a sociobiological framework. In *The Adapted Mind: Evolutionary Psychology and the Generation of Culture*, J.H. Barkow, L. Cosmides, and J. Tooby, eds. New York: Oxford University Press. In preparation

Harpending, H. 1980. Perspectives on the theory of social evolution. In *Current Developments in Anthropological Genetics*, vol. 1, J.H. Mielke and M.H. Crawford, eds. New York and London: Plenum Press

Harris, M. 1968. *The Rise of Anthropological Theory*. Chicago: Thomas Y. Crowell

- 1977. *Cannibals and Kings: The Origins of Cultures.* New York: Random House
- 1979. *Cultural Materialism: The Struggle for a Science of Culture.* New York: Random House
- 1980. *Culture, People, Nature: An Introduction to General Anthropology.* 3rd ed. New York: Harper & Row
- 1985. *Good to Eat. Riddles of Food and Culture.* New York: Simon and Schuster

Hausfater, G., and S.B. Hrdy, eds. 1984. *Infanticide, Comparative and Evolutionary Perspectives.* New York: Aldine

Hayes, R.O. 1975. Female genital mutilation, fertility control, women's roles, and the patrilineage in modern Sudan: A functional analysis. *American Ethnologist* 2: 617–33

Henry, J. 1963. *Culture against Man.* New York: Vintage Books (Random House)

Herdt, G.H. 1980. *Guardians of the Flute: Idioms of Masculinity.* New York: McGraw

- 1984. Ritualized homosexual behavior in the male cults of Melanesia, 1862–1983: An introduction. In *Ritualized Homosexuality in Melanesia,* G.H. Herdt, ed., pp. 1–82. Berkeley and Los Angeles: University of California Press

Hetherington, E.M. 1972. Effects of father absence on personality development in adolescent daughters. *Developmental Psychology* 7: 313–26

Hewes, G.W. 1973. Primate communication and the gestural origin of language. *Current Anthropology* 14: 5–24

Hill, J. 1984. Prestige and reproductive success in man. *Ethology and Sociobiology* 5: 77–95

Hinde, R.A., ed. 1983. *Primate Social Relationships: An Integrated Approach.* Sunderland, MA: Sinauer Associates

Hochschild, A.R. 1983. *The Managed Heart: Commercialization of Human Feeling.* Berkeley: University of California Press

Hockett, C.F., and R. Ascher. 1964. The human revolution. *Current Anthropology* 5: 135–68

Hoffer, C.P. 1975. Bundu: Political implications of female solidarity. In *Being Female: Reproduction, Power and Change,* Dana Raphael, ed., pp. 155–63. Paris: Mouton

Hoffman, M.L. 1982. The Development of Prosocial Behavior. In *The Development of Prosocial Behavior,* N. Eisenberg, ed. New York: Academic Press

Hoogland, J.L. 1985. Infanticide in prairie dogs: Lactating females kill offspring of close kin. *Science* 230(4729): 1037–40

Hosken, F.P. 1979. *The Hosken Report. Genital and Sexual Mutilation of Females.* 2nd rev. ed. Lexington, MA: Women's International Network News

Hrdy, S. Blaffer. 1980. *The Langurs of Abu: Female and Male Strategies of Reproduction*. Cambridge, MA: Harvard University Press
– 1981. *The Woman That Never Evolved*. Cambridge, MA: Harvard University Press
Hsu, F.L.K. 1971. Psychological homeostasis and jen: Conceptual tools for advancing psychological anthropology. *American Anthropologist* 73: 23–44
Hulse, F.S. 1971. *The Human Species: An Introduction to Physical Anthropology*. 2nd ed. New York: Random House
Humphrey, N.K. 1976. The function of intellect. In *Growing Points in Ethology*, P.P.G. Bateson and R.A. Hinde, eds, pp. 303–17. Cambridge: Cambridge University Press
– 1983. *Consciousness Regained: Chapters in the Development of Mind*. Oxford: Oxford University Press
Huxley, J.S. 1938. The present standing of the theory of sexual selection. In *Evolution: Essays on Aspects of Evolutionary Biology Presented to Professor E.S. Goodrich on His Seventieth Birthday*, G.R. de Beer, ed., pp. 11–42. Oxford: Clarendon Press
Hymes, D. 1974. *Foundations in Sociolinguistics: An Ethnographic Approach*. Philadelphia: University of Pennsylvania Press
– ed. 1964. *Language in Culture and Society: A Reader in Linguistics and Anthropology*. New York: Harper and Row
Irons, W. 1979. Natural selection, adaptation, and human social behavior. In *Evolutionary Biology and Human Social Behavior: An Anthropological Perspective*, N.A. Chagnon and W. Irons, eds, pp. 4–38. North Scituate, MA: Duxbury
– 1983. Human female reproductive strategies. In *Social Behavior of Female Vertebrates*, K.S. Wasser, ed. New York: Academic Press
Irwin, C.J. 1985. Sociocultural Biology: Studies in the Evolution of Some Netsilingmiut and Other Sociocultural Behaviors. Doctoral dissertation, Syracuse University
– 1987. A study of the evolution of ethnocentrism. In *The Sociobiology of Ethnocentrism: Evolutionary Dimensions of Xenophobia, Discrimination, Racism and Nationalism*, V. Reynolds, V. Falger, and I. Vine, eds, pp. 131–56. London and Sydney: Croom Helm
Isaac, G.L. 1978a. The archaeological evidence for the activities of early hominids. In *Early Hominids in Africa*, C.J. Jolly, ed., pp. 219–54. New York: St Martin's
– 1978b. The food-sharing behavior of protohuman hominids. *Scientific American* 238: 90–108
Izard, C.E. 1977. *Human Emotions*. New York: Plenum
Johnson-Laird, P.N. 1983. *Mental Models*. Cambridge, MA: Harvard University Press

– 1988. *The Computer and the Mind: An Introduction to Cognitive Science.* Cambridge, MA: Harvard University Press

Kagan, J. 1981. *The Second Year: The Emergence of Self-Awareness.* Cambridge, MA: Harvard University Press

Katona-Apte, J. 1975. The relevance of nourishment to the reproductive cycle of the female in India. In *Being Female: Reproduction, Power and Change,* Dana Raphael, ed., pp. 43–8. Paris: Mouton

Kaye, H.L. 1986. *The Social Meaning of Modern Biology: From Social Darwinism to Sociobiology.* New Haven and London: Yale University Press

Keith, A. 1949. *A New Theory of Human Evolution.* New York: Philosophical Library

Kemper, T.D. 1978. *A Social Interactional Theory of Emotions.* New York: Wiley

Kihlstrom, J.F. 1987. The cognitive unconscious. *Science* 237: 1445–52

King, G.E. 1980. Alternative uses of primates and carnivores in the reconstruction of early hominid behavior. *Ethology and Sociobiology* 1: 99–109

Kinsbourne, M. 1985. Parallel processing explains modular informational encapsulation. *Behavioral and Brain Sciences* 8: 23

Kinzey, W.G., ed. 1987. *The Evolution of Human Behavior: Primate Models.* Albany: State University of New York Press

Kirk, R.L. 1982. Linguistic, ecological, and genetic determinants in New Guinea and the Western Pacific. In *Current Developments in Anthropological Genetics,* vol. 2, M.H. Crawford and J.H. Mielke, eds. New York: Plenum

Kirkpatrick, M. 1987. Sexual selection by female choice in polygynous animals. *Annual Review of Ecology and Systematics* 18: 43–70

Kitcher, P. 1985. *Vaulting Ambition: Sociobiology and the Quest for Human Nature.* Cambridge, MA: MIT Press/Bradford Books

Klein, D.B. 1984. *The Concept of Consciousness: A Survey.* Lincoln and London: University of Nebraska Press

Kodric-Brown, A., and J.H. Brown. 1984. Truth in advertising: The kind of traits favored by sexual selection. *American Naturalist* 124: 309–23

Koestler, A. 1967. *The Ghost in the Machine.* London: Hutchinson

Kohn, M.E. 1963. Social class and parent-child relationships: An interpretation. *American Journal of Sociology* 68: 471–80

Konner, M.J. 1972. Aspects of the development ethology of a foraging people. In *Ethological Studies of Child Behaviour,* N. Blurton Jones, ed., pp. 285–304. Cambridge: Cambridge University Press

– 1982. *The Tangled Web: Biological Constraints on the Human Spirit.* New York: Harper Colophon Books

Krebs, D., D. Dennis, K. Denton, and N.C. Higgins. 1988. On the evolution of self-knowledge and self-deception. In *Sociobiological Perspectives on Human Development,* K. MacDonald, ed., pp. 103–39. New York: Springer-Verlag

Kroeber, A.L. 1917. The superorganic. *American Anthropologist* 19: 163–213
– 1925. *Handbook of the Indians of California*. Washington, DC: Government Printing Office
– 1963. *Anthropology: Culture Patterns and Processes.* New York: Harcourt, Brace & World (originally published 1948)
Kroeber, A.L., and C. Kluckhohn, 1952. *Culture: A Critical Review of Concepts and Definitions*. New York: Vintage Books (Random House)
Kurland, J.A. 1979. Paternity, mother's brother, and human sociality. In *Evolutionary Biology and Human Social Behavior: An Anthropological Perspective*, N.A. Chagnon and W. Irons, eds, pp. 145–80. North Scituate, MA: Duxbury
Kurland, J.A., and S.J. Beckerman. 1985. Optimal foraging theory and hominid evolution: Labor and reciprocity. *American Anthropologist* 87: 73–93
Larsen, R.R. 1976. Charisma: A reinterpretation. In *The Social Structure of Attention*, M.R.A. Chance and R.R. Larsen, eds, pp. 253–72. London and New York: Wiley
Laughlin, C.D., and E.G. d'Aquili. 1974. *Biogenetic Structuralism*. New York: Columbia University Press
Laughlin, W.S. 1968. Hunting: An integrating biobehavior system and its evolutionary importance. In *Man the Hunter*, R.B. Lee and I. DeVore, eds, pp. 304–20. Chicago: Aldine
Leach, E. 1970. *Claude Lévi-Strauss*. New York: Viking
Lee, R.B., 1979. *The !Kung San: Men, Women, and Work in a Foraging Society*. Cambridge, MA: Cambridge University Press
Lee, R.B., and I. DeVore, eds. 1968. *Man The Hunter*. Chicago: Aldine-Atherton
Leighton, A.H. 1982. *Caring for Mentally Ill People*. Cambridge: Cambridge University Press
Leighton, D.C., and C. Kluckhohn. 1947. *Children of the People*. Cambridge, MA: Harvard University Press
Lévi-Strauss, C. 1966. *The Savage Mind*. Chicago: University of Chicago Press
– 1969. *The Elementary Structures of Kinship*. Boston: Beacon Press
LeVine, R.A., 1966. *Dreams and Deeds*. Chicago: University of Chicago Press
– 1982. *Culture, Behavior, and Personality*. 2nd ed. Chicago: Aldine
LeVine, R.A., and D.T. Campbell. 1972. *Ethnocentrism: Theories of Conflict, Ethnic Attitudes and Group Behavior*. New York: Wiley
Levinson, D.J. 1978. *The Seasons of a Man's Life*. New York: Ballantine
Lewin, R. 1985. How does half a bird fly? *Science* 230: 530–1
– 1987. The unmasking of mitochondrial Eve. *Science* 238: 24–6
Lewontin, R.C., 1977. Caricature of Darwinism. Review of Richard Dawkins, *The Selfish Gene*, in *Nature* 266 (17 March): 437–77
Lewontin, R.C., S.P.R. Rose, and L.J. Kamin. 1984. *Not in Our Genes*. New York: Pantheon

Lieberman, P. 1975. *On the Origins of Language: An Introduction to the Evolution of Human Speech.* New York: Macmillan

– 1984. *The Biology and Evolution of Language.* Cambridge, MA: Harvard University Press

Lieberman, P., E.S. Crelin, and D.H. Klatt. 1972. Phonetic ability and the related anatomy of the newborn, adult human, Neanderthal man, and the chimpanzee. *American Anthropologist* 74: 287–307

Lindenbaum, S. 1974. *Kuru Sorcery: Disease and Danger in the New Guinea Highlands.* Palo Alto, CA: Mayfield

Lockard, J.S. 1980. Speculations on the adaptive significance of self-deception. In *The Evolution of Human Social Behavior*, J.S. Lockard, ed., pp. 257–76. New York: Elsevier

Lockhard, R. 1971. Reflections on the fall of comparative psychology: Is there a message for us all? *American Psychologist* 26: 168–79

Lorenz, K. 1965. *Evolution and Modification of Behavior.* Chicago: University of Chicago Press

Lorenz, K., and Leyhausen, P. 1973. *Motivation of Human and Animal Behavior.* New York: Van Nostrand Reinhold

Lovejoy, O. 1981. The origin of Man. *Science* 211: 341–50

Low, B.S., R.D. Alexander, and K.M. Noonan. 1987. Human hips, breasts, and buttocks: Is fat deceptive? *Ethology and Sociobiology* 8: 249–57

– 1988. Response to Judith Anderson's comments on Low, Alexander, and Noonan (1987). *Ethology and Sociobiology* 9: 325–8

Lumholtz, C. 1894. Tarahumari life and customs. *Scribner's Magazine* 16: 296–311

Lumsden, C.J. 1989. Does culture need genes? *Ethology and Sociobiology* 10: 11–28

Lumsden, C.J., and E.O. Wilson. 1981. *Genes, Mind, and Culture.* Cambridge, MA, and London: Harvard University Press

– 1982. Précis of *Genes, Mind, and Culture*, in *Behavioral and Brain Sciences* 5: 1–37

– 1983. *Promethean Fire: Reflections on the Origin of Mind.* Cambridge, MA: Harvard University Press

– 1985. The relation between biological and cultural evolution. *Journal of Social and Biological Structures* 8: 343–59

Lutz, C., and G.M. White. 1986. The anthropology of emotions. *Annual Review of Anthropology* 15: 405–36

MacAndrew, C., and R.B. Edgerton. 1969. *Drunken Comportment: A Social Explanation.* Chicago: Aldine

MacDonald, K. 1983. Production, social controls and ideology: Toward a sociobiology of the phenotype. *Journal of Social and Biological Structures* 6: 297–317

MacDonald, K.B. 1988. Sociobiology and the cognitive-developmental tradition in moral development research. In *Sociobiological Perspectives on Human Development*, K.B. MacDonald, ed., pp. 140–67. New York: Springer-Verlag

MacLean, P.D. 1973. *A Triune Concept of the Brain and Behaviour*. Toronto: University of Toronto Press

– 1978. The evolution of three mentalities. In *Human Evolution. Biosocial Perspectives*, S.L. Washburn and E.R. McCown, eds, pp. 3–57. Menlo Park, CA: Benjamin/Cummings

MacLean, U. 1971. *Magical Medicine: A Nigerian Case-Study*. Harmondsworth, Middlesex: Penguin Books

Majerus, M.E.N. 1986. The genetics and evolution of female choice. *Trends in Ecology and Evolution* 1: 1–7

Majundar, A.S., and A.C. Ghose. 1982. Protective properties of anticholera antibodies in human colostrum. *Infection and Immunology* 36(3): 962–5

Malinowski, B. 1944. *A Scientific Theory of Culture and Other Essays*. Chapel Hill: University of North Carolina Press

– 1954. *The Science of Culture and Other Essays*. Garden City, NY: Anchor Books

Mandler, G. 1984. *Mind and Body: Psychology of Emotion and Stress*. New York: Norton

Markl, H. 1985. Manipulation, modulation, information, cognition: Some of the riddles of communications. In *Experimental Behavioral Ecology and Sociobiology: In Memoriam Karl von Frisch 1886–1982*, B. Holldobler and M. Lindauer, eds, pp. 163–94. Sunderland, MA: Sinauer

Mascia-Lees, F.E., J.H. Relethford, and T. Sorger. 1986. Evolutionary perspectives on permanent breast enlargement in human females. *American Anthropologist* 88(2): 423–8

Masse, H. 1938. *Croyances et coutumes persanes*. Paris: Librairie Orientale et Americaine

Maynard Smith, J. 1964. Group selection and kin selection. *Nature* 201: 1145–7

– 1971. The origin and maintenance of sex. In *Group Selection*, G.C. Williams, ed., pp. 163–75. Chicago: Aldine-Atherton

– 1976. Evolution and the theory of games. *American Scientist* 64: 41–5

McClelland, D.B.L. 1982. Antibodies in milk. *Journal of Reproduction and Fertility* 65(2): 519–86

McClelland, D.C. 1951. Measuring motivation in phantasy: The achievement motive. In *Groups, Leadership, and Men*, H. Guetzkow, ed. Pittsburgh: Carnegie Press

– 1955. *Some Consequences of Achievement Motivation*. Nebraska Symposium on Motivation. Lincoln: University of Nebraska Press

– 1958. Methods of measuring human motivation. In *Motives in Fantasy, Action, and Society*, J.W. Atkinson, ed. Princeton, NJ: Van Nostrand

- 1961. *The Achieving Society*. Princeton, NJ: Van Nostrand
McClelland, D.C., J.W. Atkinson, R.A. Clark, and E.L. Lowell. 1953. *The Achievement Motive*. New York: Appleton-Century-Crofts
McClelland, D.C., and D.G. Winter. 1969. *Motivating Economic Achievement*. New York: Free Press
McClelland, J.L., D.E. Rumelhart, and the PDP Research Group. 1986. *Parallel Distributed Processing: Explorations in the Microstructure of Cognition. Volume II: Psychological and Biological Models*. Cambridge, MA: MIT Press/Bradford Books
McGuire, M.T., and M.J. Raleigh. 1985. Serotonin-behavior interactions in vervet monkeys. *Psychopharmacology Bulletin* 21: 458–63
- 1987. Serotonin, behaviour, and aggression in vervet monkeys. In *Ethopharmacology of Agonistic Behaviour in Animals and Humans*, B. Oliver, J. Mos, and P.F. Brain, eds. Dordrecht: Martinus Nijhoff Publishers
McGuire, M.T., M.J. Raleigh, and G.L. Brammer. 1984. Adaptation, selection, and benefit-cost balances: Implications of behavioral-physiological studies of social dominance in male vervet monkeys. *Ethology and Sociobiology* 5: 269–77
McGuire, M.T., and C.E. Taylor, eds. 1988. Reciprocal altruism: 15 years later. Special number of *Ethology and Sociobiology* 9(2–4): 67–256
McGuire, M.T., and A. Troisi. n.d. Deception and psychological mechanisms. To appear in *The Adapted Mind: Evolutionary Psychology and the Generation of Culture*, J.H. Barkow, L. Cosmides, and J. Tooby, eds. New York: Oxford University Press. In preparation
Mead, G.H. 1934. *Mind, Self, and Society*. Chicago: University of Chicago Press
Mead, M. 1930. *Growing Up in New Guinea: A Comparative Study of Primitive Education*. New York: Morrow
Mealey, L. 1985. The relationship between social status and biological success: A case study of the Mormon religious hierarchy. *Ethology and Sociobiology* 6: 249–57
Midgley, M. 1978. *Beast and Man: The Roots of Human Nature*. Ithaca, NY: Cornell University Press
Miller, G.A., E. Galanter, and K.H. Pribram. 1960. *Plans and the Structure of Behavior*. New York: Holt
Montagu, A. 1979. Breastfeeding and its relation to morphological, behavioral and psychocultural development. In *Breastfeeding and Food Policy in a Hungry World*, D. Raphael, ed. New York: Academic Press
- ed. 1973. *Man and Aggression*. 2nd ed. London and New York: Oxford University Press
- ed. 1978. *Learning Non-Aggression*. New York: Oxford University Press
Morris, D. 1967. *The Naked Ape*. London: Jonathan Cape

Müller-Hill, B. 1988. *Murderous Science: Elimination by Scientific Selection of Jews, Gypsies, and Others, Germany, 1933–1945*. New York: Oxford University Press. Trans. from German edition (Reinbek bei Hamburg, 1984) by G.R. Fraser

Murdock, G.P. 1967. *Ethnographic Atlas*. Pittsburgh: University of Pittsburgh Press

Murdock, G.P., and D.R. White. 1969. Standard cross-cultural sample. 1. *Ethnology* 8: 329–69

Murphy, R.F. 1957. Intergroup hostility and social cohesion. *American Anthropologist* 59: 1018–35

– 1960. *Headhunter's Heritage*. Berkeley: University of California Press

Murray, H.A. 1938. *Explorations in Personality*. New York: Oxford University Press

Nadel, S.F. 1954. *Nupe Religion*. London, Routledge and Paul

Nesse, R.M., and A.T. Lloyd. n.d. How has natural selection shaped psychodynamic mechanisms? In *The Adapted Mind: Evolutionary Psychology and the Generation of Culture*. J. Barkow, L. Cosmides, and J. Tooby, eds. New York: Oxford University Press. In preparation

Newton, P.N. 1986. Infanticide in an undisturbed forest population of hanuman langurs. *Animal Behavior* 34: 785–9

O'Gara, C., and C. Kendall. 1985. Fluids and powders: Options for infant feeding. *Medical Anthropology* 9(2): 107–22

Ogra, S.S., and P.L. Ogra. 1978a. Immunologic aspects of human colostrum and milk. *Journal of Pediatrics* 92: 546–9

– 1978b. Immunologic aspects of human colostrum and milk II. *Journal of Pediatrics* 92: 550–5

Ojemann, G.A. 1983. Interrelationships in the brain organization of language-related behaviors: Evidence from electrical stimulation mapping. In *Neuropsychology of Language, Reading, and Spelling*, U. Kirk, ed. New York: Academic Press

Ojofeitimi, E.O., and I.A. Elegbe. 1982. The effect of early initiation of colostrum feeding on proliferation of intestinal bacteria in neonates. *Clinical Pediatrics* 21: 39–42

O'Keefe, J., and L. Nadel. 1978. *The Hippocampus as a Cognitive Map*. Oxford: Clarendon Press

– 1979. Précis of O'Keefe and Nadel's *The Hippocampus as a Cognitive Map*, in *Behavioral and Brain Sciences* 2: 487–533

Omark, D.R., F.F. Strayer, and D.G. Freedman, eds. 1980. *Dominance Relations: An Ethological View of Human Conflict and Social Interaction*. New York: Garland STPM Press

Otterbein, K.F. 1985. *The Evolution of War: A Cross-Cultural Study*. 2nd ed. New Haven, CT: HRAF Press

Packer, C., and A.E. Pusey. 1983. Adaptations of female lions to infanticide by incoming males. *American Naturalist* 121: 716–28

Parker, S.T. 1985. A social-technological model for the evolution of language. *Current Anthropology* 27: 671–739

– 1987. A sexual selection model for hominid evolution. *Human Evolution* 2: 235–53

Parker, S.T., and K.R. Gibson. 1979. A developmental model for the evolution of language and intelligence in early hominids. *Behavioral and Brain Sciences* 2: 367–408

Pastner, C. McC. 1986. The Westermarck hypothesis and first cousin marriage: The cultural modification of negative sexual imprinting. *Journal of Anthropological Research* 42(4): 573–86

Peters, R. 1978. Communication, cognitive mapping, and strategy. In *Wolf and Man: Evolution in Parallel*, R.L. Hall and H.S. Sharp, eds. New York: Academic Press

Pfeiffer, J.E. 1977. *The Emergence of Society*. New York: McGraw

– 1985. *The Emergence of Humankind*. 4th ed. New York: Harper & Row

Piddocke, S. 1969. The potlatch system of the southern Kwakiutl: A new perspective. In *Environment and Cultural Behavior: Ecological Studies in Cultural Anthropology*, A.P. Vayda, ed., pp. 130–56. Garden City, NY: Natural History Press

Plutchik, R., and H. Kellerman. 1980. *Emotion: Theory, Research, and Experience.* New York: Academic Press

Popper, K.R., and J.C. Eccles. 1977. *The Self and Its Brain*. Berlin: Springer-Verlag

Porter, R H. 1987. Kin recognition: Functions and mediating mechanisms. In *Sociobiology and Psychology: Ideas, Issues and Applications*, C. Crawford, M. Smith, and D. Krebs, eds, pp. 175–203. Hillsdale, NJ: Lawrence Erlbaum Associates

Potts, R. 1984. Home bases and early hominids. *American Scientist* 72: 338–47

– 1986. Temporal span of bone accumulation at Olduvai Gorge and implications for early hominid foraging behavior. *Paleobiology* 12: 25

Pribram, K.H. 1971. *Languages of the Brain*. Englewood Cliffs, NJ: Prentice-Hall

– 1976. Self-consciousness and intentionality. In *Consciousness and Self-Regulation: Advances in Research*, vol. 1, G.E. Schwartz and D. Shapiro, eds. New York: Plenum

Pulliam, H.R., and C. Dunford. 1980. *Programmed to Learn*. New York: Columbia University Press

Radcliffe-Brown, A.R. 1952. *Structure and Function in Primitive Society*. Glencoe, IL: Free Press

Raleigh, M.J., M.T. McGuire, G.L. Brammer, and A. Yuwiler. 1984. Social and environmental influences on blood serotonin concentrations in monkeys. *Archives of General Psychiatry* 41: 405–10

Raphael, D.L. 1966. The Lactation-Suckling Process within a Matrix of Supportive Behavior. PhD thesis, Columbia University, New York

Read, C. 1917. On the differentiation of the human from the anthropoid mind. *British Journal of Psychology* 8: 395–422

Reynolds, V., V. Falger, and I. Vine, eds. 1987. *The Sociobiology of Ethnocentrism: Evolutionary Dimensions of Xenophobia, Discrimination, Racism and Nationalism.* London and Sydney: Croom Helm

Richerson, P.J., and R. Boyd. 1978. A dual inheritance model of the human evolutionary process. I. Basic postulates and a simple model. *Journal of Social and Biological Structures* 1: 127–54

– 1989. The role of evolved predispositions in cultural evolution, or human sociobiology meets Pascal's wager. *Ethology and Sociobiology* 10(1): 195–219

Rodman, P.S., and M. McHenry. 1980. Bioenergetics and the origin of hominid bipedalism. *American Journal of Physical Anthropology* 52: 103–6

Rohner, R.P. 1975. *They Love Me, They Love Me Not.* New Haven: HRAF Press

Roper, T.J. 1983. Learning as a biological phenomenon. In *Animal Behaviour, Vol. 3. Genes, Development and Learning*, T.R. Halliday and P.J.B. Slater, eds, pp. 178–212. Oxford: Blackwell

Rosch, E. 1975. Universals and specifics in cultural categorization. In *Cross-Cultural Perspectives on Learning*, R.W. Brislin, S. Bochner, and W.J. Lonner, eds, pp. 177–206. New York: Halsted Press, Wiley

Rose, M. 1980. The mental arms race amplifier. *Human Ecology* 8: 285–93

Rose, R.M., I.S. Bernstein, and T.P. Gordon. 1975. Consequences of social conflict on plasma testosterone levels in rhesus monkeys. *Psychosomatic Medicine* 37: 50–61

Rose, R.M., T.P. Gordon, and I.S. Bernstein. 1972. Plasma testosterone levels in the male rhesus: Influences of sexual and social stimuli. *Science* 178: 643–5

Rose, S.P.R. 1976. *The Conscious Brain.* Harmondsworth, Eng.: Penguins Books

Rosenberg, A. 1985a. Adaptationalism and panglossianism. In *Sociobiology and Epistemology*, J.H. Fetzer, ed., pp. 161–79. Dordrecht: D. Reidel

– 1985b. *The Structure of Biological Science.* Cambridge: Cambridge University Press

Ross, W. 1984. Beyond the biological model: New directions in bisexual and homosexual research. *Journal of Homosexuality* 10: 63–9

Rubenstein, R.A., C.D. Laughlin, Jr, and J. McManus. 1984. *Science as Cognitive Process: Toward an Empirical Philosophy of Science.* Philadelphia: University of Pennsylvania Press

Rumelhart, D.E., J.L. McClelland, and the PDP Research Group. 1986. *Parallel*

Distributed Processing. Explorations in the Microstructure of Cognition. Volume I: Foundations. Cambridge, MA: MIT Press/Bradford Books

Ruse, M. 1981. Are there gay genes? *Journal of Homosexuality* 6: 5–33

Rushton, J.P., D.W. Fulker, M.C. Neale, D.K.B. Nias, and H.J. Eysenck. 1986. Altruism and aggression: the heritability of individual differences. *Journal of Personality and Social Psychology* 50(6): 1192–8

Ryle, G. 1949. *The Concept of Mind.* London: Hutchinson

Sackheim, H.A. 1983. Self-deception, self-esteem, and depression: The adaptive value of lying to oneself. In *Empirical Studies of Psychoanalytic Theories,* vol. 1, J. Masling, ed., pp. 101–57. London: Analytic Press

Sackheim, H.A., and R.C. Gur. 1978. Self-deception, self-confrontation, and consciousness. In *Consciousness and Self-Regulation: Advances in Research,* vol. 2, G.E. Schwartz and D. Shapiro, eds. New York: Plenum

Sagan, C. 1977. *The Dragons of Eden. Speculations on the Evolution of Human Intelligence.* New York: Random House

Sahlins, M. 1960. The origin of society. *Scientific American* 203: 76–87

– 1976. *The Use and Abuse of Biology: An Anthropological Critique of Sociobiology.* Ann Arbor: University of Michigan Press

Sayre, K.M. 1986. Intentionality and information processing: An alternative model for cognitive science. *Behavioral and Brain Sciences* 9: 121–66

Schapera, I. 1930. *The Khoisan Peoples of South Africa: Bushmen and Hottentots.* London: George Rutledge and Sons

Schjelderup-Ebbe, T. 1935. Social Behavior of Birds. In *A Handbook of Social Psychology,* E. Murchinson, ed. Worcester, MA: Clark University Press

Schubert, G. 1982. Infanticide by usurper hanuman langur males: A sociobiological myth. *Social Science Information* 21(2): 199–244

– 1988. *Evolutionary Politics.* Carbondale, IL: Southern Illinois University Press

Schultze, L. 1907. *Aus Namaland und Kalahari.* Jena: Gustav Fischer

Seaborg, D. 1984. Sexual orientation, behavioral plasticity, and evolution. *Journal of Homosexuality* 10: 153–8

Sebrell, W.H., Jr., J.H. Haggerty, and the Editors of Life. 1967. *Food and Nutrition.* New York: Time

Segerstrale, U. 1986. Colleagues in conflict: An 'in vivo' analysis of the sociobiology controversy. *Biology and Philosophy* 1: 53–87

Seligman, M. 1971. Phobias and preparedness. *Behavior Therapy* 2: 307–20

Serpenti, L. 1984. The ritual meaning of homosexuality and pedophilia among the Kimam-Papuans of South Irian Jaya. In *Ritualized Homosexuality in Melanesia,* G.H. Herdt, ed., pp. 318–36. Berkeley and Los Angeles: University of California Press

Seyfarth, R.M. 1981. Do monkeys rank each other? *Brain and Behavior Sciences* 4: 447–8

Shepher, J. 1983. *Incest: A Biosocial View*. New York: Academic Press

Sherman, P.W., and W.G. Holmes. 1985. Kin recognition: issues and evidence. In *Experimental Behavioral Ecology and Sociobiology. In Memoriam Karl von Frisch 1886–1982*, B. Holldobler and M. Lindauer, eds, pp. 437–60. Sunderland, MA: Sinauer

Shields, W.M., and L.M. Shields. 1983. Forcible rape: An evolutionary perspective. *Ethology and Sociobiology* 4: 115–36

Shirokogorov, S.M. 1924–25. *Social Organization of the Manchus: A Study of the Manchu Clan Organization*. Shanghai

Short, V.S. 1980. The origin of human sexuality. In *Human Sexuality* (Reproduction in Mammals, vol. 8), C.R. Austin and V.S. Short, eds. Cambridge: Cambridge University Press

Simoons, F.J. 1978. Traditional use and avoidance of foods of animal origin. *BioScience* 28(3): 178–84

Skinner, B.F. 1984. Canonical papers of B.F. Skinner. *Behavioral and Brain Sciences* 7: 423–724

Slatkin, M. 1987. Gene flow and the geographic structure of natural populations. *Science* 236: 783–7

Smith, M.F. 1954. *Baba of Karo: A Woman of the Muslim Hausa*. London: Faber and Faber

Smith, R.L. 1984. Human sperm competition. In *Sperm Competition and the Evolution of Animal Mating Systems*, R.L. Smith, ed., pp. 601–59. New York: Academic Press

Snow, C.E., and C.A. Ferguson, eds. 1977. *Talking to Children: Language Input and Acquisition*. Cambridge: Cambridge University Press

Sober, E. 1984. *The Nature of Selection: Evolutionary Theory in Philosophical Focus*. Cambridge, MA: MIT Press/Bradford Books

Southworth, F.C., and C.J. Daswani. 1974. *Foundations of Linguistics*. New York: Free Press

Spain, D.H. 1987. The Westermarck-Freud incest-theory debate. *Current Anthropology* 28: 623–45

Spier, L. 1933. *Yuman Tribes of the Gila River*. Chicago: University of Chicago Press

Spiro, M.E. 1958. *Children of the Kibbutz*. Cambridge, MA: Harvard University Press

– 1979. *Gender and Culture: Kibbutz Women Revisited*. Durham, NC: Duke University Press

Spuhler, J.N., ed. 1959. *The Evolution of Man's Capacity for Culture*. Detroit: Wayne State University Press

Stabler, E.P., Jr. 1983. How are grammars represented? *Behavioral and Brain Sciences* 6: 391–421

Staddon, J.E.R. 1981. On a possible relation between cultural transmission and genetical evolution. In *Advantages of Diversity*, vol. 4, P.P.G. Bateson and H. Klopfer, eds, pp. 135–45. New York: Plenum

Steklis, D., and S. Harnad. 1976. From hand to mouth: Some critical stages in the evolution of language. In *Origins and Evolution of Language and Speech*, D. Steklis and S. Harnad, eds, *Annals of the New York Academy of Sciences* 280: 445–54

Stenhouse, D. 1973. *The Evolution of Intelligence*. London: Allen and Unwin

Stevenson, M. 1920. *The Rites of the Twice-Born*. London: Oxford University Press

Steward, J.H. 1955. *Theory of Culture Change*. Urbana, IL: University of Illinois Press

Strayer, F.F., and M. Trudel. 1984. Developmental changes in the nature and function of social dominance among young children. *Ethology and Sociobiology* 5: 279–95

Stringer, C.B., and P. Andrews. 1988. Genetic and fossil evidence for the origin of modern humans. *Science* 239: 1263–8

Sturtevant, H. 1964. *An Introduction to Linguistic Science*. New York: Yale University Press

Suggs, R.C. 1963. Marquesan sexual behavior. Unpublished manuscript. New Haven, HRAF

Susman, R.L. 1987. Pygmy chimpanzees and common chimpanzees. In *The Evolution of Human Behavior: Primate Models*, W.G. Kinzey, ed., pp. 72–86. Albany: State University of New York Press

Swanton, J.R. 1924–25. *Social Organization and Social Usages of the Indians of the Creek Confederacy*. U.S. Bureau of American Ethnology, Annual Report, 42: 473–672

Symons, D. 1979. *The Evolution of Human Sexuality*. New York: Oxford University Press

– 1980. The evolution of human sexuality revisited. *The Behavioral and Brain Sciences* 3: 203–11

– 1987a. If we're all Darwinians, what's the fuss about? In *Sociobiology and Psychology: Ideas, Issues and Applications*, C. Crawford, M. Smith, and D. Krebs, eds, pp. 121–46. Hillsdale, NJ: Lawrence Erlbaum Associates

– 1987b. The evolutionary approach: Can Darwin's view of life shed light on human sexuality? In *Theories of Human Sexuality*, James H. Geer and W. O'Donohue, eds. New York: Plenum Press

– 1989. A critique of Darwinian anthropology. *Ethology and Sociobiology* 10: 131–44

Tax, S. 1977. Anthropology for the world of the future: Thirteen professions and three proposals. *Current Anthropology* 36: 225–34

Taylor, C.E., et al. 1973. Asian medical systems: A symposium on the role of comparative sociology in improving health care. *Social Science and Medicine* 7: 307–18

Taylor, G.R. 1972. *Rethink: A Paraprimitive Solution*. London: Secker & Warburg

Temple, C.L. 1922. *Notes on the Tribes, Provinces, Emirates and States of the Northern Provinces of Nigeria*. 2nd ed. Lagos, Nigeria: CMS Bookshop

Thompson, L. 1916. *To the American Indian*. Eureka, CA: [Cummings Print Shop]

Thornhill, R. 1979. Male and female sexual selection. In *Sexual Selection and Reproductive Competition in Insects*, M.S. Blum and N.A. Blum, eds, pp. 81–121. New York: Academic Press

Thornhill, R., and N.W. Thornhill. 1983. Human rape: An evolutionary analysis. *Ethology and Sociobiology* 4: 137–73

– 1987. Evolutionary theory and rules of marriage. In *Sociobiology and Psychology: Ideas, Issues and Applications*, C. Crawford, M. Smith, and D. Krebs, eds, pp. 373–400. Hillsdale, NJ: Lawrence Erlbaum Associates

Tinbergen, N. 1951. *The Study of Instinct*. London: Oxford University Press

– 1968. On war and peace in animals and man. *Science* 160: 1411–18

Tooby, J., and Cosmides, L. 1989. Evolutionary psychology and the generation of culture, I. Theoretical considerations. *Ethology and Sociobiology* 10: 29–49

Tooby, J., and I. DeVore. 1987. The reconstruction of hominid behavioral evolution through strategic modeling. In *The Evolution of Human Behavior: Primate Models*, W.G. Kinzey, ed., pp. 183–237. Albany: State University of New York Press

Toth, N. 1985. Archeological evidence for preferential right-handedness in the lower and middle pleistocene, its possible implications. *Journal of Human Evolution* 14: 607

Trivers, R.L. 1971. The evolution of reciprocal altruism. *Quartlery Review of Biology* 46: 35–7

– 1972. Parental investment and sexual selection. In *Sexual Selection and the Descent of Man, 1871–1971*, B. Campbell, ed., pp. 136–79. Chicago: Aldine

– 1985. *Social Evolution*. Menlo Park, CA: Benjamin/Cummings

Turnbull, C. 1974. *The Mountain People*. New York: Touchstone

Turner, G. 1884. *Samoa, a Hundred Years Ago and Long Before*. London: Macmillan

Tyler, S.A., ed. 1969. *Cognitive Anthropology*. New York: Holt, Rinehart & Winston

Tylor, E.B. 1873. *Primitive Culture*. 2 vols; 2nd ed. London: John Murray (chapter 11 reprinted 1972 in abridged form in W.A. Lessa and E.Z. Vogt, *Reader in Comparative Religion* [New York: Harper and Row], pp. 9–19)

van den Berghe, P. 1979. *Human Family Systems*. New York: Elsevier

– 1981. *The Ethnic Phenomenon*. New York: Elsevier

– 1983. Human inbreeding avoidance: Culture in nature. *Behavioral and Brain Sciences* 6: 91–123

Vayda, A.P., and R. Rappaport. 1968. Ecology, Cultural and Noncultural. In *Introduction to Cultural Anthropology*, J.A. Clifton, ed. Boston: Houghton Mifflin

Vine, I. 1987. Inclusive fitness and the self-system. In *The Sociobiology of Ethnocentrism: Evolutionary Dimensions of Xenophobia, Discrimination, Racism and Nationalism*, V. Reynolds, V. Falger, and I. Vine, eds, pp. 60–80. London and Sydney: Croom Helm

Vining, D.R., Jr. 1986. Social versus reproductive success: The central theoretical problem of human sociobiology. *Behavioral and Brain Sciences* 9: 187–216

von Bertalanffy, L. 1968. *General System Theory*. New York: Braziller

Wade, M.J. 1978. A critical review of the models of group selection. *Quarterly Review of Biology* 53: 101–14

– 1979. The evolution of social interactions by family selection. *American Naturalist* 113: 399–417

– 1980. Kin selection: Its components. *Science* 210: 665–7

Wainscoat, J. 1987. Out of the garden of Eden. *Nature* 325: 13

Wallace, A.F.C. 1961. The psychic unity of human groups. In *Studying Personality Cross-Culturally*, B. Kaplan, ed., pp. 129–63. New York: Harper and Row

– 1966. *Religion: An Anthropological View*. New York: Random House

– 1970. *Culture and Personality*. 2nd ed. New York: Random House

Wallace, R.L. 1989. Cognitive mapping and the origin of language and mind. *Current Anthropology*. In press

Wallesch, C.W., L. Henniksen, H.H. Kornhuber, and O.B. Paulson, 1985. Observations on regional cerebral blood flow in cortical and subcortical structures during language production in normal humans. *Brain and Language* 25: 224–33

Washburn, S.L. 1959. Speculations on the inter-relations of the history of tools and biological evolution. In *The Evolution of Man's Capacity for Culture*, J.N. Spuhler, ed. Detroit: Wayne State University Press

– 1960. Tools and human evolution. *Scientific American* 63: 413–19

Washburn, S.L., and V. Avis. 1958. Evolution and human behavior. In *Behavior and Evolution*, A. Roe and G.G. Simpson, eds. New Haven: Yale University Press

Washburn, S.L., and C.S. Lancaster. 1968. The evolution of hunting. In *Perspectives on Human Evolution*, S.L. Washburn, and P.C. Jay, eds, pp. 213–29. New York: Holt, Rinehart and Winston

Wax, M.L. 1969. Myth and interrelationships in social science: Illustrated through anthropology and sociology. In *Interdisciplinary Relationships in the Social Sciences*, M. Sherif and C.W. Sherif, eds, pp. 77–99. Chicago: Aldine

Wedgwood, C.H. 1942/1943. Notes on the Marshall Islands. *Oceania* 13: 1–23

Weisfeld, G.E., and R.L. Billings. 1988. Observations on adolescence. In *Sociobiological Perspectives on Human Development*, K.B. MacDonald, ed., pp. 207–33. New York: Springer-Verlag

Weisfeld, G.E., D.R. Omark, and C.L. Cronin. 1980. A longitudinal and cross-sectional study of dominance in boys. In *Dominance Relations: An Ethological View of Human Conflict and Social Interaction*, D.R. Omark, F.F. Strayer, and D.G. Freedman, eds, pp. 205–16. New York and London: Garland STPM Press

Wells, L.E., and G. Marwell. 1976. *Self-Esteem. Its Conceptualization and Measurement*. Vol. 20, Sage Library of Social Research. Beverly Hills, CA: Sage Publications

Werner, E.E. 1979. *Cross-Cultural Child Development: A View from the Planet Earth*. Monterey, CA: Brooks/Cole

West Eberhard, J. 1975. Sexual selection, social competition, and speciation. *The Quarterly Review of Biology* 50: 155–83

Westermarck, E.A. 1891. *The History of Human Marriage*. London: Macmillan

Wheeler-Voegelin, E. 1938. *Tubatulabal Ethnography*. Berkeley: University of California Press

White, L.A. 1975. *The Concept of Cultural Systems: A Key to Understanding Tribes and Nations*. New York and London: Columbia University Press

White, N.G., and P.A. Parsons. 1973. Genetic and sociocultural differentiation in the Aborigines of Arnhem Land, Australia. *American Journal of Physical Anthropology* 38: 5–14

Whitman, W. 1947. *The Pueblo Indians of San Ildefonso, A Changing Culture*. Marjorie W. Whitman, ed. New York: Columbia University Press

Whittley, R. 1985. *The Intellectual and Social Organization of the Sciences*. New York: Clarendon (Oxford University Press)

Williams, G.C. 1966. *Adaptation and Natural Selection: A Critique of Some Current Evolutionary Thought*. Princeton, NJ: Princeton University Press

– ed. 1971. *Group Selection*. Chicago: Aldine-Atherton

Wilson, E.O. 1971. Competitive and aggressive behavior. In *Man and Beast: Comparative Social Behavior*, J.F. Eisenberg and W. Dillon, eds. Washington, DC: Smithsonian

– 1975a. *Sociobiology: The New Synthesis*. Cambridge, MA: Belknap Press of Harvard University Press

– 1975b. Some central problems of sociobiology. *Social Science Information* 14: 5–18

– 1978. *On Human Nature*. Cambridge, MA: Harvard University Press

Witkin, H.A., and J.W. Berry. 1975. Psychological differentiation in cross-cultural perspective. *Journal of Cross-Cultural Psychology* 6: 4–87

Wolf, A.P., and C. Huang. 1980. *Marriage and Adoption in China, 1845–1945.* Stanford, CA: Stanford University Press

Wood, C.S. 1979. *Human Sickness and Health: A Biocultural View.* Palo Alto, CA: Mayfield

Wrangham, R.W. 1980. An ecological model of female-bonded primate groups. *Behavior* 75: 262–99

– 1983. Ultimate factors determining social structure. In *Primate Social Relationships: An Integrated Approach,* R.A. Hinde, ed., pp. 255–61. Sunderland, MA: Sinauer Associates

Wright, S. 1943. Isolation by distance. *Genetics* 28: 114–38

– 1969. *Evolution and the Genetics of Populations. Vol. 2. The Theory of Gene Frequencies.* Chicago: University of Chicago Press

Wynne-Edwards, V.C. 1962. *Animal Dispersion in Relation to Social Behaviour.* Edinburgh: Oliver and Boyd

– 1971. Intergroup selection in the evolution of social systems. In *Group Selection,* G.C. Williams, ed., pp. 93–104. Chicago: Aldine-Atherton

Zelniker, T., and W.E. Jeffrey. 1979. Attention and cognitive style in children. In *Attention and Cognitive Development,* G.A. Hale and M. Lewis, eds, pp. 275–96. New York and London: Plenum Press

Zivin, Gail, ed. 1985. *The Development of Expressive Behavior. Biology-Environment Interaction.* Orlando, FL: Academic Press

Name Index

Subject Index

Achievement, need for. *See* n-ach
Adaptation, 7, 8, 32; and field dependence, 270. *See also* Selection; Fitness
Adaptation[al]ist paradigm, 8–11, 30
Adolescence: and identity, 197–8, 211
Adultery. *See* Multiple mates
Aggression: and the Balinese cockfight, 163; deliberate neglect of, 160n; and low father-involvement, 346–8, 348–9n; and prestige, 180; rule-bound, 185–6; and social hierarchy, 34. *See also* Rape
Agonism: culturally ritualized, 185–6; lurking in background, 185n, 208, 209; and non-verbal communication, 185, 199; and social rank, 180–3
Alcohol and 'time-out' behaviour, 89
Alexander, Richard: and the avunculate, 279–81, 292; and his challenge to anthropology, 275–6, 291; contrasted with Boyd and Richer-

son, 276; and cousin terminology, 276–9, 291; and cultural inertia, 283; and disagreement with Richerson and Boyd over transmission models, 282–3; as a functionalist, 277–9, 280, 284–5, 288; and moral systems, 285–7; and lack of proximate explanation, 277–8, 280–1, 291–2; and lack of vertically integrated explanation, 286–7; and the psychoanalyst's ploy, 286; as similar to Marvin Harris, 284–5; strengths of, 284; and use of Sahlins's reciprocity categories, 281–2, 292; and value of his approach, 288, 292
Algonkian Indians, 268
Algorithms, 6, 37, 48n, 51, 273; of altruism and social exchange, 57n, 173, 286; and evolved processors, 51, 73; and FIP, 52n, 53n, 54; and incest avoidance, 278; and the intra-individual system, 106; and male sexual jealousy,